THE RISE AND FALL OF LATIN HUMANISM
IN EARLY-MODERN RUSSIA

BRILL'S STUDIES IN INTELLECTUAL HISTORY

THE RISE AND FALL
OF LATIN HUMANISM
IN EARLY-MODERN RUSSIA

Pagan Authors, Ukrainians, and the Resiliency of Muscovy

BY

MAX J. OKENFUSS

E.J. BRILL
LEIDEN · NEW YORK · KÖLN
1995

The author gratefully acknowledges financial support from the Fulbright Commission for Educational Exchange, and the Council for International Exchange of Scholars, for a sabbatical in Göttingen in 1989-90. Additional support was generously provided by the Dean of the Faculty of Arts and Sciences and the Department of History, Washington University, St. Louis.

The paper in this book meets the guidelines for permanence and durability of the Committee on Production Guidelines for Book Longevity of the Council on Library Resources.

Library of Congress Cataloging-in-Publication Data

Okenfuss, Max J. (Max Joseph)
    The rise and fall of Latin humanism in early-modern Russia : pagan authors, Ukrainians, and the Resiliency of Muscovy / Max J. Okenfuss.
        p.   cm. — (Brill's studies in intellectual history, ISSN 0920-8607 ; v. 64)
    Includes bibliographical references and index.
    ISBN 9004103317 (alk. paper)
    1. Classical education—Russia—History—18th century.
2. Humanism—Russia—History—18th century. 3. Books and reading––Russia—History—18th century. 4. Russia—Civilization—18th century. I. Title. II. Series.
LA831.5.O39   1995
370.11'2'0947—dc20
                                         95–15028
                                           CIP

Die Deutsche Bibliothek - CIP-Einheitsaufnahme

Okenfuss, Max J.:
The rise and fall of Latin humanism in early-modern Russia : pagan authors, Ukrainians, and the Resiliency of Muscovy / Max J. Okenfuss. – Leiden ; New York ; Köln : Brill, 1995
  (Brill's studies in intellectual history ; Vol. 64)
  ISBN 90–04–10331–7
NE: GT

ISSN 0920-8607
ISBN 90 04 10331 7

PRINTED IN THE NETHERLANDS

CONTENTS

INTRODUCTION

1. *A Moving Target*

This is the story of the physical presence of the Classics in Russia, 1650–1789. In the mid-seventeenth century the tsarist court, some governmental offices (*prikazy*), and some in the Church's leadership, announced themselves to be open to the West. The proximate West was Poland, and it offered both its courtly and military culture, and the values of its Ukrainian and Belorussian clergy, who shared Orthodoxy with the Muscovites. To be sure the receptive elites took measures to shield the lower orders of Muscovy from these new values, as would subsequent Russian governments down to 1861. This was Westernization for the upper strata of society.

In the mid-seventeenth century learned Western Civilization and a Latin book-culture were still synonymous. By the end of the Enlightenments,[1] that unity was largely shattered, although everywhere centuries of Latin learning would still shape the education and outlook of every schooled European. The rhetoric of the French Revolution, for example, was incomprehensible without an education in the Classics: on a single day in 1793, addressing a decidedly non-aristocratic audience, Robespierre proclaimed, "I would gladly be one of Aristides' sons," and St. Just reminded his listeners that "oppressors arose after the time of Lycurgus who destroyed his work."[2] At that moment such orators scarcely existed in Russia, in spite of a century and a half of "Westernization." This study asks why that was so.

Tentatively, in the middle of the seventeenth century the political leaders of Muscovy took aim at a moving target. A military metaphor is the appropriate beginning for this story, because it was increasing involvement with new-style armies, navies, and fortifications

---

[1] Following a recent historiographic trend, I recognize several distinct enlightenments; see Porter and Teich, eds., *The Enlightenment*.

[2] Reynolds, ed., *Spokesmen*, pp. 126, 133. See in general, Parker, *The Cult of Antiquity*. Compare also Reinhold, *Classica Americana*, p. 102 and *passim*: "It was the Constitutional Convention of 1787 ... that the appeal to classical political theory and practice reached its peak. ... [In] the records of the Federal Convention, and *The Federalist* papers ... it is discernible that some of these were extracted from translations of Plato, Aristotle, Demosthenes, Polybius, Livy, Cicero, Sallust, Strabo, Tacitus, and Plutarch," although modern authors were cited more often.

of Western Europe which demanded a redirection of the Muscovite court's aspirations. Its target was a constellation of dynamic technologies, institutions, and habits of mind which we call Western Civilization, which gradually a few Russians and most Europeans came to regard as "superior" to those of old Muscovy, and a few even as normative for Russia's future. The target was moving in that Europe was ever changing, even in the glaringly mislabeled Dark Ages,[3] and never more so than in the early-modern period when change was catapulted along the deadly trajectory of the Gunpowder Revolution and through the carnage of its aftermath.

One example may suffice. At the end of the seventeenth century Tsar Peter embarked on his famous Grand Embassy to Europe. Among the thousands of impressions which tumbled through his ever-curious mind on that journey was an artifact as simple as the calendar. Somehow Peter came to contrast traditional Muscovy's creation-based calendar, in which the year was 7205, with those of the Year of Our Lord, 1697, in Western Europe. He learned that there were in fact two calendars in use, Julian and Gregorian, Old-Style and New-Style. Because that first journey took him to Protestant north-German lands and to Holland and England, and because his voyage was cut short before he could spend time in Catholic France, Venice, or the Empire, Peter came to regard the ways of northern Europe as more imitable than those of the south. Thus he adopted the Julian calendar still generally in use there.

As a result two centuries later the Great October Socialist Revolution would occur in November, as the February revolution had occurred in March. It is irrelevant whether Weber was correct about northern Europe or the Protestant Ethic, or whether the Gregorian calendar is a more accurate reflection of the solar cycle than the Julian. The legal use of the former was the visible target in Holland and England when Peter visited, and which he decreed to the Russian people when a new (Western) century began in 1700. The sighted target, of course, moved. But in this simple act, subsequently recorded in the *Complete Collection of Laws of the Russian Empire* as enactment #1736, old Muscovy symbolically accepted the cultural imperialism of the West. Every human society previously and since has had its own way to reckon the passage of time, and all were and are in

---

[3] I have previously recorded my debt to Jean Gimpel and Lynn White Jr., in my "Peter Tolstoi in Rome," pp. 35–41.

some manner acceptable. Peter's decision signalled his submission to the Rise of the West, the triumph of its cultural values, and a pattern of cultural Westernization through state decree.

Were all Russians so submissive? At the top of the social structure, the West ruled. No aspect of cultural subservience was more obvious than borrowing in the broad area of government, the definition of the prince's powers, his obligations, and those of his subjects.[4] Russia's rulers and elite increasingly measured their government by Western standards, accepted Western definitions of the relationships between rulers and the ruled, even when they defended their ways against the West.

In abstract terms this Westernization was unnecessary. In the bad old days Muscovites were no worse governed than the peoples of Europe. The Time of Troubles (1598–1618), the popular uprisings in 1606–07 and 1670–71 and the urban disorders of 1648 are not prima facie evidence that something was rotten in the State of Muscovy in comparison with Western Europe.[5] There was no reason why the Tsardom of Muscovy, reconstituted in the Romanov dynasty, the Orthodox Patriarchate, the boyardom, the *prikazy*, the service classes, the urban classes, serfdom and slavery, could not have survived with the changes inherent in all human institutions, right into recent times; it had its own mechanisms for reforming its military, for encouraging productivity and for taxing it, its own definitions of good and evil, and its own devices for correcting inequities. What fascinated every foreigner in Russia from Olearius in 1647 through Custine in 1839[6] was the dependent relationship the Russians more or less freely chose, once they found irresistible the military might, the religious values, the architecture, and the levels of productivity and consumption of Europe.

In the middle of the seventeenth century Muscovy began to borrow on a reckless scale. With the rational goal of national self-survival, Tsar Aleksei Mikhailovich decided to modernize his military on European models and with imported personnel. His particular

---

[4] No attempt can be made here to survey that literature, but one can note the reorientation of Tsar Aleksei to the West, recorded in Longworth, *Alexis*, Chapter 6; Peterson, *Peter the Great's . . . Reforms*, pp. 67–83. For the period discussed here see also Raeff, *Police State*.

[5] See the summary of literature on the "General Crisis" in Rabb, *The Struggle for Stability*, and compare Dukes, "Russia and the 'General Crisis'."

[6] Baron, ed., *Olearius*; Marquis de Custine, *Empire of the Czar*.

borrowing was based on the perception that Muscovy's traditional military was almost worthless in attacking a fortified place.[7] In the short period of time between his decision to import a military technology of siege and fortification, and his son's reforms in the early eighteenth century, European military engineers in the age of Vauban concluded that traditional fortified places were in fact not defensible, and Aleksei's importations required immediate replacement.[8] In short, no sooner had the leaders of the first Third-World nation set sights on a particular Western military target, than inevitably that target moved.

At the beginning of that era of borrowing, the European commitment to the Renaissance-humanist ideal of Latin education was unitary enough that it could be perceived and adopted, objections of dogma and language notwithstanding.[9] In Europe it remained largely intact over a century later. As Voltaire noted: "Homer, Demosthenes, Virgil, and Cicero have to some extent brought all the peoples of Europe under their sway and made one republic out of so many different nations."[10] But in 1650, at the end of the Thirty-Years War, the tsarist court, the most receptive element in Muscovy, was still sensitive enough to the charge of heresy not to abandon native education. It elected only to add technical or linguistic skills for a few governmental specialists to the older sequence of liturgical readings,[11] that constituted the Muscovite system of formal education.

In the middle of the seventeenth century a number of Europeans thus could look at the absence of Latin learning in Muscovy and announce that without it, the Muscovites were not Europeans and scarcely Christians. Olearius said it clearly. Individuals were forbidden to teach their offspring Latin or German.[12] "No Russian, whether

---

[7] The perception arose first during the campaign for Smolensk of 1632; see Hellie, *Enserfment*, pp. 123ff., 157ff.

[8] The impact of war on the development of the West is too vast a topic to be outlined here, but where formerly one read works like Nef, *War*, now the standard is probably McNeill, *The Pursuit of Power*. I am partial to the more recent Geoffrey Parker, *The Military Revolution*. On the appearance of fads as a phenomenon of the early-modern West, see Braudel, *Civilization and Capitalism*, I, pp. 183–333.

[9] Theoretically, of course, does not mean practically. The pseudo-Byzantine ideology of the sixteenth century, especially virulent in the reconstruction of the seventeenth, opposed any such borrowing.

[10] Cited in Jones, "A Trojan Horse," pp. 116–17.

[11] See as an introduction my "Jesuit Origins."

[12] Baron, *Olearius*, p. 175. Olearius' own Classical education is not apparent in the modern English translation as his Classical digressions were systematically omit-

ecclesiastic or layman, of high rank or low, understands a word of Greek or Latin"—such was his definitive pronouncement.[13] According to Olearius the Muscovites professed a great affinity to the Greeks, from whom they received alphabet and religion, but they exaggerated both their linguistic and religious similarities.[14]

For Muscovites, the problem was Catholicism, Rome, and by extension, Latin.[15] Late in the century a visitor could note that the Muscovites "despise liberal arts as useless torments of youth, they prohibit philosophy, and they have often publicly outraged astronomy with the opprobrious name of magic." Because they "are rude of letters, and wanting in that virtuous discipline by which the mind is cultivated, few study polite manners or imitate them."[16] A Muscovite contempt for Latin, and European pride in their Classical education, are commonplaces in the travel literature of the seventeenth century.

Foreigners noted the Russians' hostility to Latin education well into the eighteenth century:

> There is no such thing as any College that ever I heard of, or School that was appointed for breeding up Men to be qualified for [the priesthood] . . . Excepting at Kiow [Kiev] 700 Miles from Mosco, which is in Cossacks Country on the Borders of *Poland*, where the Russes seldom go for Learning.[17]

Only toward the end of Peter's reign did visitors talk about the first success of the foreign-educated teachers of the Latin Academy transplanted from Kiev to Moscow, a young prince who could deliver a "handsome Speech in Latin,"[18] as an example of the Russians' progress. When, where, and to what extent had Russian nobles been attracted to the study of Latin?

In the mid-seventeenth-century, Moscow was visited by potential

---

ted; see *ibid.*, xi. A recent collection of sixteenth and seventeenth century travellers' comments on the lack of learning and of Latin among the Muscovites is Slukhovskii, *Iz istorii knizhnoi*, pp. 76–86, 178–89.

[13] *Ibid.*, p. 238.

[14] *Ibid.*, pp. 238–41, 283–84.

[15] *Ibid.*, pp. 244–48, 249, 253, 266, 267, 272, 283, and especially 277: "The Muscovites tolerate and have dealings with people of other nations and religions, such as Lutherans, Calvinists, Armenians, Tatars, Persians, and Turks. However, they are very intolerant of Catholics and Jews."

[16] Korb, *Diary*, 1968, pp. 194–196; on the moral side of the issue, see my "On Crime and Punishment," pp. 23–27.

[17] Perry, *The State of Russia*, p. 215. Perry was correct concerning the infrequency of Russians who studied in Kiev; see Kharlampovich, *Malorossiiskoe vliianie*, I, 736–40.

[18] Weber, *The Present State*, pp. 128–29.

Latin teachers. Many were educated clergymen who professed Orthodoxy rather than Roman or Protestant Christianity, and all spoke
a Slavonic intelligible in Muscovy. They came from lands in Lithuania,
Belorussia, and Ukraine which were the targets of both Tsar Aleksei's
cautious expansionism, and of Patriarch Nikon's enthusiastic ecu-
menism. These Latin-speaking and writing Ukrainians, Belorussians,
and Lithuanians—descendants of the original Rus'—represented alien
cultural values in Muscovy. In the eyes of traditional Muscovites,
Orthodox divines from Kiev or Polock were no more welcome than
were the Protestant or Catholic mercenaries swelling the tsar's armed
forces, linguists in the *prikazy*, or Dutch entrepreneurs controlling their
industries. The violence of the urban disorder and the *raskol* was
directed against them.

2. *Principal Questions and Methods*

Commonplace generalizations about eighteenth-century Russia are
that it spawned the intelligentsia in its cultured but idle nobility, that
its clergy was largely illiterate and obscurantist, and that it lacked a
literate middle class. Education, or a lack of it, is thus crucial to our
understanding of the era.

This study's central questions are the extent to which Muscovite
society accommodated itself to European ideals of humanistic Latin
education, available after the 1640s in Moscow from a European-
educated Ukrainian clergy; and secondly, the level of Russia acceptance of secular values, found in the tales of heroic exploits circulating among the swashbuckling German and Polish mercenaries accepted
into Muscovite service.

Both questions have been previously asked. Marc Raeff, the emeritus
dean of early-modern Russian studies, has argued that in the late
seventeenth century, the culture of the Germans, Dutch, and others
living in the "Foreign Quarter (*nemetskaia sloboda*) was of great importance in the formation of young Peter's outlook," and for the *secular*
elite; the Latinizing influence of the Ukraine and of Kiev's Academy, however, "was mainly felt in *ecclesiastical* circles (my Italics—
MJO)."[19] From these roots would spring a more general thirst for

---

[19] Raeff, "The Enlightenment," p. 25.

European education among Russia's elites. Through the compulsion of the Petrine service system, "education did take hold in Russia, particularly among the nobility. . . . No more than a generation after Peter's death education was accepted as a matter of course by the majority of nobles and in many instances even eagerly sought after."[20] Another respected study proclaims that, by 1761, this triumphant education was a Latin course of study, and that it was broadly successful across the elite levels of Russian society: "For the Old Believers and for most Orthodox peasants, Latin, German, and French were equally alien, Roman and Protestant equally anathema, Voltairian and Freemason equally incomprehensible. *But for the court and the gentry and the clergy, at the end of Elizabeth's reign Latin was taken for granted as the gateway to education* (my Italics—MJO)."[21] This study reexamines these historiographic conventions.

Did both the Russian gentry and the clergy accept Latin education? When? A reexamination of the evidence from the history of book-publishing, from the study of the Latin language, and from private libraries in Russia, should clarify the extent to which various social strata converted to humanist values in the eighteenth century.

To anticipate its conclusion, this study also chronicles the amazing durability of a much-maligned Muscovite culture. In steadfast resistance to the irresistible, virtually every member of every social group in Russia rejected Latin learning throughout the entire early-modern period from the Peace of Westphalia to the French Revolution. They resisted Latin culture from the sanctioned arrival of humanists from Ukraine in Moscow in the 1640s, until the attempt to impose a national public school system on the nation in the 1780s. If at times it seemed that the Latin-rooted culture of Western Europe had gained a real foothold in Russia, particularly among the nobility, the reader is cautioned: The nineteenth-century Slavophiles were correct when they applauded the undisturbed survival of old Muscovite attitudes, tastes, and mores into their own age, not only among the peasantry, but among nests of gentlefolk as well. Throughout this is a study of fickle fads among the tiniest of elites.

This durability of Muscovite values was not the preservation of simplicity, ignorance, or obscurantism. Nor was Muscovy a unified, unstratified culture. Cultural anthropologists remind us that every

---

[20] Raeff, *Origins*, 133.
[21] See Treadgold, *The West in Russia. I*, p. 115.

human society, even the most "primitive"—which assuredly seventeenth-century Muscovy was not—is held together by complex structures of family, clan and kinship, religion and ritual, work and lei-
sure, and politics. Peasant values are neither simple nor stupid, and
Muscovite popular religion was neither. In this anthropological sense,
at every level of a complex hierarchical society, Muscovite thought
was rich and nuanced. The story told here is not the resistance of
unlettered peasants to some "higher" level of culture. Rather most of
Muscovy resisted Latin and endured because its culture was satisfy-
ingly complex, had psychological resonance, and was centered on a
firmly held Christian faith.

The small numbers of Russians who did prove susceptible to the
West have been consistently exaggerated for decades by historians in
East Germany, the Soviet Union, and in the West as well. Most
pernicious has been the single-minded, Marxist-inspired, pursuit of a
"Russian Enlightenment."[22] It produced a massive literature. Scarcely
thirty years ago the idea was an occasional theme for a few incom-
petent scholars in the Soviet Union.[23] But Dietrich Geyer has outlined how the idea of a Russian Enlightenment took hold, primarily
in Soviet and East German scholarship.[24] The 1960s witnessed an
explosion of literary studies of the eighteenth century, championed
by Pavel Naumovich Berkov (1896–1969), and catalogued in K. P.
Stepanov & Iu. V. Stennik, *Istoriia russkoi literatury XVIII veka. Bibliograficheskii ukazatel'*, which he edited.[25] Simultaneously Russo-German
cultural and scientific contacts were explored by Eduard Winter and
his school in East Germany, as Helmut Graßhoff and Ulf Lehmann
were publishing widely on Russian literature's links to Europe,
particularly to German letters.[26] In West Germany Erik Amburger

---

[22] This historiographic mania is explored at the end of Chapter IV below. All
references in the notes are given in short titles; for complete citations, see the List
of Works Consulted.

[23] See for example, Sholom, "Prosvetitel'skie idei," which argues that the Ukraine
imported its enlightenment from Russia.

[24] For the following, Geyer, "Aufgeklärte Absolutismus," pp. 176–189. The long-
time field-marshal of Soviet eighteenth-century literary studies, P. N. Berkov, catalogued the first phases of the scholarly explosion in his *Vvedenie v izuchenie*, pp. 18–
19, 231–250. I myself reexamine the process in Chapter III below. Authors and
works mentioned here can be found in the Bibliography.

[25] Berkov's own reflections of the joys of book owning are in his "Biografiia moei
biblioteki," pp. 220–26.

[26] They produced such odd volumes as Graßhoff et al., eds., *Humanistische Traditionen*,
in which, the title notwithstanding, there are no references to Erasmus, Cicero, or
Montaigne, but seven to Lenin and five to Marx.

was publishing on related topics, and W. Gesemann began to look at the popular mind. A new generation of scholars like Heinz Ischreyt in the West and Erich Donnert in the East entered the field. Into this flood stepped the unsavory M. M. Shtrange (his early career involved shipping Soviet citizens from post-war France to the Gulag) with a book on the cultural activities of seventy-four educated non-nobles. Eventually five volumes of the *Svodnyi katalog russkikh knig* (1963–67), sometimes mistakenly assumed to represent the output of Russian presses, were followed by the promise of other catalogues of Russian publishing, and also by the pioneering work of S. P. Luppov, who attempted to identify the literary public through the study of private libraries in Russia. The result was the discovery of a *Russian Enlightenment*.

In the end Soviet scholars did note exceptions and qualifications: education did not necessarily equate with liberal enlightenment, and conservatives like Shcherbatov could flourish; Pugachev's uprising made championing enlightenment more risky politically; traditional pretender- and utopian-thinking continued to appear, unaffected by enlightenment; secret societies, including freemasonry, were not as enlightened as they might have been; but there was a Russian Enlightenment. Geyer could conclude, this Russian "Enlightenment and Enlightened Absolutism were really the same." Scholars could assume Catherine's policies were grounded in an enlightened public.

Such glowing judgements were possible because the requirements for membership among Russia's enlighteners were kept generously low by East-German and Soviet scholars. Only the most traditional and ignorant village *pop* was unqualified for inclusion;[27] later membership in a class other than the serf-owning nobility automatically qualified one ("sons and daughters of the people"), as did descent from the impoverished gentry,[28] and in general a hostile attitude toward serfdom rather than a religious test became the barometer of "enlightenment" in a Russian.[29]

My measuring rod is different. It involves a comfort with the ancient Classical authors, a mental characteristic acquired in the schools Russians attended in youth, visible in literary activities, and measurable

---

[27] Eduard Winter, "Die Aufklärung," pp. 283–294, said it could include everything from the Baroque to Romanticism.
[28] *Ocherki russkoi kul'tury XVIII veka, II*, p. 43.
[29] See Donnert, *Politische Ideologie*, pp. 76–77.

in their consumption of books. "Who among Russia's social strata and nationalities read Cicero, when did they do so, and what difference did it make?", could be my sub-title.

Two caveats, suggested by earlier readers of this study: First, I am aware that peasants did not read Cicero in the West or in Russia. This is a study of small elites, and it concludes before the major drive for popular education in the West, to say nothing of Russia. Second, the ideal and most meaningful way to measure Latin influence in Russia would be to trace the impact of an individual author like Cicero, throughout the period. Such studies have been attempted, for example by both Pavel Berkov and Wolfgang Busch, who sought Russian familiarity with Horace, the most widely disseminated ancient in Russia. Both concluded that the effects of any author was so slight prior to 1800 as to preclude satisfactory monographic study.

In default, the history of Latin humanism in Russia has been studied in several other, less satisfactory, ways. One is through the biography of individual Ukrainian humanists working in Russia, another is through the institutional histories of their schools, and a third is through the impact of humanism and pagan authors on early-modern Russian literature. The results of this scholarship appears here in a sizeable secondary bibliography.

My own contribution lies elsewhere. I have reexamined the output of the printing presses in Russia, I have also attempted some vignettes in comparative intellectual history, exploring the thought of representative thinkers and specific works in the mirror of their receptivity to Classical pagan thought. I have also tried to break new ground in the social history of education in Russia, trying to explain more precisely who actually studied Latin, and what it meant for book culture. Finally—and this is perhaps the most novel aspect of the present work—I have sought to investigate every available private library description in Russia between 1650 and 1789, and to ask the extent to which Latin authors were represented. These libraries, incomparably few in a European context, nonetheless suggest the resistance to this order of Europeanization by most in Russian culture, including those nobles most often identified as the *Kulturträger*, those who reputedly brought the West to Russians.

The private library requires a comment. Humanism was an educational program. It is not easy to define, today or in times past or places distant, the precise effect of an education on the individual. The likely effects of a Jesuit or Harvard education, a public or ex-

pensive private high-school education, may be well enough understood for parents to make meaningful decisions. One suspects, however, that they make choices on the basis of what they hope that a
particular schooling will accomplish rather than on the basis of a
guarantee that their hopes will be realized. It is, I suspect, a historical constant that educators disappoint or frustrate as many parents
as they satisfy.

All methods of assessing the effects of schooling in history are
unsatisfactory. In the case of eighteenth-century Russia it is difficult
to trace the subsequent careers of pupils from class rosters. Some
class-lists are available, for many clerical academies for example, but
often as few as ten percent of the names can be traced forward to
eventual careers. Starting from the other end of the problem, with
lists of well-known writers, teachers, artists,[30] or with the *demokraticheskaia
intelligentsiia*, produces almost equally dismal results when one attempts
to unearth meaningful details of individuals' educational origins.

In part this essay approaches the effects of schooling through a
study of subsequent book ownership. The limitations of such research
are apparent: How good is the sample? What percentage of book
owners had their effects catalogued, and how many lists survived?
Even if all had the inclination, what percentage of school graduates
had incomes to buy the books they wanted? How accessible and
how costly were books, Russian editions as well as foreign, in Moscow or in the provinces, and in what shops and at what dates? Which
titles did an individual long to purchase, but find unavailable? Which
important books did a wife, friend, or bureaucrat quietly remove
before cataloguing? To what extent are our personal libraries exactly
what we want it to be? What do our libraries say about our interests, lives, and passions? Beyond practical concerns are intellectual
ones so complex that one despairs at posing them: Does ownership
of a book signify interest, or agreement with its contents? Are books
owned actually read? Do they influence the mind or the personality
of a reader in some knowable way? Does failure to own a book
indicate lack of influence?

Judging a book by its cover is less perilous than judging a man by
his book covers. One avoids Lansonism—attributing influence to

---

[30] See for example Perkins, "Mobility," p. 226 and passim, where she notes that
for one of the most visible and illustrious social groups, students of the Academy of
Fine Arts 1758–1854, biographical information is lacking for sixty percent of students.

possession alone[31]—but judging schooling by its graduates' libraries
is obviously unsatisfactory. It has been done: The publication of the
catalogue of one private library noted, "The basic source for the
reconstruction of P. F. Zhukov's life will be the books in his library."[32]
The recently deceased dean of Soviet scholarship on book-owning,
S. P. Luppov optimistically proclaimed that "a book collection reveals
the tastes, interests, inclinations, and even the whims of its owner."[33]
Ultimately the impact of schooling is found in the quality of graduates'
minds, in mental habits not found or less likely found among others
not so instructed. But combined with institutional and traditional
intellectual history, collective book lists can tell us much.

Readers of an earlier version of this essay pointed out the obvious,
that there are few pleasant ways to present the contents of a private
library to a reader. Individual titles by any Classical author do not
appear frequently enough to allow them to be grouped and discussed
topically: Who in Russia read Cicero on duties?, for example. The
comprehensive treatment of any individual collection inevitably wan-
ders from the thrust of the argument, while overly truncated discussions
distort the texture of the libraries. The resulting compromise here
will not satisfy all, but I do try to avoid simply listing authors in an
intellectual game of name-dropping.

Because Soviet historians previously directed enormous resources
to the history of the book,[34] because the foundations of Marxist history
writing are being challenged while many formerly Soviet historians
remain uniquely Soviet,[35] because a massive Soviet project on early-
modern book history seems now drawing to a close but everywhere
influences historians, I attempt a fair survey of the vast Soviet literature on book culture in Russia. I hope to impart, along with my
own conclusions and questions, a sense of where Russian, and Western,
scholarship stands today.

Inevitably, I also raise two sensitive contemporary issues, the role
of religion and religious authors in Russian life, and the role of non-

---

[31] See Raeff, review in the *AHR*, Vol. 95, No. 2 (Apr. 1990), p. 548.

[32] Gorfunkel' & Nikolaev, *Nachalo universitetskoi*, p. 5.

[33] Luppov, "Izuchenie istorii bibliotek," p. 21.

[34] See the survey by Zaitseva, "K 15-letiiu," pp. 5–12. I first talked about my
dissertation publicly at the invitation of P. N. Berkov at Pushkinskii Dom; he had
played a major role in beginning the investigations surveyed in this essay. See Kasinec,
"P. N. Berkov," pp. 35–48. The nineteenth volume in the series on books and
publishing in early-modern Russia appeared in 1991.

[35] Torke, "The History of Pre-Revolutionary Russia," pp. 97–109.

Russians in the culture of the early Russian empire. The original importers of Latin books into Muscovy were clerics, and they were non-Russians. Both facts were consistently slighted by the Soviet historians whose scholarship I exploit.

Above I noted that I address broad assumptions about Russian education in the work of Professors Raeff and Treadgold. I also reexamine other accepted themes of Western historiography. A liberal-émigré school, wedded to the old intelligentsia, to aristocratic and democratic opposition to tsarism, and matured abroad in nostalgia and anti-Communism, is characterized by a modernist disdain for the religious traditions of the Russian people, by class prejudices favoring a secular nobility as the more likely cultural mediators than an obscurantist clergy, and by a blindness to Russian imperialism. I address both issues, the positive role of religion, and the question of the empire, directly.

The meaningful divisions in Russian culture 1650–1800 had little or nothing to do with one's legal *soslovie* at birth, with income, with relationship to the means of production, including serfdom, or to rootlessness, alienation, or any such a-priori or metaphysical constructs. The significant divisions in early-modern Russian culture, like those in the West, were those born of education: particular educations opened and closed minds as they opened and closed careers. While class origins might determine which particular school one might attend, and while the enserfed peasantry in general was spared education other than the traditional Orthodox variety available in home and parish, imported concepts of education were not available exclusively to one "class."

Since this manuscript was first drafted, Paul Bushkovitch's *Religion and Society in Russia* has appeared. Although our work was independently conceived, and he deals with the period prior to formal schooling in Russia, we are of one mind. Professor Bushkovitch begins his work by noting the cultural stratification of Muscovy. He explores the popular cult of relics and icons after 1550, for example, and shows how this popular religion based on saints' lives was rejected by other strata: the boyars were spectators of these cults, "not . . . participants."[36] Popular faith was sharply challenged by a new philosophical Christianity of the elites, symbolized by Slavinec'kyj and other

---

[36] *Religion and Society*, p. 113.

Ukrainians after 1650. Their arrival signalled a Church schism and one in society, since the alien Kievan preachers "in Moscow preached mainly to the court, the tsar, his family, the boyars, and the clergy of the capital, not to the masses."[37] My reading of Muscovite private libraries confirms this perception of distinct cultural strata in the seventeenth century, and clearly indicates that they remained distinct for another full century.

A second recent book will come to the mind of specialists. A Dutch scholar has recently published a study of the classics in Russia from 1700 to 1855, although only brief introductory chapters treat the eighteenth century. He justifiably notes that "the reception of the ancient classics, of the education in the classical languages, and of the translations from Greek and Latin in the work of the new [Russian] classics has never been investigated for Russian literature in a systematic-historical way."[38] My work complements that of Professor Wes. We agree that "the history of the classical tradition is an aspect of the history of Russia's orientation to Western Europe in general. It is an aspect of the Europeanization of Russia." His treatment of the seventeenth and eighteenth centuries can be delightfully episodic and anecdotal, since he knows that "education in Latin and Greek was made a structural part of the Russian system of education [only] in the first quarter of the nineteenth century," not before. It is there, in the nineteenth-century reintroduction of Latin studies, that his systematic interest rises, a full generation after the present study ends. My own work in several respects bridges the gap between Bushkovitch's account of a culturally stratified Muscovy, and Wes' theme, the general acceptance of the idea that "knowledge of the two classical languages became a prerequisite for anyone wanting to study anything at a university" in the Golden Age of Russian literature.

Cultural divisions in the early-modern world, it should be said at the outset, did not produce political or national resistance. Indeed the opposite was true. While some Ukrainian humanists avidly supported Peter's reforms, others resisted; but there was no major movement to reject the linking of Ukraine and Russia, and no Ukrainian "nationalism." There was no movement within the Ukrainian Church to return to Catholic Polish rule. Although traditional Muscovites sometimes criticized the Slavic spoken or written by the Ukrainian

---

[37] *Ibid.*, p. 174.
[38] M. Wes, *Classics in Russia*, intro.

clergy, there was no Ukrainian language movement. Although some Ukrainian hierarchs had difficulties in their Russian dioceses, and many Russian pupils resisted the lessons imposed by their Ukrainian humanist schoolmasters, the conflicts described here were cultural, not political. They did not broach the questions, are Ukraine, Belorussia, and Lithuania separate nations, and should they remain part of the Russian empire?

The study of Russian educational institutions between 1701 and 1782 affords a few preliminary generalizations.[39] Socially, schools in Russia were open to the male offspring of the free classes, nobles old and new, clerical sons, urban sons, and even the sons of peasants whose fathers were in the army and navy. Enserfed peasants, as private property, could not be offered education by the state without violating property rights, but soldiers and factory serfs were. All Petrine schooling was legally *vse-soslovnyi*, that is, open and theoretically available to all non-serfs, either with mixed student bodies of nobles and non-nobles on the same benches, or in parallel institutions, as in mathematical schools after 1715.

In terms of content and instruction, schooling in Russia can be divided into two great traditions. On one side was the Muscovite, marked by a primarily liturgical attitude toward book-knowledge, sacred and profane, codified back in the days of *Domostroi*, expressed in a *Ladder of Literacy* of primer, Book of Hours, and Book of Psalms, and by a hostility to most book learning exceeding those parameters.[40] Whatever we moderns think of such an education, it imparted a durable, practical, intellectually and psychologically satisfying vision of human life and of the role of the individual in human society, and in the divine plan of the universe. It was grounded in parish and family, rather than in the schoolroom. Long before Peter the Great the Muscovite state had successfully grafted onto that ancient Orthodox education the idea of service: certain members of Christian Orthodox society might require more literacy in their God-ordained role in life, some of the urban classes might require arithmetic, some

---

[39] I have recorded my objections to Black, *Citizens for the Fatherland*, in *CASS*, Vol. 15, No. 4 (Winter, 1981), 577–78. More reliable are the older studies by Demkov, *Istoriia russkoi pedagogii. II*, and Rozhdestvenskii, *Ocherki po istorii sistema*.

[40] The classic analysis remains that of Kliuchevskii; see my translation "V. O. Kliuchevskii on Childhood."

prikazchiki might acquire a technical skill, language, or learning necessary to their tasks, without mortal danger to their souls. Some clergy, by extension, might need to study the languages and the damning thoughts of heretics to combat them, and some courtiers might make weekly digests of secular news from the courts of heretical Catholic and Protestant Europe: such were the compromises and practical adaptations already made when this study commences. A half-century and more later every school established by Peter the Great's state was based on the assumption that this old Muscovite Orthodox educational *Ladder of Liturgical Literacy* would not be disturbed, that it would continue to form the basic "elementary" moral and vocational education of all Russians, no matter what language or technical skill might later be added to it.

The second great tradition was alien Ukrainian humanism. Even when the religious Orthodoxy of its proponents was not questioned, it differed from the Muscovite in that the Latin language was its essential core. Because Ukraine had been part of the Europe-centered Polish-Lithuanian state for centuries, acquiring a familiarity with the grammar, poetics, rhetoric, and philosophy of the ancient pagan world was its fundamental educational curriculum. Its appearance in Moscow is the background for this essay.

The alien nature of these humanists is recognized in these pages by the heuristic use of an alternate spelling of their proper names, that preferred by contemporary Ukrainian scholars. This is a conscious effort to rescue their native and alien identities from the homogenizing of Soviet-Russian historians. This eye-catching and unorthodox usage is meant to underscore the distinct cultures of Muscovy and early-modern *Rus'*, the Belorussian and Ukrainian peoples of the Lithuanian-Polish state.[41]

Because this study attempts to distinguish between adherents of Muscovite educational traditions, and those of Western humanism, I emphasize the alien geographical and educational roots of many individuals otherwise rightfully considered Russian. When, for example,

---

[41] The background of political relations between Moscow and Ukraine can be handily found in Vernadsky, *The Tsardom of Moscow*, Part I, Chapters 4 and 5. I have already used the form Teofan Prokopovych instead of the usual Feofan Prokopovich, and will consistently use Simeon Polockij instead of the Russian Polotskii, and Polock instead of Polotsk. As a general rule I adopt the system found in the publications of the Harvard Ukrainian Research Institute, while recognizing that they are inconsistent.

I detect non-Muscovite reading habits in savants like Jacob Bruce/ Brius, I emphasize his family's foreign origins, rather than his father's service to Muscovy, or his birthplace. Consistent with the nature of this inquiry, my distinctions are those of education, reading, and cultural orientation, rather than national citizenship.

The confrontation between Muscovy and alien Ukrainian humanism was not a unique occurrence. The Renaissance can be read as such an encounter. Another was the original clash between the pagan Classical world and the Judeo-Christian. In antiquity Western Christianity, while skeptical about many aspects of Classical *paideia*, eventually and painfully came to an uneasy compromise with Hellenistic rationalism, Classical legalism, and the social inequalities of the ancient world. It has been argued that in the West, it was not Christianity but paganism that emerged triumphant. In the main, "the long Classical quest for humanism was scarcely interrupted by the Christian movement."[42] In this light the *historical* question addressed here is the response of traditional Muscovite Orthodoxy to this Christianized Roman *humanitas* in early-modern times.

Finally, concerning the often-repeated and fully-justified charge, 'Sure, the Russians owned books, but did they read them?', we can note that most libraries discussed here were not those of monied professional collectors—early-modern Russia boasted not a few—but those of people who used their books in their daily lives. That fact, plus the judicious recourse to individuals' educations, and to the examination of texts they wrote, brings us close to the interconnections between schooling and culture in eighteenth-century Russia.

3. *Contexts and Acknowledgements*

It was a minor family joke as I grew up to question whether my hardware-store owner-plumber father had graduated from high school (he had). But from time to time he would confound us children with a Latin phrase which he learned in public school, and infrequently he could be seen late at night quietly thumbing through a slim red volume of *The Master Classics*. In them bits of Anacreon, Aristophanes, Euripides, Herodotus, Homer, Horace, Pliny, and Plutarch spoke with

---

[42] Here I follow the formulation of Weltin, *Athens and Jerusalem*, p. 236.

numerous moderns. My own Latin studies in a Catholic high school would follow, as would a winter snowbound on an island off the coast of Alaska, when I first read translations of Homer and Plato, Marcus Aurelius' *Meditations*, Epictetus' *Discourses*, and Plutarch's *Lives*, as well as Erasmus, Montaigne, and Grotius. Readers of my generation might recall the ubiquitous advertisements for a book plan called the "Classics Club" which shipped antique-looking volumes from Roslyn, New York, but I would reach a considerable age before I realized that a chain of education and tradition linked these family episodes to the inquiry in this book.

The old Latin curriculum has been dying since the end of the Enlightenments, but for many even in an America born modern, the language remained widely available until the Second World War and beyond. The decades between the end of my father's education and the beginnings of my own saw many public schools abandon Latin, and the pages of Classical journals bristle with pleas for its revival in more pleasant and relevant guises, lest it slip away as had Greek earlier.[43] Classical scholars celebrated Horace's Bimillennium, recorded the revival of both religion and of Classical studies in Stalin's USSR (sic!), and attributed the success of Hitler to his banishment of Latin from the gymnasia of the Third Reich; the Nazis realized, it was argued, "that their schemes [could not] be firmly rooted in a population whose educated classes have been grounded in Latin and Greek."[44]

More recently the two-centuries-old fight to save Latin in America has been revived with appeals to the cultural traditions of Western Civilization. The 1980s were identified as "a period of deep, comprehensive, and accelerated historical change," in which only the guidance of the Classical past could provide clear direction.[45] For some aesthetic concerns were paramount; the impact of models, myths, and metaphors from antiquity on the theater, dance, music, and visual arts of the twentieth century pointed to a "present-day vitality of the classical tradition,"[46] disproving literary historians who earlier saw it fading already in the eighteenth century. That was when a *Literary*

---

[43] Peterson, "Who Killed Cock Robin?"

[44] Flickinger, "Horace's First Bimillennium," and "The Classics in Russia."

[45] Freis, "The Classics and a Contemporary Liberal Education." Freis includes a wonderful story about President Harry S. Truman and the living influence of Plutarch on his political decisions; *Ibid.*, 352–353.

[46] Rutledge, "Greece and Rome."

Revolution, paralleling the *Industrial Revolution*, began in England, and broke the spell of the antiquity, allowing the populist *Voices of the People* to ring through.[47]

Recently the contribution of the Classics to the birth of America has been celebrated,[48] and ancient authors have been brought into the feminist camp.[49] One political writer reminded us that the ancients first knew how to know, were still sure guides to moral behavior, had erected the foundations of modern jurisprudence, and had created the family values treasured by modern conservatives.[50] But most important, teachers of Latin have rallied behind E. D. Hirsch's *Cultural Literacy: What Every American Needs to Know* and his campaign against "educational formalism." His 5000-item, 63-page catalogue of things one needs to know to be literate in the West's cultural traditions, contains 271 items which from Classical antiquity which remain vital two millennia later.[51] If the study of Latin has faded, the ideas of Classical authors remain available in translation.[52] Latin learning remains essential to the West, two centuries after Catherine the Great and the French Revolution. It is remarkable that so little is understood about the fate of Latin and the Classics in Russia at the height of its influenced in Europe itself.

I owe thanks to many. I am grateful to my friends and Fulbright referees, Professors Daniel Field, John Alexander, and Franklin Walker, and to the German Fulbright Kommission, for recognizing that this essay was better drafted in a European library and setting. In Göttingen I thank my host, Prof. Dr. Manfred Hildermeier, and Dr. Trudi Maurer, Frau Barbara Kausch, Werner Benecke, Doris Klingberg, and Prof. Dr. H. Wellenreuther of the Seminar für Mittlere und Neuere Geschichte, Georg-August Universität; also Prof. Dr. Andrzej de Vincenz and Dr. Hans Schultze of the Seminar für Slavistik, which opened its treasures to me; also the staff of the reading room of the Niedersächsische Staats- und Universitätsbibliothek Göttingen; and to the ladies of the Klausberg Kafe who contributed so much to the quality of life in the Internationalbegegnungszentrum.

---

[47] See Curtius, *Europäische Literaturgeschichte*, pp. 252–254 and passim.

[48] Rexine, "The 350th Anniversary of the Boston Latin School." See now especially Carl J. Richard, *The Founders and the Classics*, Cambridge, 1994, which I read after this essay was completed.

[49] Harwood, "Latin for All Americans."

[50] Kirk, "What did the Americans Inherit."

[51] Reedy, "Cultural Literacy and the Classics."

[52] "Greek and Latin Literature in Translation"; and "1988 Supplementary Survey."

Professors David Konig and Rick Walter did everything one could expect of a Chair, and more. Thanks too to Dr. Frank Sysyn for comradeship and advice during my research, and more generally to Orest Pelech, Dan Schlafly, Ed Weltin, Theodore H. von Laue, and to many friends in the Study Group on Eighteenth-Century Russia. The interlibrary-loan department of Olin Library was cooperative and understanding. I owe thanks too to several patient groups of students in History 448 and 449 and seminars in Russian intellectual life at Washington University, on whom I tested these ideas, so alien to most of their assigned readings. Readers of earlier versions of this manuscript, Professors John Alexander, Marc Raeff, and Donald Treadgold, and others, were conscientious and willing to share criticism. I strove to address, if not to satisfy, all their concerns.

Special thanks are due to Roderick E. McGrew who has long been ready to teach, to listen, and to advise.

> Verum etiam amicum qui intuetur, tamquam exemplar *aliquod intuetur sui.* He who looks upon a true friend, looks as it were, upon a sort of image of himself.[53]

Finally, my wife Beth and my daughter Heidi, willingly or not, tolerated, shared, and participated in every stage of this project. I acknowledge and appreciate their love, forbearance, and support. This work is for them.

---

[53] Cicero, *De amicitia*, 23, vii. Unless otherwise indicated, citations of classical authors throughout are to the standards bilingual editions in the Loeb Classical Library. In the interpretation of the pagan Classics I have followed Moses Hadas. I cite his respected guides to Greek and to Roman literature because it seemed preferable to adopt one consistent voice in discussing authors removed from my own area of expertise.

CHAPTER ONE

BOOK CULTURE IN MUSCOVY

1. *Humanism and Book Culture in the 17th Century*

To understand the role of Latin and the Classics in early-modern Russian culture, it is essential to recall at least in broad outlines the history of humanism and education in Europe since the Renaissance, especially for social groups other than the clergy.[1]

Although Latin and schooling had long been synonymous, around 1500 old life was breathed into the schools.

> In the early sixteenth century a new spirit came into the English schools, the spirit of humanism. The humanists spurned as barbarous the utilitarian Latin of the Middle Ages, and cultivated the classical elegances of Cicero and the Augustan poets. The study of Latin meant for them the study of the classics and the reading and imitation of the best classical models.[2]

In adopting this consciously antique curriculum the English belatedly duplicated a continental process begun almost a century earlier, in Italy between 1402 and 1450, one already in evidence across the map of Europe.[3] The program emphasized pagan authors of Rome, rather than medieval Christian Latin texts.

This revival of the antique Classics constituted a revolution in European education as radical as anything later proposed by Locke or the philosophes: it sought to return to a starting point, to recapture an ideal from the past. Furthermore,

---

[1] This line was written on the day that the *New York Times*, December 30, 1990, p. 9, noted yet another attempt to revive Latin teaching in America, arguing for "an exercise for the brain muscle," and bemoaning "a severe shortage of qualified Latin teachers."

[2] Clarke, *Classical Education*, p. 3. See in general on Humanism the collection by Rabil ed., *Renaissance Humanism*, and Goodman and MacKay, eds., *The Impact of Humanism*.

[3] See Grendler, *Schooling in Renaissance Italy*, pp. 117–119; the rediscovery in 1392 of Cicero's *Epistulae ad familiares* was "the most important discovery for the curriculum"; p. 121.

the revival of learning involved not only the reading and study of the
classics but also the attempt to recover the ancient way of life, and the
ancient way of life included the educational methods of antiquity. . . .
The English grammar school as it was established in the sixteenth
century, and continued for some three centuries after, was essentially
the grammar school of the ancient world.[4]

By the middle of the century, an English Etonian "would have felt
quite at home in the schools of the time of Quintilian [b. ca. 35] or
Ausonius [d. ca. 393]."[5] It was a remarkable goal.

The chief European architect of this revitalized old learning, although its origins antedated him, was Erasmus' *De Ratione Studii* (1511).
It dictated the study of Plautus, Terence, Virgil, Horace, Cicero,
Caesar, and Sallust.[6] Of course, initially there was animated opposition
to mastery of the pagans on the part of the Church, but in England
already by 1528 Cardinal Wolsey himself had outlined an "exclusively
pagan course of reading" for schoolboys.[7] This wholesale adoption of
a pagan curriculum was arguably the major educational innovation
of early-modern times.

This Europe-wide phenomenon had the primary effect everywhere
of making education more attractive to those not destined for careers in the church, particularly the various nobilities, who early set
high standards of learning for themselves.[8] As a single illustration of
the phenomenon from German-speaking Europe, one can consider
the example of one Wolff Helmhards von Hohberg (1612–1688), a
rustic Austrian nobleman, a moralist, a Classical poet of some stature,
and the author of an often-reprinted guide to estate management,

---

[4] *Ibid.*, p. 3.

[5] *Ibid.*, p. 4; for France, the revival, including the direct appeal to Quintilian, can
be sampled in Philippe Ariès, *Centuries of Childhood*, p. 176 and *passim*.

[6] There is an unbroken chain between the inclusion of Plautus and Terence here
and the ritualistic school plays of our gymnasia and high schools. See Clarke, *Classical Education*, p. 10.

[7] *Ibid.*, p. 6. Muscovy would first address pagan knowledge only in the 1680s in
the infamous ecclesiastical conflict between Latinophiles and Grecophiles. The ad-
vocates of Latin authors, pagan and Christian, were defeated. See Kharlampovich,
"Borb'a shkolnykh vliianii"; Kliuchevskii, "Zapadnoe vliianie i tserkovnyi raskol,"
pp. 380, 448–51, and *passim*. In English, see Florovsky, *Ways of Russian Theology*, I,
pp. 105ff.

[8] J. H. Hexter, "The Education of the Aristocracy," pp. 61ff. Ariès, *Centuries*,
p. 174: "In the fifteenth century and still more in the sixteenth, the college altered
and enlarged its recruitment. Formerly composed of a small minority of scholarly
clerics, it opened its doors to an increasing number of laymen, chiefly from the
nobility and the middle class, but also from lower-class families. It thus became an
essential social institution."

one which allowed countless of his peers to survive wealthy and productive the gradual dismemberment of feudalism.

How does one explain von Hohberg? The three threads, moralist, poet, and business-minded landowner, were unraveled a generation ago.[9] All led back to the Renaissance humanists' Classical revival, and its educational potential, even for the rustic European nobility.

von Hohberg's persona as a *moralist* can be traced back to 1260 when a Florentine, Brunetto Latini, wrote a lay encyclopedia in French. The *Trésor* contained a chronograph and books on ethics and on rhetoric.[10] Ultimately the morality would nourish Francesco Petrarca, Dante, and eventually Erasmus himself, who in turn would found a whole culture of *Tugend* (virtu), of noble virtue, visible in Castiglione's Italian mirrors for princes and knights, *Institutio principis Christiani*, and *Enchiridion militis Christiani*. This humanistic virtue could be found subsequently in France in Ronsard (1525–85), and in Spain in Balthasar Gracian's *El Héroe* and *Oráculo manual y arte de prudencia* (1653), the culmination of the movement. At the root of this tradition stood humanism, Cicero's philosophical writings, Seneca and Boethius, and Roman *Humanitas*. It celebrated the image of a St. Ambrose, who had been a high Roman official before he became a bishop, a prince of the Church. He was a living symbol of the possibility of integrating pagan and Christian notions of virtue, and he mirrored the dual-faceted civic morality of Western nobilities. von Hohberg, Latin-schooled and well travelled, became an Imperial spokesman for this moral culture.

The key to von Hohberg's *verse* was a youthful commitment to humanistic education, later visible in his personal library, and typical of his social class. Brunner discovered that numerous nobles in the seventeenth century in both Catholic and Protestant Europe had pursued the Latin education of the humanists, that it was both remarkably widespread and uniform, and that it subsequently guided the reading habits of many for life.[11] A sequence of home study, followed by a Latin grammar school (based on Cicero's *Letters* and *De officiis*, Terence, and Erasmus' *Colloquia familiaria*), then by university, and capped by a *Kavalierstour*, led almost invariably to a personal

---

[9] For the following Brunner, *Adeliges Landleben*. Brunner was much influenced by the work of Paul Hazard.

[10] For this paragraph, Brunner, *Adeliges Landleben*, 79–80, 103–134.

[11] *Ibid.*, 152–166, esp. p. 157; see also his broader "Österreichische Adelsbibliotheken," pp. 155–167.

library which contained *De officiis*,[12] Petrarch's *Canzoniere*, and Ariosto's
Orlando furioso. After Cicero, the pagans most often found in these
nobles' libraries were Aulis Gellius' *Noctes Atticae*, the transmitter of
the idea of *Humanitas* from Homer to the eighteenth century, and
the history of Valerius Maximus, containing the best examples of
civic virtue in real lives.

Every noble library contained at its heart a good selection of religious literature. Scripture, prayer-books, hymnals, patristics, the works
of medieval mystics and scholastics, and of the moderns, Luther and
Melanchthon or Bellarmine, depending on one's creed, were always
represented, no matter how distanced the individual was from the
Church. Every sizeable library also had countless grammars and
dictionaries, but its core remained ancient letters, above all Plato
and Aristotle, Cicero and Seneca, followed by the humanists, often
including the feigned Stoic, Justus Lipsius,[13] as well as a bit of mathematics, astronomy, herbals and medicine, alchemy, history and geography, and the like. Only after this common core was confirmed,
did the noble libraries branch into their 'professional' sections, those
holding modern literature, the scientific revolution, law, or theology.

Otto Brunner had been aware of thirteen seventeenth-century
Austrian noble libraries. A study of over twenty-five aristocratic libraries from Franconia[14] produced remarkably similar conclusions: a
noble's education in the seventeenth century was synonymous with
the nexus of religion, eloquence in the Latin language, and the fruits
of the *Kavalierstour*,[15] Bibles, herbals, some volumes of the Latin pagan
Classics, "especially Cicero," and the humanists, above all Erasmus'
Colloquia familiaria. No seventeenth-century library lacked religion,
irrespective of the free-thinking or the piety of its owner.

The third key to understanding the bucolic noble von Hohberg
was the intellectual tradition behind his celebrated book, the *Adeliges*

---

[12] Nothing, Brunner insisted, was more important than this book; in print in 1465,
in German in 1488, it remained "the best book on Morals that has been or could
be written" until the time of Frederick the Great. Brunner, "Österreichische
Adelsbibliotheken," p. 160.

[13] Affecting stoicism, Lipsius bore in his "heart the Catos, Brutuses, and Senecas,
and ... would succumb to death rather than to dishonor." Quoted in Smith, *Origins
of Modern Culture*, pp. 270–71.

[14] For the following, Pleticha, *Adel und Buch*, especially the conclusion and pp.
228–29.

[15] For the following Brunner, *op. cit.*, 237–259; see also his "Das "Ganze Haus,"
pp. 33–61.

Landleben of 1682.[16] This was a guide to managing one's estate, with
sections on the land and its mills, ovens, and salt-works, on the duties
of the *Hausvater* and the *Hausmutter* and their concerns ranging from
the annual *Arbeitskalendar* to the *Hausapotheke*, on the technology of
the winery and of the kitchen-medicinal—and flower-gardens, on
agriculture and animal husbandry, on beekeeping and silk worms,
on estate hydraulics from health springs to millraces, angling to beaver
dams and forestry. Brunner found that the book was based on Greek
and Hellenistic texts, especially on Xenophon and Aristotle as transmitted to early-modern times, on humanism including Latini's *Trésor*,
and on a practical fund of German *Agrarliteratur*. It was, in short,
part of an unbroken Western intellectual history running from Greece
to Rome to the revival of Classical Latin to the schooling of the
humanists. Furthermore, because it was grounded in the Aristotelianism of the schools, this *Oeconomia domestica et ruralis* could itself in the
eighteenth century become an academic concern. It was the root of,
for example, a Christian Wolff who could write ably on science, ethics,
economics, and politics. von Hohberg stands as a symbol of the impact of humanism on early-modern, non-clerical culture.

Most remarkable was a humanistic melding of Christianity and
paganism. The reading habits of an educated noble in seventeenth-
century central Europe shared spiritual texts with his earlier less-
educated forebear. After the Reformation and the spread of printing
Scripture came to stand side by side with Cicero, Virgil, and Horace,
with Homer, Aesop, Apuleius, Ovid, Herodotus, Xenophon, Valerius
Maximus, Suetonius, and others, with Seneca, Pliny, and Plutarch,
plus whatever humanists or modern authors one happened to own.[17]
Among the urban classes of the seventeenth century the preponderance
of religious reading materials was much greater, but when formal
secondary or higher education was available, a library of ancient
authors, especially Cicero, was to be found, even among those of
modest means.[18]

Quite ordinary German nobles' libraries of the sixteenth century
had counted perhaps fifty to a hundred volumes. By 1600 they or-
dinarily ranged upwards from a hundred volumes, and the Latin

---

[16] For the following, Brunner, *op. cit.*, 237–259; see also his "Das Ganze Haus,"
pp. 33–61.
[17] Engelsing, *Die Bürger als Leser*, pp. 27ff.
[18] *Ibid.*, Chapter 4, "Die Lektüre der bremer Bürger im 17. Jahrhundert," pp.
46–55, esp. pp. 50, 54.

Classics assumed a greater significance. By the end of the seventeenth century, private aristocratic libraries of four or five hundred
volumes were not uncommon, and those of clerics, of prince-bishops
"did not in any way differ from the book collections of their contemporaries. Not once did theological works predominate," so great was
the weight of the pagan Classical authors.[19]

Education transformed the early-modern nobility. Classics joined
Christianity. A nexus of religion, Classicism, and humanism came to
characterize elite non-clerical education in seventeenth-century Europe. German evidence is emphasized here, for a vast scholarly literature suggests that the German-speaking realm and Russia were
closely comparable. But the impact of humanism is a story generally
unappreciated in Soviet histories of education and book culture, which
tended dialectically to dismiss out-of-hand all Latin study as archaic
"scholasticism," and disparaged its religious content as well. At the
moment that Western Europe was to become a cultural model for
the Muscovite court, this was the moving cultural target in the middle
of the seventeenth century, about a century after the first printed
book appeared in Muscovy.

Otto Brunner was not a Russian historian, but he was convinced
that this great synthesis of Christianity, Latin-pagan culture, the
Christian-Renaissance revival, and the emerging aristocratic ethos did
not reach Muscovy: "The Greek east," he noted, "never resolved
this fundamental tension between pagan-secular and ecclesiastical
values."[20] This chapter examines the educational and book culture of
late Muscovy, asks whether and where the Classics were found, and
seeks their significance.

2. Muscovite Book Culture and Soviet Historiography

A. Attitudes Toward Books and Printing

Contrasted to Western Europe in the seventeenth century, Muscovy
was a bookless wasteland. According to the leading Soviet historian
of the book, this changed at mid-century with the "culturally enlight-

---

[19] Pleticha, *op. cit.*, 20–70, here esp. p. 70. This section, designed to anticipate the
library holdings of Muscovy, necessarily slights the theme of literacy; see the recent
summary by Houston, *Literacy in Early Modern Europe.*

[20] *Ibid.*, p. 80.

ening activities of Ukrainians and Belorussians" who founded Muscovy's first schools,"[21] and with the beginnings of secular publishing in Muscovy. In the 1640s the press in Moscow began to circulate printed books among the various strata of the population, and the first sizeable libraries appeared, characterized by "a large number of secular books and by books in foreign languages." "A sharp increase in the interest of Russians for literature of secular content was the chief characteristic of the second half of the seventeenth century," even among Muscovy's simple folk.[22] This chapter examines these propositions as they are routinely repeated in Soviet historiography and in Western histories of Russian book.[23]

Concerning the origins of the printed book in Muscovy, very little need be said here.[24] For almost a century it consisted solely of liturgical books. During the first hundred years of printing books in Moscow, if the press made more copies of books available to larger numbers of readers, it had no measurable impact on the kinds of books Muscovites consumed. When Soviet scholars paraded the isolated mid-seventeenth-century appearance of "secular" books in Muscovy, the *Ulozhenie* or a translated infantry manual, as evidence of the rise of

---

[21] Compare Winter, *Frühaufklärung*, p. 272: With the arrival of the White Russian Simeon Polockij, because he began Latin schooling and prepared translations for a large part of the population, the *Frühaufklärung* could begin.

[22] Luppov, *Kniga v Rossii v XVII veke*, conclusion, pp. 213–215. The story of libraries in seventeenth-century Muscovy, those of the *prikazy*, of the monasteries, of Nikon, and of other individuals, has been told without Luppov's pseudo-Marxism, and without the artificial religious-secular division, by Slukhovskii, *Bibliotechnoe delo*, but the works of Luppov have become the standard.

[23] Compare, for example, Luppov, *XVII veke*, pp. 30ff. with [Rogov], "Knigopechatanie," *Ocherki russkoi kul'tury XVII veka*, pp. 155–169, and with Barenbaum, *Geschichte des Buchhandels*, pp. 28–40.

[24] The nationalistic bibliography is already so inflated that even Soviet scholars have complained. The value of these mountains of publications on Muscovy's tragic first printer, Ivan Fedorov, has been questioned by Dneprov, "Relentlessly Running in Place." The worst excesses of Soviet eulogy can be avoided with the standard German survey, Appel, "Die Anfänge des Buchdrucks." One reason for the excesses was a strain of new anti-Normanism, the charge that the Russians received print from the Germans, an allegation violently contested during and after the Second World War; the first printer was, in fact, German: Wynar, *History of Early Ukrainian Printing*, pp. 9–13; but see Tikhomirov, "Nachalo Knigopechataniia," and "Moskva i kul'turnoe razvitie," pp. 267, 311ff. The standard works are by Nemirovskii, *Vozniknovenie knigopechataniia, Nachalo knigopechataniia na Ukraine, Ivan Fedorov v Belorussii*, and most recently, *Ivan Fedorov okolo 1510–1583*. Note also the bibliography of twenty years of Fedoroviana subsequent to the discovery and publication of his first primer: Botvinnik, "Istoriografiia izucheniia "Azbuki." On the primer itself, see my *Discovery of Childhood*, pp. 14–16.

the secular, they gave mute testimony that nothing worthy of the word had appeared from a Muscovite press between 1575 and 1650, and very little thereafter.

The gap between Muscovy and Orthodox Eastern Europe was enormous and easily established. A list of books published in Cracow between 1506 and 1548[25] leads to two obvious conclusions. First, the vast Polish-Lithuanian realm had participated in the print revolutions of Western Europe, and Moscow did not. By general European standards Cracow was slow to found a press and relatively provincial long after it did. But insignificant little Cracow alone in the first half of the sixteenth century could boast six or seven productive printers, and in fact seventeen separate printing companies, before Moscow had its first. Second, Poland was part of Western Civilization, and Muscovy was not. Long before Moscow could print a simple single-sheet ABC book or a Gospel in Church Slavonic, provincial Poland was cranking out Latin editions of Cicero's *De officiis*, of Eutropius' ten books of Roman history,[26] of Demosthenes, Pliny, and Hesiod, Aristotle's *De anima*, and Erasmus, in addition to the standard Christian fare of missals and psalters, and Polish-language works of divines, schoolmasters, and Christian polemicists of the early Reformation.

It is a commonplace that Muscovy missed the Renaissance—in terms of technology and attitudes toward nature she missed the Middle Ages as well.[27] She missed almost entirely its concomitant print revolution.[28] Soviet scholarship held that Muscovite culture was "not at all so distant from that of the era of the Renaissance as is commonly

---

[25] Nemirovskii's major works are listed above; here "Izdaniia pervoi pol'skoi tipografii," pp. 5–27.

[26] It was "used as a school text until modern times"; Hadas, *Latin Literature*, p. 371.

[27] Wes, *Classics in Russia*, p. 3; see also my "Peter Tolstoi in Rome."

[28] Early in the process of canonizing Fedorov, a massive book display was assembled to commemorate the 375th anniversary of his death. It consisted of Muscovite, Belorussian, and Ukrainian editions, as well as the manuscripts he challenged. Covering over a century and a quarter of Slavonic printings, the display cases held just three works on mathematics. One was a textless table of sines and cosines, one a tradesman's ready reckoner, and the third Magnitskii's *Arithmetika* of 1703. The display was almost exclusively one of Epistles, breviaries, Gospels, primers, and Minea, the trappings of Orthodox ritual alone. See "Doklady i soobshcheniia . . ." One piece of Fedorovian excess in Sapunov, "Ivan Fedorov i Renessans," which argues that, because a letter by Fedorov mentions a cannon, he can be compared to da Vinci and Dürer. The older literature prior to Soviet chauvinism was more modest. See, for example, Ptashitskii, "Ivan Fedorov."

assumed."[29] Thus it took a heretical historian to declare that there were two East-Slavic cultural communities in the sixteenth century, Muscovy and the "Lithuanian-Russian" state, the latter including the Ukrainians and Belorussians. Only these westerly peoples, linked culturally to Poland and Western Europe, had a Renaissance.[30]

Some voices in Muscovy made a virtue of booklessness. The most eloquent was one Silvestr, a monk who was a confederate of Tsar Ivan IV in the middle of the sixteenth century. He was the likely compiler of the *Domostroi*, the "House-Orderer," or Book of Household Management.[31] It survives in some forty manuscript copies. It is so infamous in the history of Russian education for its brutality toward children and women that V. O. Kliuchevskii felt compelled to apologize for it.[32] Dmitrij Cizevskij found *Domostroi* to be alien to Europe, "totally different" from contemporary manuals of behavior, noting that such books in Western Civilization always gave "serious treatment of moral problems," while *Domostroi* did not.[33]

Kliuchevskii, however, detected the fact that *Domostroi* preached a vision of life that was to its core anti-book, anti-intellectual, and indeed anti-intellect. Long after the dawn of the modern world, when elsewhere the printing presses of the Renaissance, Reformation, and Counter-Reformation were seducing all with reading, this major Muscovite cultural statement condemned reading and all idle

---

[29] Alekseev, *Iavleniia gumanizma*, p. 38. His views subsequently moderated. Outrageous claims have long been made for literacy and for philosophizing in ancient Kiev Rus'; while the topic is beyond the scope of this essay, see the convincing debunking by Franklin, "Booklearning and Bookmen in Kievan Rus'." In English, the hostility to learning in Muscovy was summarized by Lewitter, "Poland, the Ukraine and Russia," pp. 159–162.

[30] Nemirovskii, *Frantsisk Skorina*, pp. 79, 81, 94.

[31] The former standard edition was Orlov, ed., *Domostroi*; see also Ryan, ed., *Domostroi* (reprint of Zabelin's ed. of 1882), and the new edition, *Domostroi*, Kolesova, ed., with variant readings and sources. The long-awaited English version has appeared, Pouncy, trans., *The Domostroi*. In German see Müller, ed., *Altrussisches Hausbuch "Domostroi"*. Pouncy, "The Origins of the Domostroi," casts doubt on its connection to Silvestr', but ascribes it "probably" to 1550–1560 to a "secular" audience, for whom however "Biblical models" rang true. See also Bushkovitch, *Religion and Society*, pp. 47–49.

[32] "V. O. Kliuchevskii on Childhood," pp. 445–47. For sources available to "Silvestr'" see Müller's "Nachwort," *Altrussisches Hausbuch*, pp. 137–138, and Pouncy, *op. cit*. Müller does point out that a large part of Chapter 20 of *Domostroi*, "The Praise of Women," is based closely on Proverbs 31: 10–31. "Who can find a virtuous woman? for her price is far above rubies . . ., she is like the merchants' ships; she bringeth her food from afar . . ."; p. 138.

[33] Cizevskij, *Russian Literature*, pp. 305–06.

philosophizing as sure paths to sin, and ultimately to perdition.[34] A century later the proud old-ritualist archpriest Avvakum during the great Russian Church schism would faithfully echo its contempt for learning. "I am unschooled in words, but not in understanding. I am unschooled in dialectics and rhetoric and philosophy," he would boast, "but I have Christ's understanding within me."[35]

Popular Muscovite culture was absorbed with this fundamental mistrust of books, which would survive into Old Belief. Paul Bushkovitch, however, reminds us that Muscovite culture was stratified, and the elites followed quite different norms. There the reading of manuscript collections, and eventually printed books, was more common. There the printed book slowly made its mark. Among the elites of the court and the Church other cultural patterns pertained.

B. *The Repertoire of Books: How Secular?*

Manuscript books in Muscovy were limited to a small cluster of Eastern Orthodox patristics, Scripture, the Psalter, and the books of Church ritual. When one surveys all the manuscript book titles mentioned in medieval "Russia"—it has been done—one comes away with the picture of a very limited and circumscribed cultural world: Psalms, Gospels and Epistles, individual saints' lives, liturgical service books,[36] and collections like the Prolog and the Menology (Menea; the lives of saints arranged by the calendar), small collections of the Eastern

---

[34] The disturbing passage is one where Silvestr' tells his son that one child, according to his birth, might be taught "reading, writing, and singing," another icon painting, another still silver-smithing or a different craft, clearly indicating that literacy had no value in itself, that it was merely another skill or trade. See Müller, *op. cit.*, p. 124.

[35] Avvakum, *The Life*, Brostrom, ed., pp. 100, 101. Avvakum praised simple speech, and "those wise without books" (neknizhnye mudretsy); see Robinson, "Zarozhdenie kontseptsii," p. 47.

[36] A full set of the service books, cited often here, was a small library of about twenty folio manuscript volumes; it would consist of twelve volumes of the Minea or Minoeon, the services and hymns for the festivals of the saints, one for each month; the Octoechos in two or three volumes, the hymns for the days of the week with other hymns; a volume containing the Psalter and the Hours; the book of Psalms; a volume of daily prayers and the Ectinias; two volumes of the Fast Triods or the period of Lent and the days of Pentecost; a volume of the Gospels; the Book of Offices with the rites for baptism, marriage, burial, etc.; and a regulation on how to use the rest. See Robert Pinkerton in Platon, *The Present State*, pp. 25–26. In practice, the list was usually shorter. Stocking a church in 1686, for example, required "evangelie naprestol'noe, sluzhebnik, mineia obshchaia, prolog vo ves' god, psaltyr uchebnaia, triod tsvetnaia"; see the document in *Russko-belorusskie sviazi*, p. 341.

Church Fathers, and the local chronicles—in short, a spiritual repertoire which can only proclaim that old Rus' and Muscovy had little
in common with the West intellectually.[37] Abbot Dosifei, who gathered
the initial collection for the Solovetskii monastery's overwhelmingly
liturgical library in the age of Columbus was typical not only of the
church, but of society at large.[38] The dynamic Romanov restoration
of the seventeenth-century changed the situation little. Only three
percent of the population read beyond the abecedarium, and the
entire purpose of an expansion in the printing of Orthodox primers
at mid-century was "to ensure that priests learn how to recite the
liturgy and perform the rites properly."[39]

Book culture in sixteenth-century Muscovy differed from post-
Renaissance-Europe in that more individuals, both lay and clerical,
read books directly related toward the salvation of their souls in traditional ways recorded in *Domostroi*. Some in society were more secular
or cosmopolitan, some were oriented toward the values of the steppe
peoples, and some were attracted to the culture of those representatives
of the West who lived among them. But Muscovite Orthodox believers
rejected the heretical West, rejected its roots in the Latin culture of
antiquity and the Medieval West, and rejected the neo-Roman humanistic values of its elites. At least since the fall of Constantinople
in 1453 increasingly they saw themselves as the God-ordained pre-
servers of a one, true, life-giving, Christianity. Although Muscovy's
merchants could trade with Protestants and her diplomats deal with
the Ottoman and the Catholic Empires, the story of sixteenth-
century Russian book-culture was still of one directed to the values
of the next world. Their claims to have the exclusive route to salvation
amused foreigners,[40] but that path was precisely where their values
lay, and it relied minimally on reading or the book.

---

[37] Rozov's two monographs are his *Kniga drevnei rusi* , and *Kniga v Rossii v XV veke*.
Elsewhere Rozov has noted that the total number of books for the period 1200–
1500 is outrageously low: "K opredeleniiu poniatiia 'kniga,'" pp. 11–19. See also
his essays on medieval Russian readership, "Chitateli russkoi knigi," and "Russkie
biblioteki XV v. i ikh chitateli," pp. 51–59. See, by way of contrast, on the West,
Curtius, *Europaische Literaturgeschichte*, or Bolgar, *Classical Influences on European Culture,
A.D. 500–1500*.
[38] Rozov, "Solovetskaia biblioteka." See also his "Nekotorye problemy." Note also
the broader statement covering the fifteenth through seventeenth centuries in
Slukhovksii, *Bibliotechnoe delo*, pp. 25–32.
[39] See respectively, Gary Marker, "Literacy and Literacy Texts," and his "Primers
and Literacy."
[40] Olearius, *op. cit.*, p. 233.

Soviet scholarship was virtually unanimous in proclaiming the rise
of secular reading as the essential trait of the seventeenth century.
The Muscovite "library became larger than in preceding periods,
growing in size and changing composition" as secular books replaced
religious. The first Romanov, for example, owned thirty-two books,
mostly of an "ecclesiastical-theological character." Although the young
Aleksei Mikhailovich had only fifteen books, he had "more secular
books than his father." His brother Ivan, although he died at age
6, had more books, ninety-nine, and "the range of secular books
widened."[41]

For Soviet scholars, the same pattern held true for broader courtly
circles: During the Time of Troubles M. Tatishchev had but five
books, but Prince V. V. Golitsyn had amassed a collection of 266
books in 1689, no fewer than a hundred of them secular.[42] Among
the clergy, the former Patriarch Filaret in 1637 owned 155 books,
printed and manuscript, with only a few of them secular, but by
mid-century Patriarch Nikon's library was far larger, 1282 books,
with at least 154 of them secular. By the end of the century Paul,
Metropolitan of Sarai and the Don region, and Afanasii, Archbishop
of Kholmogory, had very large collections, bristling with secular books,
with books in Greek, Polish and German, and with globes and maps
as well.[43]

These scholars argued that even monastic libraries shared this
tendency to increasing secular content, as did the books of the bureaucrats of the *prikazy*, town-dwellers, and peasantry, although sources
for such groups were scarce.[44] One scholar found that ten percent of
the private surreptitious reading of monks in the Kirillo-Belozerskii
monastery and in the Troitse-Sergieva *lavra* in the fifteenth century
included "items of secular content."[45] Another study argued that the

---

[41] Baklanova, "Russkii chitatel'," pp. 171–72. There are two methods of ascribing
texts to owners, and written notes, and inventories after death; the latter endowed a
child with a sizeable library. Soviet literary historians' equivalent of Baklanova's
search for the "secular" is the search for "*belletristiki*," evidence of pure literary in-
tent. In the hands of Ia. S. Lur'e and colleagues, the scholarship is done with grace
and sophistication. See *Istoki russkoi belletristiki*. This was a phenomenon of the manuscript; a recent article, for example, found only one piece of printed *literature*, so
defined, in the entire 17th century; see [Rogov], "Knigopechatanie," p. 156.

[42] Baklanova, pp. 173–76. See Ikonnikov, *op. cit.*, pp. 1072–79.

[43] Baklanova, pp. 176–78.

[44] *Ibid.*, pp. 176–78.

[45] Dmitrieva, "Svetskaia literatura."

number of printed books "of secular content" in the northern Solovetskii monastery jumped from a mere two in 1645 to sixty-five in 1657.[46] Sales records at the Moscow Printing Court for the years 1650–53 and 1663–65,[47] seemed to demonstrate that secular books were purchased by a wide spectrum of society, "from patriarch and boyar to courtiers."

This consistent preoccupation of Soviet scholars with the triumph of secular can be questioned. Luppov's attention to a translated infantry manual, for example, must be balanced by the fact that of 1,187 copies of it printed, 992 or 84% remained on the shelves unsold, at a moment when 304 of the 313 copies of the monthly liturgical guide sold, when 126 of 128 copies of an edition of the Gospels sold. When the infantry manual was selling less than nine copies per month, editions of Scriptures and of the Psalter sold at the rate of 323 and 286 copies per month respectively.[48] Soviet scholars invariably pointed to the sales (perhaps 2400 copies) of the secular *Ulozhenie*, but no other printed book of the century was ordered to be distributed to "all the chancelleries and . . . provincial towns."[49] The putative increase in the fund of secular books at Solovetskii was due to the arrival of sixty copies of an *"azbuk uchitel'nykh pechatnykh v tetratekh,"* almost certainly the 1657/(7165) *Bukvar' v tipografii pervoe izdadesia,* issued by Patriarch Nikon and Tsar Aleksei, the first full primer printed in Moscow since Burtsev's edition of 1637.[50] The inventories for 1666 and 1676 indicated that they had been dispersed.

Soviet scholars inflated the "secular" list. They included as secular the *Grammatika* of Meletij Smotryc'kyj.[51] The author was a monk, he wrote to make the study of Scripture intelligible, and he began his grammar with question-and-answer catechistics. Primers throughout the East-Slavic world routinely specified that the entire goal of reading was access to Scripture, *"chelovekom khotiashim ouchitisia knig bozhestvenago pisania* (for he who wishes to read the books of divine

---

[46] Kukushkina, *Monastyrskie biblioteki,* Table 10, p. 169.

[47] Luppov, *Chitateli izdanii moskovskoi tipografii,* pp. 15, 20 and passim; subsequently he published an alphabetical listing of, and a geographical index to, the names of these buyers. See his *Pokupateli izdanii moskovskoi tipografii.*

[48] *Ibid.,* 12, 48, and *passim.*

[49] *The Muscovite Law Code (Ulozhenie),* Richard Hellie, trans., p. 2.

[50] See Zernova, *Knigi kirillovskoi pechati,* pp. 69, 85.

[51] *Ibid.,* pp. 169, 172, 175. The modern facsimile edition is Smotrit'skii, *Gramatika,* Nimchuka, ed.

writing)." They opened with a selection from vespers, other prayers, and a catechism.[52]

In their zeal to crush religion in the past and present, Soviet historians categorized everything as "secular content" up to and including the Bible's Book of Proverbs.[53] Soviet scholars regarded as "secular" every mention of a chronicle. Calling the oldest Kievan-era chronicles "secular" is like calling the New Testament "natural science" because it indicates that the sun comes up in the morning. One need only think of the *Primary Chronicle*'s attribution of Christianization to Vladimir's escape from a debauchery, parallel to Solomon's even to the number of his concubines, to the miraculous healing of his eyes, to the fulfillment of a prophecy,—to everything Christian, in short, except to the actual politics of religion in the Byzantine empire in the ninth century. Since the Chronicle was written by a monk, it opens with a biblical division of the tribes and with the story of St. Andrew's proselytizing in Kherson, is studded with Scriptural citations (often omitted in translations sanitized for modern students), and has as its chief theme the conversion of the Rus' into "a new Christian people, the elect of God," it requires a cynical modern mind to deem it "secular."[54]

Soviet scholars also included as secular the Russian redactions of Byzantine Christian compilations, the ninth-century Chronicle of George Hamartolos and the sixth-century Chronicle of John Malalas,[55] the Chronograph's "Aleksandriia," the version of the story of Alexander the Great wholly and closely interwoven with Christian motifs and fantastic pilgrimages,[56] and the *Sinopsis* (1674) of Inokentij Hizel'

---

[52] See the recent edition by Roberts, *The Slavonic Calvinist Reading-Primer*, and Okenfuss, *op. cit.* I have not discovered evidence concerning how Orthodox Muscovites reacted to Smotritskii's advice to the newly literate—he was a Belorussian divine who composed his grammar outside the realm of the Muscovites—to read the pagans, Homer, Hesiod, Ovid, Virgil, and others, although that advice made perfect sense in the fully Western Lithuania from which he came. See Dvoichenko-Markova, "Iz istorii russko-rumynskikh kul'turnykh vziamosviazei," p. 270.

[53] Kukushkina, *op. cit.*, p. 169; Dmitrieva, *op. cit.*, p. 153, includes under the rubric "secular" a collection entitled "Excerpts from Old and New Testament Histories."

[54] See Cross & Sherbowitz-Wetzor, trans, *The Russian Primary Chronicle*, pp. 51–54, 93–119, and *passim*.

[55] Cizevskij, *op. cit.*, p. 24. On the Russian Chronographs of 1512 and 1617 see *Ibid.*, p. 310, and the classic, Popov, *Obzor khronografov*. See also Tvorogov, *Drevnerusskie khronografy*.

[56] Cizevskij, *op. cit.*, p. 26. Dmitrieva specifically distinguishes it from the "Serbian" *Aleksandriia* which is more secular. See Fennell and Stokes, *op. cit.*, p. 139. The old standard study is Istrin, *Aleksandriia russkikh khronografov*. The new standard reference

(Innokentii Gizel'). This Prussian Protestant convert to Orthodoxy went to Kiev, befriended Mohyla, taught at the Academy, and conducted a famous three-day theological debate with a Jesuit. Based largely on the *Kronika Polska* of Stryikowski, his book repeated all of the theological elements of the conversion of the Rus', attributed the translation of Greek books into Slavonic to "the Holy Spirit" (p. 68), and accepted a spiritual rather than a political or genealogical interpretation of the "Holy Martyrs Boris and Gleb" (p. 153). Even a late edition published by the Academy of Sciences concluded with a prayer and a blessing.[57]

The *Stepennia kniga* was regarded as secular in spite of its typical sixteenth-century ecclesiastical style in which "the religious aspect of history is strongly brought to the fore," and in which the Tsars of Moscow emerge triumphant as "God appointed holders of the sceptre, who, like the trees in Paradise, were planted by God."[58] Soviet scholars of the book also deemed secular the "Tale of Barlaam and Josaphat," a Christian version of the story of the Buddha, in which Josaphat struggles against his pagan father, brings his country to Christianity, and is pursued by dragons and unicorns.[59]

Religious motives guided all Muscovite compilers. In the Polish and Ukrainian translations of the *Magnum Speculum Exemplorum*, which later found their way into the Muscovite manuscript tradition, individual stories were included specifically because of their "religiosity," that is, their resonance with the "well-known and traditional Slavonic lives of the saints from such collections as patericons, the Prolog, and *Cet'i Menei*."[60] The scant information about the ancient world in

---

work for old-Muscovite literature of this period is now the *Slovar' knizhnikov i knizhnosti drevnei Rusi*.

[57] Gizel', *Sinopsis*, 5th ed., St. Petersburg, 1762. In all there were twenty five civil-script and Cyrillic printings in Russia by 1762. Sumtsov, "Innokentii Gizel'." On Biblical elements in its history of the early Slavs, see Black, *G.-F. Müller*, p. 33. All geographies are deemed secular, even manuscripts which contain nothing more than the distances from Moscow to other cities, as useful for the pilgrim as for the diplomat. See V. A. Petrov, "Geograficheskie spravochniki XVII v."

[58] Cizevskii, *op. cit.*, pp. 158, 302–04; Luppov too regards it as secular; see his *XVII vek*, p. 98. On its seventeenth-century infiltration into the books of saints' lives, see Kuchkin, "Pervye izdaniia russkikh Prologov," pp. 139–154.

[59] Cizevskij, *op. cit.*, pp. 27–28, 91. The standard modern edition is Lebedeva, ed., *Povest' o Varlaame i Iosafe*. While book historians regard it as secular, its appearance in a seventeenth-century collection depicted the principals with halos and with the descent of the Holy Spirit. See the illustrations following p. 160 in *Literaturnye sbornik XVII veka. Prolog*.

[60] See Lewin, "Polish-Ukrainian-Russian Literary Relations," p. 259, citing the work of Derzhavina, *'Velikoe Zertsalo'*.

Muscovy came via Polish satirical novellas known as the *facetiae*. There
by the late seventeenth century, a Muscovite could read a paragraph
"About Caesar Augustus and the poet Virgil," about Socrates, about
Demosthenes or Diogenes, or about Alcibiades, "prince of Athens,"
or Scipio Africanus. If such lofty topics happened to be interspersed
with Christian parables and tales of "How the woman taught the
bear to read,"[61] they at least offered late Muscovite and eighteenth-
century Russian readers a taste of Classical antiquity inaccessible
earlier. Although translated Polish and Latin works sometimes merged
Classical content with traditional saints' lives,[62] religious values dictated selection and set tastes.

Soviet scholars called "secular" the *Stoglav*, the decisions of the
Church Council of 1551, the *Paleia*, an exposition of Biblical history,
with notes derogatory to Judaism, the *Pilgrimage of Abbot Daniil*, a tale
of a hierarch from Chernihiv who travelled to Palestine in 1106–
1108 to observe the Easter Liturgy at the Holy Sepulchre,[63] and the
Epistle to the Ugra, 1480, written by Archbishop Vassian of Rostov,
which places the deed of the "pious, Christ-loving, well-born, God-
crowned, God-confirmed . . . [and] most glorious and shining sovereign amongst tsars" along side those of Constantine the Great, Moses,
Joshua, Judah, Gideon, Samson, and David, among others.[64] Such
were the doubtful techniques of Soviet scholarship.

The growth of secular publishing and reading in seventeenth-century
Moscow is a carefully nurtured Soviet myth. The printing press remained firmly in the hands of the Patriarchate, and although there
was the slightest wavering at mid-century, no Patriarch from Filaret
through Adrian tolerated its use for "secular" purposes. This is the
single greatest distinction between Muscovy and the West, including
the Polish-Lithuanian state. The exceptions, and they were just that,
numbered no more than seven books or 1.45% over the entire century:

[61] Derzhavina, *Fatsetsii*, pp. 105, 109, 111, 116, 140, and *passim*. Popular themes
also included Alexander the Great and the Fall of Troy; see Egunov, *Gomer v russkikh
perevodakh*.
[62] See Ziolkowski, *Hagiography and Modern Russian Literature*, intro, esp. 19–23.
[63] Cizevskij, *op. cit.*, 60–62, 143, 253.
[64] Fennell & Stokes, *op. cit.*, p. 142. One wonders too what Karl Heinrich Rengstorf,
editor of *A Complete Concordance to Flavius Josephus*, Leiden, 4 folio vols., 1973–83,
would think of his life's subject being flaunted as rampant secularism, when after 20
years of labor, he dedicated his work to "three renowned centers of theological
scholarship and teaching, the theological faculties "Tubingense, Ludensis,
Aberdonensis."

an illustrated soldiers' manual by Walhausen, a table of sines and cosines without text, a practical arithmetic text with multiplication tables—these solitary printings are evidences of a cultural unity of Patriarch and Tsar, of Church and State, in the Romanov restoration. Both culturally and statistically they were insignificant when the Psalter was reprinted at least forty-four times, the liturgical service book twenty-eight times, the Breviary twenty-seven times, and the Gospels twenty-two times. Furthermore, the press runs of these liturgical texts printed grew steadily over the century.[65]

The idea of a secular printing press in Muscovy was a complete fabrication of recent Soviet historiography. Publishing in Moscow was rigidly controlled the the Church and remained wholly religious in its content until the eighteenth century.

C. *The Manuscript Tradition and Reading*

Perhaps manuscripts were more secular than printed books in seventeenth-century Moscow? It is sometimes suggested that the presence of Greek manuscripts in Muscovy and other popular reading materials attested to the steady secularization of society. In some ways a flurry of recent studies has reinvented the wheel, since it has long been recognized that manuscripts in Muscovy became more varied in content during the hospitable and receptive era of Ivan III; a Western dynastic marriage, Italian architects at work building the Kremlin walls, erecting cathedrals with Renaissance scallop decorations, designing "faceted palaces" with stonework identical to that of the Sforza's in Milan, and leaving "Deo-gratia" Latin inscriptions over entry gates—one could only expect to find reflections in literary life and manuscript production as well.[66] The sixteenth century was quite another matter.

---

[65] Amosov, "Zametki o moskovskom staropechatanii," pp. 5–12; Luppov, *XVII vek*, p. 29. For a recent study of one of richest and best endowed monastery and of its book collection on which a century of Muscovite book publishing had almost no visible impact, see Popesku, "Osnovnye istochniki XVII veka," pp. 26–38. The near frantic search for anything vaguely secular continued a decade after Luppov wrote. See [Rogov], "Knigopechatanie," *Ocherki*, p. 156, where the *Testament* of the Greek Emperor Basil to his son Leo the philosopher is included, along with prayer-book-primers.

[66] See for example Stökl, "Das Echo von Renaissance"; Winter, *Rußland und das Papstum*, I; Sacharov, "Über den Kampf gegen das 'Lateinertum' in Rußland," pp. 92–105; Medlin & Patrinelis, *Renaissance Influences*, good on the handful of Greeks in Moscow.

Twenty-two Greek manuscripts were transcribed in Moscow, Tver, or Novgorod in the fifteenth and sixteenth centuries.[67] Most were done by Greeks who took them along when they left Muscovy, but their content added almost nothing to the repertoire already available in manuscript: they were service books and scripture, a bit of patristics, and the decisions of the old Councils of Nicea and Ephesus. Greek manuscripts provide no evidence of an intellectual infusion from afar. When Arsenii Sukhanov later departed Moscow for Greece in search of manuscripts for Nikon in October of 1653, there existed thirty-two Greek manuscripts in Moscow, none of them departing from the standard fare of Muscovite clerical bookmen.[68] Greeks did not necessarily champion the contemporary West. "Like Savonarola," the quintessential Greek in Moscow, Maksim Grek, "condemned the revival of pagan classical culture," since the Latins placed dialectical philosophical truth before spiritual truths.[69]

If more copies of reading material circulated among Muscovy's lower orders with the arrival of the printing press, it was virtually unchanged in its ecclesiastical and liturgical content.[70] Actual references to books in peasants' homes are understandably rare, but the book holdings of parish-church collections in two districts in 1629 included 267 printed books and 135 manuscripts, and from their titles one can glean some information on the "popular" reading materials in thirteen scattered churches. The most common books were the general and monthly Menology of the Saints, the Oktoich (Oktoechos) which together with the Triod' (Triodion) contained the liturgical chants for the entire year, and the Hexaemeron, the Psalter, Gospel, and Epistle, and the Prolog, the other service books. No *Domostroi* was found, and no foreign or translated books. Muscovite book culture remained almost wholly liturgical a half-century after the introduction of printing in Muscovy.

From the chance-survival of holdings of remote parishes one can

---

[67] Fonkich, *Grechesko-russkie kul'turnye sviazi*. The search for Greek manuscripts in Russia was originally a nationalistic response to Polish reports of the Time of Troubles that there existed no tsarist library, and no collection of Greek learning in Muscovy, thus undercutting the validity of the idea of "Third Rome." See Tikhomirov, "O biblioteke moskovskikh tsarei."

[68] *Ibid.*, pp. 10–70, esp. 45, 67, 68–70. The collection of Greek manuscripts held by the Ministry of Foreign Affairs, based on the older *Prikaz* collection, was studied by Belokurov, *O biblioteke moskovskikh gosudarei*, pp. cxxxvi–clxxxix.

[69] Zenkovsky, "The Ideological World of the Denisov Brothers," p. 63.

[70] Kopanev, "Volostnye krest'ianskie biblioteki," pp. 59–70.

trace the arrival of the printed book in the seventeenth century. Gospels, Epistles, Psalters, Oktoechos and Hexaemeron existed in multiple manuscript copies already in 1589–90. By 1676 and 1683 printed versions of the same texts coexisted. The repertoire of printed books available in parish collections in the late seventeenth century was not much expanded beyond the traditional cycle of Scripture, service books, and limited patristics available a full century earlier, at the dawn of Muscovite printing.[71] A century ago Ivan Zabelin published the book collection of the Church of All Saints at Izmailovo from 1687, and it showed a cycle of liturgical works exclusively.[72]

B. V. Sapunov attempted to quantify the ownership of books in Muscovy.[73] Using owners' marks to reconstruct libraries, he showed that the manuscript books of an Old-Believer contained nine titles deemed "secular" by the standards of Soviet scholarship: a Chronograph, Flavius Josephus, the *Stepennaia Kniga*, "Barlaam and Josaphat," among others, none of them outside the range of writings long accepted as routine for the seventeenth century. He established that peasants, 91.4% of the population, owned twenty-one books or 2.6% of his sample. Not surprisingly he discovered that the clergy, monasteries, and churches, owned two-thirds of all the printed and manuscript books in Muscovy, even though the "feudal" orders, the clergy, service classes and the army together comprised less that four percent of the population. In short, the new empirical research shows that the spread of books throughout the population had not actually proceeded very far; nor had the repertoire varied very much.[74]

Sapunov's work quantified the known ninety-three libraries and the 11,261 identifiable books from seventeenth-century Muscovy.[75] Of those manuscript and printed books, 544 or 4% were printed in the Ukraine. Books imported from the Ukraine, ninety percent of them from Kiev, were the liturgical books, Psalters and *Kanoniki*, Ostroh (Ostrog) Bibles, and the like. Ukrainian books were the most important category of non-Muscovite books circulating in Moscow between

[71] Kopanev, "Knizhnost' severnoi volosti," pp. 394–399.

[72] Zabelin, *Domashnyi byt russkikh tsarei*, Vol. I, part 1, p. 498.

[73] Sapunov, "Kniga i chitatel'," pp. 61–74.

[74] Luppov, *XVII vek*, pp. 76–96, and Baklanova, *op. cit.*, esp. pp. 183–89.

[75] See here Sapunov, "Ukrainskaia kniga," *Istoriia knigi*. See also the study, to be discussed below, "Antichnaia literatura," based on the same source base. In his "Izmenenie sootnoshenii rukopisnykh i pechatnykh knig," pp. 37–50, he worked with the total 223 descriptions and the 16,914 books from the sixteenth and seventen centuries.

the Smuta and Peter the Great, but their distribution may suggest
book hunger among the clergy, and may reflect the need for new
editions in the age of the Schism. It does not mirror secular intellectual
curiosity. However important were their subtle theological differences
to the *Raskol*, the books Muscovites imported from Kiev were the
same liturgical books they themselves produced in limited numbers.

The seventeenth century did witness a flurry of translations from
the outer world. It was "astonishing in its variety, its haphazard choice
of material, the frequently poor quality of its translations, the colour-
fulness of its language and not least, in the limited popularity of the
majority of the translations."[76] Some "secular" tales like the Serbian
Alexandria or the Tale of Dracula were copied in the 1480s and 1490s,
only to virtually disappear for over a century, as not in accord with
the sixteenth-century Church's ideological role.[77] Beginning with the
victory of the Josephites over heresy early in the 1500s, and culminating in the era of cultural classicism[78] at mid-century with the
production of standardized and standardizing patericons, genealogies,
law codes, church statutes, and the *Domostroi*, the Church's emphasis
was on uniformity, conformity, and on the imitation of an idealized
Orthodoxy of old Byzantium.

The architect of this sixteenth-century classicism was Metropolitan
Macarius. He compiled the Great Menology and the Book of Degrees,
fundamental texts for Ivan IV's political ideology. He did little re-
writing of the "sacred" Byzantine or Muscovite texts, and instead
limited himself to editing and compiling—the activities of a preserver,
rather than a creator: "Russia's cultural heritage had to be catalogued,
and interpreted, so that it, like the empire, might stand forever."[79]
This atmosphere could at first welcome Fedorov's printing activities,
and just as easily drive him to more hospitable refuge in East-Slavic
Orthodox lands outside the control of the conservative Muscovite
clergy. This chronology accounts for the fact that "secular" books
were more apparent at the Kirillo-Belozerskii and Troitse-Sergieva
monasteries at the end of the fifteenth century than they were a

---

[76] Cizevskij, *Russian Literature*, pp. 326–331, for the standard survey of translated
texts in the seventeenth century, not much altered by recent scholarship. The old
classic, on which all scholarship still relies, was Sobolevskii, *Perevodnaia literatura*.

[77] Fennell & Stokes, *Early Russian Literature*, pp. 139–40.

[78] On the concept, which I find useful in understanding Muscovy in the middle
of the sixteenth century, see von Grunebaum, "The Concept of Cultural Classicism,"
pp. 98–128.

[79] Miller, "The Velikie Minei Chetii," p. 365.

century later. It also accounts for the huge flood of manuscript saints'
lives, the material traces of the cults of miracles, relics, and saints
which dominated popular religiosity from 1550 to 1650.[80]

In the long run Macarius' cultural classicism was successful in freezing the publishing of books and the reading habits of Muscovy. It
created the milieu in which tampering with the inherited Church
was the greatest of all sins. In the meantime, the reading manuscript
traditions of Muscovy remained every bit as religious as the repertoire of printed books.

D. *Avvakum as a Mirror of Traditional Muscovy*

The most eloquent and authentic voice of the reading habits of old
Muscovy was the archpriest Avvakum.[81] Like the Ayatollah Khomeini
in our day, Avvakum rose up in indignation at the destructive influence
of the new and the Western, all of it the Devil's work. His life had
a single thread in an adamant rejection of compromise with the
Greeks, Ukrainians, and the Polonized courtiers who commanded
the attention of his tsar in the middle of the seventeenth century.

Avvakum's was no unlettered peasant. His sophisticated autobiography was part folk-tale and part Scripture, part peasant humor and
part sermon, part saint's life and part liturgy.[82] It also mirrored one
traditional strain of Muscovite literary culture. It praised booklessness,
save only the *Ladder of Literacy* leading to the liturgy. It expressed a
psychological preference for unlettered simplicity—although it could
be quite ingenious in its citations from a select corpus of learning.
Avvakum took pride in being "unschooled in dialectics and rhetoric
and philosophy,"—this being the commonplace description of the
content of the alien Ukrainian humanism that was beginning to
penetrate his church.

Avvakum was not alone. His friend the monk Epifanii, with whom
he endured the persecutions of the tsar and official Church, was also
proud that he "had not studied rhetoric, philosophy, or grammar to

---

[80] Dmitrieva, *op. cit.*, pp. 146–163. On the growth of the Kirillo-Belozerskii monastic collection, see the early work of Rozov, "Iz istorii kirillo-belozerskoi biblioteki";
on the cult of saints, Bushkovitch, *Religion and Society*, Chap. 5.

[81] Quotations below are from the standard translation, Avvakum, *The Life*, Brostrom,
trans. The critical edition, used by Brostrom, is that edited by Robinson, and the
newest biography that by Zhukov, "Avvakum Petrov." See also Brown, *Seventeenth
Century*, pp. 61–73.

[82] Vinogradov in Avvakum, *op. cit.*, p. 144.

get his healthy reason," proud that he had not gone to Athos to study "Platonic or Aristotelian" learning, proud that he "had not studied rhetoric or grammar in [his] youth."[83] Even in the Ukraine, of course, there remained dissenting anti-Latinists, including one Ivan Vishnevskii, who mistrusted schooling. He said that "a rhetorician and a philosopher cannot be a Christian," and with Avvakum, sought the old simplicity of life and of speech.[84] He rejected the values of Latin pagan education, as had many in Europe a century and a half earlier. There were recidivists: the well-known Andrei Denisov (1674–1730), organizer of a sectarian community in the Russian north, had been a student of the "rhetorical, philosophical, and theological sciences" at the Kiev Academy, and had then rejected schooling for the older, simpler values of Old-Belief.[85]

For such men the individual's choice was clear: either to pursue the disciplines of the Latin schooling of the Ukraine, or to limit study to the Breviary, Psalter and Gospels, and to remain a simple man "agreeable to God." One chose the apostles Peter and Paul or the pagan Aristotle; one aligned oneself with the authority of the Latin scholars or in good conscience chose a naive belief in Christ and the simplicity of the Apostolic faith.[86] Faced with these alternatives, the *pop* Ivan Nasedka of the Dormition Cathedral in Moscow defended ignorance and piety, and the absence of schools in Moscow. Soviet scholars regard Avvakum as "the bearer of the democratic ideas of the equality of the people";[87] the phraseology is Marxist cant, but indeed he was a populist symbol of the unity of Muscovite Orthodox culture, on the eve of the double onslaught of the Ukrainians' humanistic Latin culture, and the court's adoption of a Polonized reading list of adventures and romances.

Avvakum recognized the traditional texts of Muscovite religious life, those as *Domostroi* had put it, not harmful to the pursuit of Eternal Life. "Forgive me," wrote Avvakum, "I will chat with you a bit more

---

[83] Robinson, "Avtbiografiia Epifaniia," pp. 102–108. On the initial opposition to Mohyla's Latin humanism among Ukrainian clerics in Kiev, see Sydorenko, *The Kiev Academy*, pp. 26–37.

[84] Robinson, "Zarozhdenie kontseptsii avtorskogo stila," pp. 46–47.

[85] Tschizewskij, "Das Barock," pp. 16–17; Zenkovsky, "The Ideological World of the Denisov Brothers," p. 53.

[86] For this paragraph Florovskij, *Le conflict de deux traditions*, pp. 172, 177ff. These were the words of an Orthodox cleric from Galicia, Jean Vychensky, in the early seventeenth century.

[87] Eleonskaia, *Russkaia publitsistika*, p. 82.

about my ignorance. Once I did a stupid thing, so help me; I transgressed the commandment of my confessor, and because of this my house was punished." What stupid thing had led to all of his misfortunes? "I traded [the book of St. Efrem the Syrian, d. 373] for my cousin's horse,"[88] that is, he disobeyed his confessor, and he sought something of this world over the teachings of the Church. With that inevitably his household realm and the locus of his Faith, his *dom*, came to ruin.

One of Avvakum's acceptable authors was Dionysios the Areopagite. For him, Dionysios' cosmography, his sure knowledge that an eclipse "shows God's wrath against men,"[89] was every bit as "scientific" as the new texts the Ukrainians and Poles were translating from Renaissance Europe. "And in the time of King Hezekiah there was a sign: the sun went backwards in the twelfth hour of the day, and in the day and night were thirty-six hours. Read Dionysios' book; there will you learn of it at length." Patristics contained truth, not the Latins' error.

He was equally clear on new printed Ukrainian books. The monk Fedor, "uncommonly stern was the ascetic life of that Fedor," "had only a Psalter from the new printings in his cell then; he still knew only a little bit about the innovations. And [Avvakum] told him about the new books in detail. He grabbed the book and tossed it into the stove then and there, yes, and he damned all innovation."[90] Muscovite culture appreciated the true conservatory nature of Orthodoxy, rejected the new theologies, and the cursed printed books that held them.

For Avvakum the problem was more fundamental than the printed book or the externals of religious observance; it went to the use of language itself. His Faith was expressed in a "Russian" and "natural" language, while his enemies spoke "Hellenic," Greek, or worse, Latin. That critique of linguistic innovations became in time, among certain Old Believers, a defense of schoollessness. For example, the *starets* Avraamy, investigated for his incautious criticisms of tsar Peter, could boast in self-defence, "I have not studied rhetoric or philosophy, nor

---

[88] Avvakum, *The Life*, p. 101.

[89] For these passages, *Ibid.*, pp. 37–39, 208–11.

[90] *Ibid.*, pp. 89–91. Those Soviet scholars who are unhappy making Polockij and the Ukrainians the founders of modern Russian literature argue that such real-life heroes as this Fedor in Avvakum's writings were its birth; when Polockij succeeded him with "allegorical heroes," to be followed later by "purely fictional heroes" in Kantemir, Sumarokov, and Trediakovskii, the genuinely "Russian" roots had been established. See Demin, *Russkaia literatura*.

do I know the grammatical studies." In so many words he, like
Avvakum, clearly identified the enemy as the vertical curriculum
(grammar, rhetoric and poetics, and philosophy) of the Kievans'
Academy, the foreign languages upon which it was premised, and
the speech it encouraged.[91]

The attitudes of Avvakum and Avraamy were defensible and eloquent statements of old-Muscovite book values. The long history of
Old-Believer defiance and survival is testimony to their sincerity, and
to the appeal of the unlettered oral tradition of many in that society.
It was not obscurantism or ignorance to defend the old ways, nor
was it obtuse to reject the ills associated with the spread of the printed
book, the "seductions of this vain age."[92] "Shaving one's face, whether
with bladed razors or electric apparatuses intended for the same
purpose, is highly unacceptable," announced the leader of an Iran
returned to its religious roots. Like the Ayatollah Khomeini in the
1970s, Avvakum three hundred years earlier saw simple God-fearing
people tempted by a Satan-West, its books, and worldly pleasures;
when the formerly God-blessed civil authority in each case abandoned traditional ways, adopted Western military arts, supported a
"modern" version of the clergy, and permitted foreign innovation in
religions, the pious necessarily rejected the state and went over to an
integral defence of religious values.

Avvakum and his compatriots are not important because they
represented a popular culture's rejection of elite Western education.
They are significant because they were shrewd and, by their own
standards, well-read Christian clergy and literati, who rejected the
division between elite and popular religious culture in their own land.
Their religious fundamentalism was not a calculated pose, but an
integral insistence on the cultural values of the Muscovite Christian
commonwealth, grounded in the conviction that theirs was the one
true faith, and the one true Christian realm. Their opposition to the
Ukrainians, to Latin, and to studying "to philosophy" was not peasant obscurantism, but an intellectual rejection of a bifurcation of
cultures, unthinkable in their scheme of one Redeemer, one true Faith,
one Salvation, and one holy God-ordained Tsar.

---

[91] See Baklanova, "'Tetradi' startsa Avraamiia," and Siromakha, "Nikonovskaia
knizhnaia spravka," pp. 445–451.
[92] Avvakum, *The Life*, p. 84.

3. *Ukrainian Humanism's Challenge to Muscovite Culture*

A. *The Alien Nature of Ukrainian Humanism*

Prior to Soviet historians' claims to have discovered the triumph of the secular a half-century before Peter, there was an historical consensus. It was an image of seventeenth-century Muscovy that we knew from Kliuchevskii, from Platonov, and from Father Georges Florovsky, among others, including historians of the Schism.[93] It addressed the complex interrelationship of numerous cultural elements, Muscovite religiosity, Ukrainian humanism, Polish court culture, Western technology, the role of the Church in pre-modern societies, and international politics in the age of Westphalia.

For these scholars, Muscovite culture meant the arrival of alien learned Greeks and Ukrainians in Moscow, of their bringing with them Western Christian vernacular and Latin cultures unacceptable to most Muscovites, clerical and lay (lacking formal schools, the distinction scarcely existed),[94] and of violent protests by a society ready to die for the old, Orthodox, Muscovite ways.[95] Here we treat the coming of the Ukrainians. The political relations between Muscovy, Poland, and the Ukraine were complex. The historiographic conventions are also confused, divided as they are between Great Russians and Soviets who talk of the inevitable gathering of the "Russian"

---

[93] Kliuchevskii, *The Seventeenth Century*, Chap. 14 and *passim*; Platonov, *Moscow and the West*; Florovsky, *Ways of Russian Theology*. See also, Lewitter, "Poland, the Ukraine and Russia."

[94] The idea that Ukrainian ecclesiastical culture was Western and Muscovite was not is not a new one, of course. One older statement is in Winter, *Byzanz und Rom*. More recently see Subtelny, *Ukraine*, and Sysyn, "Concepts of Nationhood in Ukrainian History Writing." The official Soviet view of Ukrainians and Russians, fraternal peoples united to fight off the intrigues of Polish "feudals" and agents of the Vatican, can be sampled in Pushkarev, "Kul'turnye sviazi Ukrainy i Rossii." The ongoing Soviet attack on Ukrainian nationalism, the Harvard Ukrainian Institute, Richard Pipes, and others, can be seen in Kondufor et al., "Kritika sovremenykh burzhuazno-natsionalisticheskikh fal'sifikatsii." A pioneering study of the Slavinec'kyi-Polockij-Rostovs'kyj-Javors'kyj-Prokopovych tradition, discussed here, based on their libraries, was Brückner, *Die Europäisierung Rußlands*, pp. 195–213, which discussed the forbidden theme, the *Moglichkeit einer Polonisierung Rußlands*; new libraries have dated the work.

[95] The literature is voluminous and cannot even be sketched here, but the best short introduction is probably Zenkovsky, "The Russian Church Schism," but also his *Russkoe staroobriadchestvo*. Andreev, *Raskol i ego znachenie*, has an interesting chapter on the Raskol as a movement against "Western novelties." A classic Soviet account of the Schism as class-struggle is in Nikol'skii, *Istoriia russkoi tserkvi*.

lands, and Ukrainian nationalists who detect the ravages of Russian imperialism.[96]

Five steps led to the acquisition of the eastern Ukraine and Kiev by the Muscovites in 1654. One was the transfer of the region (never a part of Muscovy) from Orthodox-Lithuanian to Polish—Catholic administration in 1569; another was the rise of the Cossack hosts; a third was the incessant rebellion of those Cossacks and peasants against Polish rule after 1624, culminating in the uprising of Khmel'nyts'kyi in 1648. The final was taken in Pereiaslav in January 1654 when representatives of Ukraine considered four more or less viable options: a continuation of Polish rule, overtures to the Ottoman empire, to the Horde, or to a reluctant tsar in Moscow. The significance of a recognition of Muscovite sovereignty is hotly debated, but in 1654 in fact, and after 1667 de jure, the eastern Ukraine politically became part of Muscovy.

In the process of uniting eastern Ukraine and Muscow, it should be noted, Moscow's diplomacy was half-hearted, inept, and lacking any sense of historic mission; the popular enthusiasm of Muscovites for their brother Slavs was decidedly muted; the hostility of the Ukrainian hierarchy to the Moscovite Patriarch was intense; and the only people who seemed to celebrate the union of nominal ethnic brothers and co-religionists were Ukrainian scholars already in Muscovite employ, and the tiny Westernized elite of Moscow.[97]

The meaningful divisions in mid-seventeenth century Muscovite society were those stemming from education and geography, and the legal categories confirmed by the *Ulozhenie*.[98] The patterns of book ownership help us to understand them better. The Muscovite state had not yet annexed the alien cultures of educated clergy and townsmen of the Orthodox Ukraine, Belorussia, or Baltic regions. They were alien. They had never been Muscovite, and their churches were not centered on Moscow, the Kievan Metropolitanate being subjected

---

[96] The most recent and clearest statement of the divisions can be found in Pelenski, "The Contest," in Potichnyj, ed., *Ukraine and Russia*, pp. 3–5.

[97] See Edward L. Keenan, "Muscovite Perceptions," and Hans-Joachim Torke, "The Unloved Alliance," in Potichnyj, ed., *Ukraine and Russia*, pp. 35, 50–51, and passim.

[98] The authoritative Soviet edition is now *Sobornoe Ulozhenie 1649 goda*; note too the new magnificent English translation by Richard Hellie, *The Muscovite Law Code (Ulozhenie) of 1649. I. Text and Translation*, and the German version, *Das Sobornoe Ulozhenie von 1649*.

to Moscow's Patriarchate only in 1686, over the heated objections a learned Kievan hierarchy.[99]

It must be stated forcefully. Orthodox Eastern Europe outside of Muscovy was culturally European. Muscovite territorial expansion westward before Peter the Great usually meany the eradication of Europe, that is, the closing of the Latin presses in the areas Russia acquired.

Outside Muscovy, for example, a modest provincial publishing activity was associated with the Latin Academy at Vilnius in Lithuania. It alone published twice as many editions as the Muscovite press, and it produced both Polish and Latin editions of Augustine, three Latin editions of Cicero's *Epistolae* for use by schoolboys, Cornelius Nepos on the Trojan War, and Virgil's *Georgics*.[100] Cicero was, in fact, the first author debated by the students, their disputations being published just two years after the opening of the school as *Assertiones theologicae, philosophicae et rhetoricae in gymnasio Viln[ensis] . . . 1577 16 Aprilis defendendae.*[101] The first Muscovite printer, Ivan Fedorov, issued a primer in 1574, but it was only when he escaped Muscovy and resumed his work in the more congenial environs of Ostroh that an identical primer could include the fundamentals of Greek as well. What is significant about the well-known network of Orthodox Brotherhood schools and presses throughout Poland-Lithuania then is the fact that they were founded in the last quarter of the sixteenth century—the famous statute for the Lviv Academy is dated 1586. They were created within the spirit of Western humanism, with its respect for ancient pagan authors and its appeal to the sons of a non-clerical audience.[102] They constituted the non-Muscovite Orthodox community's reaction to the Counter-Reformation and official Polish Catholicism. The movement was most vigorous in Belorussia and Lithuania between 1569 and about 1635, thereafter in Kiev with the rise of Peter Mohyla.

Chernihiv (Chernigov) in the Ukraine had an active press only after 1680. Although since 1667 and the Treaty of Andrusovo it

---

[99] See the essays by Hrushevsky and Pritsak in *From Kievan Rus' to Modern Ukraine*, and Sydorenkò, *The Kievan Academy*, pp. 49–50.

[100] Cepiene *et al.*, *Vilniaus Akedemijos Spaustuwes Leidiniai 1576–1805*, pp. 34, 48, 103, 152. Nepos' work was presumably an extract from his *Chronica*, the first Roman attempt at universal history, rather than the *De viris illustribus*, which almost everyone owned.

[101] *Ibid.*, p. 14.

[102] Compare the primers in Botvinnik, *Otkuda est' poshel bukvar'*, pp. 14–41. Winter, *Frühaufklärung*, p. 322.

belonged to Moscow, and although in its first twenty years of existence it faithfully published the traditional list of psalters, service books,
and prayer-books, it also published Polish and Latin editions of the
works of local and Kievan divines, a phenomenon impossible in
Moscow.[103] In Kiev itself, the Slavonic press was traditionally Orthodox in its repertoire in the first half of the seventeenth century, pro-
ducing Eastern patristics, service books, Menologies and the like in
multiple editions, with only occasional innovations,[104] although the
Academy thrived on Latin books of Polish presses and taught Cicero's
Orator as early as 1635. If the list of Slavonic books from Kiev resembled Moscow's, their contents did not, since they were not controlled by a resident conservative patriarch. Kievan books appeared
"as if on foreign presses run by private individuals, without the approval of Church authorities, and no one knew if they themselves
had been initially corrected from Greek or Old Slavonic copies."
Kiev was a relatively free marketplace of books and printing compared to Moscow, and their Ukrainian co-religionists were "foreign."[105]

In the urban Orthodox areas of Lithuania and Belorussia book
culture had long been European and vastly different from provincial
Moscow.[106] A half century before Moscow, in 1517–19, in Praga/
Warsaw, and in the 1520s in Vilnius, there were active Orthodox
Slavonic presses, publishing activities associated with the name
Francisca Skorina. There were other flurries of activity in the 1560s
and 70s, especially with the arrival of Fedorov from Moscow, but
between the 1580s and the 1620s the major centers of Slavonic
publishing were the Typography Mamonicha in Vilnius, and a bit

---

[103] T. N. Kameneva, "Chernigovskaia tipografiia," pp. 255–279. It should be noted
that this provincial press, while operating relatively unhampered in its first decades,
published the religious polemic of the European *Frühaufklärung*, but with ecclesiastical control in the Petrine era, the Latin and Polish publications ceased, and it published
almost exclusively Slavonic editions of Psalters and liturgical books, plus 175 editions of the state's *ukazy*.

[104] Guseva, "Vzaimosviazi ukrainskikh tipografii." An old classic, Titov, *Materialy
dlja istorii knyzhnoi spravky*, has been reprinted. Note also, [Kameneva & Guseva],
Ukrainskie knigi kirillovskoi pechati, which excludes the non-Slavonic press in the Ukraine.

[105] Makarii, *Istoriia russkago raskola*, pp. 105–109.

[106] For the following, *Kniga Belarusi 1517–1917*; see also *Belorusskii prosvetitel' Fransisk
Skorina*, the newest fully-illustrated folio, *Frantsisk Skorina—belorusskii gumanist*, and
Nemirovskii, *Frantsisk Skorina*. See also Botvinnik, "Istochniki i literatura o Lavrentii
Zizanii," pp. 200, 237. The works of Zyzanij are being reprinted: *Hrammatika Slovenska*.
The very first Cyrillic printer, in Cracow in 1491, was in fact a German, Shviapolt
Fiol (various spellings), who was born in Neustadt on the Esch in Franconia; see
Wynar, *History of Early Ukrainian Printing*, pp. 9–23, who surveys the relevant literature.

later, the Press of the Vilnius Orthodox Brotherhood, which published the polemical and linguistic writings of the Zyzanij (Zizanii) brothers. By the 1630s Slavonic publishing had spread to Kuteino and Mohilev as well, but with the mid-century intrusion of Muscovite political and ecclesiastical influence, these independent activities were closed down.[107]

There had been a Renaissance among the non-Muscovite, Orthodox Eastern Slavs. At the famous school of Prince Kostiantyn Vasyl' Ostroz'kyi (Konstantin of Ostrog) one could find "orators equal to Demosthenes," and a "Latino-Greek-Slavic school of the Liberal Arts."[108] There humanists' learning touched cleric and urban classes alike. The works of the ancients on science—Lucretius, Pliny, Hippocrates and Strabo—circulated among the patrons of these schools.[109] In the sixteenth century, the presses of Lithuania produced 324 editions, fifty of them in Belorussian, but almost half, 151 in Latin; in the golden age, 1600–1625, a further 374 books were printed, 56 in Belorussian, 202 in Polish, and 107 in Latin.[110] Nothing bespeaks more eloquently the divide between the Orthodox clergy of the Polish-Lithuanian state and those in Moscow. In Muscovy the printing press arrived unbelievably late, and a Latin press was not tolerated as it was among other Orthodox Eastern Slavs.

Soviet historians of the book were loath to affirm the striking separateness of these literate Ukrainian, Lithuanian, and Belorussian cultures from that of Muscovy.[111] Western literary scholars on the other hand, pointed to the sharp distinction between Muscovy, where down to the age of Olearius it was difficult to find a Latin reader, and the Ukraine, where as far back as the Mongol age one finds evidence of Western educations. In Kiev the reading of Latin and a knowledge of antiquity flourished in the seventeenth century after Metropolitan Peter Mohyla's "wholesale adoption of Western educational methods."[112] Some of his clergy correctly complained that "nowadays they

---

[107] *Kniga Belarusi*, p. 121.
[108] Florovsky, *Ways*, pp. 42–43.
[109] See Bilevich, "Staropechatnye inostrannye knigi estestvennonauchnoi tematikí."
[110] Anushkin, *Na zare knigopech ataniia v Litve*, p. 13.
[111] See my review of *Ocherki russkoi kul'tury*, in the *JfGO*, Vol. 37 (1989), No. 3, p. 434. By way of contrast, see the attempt to define the term "Western Rus'" by the fine scholar of seventeenth-century Muscovite literature, Robinson, "Zarozhdenie kontseptsii avtorskogo stilia," p. 33.
[112] Lewitter, "Poland, the Ukraine and Russia," p. 415; Busch, *Horaz in Russland*, p. 13. On the triumph of Latin in Kiev under Mohyla, see Sydorenko, *The Kievan*

do not learn wisdom from the Holy Spirit, but from Aristotle, Cicero, Plato, and other pagan philosophers." But with urban elites long acquainted with the culture of their Polish Catholic governors, Latin triumphed.[113]

When these Ukrainian humanists arrived in Muscovy "everything went haywire."[114] In literary circles, for example, the origins of Muscovite poetry can be traced to a small group of versifiers, the Princes S. I. Shakhovskoi, I. M. Katyrev-Rostovskii, and I. A. Khvorostinin, inspired by Polish, Belorussian, and Ukrainian literature during the Time of Troubles. They were succeeded by a *prikaznaia shkola* of poets during the reign of the first Romanov, including Aleksei Romanchukov, named ambassador to Persia, Vasilii Volkov of the "upper *prikaz* bureaucracy, and Mikhail Iur'evich Tatishchev, among others. After the middle of the century a third group arose, the *Novoierusalimskie poety*, poets of the New Jerusalem monastery, one of three monasteries built and supported by Patriarch Nikon. They were distinguished by the direct influence of "Ukrainian and Polish poetry," by their Latin educations, by their private libraries, "the mark of a professional writer in modern times," and by their ability to use the ancient authors Homer and Virgil, Demosthenes and Cicero.[115]

Ukrainians were distinguished from Great Russians by their ability to synthesize pagan-Roman literary elements with the Christian.[116] While the issue of the Kurbskii-Groznyi Apocrypha is beyond the scope of the present essay, it is suggestive that in it one can contrast the Muscovite "tradition [of Ivan] with the Latin tradition in the Polish-Lithuanian state," with Cicero the divide. Indeed Kurbskii was a Classicist, at home with Plato, Aristotle, Dionysios the Areopagite, Tertullian, Jerome, Ambrose, and Cicero, all largely unknown in Ivan IV's Moscow.[117]

Academy, pp. 13, 108–113, and *passim*. Note also Medlin & Patrinelis, *Renaissance Influences*, pp. 130–135.

[113] See Hippisley, *The Poetic Style of Simeon Polotsky*, p. 4.

[114] Serman, review of Demin, *Russkaia literatura*, in *SGECR*, No. 6 (1978), 81–90.

[115] Panchenko, *Russkaia stikhotvornaia kul'tura*, pp. 26–33, 36–43, 103–115, 130, 134–35, 140–44, and *passim*. See also Bushkovitch, *Religion and Society*, Chap. 6.

[116] Uspenskij & Zivov, "Zur Spezifik des Barock in Rußland."

[117] Freydank, "A. M. Kurbskijs Rezeption der humanistischen Bildung," p. 807. See on Kurbskii I. N. Golenishchev-Kutuzov, *Gumanizm u vostochnykh Slavian*, pp. 30–33. Thus one can again quote the older scholarship of *vliiania* rather than the Soviet convention of *sviazi*: "The noted teachers Epifany Slavinec'kyj and Simeon Polockij brought West-European learning to Moscow, and made the development of new pedagogical ideas possible." Demkov, "Vliianie zapadno-evropeiskoi pedagogiki," p. 34.

Soviet historiography of this era once produced two antagonistic books. In 1958 M. P. Alekseev had sought East-Slavic *Humanism* in the feeble ties between Russian letters and the literatures of Europe in the fifteenth through seventeenth centuries. He was immediately challenged by I. N. Golenishchev-Kutuzov. He argued instead it was to be found exclusively in the literature of "West Russia," in the culture of "Galician Russia and the Russian land of Lithuania." There, not in Moscow, schooling and printing flourished, there translations were made of medieval European literature, and there Latin was known.[118] A politically correct Alekseev survived and flourished as a major scholar in post-Stalinist Russia, while Golenishchev-Kutuzov's book instantly became a bibliographic rarity.

When the boyar F. M. Rtishchev summoned to Moscow the first of the famous Ukrainian monk-scholars, Epifany Slavinec'kyi (Epifanii Slavinetskii), and Arsenij Satanovs'kyi, it was the beginning of a flood of alien learning which would last well over a century. A small army of "Orthodox" schoolmen existed abroad because in the seventeenth century, significant numbers of Ukrainian and Belorussian youth had converted to Catholicism, passed through the vertical Latin curriculum of the grammar school, college, and university of Central and Western Europe, travelled, returned, were re-attested in their Orthodoxy, took monastic vows and were certified to teach in the growing network of Orthodox Brotherhood schools.[119]

By the middle of the seventeenth century, the future Academy at Kiev had emerged as the most serious of these Orthodox Latin schools, under the leadership of Metropolitan Peter Mohyla.[120] Teachers and students of these Belorussian and Ukrainian schools would play a major role in fomenting the Schism in the Muscovite Church in the 1650s; collectively they would enjoy the protection of the Tsar's court until the 1690s, when the traditional Muscovite clergy would briefly

---

[118] Contrast Alekseev, *Iavleniia gumanizma*, with Golenishchev-Kutuzov, *Gumanizm u vostochnykh Slavian*.

[119] See Okenfuss, "Jesuit," and the literature cited there. Edward Keenan, "Semen Shakhovskoi," p. 804, has recently written of the "juggernaut of the Counter-Reformation" which rolled through Poland and the Ukraine, to which schools were an Orthodox response.

[120] Note the special issue of *HUS*, Vol. VIII (1984), devoted to the institution, and especially Sevcenko, "The Many Worlds of Peter Mohyla," pp. 9–44. The quality of the Latin used and taught there has received scant attention, but see Bezborod'ko, "Uchebnaia latyn' na Ukraine," which also contains a list (p. 86) of Latin philosophy courses available from Kiev. See also Nichik, "Sobranie kursov ritoriki i filosofii," pp. 80–87. See also Treadgold, *The West in Russia*, esp. Chapter 3.

silence them, but they would reemerge under Peter as a major component in Russian cultural and ecclesiastical life.

The most important attribute of these non-Muscovite Orthodox
divines is that they belonged heart and soul to a Western Civilization alien to the book habits of Muscovites. Beginning in the fifteenth century Ukrainians, "Rossicus, Ruthenus, Roxolanus, de Russia," began to appear in the records of the universities of Cracow,
Padua, Bologna, and Prague; by the sixteenth century they were in
German schools, at Wittemberg, Greisfeld, Rostock, and others, and
even in Basel and Paris.[121] They were educated in the rhetorical
traditions of the Latin colleges of the West. No fewer than thirty-two
Kievan texts of rhetoric exist from the seventeenth century (eighty-
five from the eighteenth), all in Latin, before the very first "Russian"
text appeared in 1699. Such was the cultural divide between the two
educations, native Muscovite and immigrating Ukrainian, and travellers such as Olearius were aware that native Muscovites, ecclesiastical and lay, lacked the Classical languages.[122]

Perhaps only with the dissolution of the Soviet Union and the
emergence of a virulently nationalistics Ukraine are we prepared to
recognize the obvious, that is, the enormous difference between most
cultured Ukrainians and Muscovites in the seventeenth-century age
of unification. However similar the folk-ways of the common East-
Slavic people, and whatever their common religious heritage, their
elites had grown culturally apart in the centuries of Polish domina-
tion of Ukraine, the age of the Renaissance and Reformation.

B. *The Coming of the Ukrainians and Their Books*

Among the first to arrive was Slavinec'kyj.[123] Educated and later a
teacher in the Kiev Brotherhood School, Epifany studied abroad,

---

[121] Golenishchev-Kutuzov, *Gumanizm u vostochnykh Slavian*, p. 11.

[122] See Grabosch, *Studien zur deutschen Russlandkunde*, p. 30, and Vomperskii, *Ritoriki
v Rossii*, pp. 12–72, for seventeenth-century editions. The famous "Russian" rhetoric
of Archbishop Makarii, early 17th century, often hailed as native, has now been
shown to be a copy of Melanchthon's Latin text, originally published in 1531, but
specifically an edition of 1551. See Eleonskaia, *Russkaia oratorskaia prosa*, pp. 26–40.
There was, of course, some clerical opposition to the Latinizing of Ukrainian Orthodox schooling. See Sydorenko, *Kievan Academy*, pp. 34ff.

[123] See Luppov, *XVII vek*, 126–128. The most recent search for his biography is
Iakimovich, *Deiateli russkoi kul'tury*, pp. 7–11. A well-known description of a vast Ukraine,
in which "les Cosaques" are identified as the *Rus*, is Sieur de Guillaume Beauplan,
Description D'Ukrainie, Paris, 1661, now available in an English edition from the Harvard

before he came to Moscow in 1649, began translating works from the Greek, and became an aide to Patriarch Nikon. He translated some of Thucydides, Pliny, Copernicus, and Vesalius, although more important at the time were theological and liturgical translations for the Patriarch, based on West-European rather than Greek editions;[124] his scientific and Classical work remained in manuscript and there is scant evidence that anyone read it. His small private collection of seventy-two books were about equally divided between Latin and Slavonic (38 and 34 books respectively), and the former included such grammar-school Classics as Plutarch, Livy, and Aristotle, as well as Hippocrates.[125]

Another private European library in Moscow was that of Arsenii the Greek.[126] He, in perfectly normal fashion for Greeks of that age, had studied in Venice, in Padua, and with the Jesuits in Rome. He was found in Kiev by Patriarch Paissios of Jerusalem en route to Moscow in January of 1649. Brought along as someone who could speak "Russian," he was left behind to teach the standard grammar-school curriculum, that is, "*do retoriki*," but within a month he was imprisoned at the infamous northern Solovki and his property confiscated. Among his sixty books, in addition to linguistic materials, Scripture, service books and saints' lives, were the works of John Damascene, John Chrysostom, Cyril of Jerusalem, and as grounds enough for imprisonment, Thomas à Kempis. He also owned Flavius Josephus. But his library betrayed his education; it contained editions of Plutarch, Aristotle, Homer (in Greek and Latin), and Isocrates' *Address to Philip*. One can only wonder what else was contained in the library in this vein, for the hapless Muscovite clerk charged with cataloguing the heretic's possessions recorded only a generic

---

Ukrainian Institute. Slavinetskii brought his own Latin dictionary with him, a manuscript copy of Ambrosius Calepini, published first in Basel; see Nimchuk, ed., *Leksikon latins'kii*, which reprints the Slavic-Latin edition prepared in Moscow, which was being recopied well into the eighteenth century. See also Bushkovitch, *Religion and Society*, Chap. 7.

[124] He was almost certainly also the translator of Erasmus, although it did not circulate; See Alekseev, "Erazm Roterdamskii," pp. 275–330. Kharlampovich, *Malorossiiskoe vliianie*, pp. 375–77, discussed his religious translations; a collection of Gregory the Theologian, Basil the Great, Athanasius of Alexandria, and John Damascene was published in Moscow in 1665; see *Slavianskie knigi kirillovskoi pechati*, item 233.

[125] The Classics were less in evidence in the library of his untravelled pupil, the monk Evfimii, the famous opponent of Medvedev; see Luppov, *XVII vek*, 128–31.

[126] Fonkich, *Grechesko-russkie*, pp. 108–25; see also Avvakum, *The Life*, pp. 264–65. Luppov did not describe his library.

entry: "plus 17 books, small and medium, in Latin."[127]

Another foreign library belonged to Arsenii Sukhanov.[128] It was the result of a shopping expedition. A Muscovite monk, Arsenii had visited Greek monasteries in 1649–50 and 1651–53 and returned, before he was dispatched by Patriarch Nikon again in October of 1653 to collect texts needed to correct Church books. Most of the nearly 500 volumes that he brought back were therefore ecclesiastical, liturgical, and ritualistic in content, but his excess baggage included Greek letters: Strabo's *Geography*, three volumes of Homer,[129] two each of Sophocles, Demosthenes, Plutarch and Hesiod, plus Aeschylus, Thucydides, and seven volumes of Aristotle. Deposited into Nikon's Patriarchal Library, after his fall they were removed to New Jerusalem on the banks of the Istra.

There is little external evidence for the education of Paul, Metropolitan of Sarai and the Lower Don, who died in 1675. He was probably the first of the Kievans to reach the Muscovite hierarchy.[130] At first glance his seems a typical Muscovite clergyman's library, with numerous psalters, liturgical service books, catechisms, patristics, saints' lives, breviaries, and Testaments. But his educational heritage showed through. He owned Virgil in duodecimo, a Cicero (*Kniga Kikeronova*) in quarto, as well as another volume of Cicero's *Orations*. He owned a "Mirror of Life" in Latin, a *Kniga Plutarkha, Greko-Latinskaia*, a *Kniga Iustina*, a *Kniga Livieva* (Livy), and a *Kniga Aristoteleva, Greko-Latinskaia*. Reflecting the highest form of the old Kievan Academy, he retained a *Kniga Dialektika, rukopisnaia, Latinskaia*, a *Kniga Filosofiia rationalis, rukopisnaia, Latinskaia*, and a *Kniga drugaia Filosofiia, rukopisnaia Latinskaia*, presumably his old college notebooks.

The most impressive European library in Muscovy was the Polockij-

---

[127] Fonkich, *op. cit.*, 125–37. His library was unknown to Luppov. Education never assured virtue; the seamier side of his life is sketched by Bostrom in Avvakum, *The Life*, p. 258. Also from Slavonic Poland-Lithuania was the monk Dionysius who arrived in 1655, worked at the Moscow Printing House, and taught Greek to a future Muscovite bishop. He owned sixteen books, including the *Iliad*, the *Odyssey*, and Polybius.

[128] For the following, Fonkich, *op. cit.*, pp. 70–102, is especially good on the voyage; on contents, see Slukhovskii, *Bibliotechnoe delo*, pp. 119–20. Luppov does not deal with his library. Similar was the collection of the Lichud brothers, Moscow's first Greek grammar-school-college teachers, but the description of their books is sketchy; see Luppov, *XVII vek*, pp. 146–47, and Okenfuss, "Jesuit Origins."

[129] On the importation of Homer see Egunov, *Gomer*, pp. 16–7.

[130] For the following, the description published by Undol'skii, "Biblioteka Pavla."

Medvedev collection.[131] Simeon (born Samuil Gavrilovic Petrovskij-Sitnianovic) was born in 1629 in Belorussia,[132] studied at Kiev, taught in the Brotherhood school in Polock before migrating to Moscow in 1663. He was the chief clerk at the Church Council of 1667, wrote stinging anti-Old-Believer polemics, became the court preacher and the tutor to the Tsar's children, and a major force in the creation of modern Russian literature. He was, as a European and a European-educated clergyman, grounded in the Latin Church Fathers Augustine and Jerome (as well as John Damascene, Chrysostom, and Athanasius), and his recent investigator, Hippisley, notes that his editions of Saints Augustine, Jerome, and Thomas Aquinas mysteriously disappeared between an early listing of his private collection and the final one. His was a European's library, with no books in Slavonic; it was chiefly Latin, nearly half, to a lesser extent Polish. It was a significant Classical library, including Aristotle's *Organon* and *Politics*, Cicero's, Sallust's and Virgil's *Works*, Seneca's *Tragedies*, Plautus' *Commedies*, Cato, Plutarch, Terence, as well as the humanists, Lipsius, Erasmus, and others.[133]

These European libraries built around a Classical education were not the property of Ukrainian churchmen alone. Prior to influx of Ukrainian divines into the Muscovite Tsarist and Patriarchal courts, the streets of Ukrainian towns were populated with Latin readers:[134] An Armenian *Bürger* living in Lviv, Nikolai Avedikovich, owned Aristotle, Xenophon, Virgil, and Cicero of the ancients, Petrarch,

---

[131] Luppov, *XVII vek*, pp. 118–126, said they could not be separated, but Hippisley, "Simeon Polotsky's Library," pp. 52–61, separated them. See also Cizevskij, *History*, pp. 346–57. The literature on Polockij is large. In English the best study of his literary career is Hippisley, *The Poetic Style of Simeon*. See the biography by Pushkarev, "Simeon Polotskii," with bibliography, and more recently, *Simeon Polotskii i ego knigoizdatel'skaia deiatel'nost'*. See also the latest bibliography, that in Sazonova, *Poeziia russkogo barokko*, pp. 244–262. A study of his student and colleague Medvedev is Kolosova, "'Sozertsanie kratkoe' Sil'vestra Medvedeva," pp. 207–29, and his library is described in Hughes, *Sophia*, p. 171. See also Lewitter, "Poland, the Ukraine and Russia," p. 420.

[132] He was a foreigner; in 1669 his brother was called an *inozemets* by the Posol'skii Prikaz; see *Russko-belorusskie sviazi*, pp. 58–9; Polotskii's teaching of Latin was a governmental, not a churchly appointment; see *Ibid.*, pp. 192, 268–69. Late in his life he signed himself as follows: "Ex libris Simeonis Piotrowski Sitanianowicz Jeromonachi Polocensis Ord(inis) S(ancti) Basilii Mag(ni), A(nno) D(om)ini 1670 Aug(usti) 26 Moscovie"; Simeon Polotskii, *Virshi*, p. 7.

[133] On the expropriation of the Kievan past, see Pelenski, "The Origins of the Official Muscovite Claims."

[134] For this paragraph, Isaevich, "Krug chitatel'skikh interesov," pp. 65–76.

Erasmus, and Jean Bodin of the "moderns." In a law court the typographer Andrei Skol'skii could cite Sallust, Livy, and Seneca. In the preface to an edition of the Gospels of 1639, M. Slezka cited Plato, Caesar, Cicero, Virgil, Plutarch, and Lucian.

Jan Andrej Bialocki (Belobotskii), was of Polish gentry origins. Born in Peremyshl' in the Ukraine, well educated and travelled, he had studied in France, Italy, and Spain before reaching Riga, Smolensk, and finally Moscow in 1681, where he was awarded Muscovite nobility. He taught Latin at court, and like the divine, Polockij, he turned his hand to poetry, writing in "Russian," but he based his work on Polish, German and Latin originals, including the Renaissance rhetoric by Raymond Lull.[135]

Forty-three catalogues of private libraries of only "the urban classes" in the Ukraine for the early period 1560–1653 have been located. They include an astonishing

85	mentions of books by	Cicero,
58	"	Aristotle,
34	"	Plutarch,

as well as the works of Virgil, Ovid, Livy, and many others. How did these foreign libraries compare to those of Muscovites? The libraries discussed above were those of foreigners, Slavinec'kyj, Arsenii, Polockij, Medvedev, Sukhanov, and they accounted for virtually the entire penetration of the Classics into Muscovy, save only a few scattered volumes.

B. V. Sapunov, as noted above, developed a data-base of a meager 11,259 manuscript and printed books, every title known to have existed in Muscovy. In 1983 he extracted every mention of a Greek or Roman author, arguing that "the number of citations in descriptions of libraries of the works of one or another author indicated the level of his popularity among the Russian reader in the 17th century."[136]

Aristotle	25 mentions	Hippocrates	2 mentions
Homer, *Odyssey*	10 "	Aesop	2 "
Homer, *Iliad*	1 mention	Anacreon, *Odes*	1 mention
Plutarch	7 mentions	Aristophanes	1 "
Hesiod, *Works & Days*	5 "	Aristeas	1 "

---

[135] Lewin, "Polish-Ukrainian-Russian," pp. 260–61. Bialocki accompanied the famous Muscovite mission to China. See also Brown, *Seventeenth Century Russian Literature*, pp. 129–30 and *passim*; also Vomperskii, *Ritoriki*, pp. 38–53.

[136] Sapunov, "Antichnaia," here p. 71, and other titles cited in endnote 73 above.

Demosthenes	5	mentions	Aeschylus	1	mention
Herototus	3	"	Cato	1	"
Sophocles	3	"	Livy	1	"
Josephus Flavius	3	"	Plato	1	"
Pliny, *Cosmograph.*	2	"	Pythagoras	1	"
Strabo	2	"	Polidorus	1	"
Cicero	2	"	Theocritus	1	"
			Thucydides	1	"

Besides these there were allusions indicating the existence in Muscovy of the works of Xenophon, Diodorus Siculus, Ptolemy, Galen, Quintus Curtius Rufus, Seneca, and Virgil, although they never appeared in a catalogue of a library.

Looking at this slim list, one can agree readily with Cizevskij's judgement on Muscovite translations: "The classical poetic works aroused no interest."[137] To that one might add, nor did the Classical rhetorical, historical, moral, political, philosophical, or scientific works, judging by the records of ownership and translation. Most of these books belonged to resident foreigners, Ukrainians, Belorussians, and Greeks. The only seemingly interesting number, twenty-five mentions of Aristotle, was not a measure of his "popularity," but a recognition of his ubiquity in European education, from poetics and rhetoric to politics and physics. The total number of mentions Aristotle in pre-eighteenth-century Muscovy, incidentally, was about equal to the number of printed editions of his works currently available in Germany in the 1680s.[138]

The growth of humane secular learning was not an organic development within Muscovite society, but the struggle of Kievans—Polockij and his coterie of Medvedev, Istomin, Magnitskii, Polikarpov, and Kopievskyj in the first round, Teofan Prokopovych and Havryjil Buzyns'skyj (Gavriil Buzhinskii) only slightly more successfully in the second—the struggle of Ukrainian humanists to make themselves heard above the din raised by an avalanche of psalters and liturgical books.

The evidence of private libraries makes it absolutely clear that the "West Russians," the clerics from Ukraine, Belorussia, and Lithuania who began to appear in Moscow in numbers after 1640, had had

---

[137] Cizevskij, *History*, p. 328.
[138] See Ashworth, "Changes in Logic Textbooks," and Riedel, "Aristoteles-Tradition." Textbooks for librarians parade the Classical content of a pre-Petrine school library, but the Lviv Brotherhood school was not in Muscovy. See Abramov, *Istoriia bibliotechnogo dela*, pp. 27–8.

different educations, and subscribed to different cultural norms that
their nominal Muscovite co-religionists.

C. *The Significance of Polockij and Ukrainian Humanism*

Many visitors to seventeenth-century Muscovy had the humanists'
education. Iurii Krizhanich, for example, the early voice of Slavic
unity, was exiled to Tobol'sk, and took along Homer, Plato, Aristotle,
Plutarch, Polybius, Livy, Virgil, and Cicero from his Jesuit education: "Cicero, a Roman, writes about his nation as follows: I have
always thought that our people are more ingenious than the Greeks,
and whatever we have adopted from them we have corrected and
improved." The Slavs, and especially the Muscovites, lacked this
education: "We are called barbarians, savages, beasts, thieves, and
cheaters only because of our illiteracy, laziness, and stupidity."[139]

The chief representative of Ukrainian humanism in Moscow was
Simeon Polockij. He was a major disrupter of Muscovite values.
Contemporary "Orthodox churchmen on both sides of the Schism
suspected his theology," and he is now credited as "the first to lead
Russians astray with Latin ideas." His Jesuit education touched many,
being a major influence on the "new humanistic school" of icon
painters around Simon Ushakov which shook the foundations of
Orthodoxy in the 1660s and 1670s.[140] He taught Latin to clerks of
the Chancellery of Secret Affairs (*Prikaz tainykh del*) and at court shortly
after his arrival in Moscow. As the tutor for the 12-year old Aleksei
Alekseevich and the 10-year old Sophia Alekseevna he compiled a
primer. His major debts in that enterprise were to the foreign editions of the Zyzanij brothers and others in Belorussia and the Ukraine.
He used the Polish *Psalterz Dawidow* (1578) by Jan Kochanowski in
the composition of his rhymed Psalter.[141] Polockij and the Germans

---

[139] Krizhanich, *The Politika*, Letiche & Dmytryshyn, trans., pp. xxvi–xxix, xxiii,
47, 87, 110.

[140] See Hippisley, *The Poetic Style of Simeon*, p. 14; Hippisley, "Emblem," pp. 167,
180; the quote is from S. Liubimov, 1875. On icon painting, see Andreyev, "Nikon
and Avvakum," and especially the perceptive pages in Hughes, *Sophia*, pp. 134–150.
See also Baehr, "Regaining Paradise," where the visual image of a Christlike Emperor
is traced back to Ushakov's revolutionary "icon," inspired by Polockij, "Planting the
Tree of the Russian State."

[141] Polotskii, *Virshi*; Setin, "'Bukvari' Simeon Polotskogo," pp. 93–104; Derzhavina,
"Simeon Polotskii v rabote," pp. 116–33. On his syllabic verse, see Brown, *17th
Century*, pp. 109–129. Unfortunately nothing survives of his tutorials for Sophia; see
Hughes, *Sophia*, 23–24, 32–35.

at court were responsible for the birth of Russian theater in 1672.[142] He also took the first step toward transforming the old Cyrillic script into a more modern "European" typeface.[143]

In terms of politics, Polockij was the first to use the word *tyrant* in Muscovy in the sense of an evil or cruel tsar.

> He who wishes to know who is a tsar and who a tyrant must read the books of Aristotle.[144]

One of the most frequently used political metaphors of the age, that of Peter as the Tsar-Sun, had its origins with the alien Polockij. Polockij and his followers represented a distinctive "southwestern Russian ideology," for which it was perfectly acceptable to mix the Christian God with pagan gods, and to merge the Christian heaven with Olympus.[145] Such innovations indicate that Polockij's education and cultural values were far removed from those of Muscovites like Avvakum.

Latin learning linked Polockij to the Moldavian of Greek descent, Nikolai Spatharios-Milescu (1636–1708). Educated in Constantinople and Italy, probably at Padua, he had been in Germany, Stockholm, and Paris, where he published an anti-Calvinist tract, before entering Muscovite service in 1671. There he befriended Polockij, as well as the head of the Foreign Office, A. S. Matveev. For Matveev he proposed an ambitious cycle of translations of the Classics. They were to include Plato and others "of the Academy," Cicero, Pliny, Tacitus, Virgil, Varro, and Martianus Capella (whose listing of the seven liberal

---

[142] See Robinson, "Pervye russkii teatr," and other articles in this volume. A sanitized Soviet account, which understates foreigners, Ukrainians, Latin, and Western themes, is Aseev, *Russkii dramaticheskii teatr*, pp. 89–117. See also P. Lewin, "Polish-Ukrainian-Russian," pp. 265–67.

[143] The subsequent steps in the eventual development of the civil script were taken by Menshikov's draughtsman Kühlenbach, by the Dutchman Christopher Brant, and by Peter himself; see Kaldor, "The Genesis of the Russian *Grazhdanskii Schrift*." On the contribution of Oxford University Press and Peter personally see the account in [Daniel Defoe], *An Impartial History*, p. 80.

[144] Bochkarev, *U istokov russkoi istoricheskoi dramaturgii*, p. 43; see the brief political note on Polockij in Wes, *Classics*, pp. 18–19.

[145] Uspenskij & Zivov, "Zur Spezifik des Barok," pp. 25–35. It is the contention of this essay that the Muscovite mentality never died. "When Sergei Trubetskoi, professor of philosophy at Moscow University, published his *Metaphysics in Ancient Greece* (1890), a study of the classical antecedents of Christianity, he was viciously attacked by influential clerics who objected to any linking of Christianity with pagan philosophy." Rosenthal and Bohachevsky-Chomiak, eds., *A Revolution of the Spirit*, p. 19.

arts literally shaped European education),[146] and others "of the Latin sages," Diodorus Siculus, Strabo, and others "of the Greek historians," Eusebius, Justinian, Clement of Alexandria, and others "of the Christian Greek Fathers," and Lactantius, Jerome, and Augustine "of the Latins."

Such a proposal was too heathen and too heretical for Muscovite traditionalists. The pious monk of the Chudov monastery, Evfimii, damned it. His "Discussion, whether it would be useful for [Muscovites] to teach grammar, rhetoric, philosophy, and theology," was an anti-Latinizer tract which identified Spatharios and his Ukrainian friends as the implacable enemies of Muscovite values.

Polockij's Polish and Latin verses from his early Kievan period before 1653 included a Classical educational reflection.

THE SEVEN LIBERAL ARTS

When you seek to know, what is included in *Grammar*,
The gates to wisdom open before you. (Thereafter),
As an ostrich is guided by the look of her own eggs,
So are you attracted easily by the book.

A fine eloquence is encountered in *Rhetoric*,
If, when reading, we harken to our teachers.
When we heed them either we then orate with ease,
Or perhaps we have no aptitude for declamations?

A sufficient grasp of *Dialectics* Plato rightfully
Regarded as the mother of all the Sciences.
Indeed it is true that they lead us to wisdom,
Enlighten our reason, and untie thorny knots.

Arithmetic is the wisdom to calculate
Whatever is needed with ease.
Geometry measures whatever is necessary,
Its size or height, even to heaven itself.

Astrology takes note of the course of the heavens,
And the future is easily determined by the stars.
A fine melody is comprised of various voices,
And *Music* creates it as well as a symphony.

---

[146] Hadas, *Latin*, p. 406.

Elsewhere in these youthful verses Polockij revealed his education in
Stoicism, a studied indifference to the things of this world:

> (*Gloria inconstans est*)
> Why is the fame of this world so fleeting?
> Why does its joy know not even one hour of repose?
> . . .
> Tell me, where is Tully the most eloquent?
> Where is now Aristotle the most wise?
> . . .
> Fortunate indeed is he whom this world spurns.

And in an epigram he captured the self-irony than came with an
awareness of the transitory nature of human life—here today, gone
tomorrow—more apparent in a pagan Classical education than in
the Christian message of Life Eternal and the Communion of Saints.

> *Homo*
> Man is a bubble, a glass, ice, a fantasy, dust, a bit of straw;
> a dream, a kopeck, a voice, a sound, a breeze, a flower;
> man is a nothing, until he calls himself king.[147]

Polockij's mature educational tracts revealed his values to have been
two-sided. On the one hand he was an East-Slavic monkish book-
man, albeit Jesuit educated, and thus he was the heir to the old
Slavic primer tradition. His primers, designed initially for the tsar's
children, borrowed more from Lithuanian than Muscovite traditions.
If they were stylistically and doctrinally innovative, they still announced
that the old Slavonic *Ladder of Literacy* need not be abandoned for
beginning learners. As a Latin humanist, he advocated a learning
that began with the breviary and psalter, but continued through the
study of grammar, rhetoric, dialectical reasoning and arithmetic. Such
studies prepared the young for health, happiness, and a useful life in
this world, not merely for the bliss of the saved in the hereafter.[148] In
his *Garden of Many Flowers* (1678) he discussed the pagans, Plato and
the Academy, as well as the stoic philosophy of Thales of Miletus.[149]

---

[147] Polotskii, *Virshi*, pp. 120–22, 172–4. 193–4. My translations.

[148] Okenfuss, *Childhood*, pp. 19–22. One of the best studies of Polotskii's educational thought, emphasizing both its compatibility with Greek Orthodoxy and its
roots in the brotherhood schools of the previous century, is Smirnov, "K voprosu o
pedagogike."

[149] Polotskii, *Izbrannye sochineniia*, pp. 68–69, and *passim*.

He instructed his wary Muscovite readers in the lore of Caesar, Socrates' pupil Aristippus, Aristotle, Diogenes, Epicurus, Homer, Plato, Pliny, Strabo, and the Emperors Titus Flavius, Vespasian, and Trajan.[150] Typical of his atypical worldliness was his resurrection of the ancient debate as to whether a philosopher could be married:

> . . . it is impossible to sit among one's books
> When wife and children draw you away from them.
> Epicurus was a rabid voluptuary,
> Yet he forbade any wise man to marry.
> And Theophrastus in his book also prohibited it,
> Predicting that marriage was an obstacle to wisdom . . .[151]

His educational vision was shaped by the resurrected ancients, as he found his goal, the education of "the total man," or as we would say, "the complete personality," in Diogenes the Stoic.[152]

His schooling was that of the Western college where Latin ruled, where the seven liberal arts were taught, where Cicero and Quintilian ruled rhetoric, and where Plutarch, Flavius Josephus, and Herodotus ruled history. The source of this curriculum was Erasmus, *De civilitate morum puerilium* (1530), translated for the Muscovites by Polockij's colleague, Slavinec'kyj the Forerunner.[153] When Polockij speculated on the ages of human life, as did contemporaries like Comenius, he borrowed from the legacy of Pope Gregory the Great. This Hildebrand, expoited by Polockij, symbolized the ability of the Roman Church to coexist "freely and even victoriously with the pagan world," a position rejected by most learned Muscovites of the age.[154]

Polockij's advocacy of the Latin college did not lead to the foundation of an academy. Only after his death would a first compromised Grecophile incarnation open in 1685 in the school of the Lichuds.[155] Eventually and inevitably it would teach Latin as well, and be shuttered for the effort, but its pupils would spread the word. Their efforts in the 1690s would touch the tsarist family. The monk Karion Istomin, would advocate the vertical curriculum of grammar, syntax, poetics,

---

[150] *Ibid.*, pp. 268–72.

[151] *Ibid.*, p. 61.

[152] Eleonskaia, *Russkaia publitsistika*, p. 145.

[153] *Ibid.*, pp. 153, 161, 163, 164, 172.

[154] See Max J. Okenfuss, "The Ages of Man on the Seventeenth-Century Muscovite Frontiers of Europe," *The Historian*, Vol. 56, No. 1, 87–104.

[155] On the opening of the Lichuds' academy as evidence of a temporary lessening of Ukrainian influence on Moscow's cultural life, see Kharlampovich, *Malorossiiskoe vliianie*, pp. 402–405.

rhetoric (with subtleties, the *trivium*), dialectics, arithmetic, geometry, philosophy, astronomy, philology, and music (ditto, the *quadrivium*), to his charge, Aleksei Petrovich (b. 1690), son of the future Peter the Great,[156] and prior to his crude reeducation at the hands of Menshikov. For Polockij the Bible was literature. Humanistically educated, for him the Scriptures sang with verse and hymn, clear evidence that poetry was pleasing to God. For his archenemy Avvakum, even the pretense of poetics or literary style, was tantamount to the deadly sin of pride,[157] always to be avoided in favor of plain, simple speech. It was not merely the institution of the college or the heresy of the Latins which made the Ukrainians anathema to traditional Muscovites, it was their use of language itself. Among the clerical elites, Muscovites and Ukrainians represented two separate civilizations.

4. *The Impact of Polish Court Culture*

A. *The Opening of Muscovy by Tsar Aleksei*

The second major crack in the monolith of old Muscovite liturgical book culture was the Polonization of the tsarist court and of those *prikazy* that dealt regularly with foreigners and foreign learning. It too became visible in libraries. The chief characteristic of this mid-seventeenth century sub-culture was not so much its growing secularism, as its rapacious, wholly unsystematic eclecticism.[158] This was the culture that began to import the relatively new Western news-sheets, eventually to read translations at court,[159] a culture fascinated with all the varieties of history, with genealogy and with the chronicles from Poland and Lithuania, with the Trojan War and with Baronius' *Church History*, paving the way for the popularity of Pufendorf as historian two generations later. This was the courtly culture which added cosmology to the older chronicle and chronograph, as the mark of a curious mind. More often than not Poland was the direct intermediary.[160]

---

[156] Bogdanov, "Pamiatnik russkoi pedagogiki," pp. 131–139. I am grateful to Professor Daniel C. Waugh for this reference.

[157] Panchenko, "O smene pisatel'skogo tipa," pp. 112–117.

[158] Contrast Luppov with Cizevskij, *History*, pp. 326–31. The best Soviet work on this theme is perhaps Glukhov, *Rus' knizhnaia*, pp. 157–205.

[159] See Schibli, *Die ältesten russischen Zeitungsübersetzungen*.

[160] See Peter Kosta, *Eine russische Kosmographie*; this is the tale of a cosmography

This was the world of Tsar Aleksei Mikhailovich's court after his
Polish trip in 1655, of the Foreign Office, of the *Prikazy* for apothecary and for foreign troops, the world of the "Westernizers," A. L.
Ordin-Nashchokin, F. M. Rtishchev, A. S. Matveev, and later of
V. V. Golitsyn, and of an ambitious ecclesiastic, Patriarch Nikon
himself, and of a few other clerics in Moscow of his type.[161] It was
the culture which favored the printed book over the manuscript, although the printing press would remain in traditional Church hands.[162]
This was the world of unsystematic education but of endless curiosity,
in a word, the earthly world which produced Tsar Peter.

A vast and eclectic array of medieval and early-modern European
works had been translated previously into Slavonic in the Ukraine,
Lithuania, and Belorussia in the late fifteenth and sixteenth centuries;
now they were imported to the Muscovite court. They included a
history of Troy by Guido de Columna, tales of Dracula, of Tristan,
and of Appolonius of Tyre, and the Polish chronicles of Bielski and
of Stryikowsky, among many others.[163]

Western tales of chivalry and adventure, often first translated into
Serbo-Croatian or Polish, were then rendered in Slavonic in the
Ukraine, and then reappeared in Moscow in the 1650s and 1660s.
Sometimes, as in the case of the "Tale of Bova, the King's Son," an
import from medieval France, the brave knight became in Muscovy
a defender of the Faith, adding a religious theme absent in European redactions. Elsewhere in these tales, as in "Savva Grudtsyn,"
the traditional 'pact with the Devil' became a tale of Muscovite
corruption by the West. Once opened to this literature, the court
would set tastes in aristocratic reading for a century and more. The
seventeenth-century collections of this material were more read than
printed books.

---

which had seen 41 editions in numerous languages 1570–1612, which was out of
date when it was Polonized about 1640, and more antique still when Russified, with
additions from Marcin Bielski's *Kronika*. See in general Sobolevskii, *Perevodnaia*. On
the Trojan War, see Egunov, *Gomer*, pp. 18–28.

[161] The interlinked fate of the service classes and the hierarchy is emphasized in
Neubauer, *Car und Selbstherrscher*. See also Torke, *Die staatsbedingte Gesellschaft*.

[162] Sapunov, "Izmenenie."

[163] Standard accounts include Gudzy, *History of Early Russian Literature*, pp. 397–
431, Cizevskij, *History of Russian Literature* pp. 326–31, and now Likhachev, *A History
of Russian Literature*, pp. 465–496, with very good bibliographies of Soviet and Western works and of translations; but see also Golenishchev-Kutuzov, *Gumanizm*, 64–65,
for the Ukrainian transmission.

In the beginning this was an opening hidden from the view of most Muscovites. Prohibitions of Western-style clothing and haircuts continued to be issued. Nikita Romanov, the tsar's cousin, violated the rules and lost his Western dress in the 1650s, as would other boyars in the 1670s. Prior to Aleksei's own conversion he would, at Nikon's behest, order all musical instruments to be confiscated and destroyed, and Olearius had reported five wagon-loads were burned. In comparison to music and clothing, reading could be private, and one suspects that literary culture could be transformed more easily for that reason. Minds and libraries could be enriched quietly, long before there was a Peter the Great to open the doors publicly.[164]

Foreign technicians and mercenaries, eventually clustered in the infamous Foreign Settlement in Moscow, represented the second cultural challenge to Muscovy. Their impact on the military and on court life is generally appreciated. Less obvious was their subtle influence on the reading habits of the elites with whom they came in contact. The first evidence came in the libraries of courtiers and leaders of those *prikazy* that dealt directly with Europe.

B. *Polonized Book Culture at Court*

One fascinating glimpse into this world, foreign-tainted and open to the learning of the ages, was the library of the Apothecary *Prikaz*. Almost exclusively in Latin, its core was naturally in pharmaceutics, chemistry, natural history, medicine, and alchemy. One notes a copy of Andreas Vesalius, *De humani corporis fabrica* (Basel, 1555), presumably one that Slavinec'kyj earlier used, as well as a copy of Galen (Basil, 1561). One notes Samuel Marolois, *Opera mathematica* (actually in French) and one of his works on architecture, Vincenzo Scamozzi, *L'idea della architettura universale* (Venice, 1615), and da Vignola, *Le due regole della prospetiva practica* (Rome, 1664). One finds Latin Old and New Testaments, an Italian Bible, the works of Cyril of Alexandria, Gregory the Great, and Piscator's *Epitome* of Augustine. Someone collected Cicero's *Opera*, Tacitus' *Opera* (as well as Justus Lipsius' commentary), Aristotle *Omnia quae extant opera*, Plutarch "*Summi et philosophi et historici opus*," a Latin Xenophon *Opera*, a history of the

---

[164] Olearius, Baron, ed., pp. 262–263. He is cited with other material in a recent unpublished evocation of the anti-foreign spirit of mid-seventeenth-century Muscovy in Lahana, "Breaking the Rules in Muscovy."

Jesuits, and Marsilius of Padua's *Defensor pacis*.[165] This list documents the eclectic receptivity of Westward-looking *prikaz* culture in the second half of the seventeenth century.[166]

Private collections were mirrors. The library of the young Aleksei Mikhailovich has been reconstructed. The tsar's education was traditional, represented by the *Ladder of Literacy* of *azbuka*, Psalter, breviary, and Epistles. However, already in his youth "German printed sheets" and a grammar and dictionary "of Lithuanian printing" appeared. The bulk of his personal library was collected later in his life, after the nearly bookless 1650s when he discovered the West. In the end it ranged from news reports translated from German and Polish, to herbals, to the works of the house tutor Simeon Polockij, to works on the liberal arts commissioned of his aide, Milescu-Spatharios.[167] The reconstruction of this library by the dates of acquisition allows one to see how the new overlay but did not disturb the traditional in the tsar's education.

His son Aleksei Alekseevich (1654–70) had a slightly larger collection, which included the new courtly mix of chronicles and works on geography, linguistic materials, and a bit of mathematics, an unidentified book entitled "Monarchy," and something by Aristotle.[168] As we would expect after a quarter century of Kievans at court, the library of Tsar Fedor (1661–1682) was slightly larger, slightly more varied. After his voluminous collection of Scripture and service books, he had the *Titularnik*, *Stepennaia kniga*, and the *Zertsalo Velikoe*, chronographs, the Polish (Stryikowski) and "Russian" chronicles characteristic of the group, descriptions of Amsterdam and of Rome, two copies of the one little military manual published in Moscow, copies of the

---

[165] For the above, "Spisok knig aptekarskogo prikaza," pp. 428–33. The library was lost in the recent tragic fire in the Academy of Sciences Library. The other comparable collection was that of the *Posol'skii Prikaz*; it was listed in its 1696 form in Belokurov, *O biblioteke*, pp. 66–80.

[166] A century later these books belonged to the Academy of Sciences, and theology still constituted the largest segment of its collection. *Istoriia Biblioteki Akademii nauk*, p. 147.

[167] Waugh, "The Library of Aleksei Mikhailovich," and for an earlier problem, his "The Unsolved Problem of Tsar Ivan IV's Library." The published versions of the libraries of Aleksei, his father and his sons, are in Ivan Zabelin, *Domashnyi byt russkikh tsarei*, Vol. I, Part 2, 591–607. See also Longworth, *Alexis*, Chap. 4, and on his aide, Belobrova, ed., *Nikolai Spafarii*. I have not seen the older works by D. T. Ursul.

[168] Luppov, *XVII vek*, pp. 113–14, omits comment on his religious books, the bulk of his collection.

increasingly common remedy-books (*lechebniki*), three singing-books of unknown content (Luppov counted them as secular, but they could as easily have been the infamous books of Kievan church singing, distributed by Polockij, the family's tutor). His "literature" scarcely extended beyond the usual tales. The great bulk of his collection, sixty-four titles out of a total of 280, were service books of the liturgy, Scripture, historical works, the Greek Fathers (15 titles), and saints' lives (10). Unfortunately the influence of Polockij cannot be measured as the Muscovite scribe garbled hopelessly the identities of his forty-one Latin books.[169]

The books of a few courtiers began to reflect this same mixture. This conversion of the courtier was the first step in the long-term attempt to transform Muscovy's old elites into new.[170] Boris Ivanovich Morozov, Moscow's chief minister during the early years of Aleksei's reign, had seventeen books; they included the Tacitus with Julius Lipsius' *Commentary*, Cicero, and Galen, and the rest were traditional religious materials.[171]

Just three collections in Muscovy approached the texture of the gentleman's library in the contemporary West. Paltry in relative size, one belonged to Artamon Sergeevich Matveev, head of the Ukrainian *Prikaz* (1669) and then the Foreign Office. He had a Scots wife. A well-known devotee of Western tastes and organizer of a domestic theater group, he recruited twenty-six Belorussians to study comedy acting in the German suburb. He would be tried for sorcery, and killed in the *strel'tsy* uprising of 1682.[172]

Matveev's seventy-seven foreign-language books, over sixty percent of them in Latin or Greek, included theology and Scripture, Athanasius, Chrysostom, the Roman Martyrology, and a Polish Missal. He held Cicero, Aristotle, Justinian, Seneca, and Virgil, Quintus Curtius, as well as travel literature, chronicles, histories, works on architecture, apothecary and home remedies, genealogy, and Polish

---

[169] Luppov, *XVII vek*, pp. 115–116. Since Luppov wrote the library has been reexamined by Lebedeva, "Lichnaia biblioteka tsaria Fedora Alekseevicha," pp. 56–64. The list is in Zabelin, *Domashnii byt*, I, Pt. 2, 599–607. No catalogue of the books of Sophia Alekseevna was made; see Lindsey Hughes, *Sophia*, p. 171. Lacking the descriptions of the libraries of Muscovite women there is nothing to compare to Moore, *The Maiden's Mirror*.

[170] See Shatz, trans., "Evgenii Onegin," and his "Zapadnoe vliianie," and Shatz, trans, "Western Influences in Russia."

[171] Luppov, *XVII vek*, p. 111.

[172] *Russko-belorusskie sviazi*, p. 114, dated 1673; Belokurov, *O biblioteke*, pp. 69–74.

law.[173] He gave his son, Andrei (b. 1666) a Classical education, one
of the first in Muscovy. The Polish ambassador reported of him,
"Artamonovich has an extensive mind, speaks Latin, loves to read; is
attached to foreigners; with rapture he listens to everything European. I advised him to apply himself to the study of French. At the
age of 22, I assured him it was not difficult to learn that language.
In this way he could attain his wish—to read the ancient and the
new writers."[174]

Another belonged to the boyar Vasilii Golitsyn, head of the Foreign
Office (1682) and favorite of Sophia. In the 1670s his household
acquired a case of apothecary goods including all sorts of medicines,
a printed text of the story of Barlaam and Josaphat, and a German
book on land surveying. He too had a large collection of religious
and liturgical books, a smaller number of chronicles and law codes,
a book on veterinary, some of the works of the Ukrainians, Polockij
and his pupil Medvedev, Dmytro Tuptalo-Rostovskyi, Lazar
Baranovych, as well as the Koran, translated from the Polish.[175]

The third such library was, surprisingly, that of the peasant-born
prince of the church, Patriarch Nikon.[176] It is quite ordinary to think
of English divines, German monks, and French Cardinals as active
players in politics, but rarely are Russian prelates so depicted. Patriarch
Nikon's book habits belonged to the world of Boris Morozov, Fedor
Rtishchev, and Afanasii Ordin-Nashchokin, just as they were co-
participants in court politics, subject to the same rules of patronage,
faction, clique, familial connections, status, rank, and parvenu wealth.[177]

The professional part of Nikon's library was well stocked with
patristics, including eleven volumes of John Chrysostom, the works

---

[173] Luppov, *XVII vek*, pp. 102–07; the full extent of his religious books is unknown since all of his Slavonic books were dispersed separately. Luppov notes the
missing books, but presents statistics which suggest the foreign books were the entire
collection. See Belokurov, *O biblioteke* , pp. 69–74, where the collection is included
in its eventual resting place, the library of the *Posol'skii Prikaz*. See also Lahana,
"Breaking the Rules," 8–9, where his library is discussed in the context of his trial
for sorcery, and on herbals, Slukhovskii, *Russkaia biblioteka* p. 161.

[174] Matveev, "Zapiski Andreia Artamonovicha Grafa Matveeva," p. iii.

[175] Hughes, *Russia and the West*, pp. 87–88. The neglected classic on Polish influence
is still L. R. Lewitter, "Poland, the Ukraine and Russia."

[176] On the Polonized library of Golitsyn, see Hughes, *Sophia*, p. 170, and Zabelin,
Domashnyi byt, Vol. I, Pt. 1, 563. For the paragraphs below, Luppov, *XVII vek*, pp.
102–07, 107–10, 133–36.

[177] It is probably also time to abandon the Soviet convention of using initials to
identify Russians, since they often use it to mask monastic names: F. Prokopovich.
It does not reflect early-modern or nineteenth-century usages.

of Dionysius the Areopagite, of Basil the Great and Gregory the Theologian, and also many Christian liturgical and scriptural texts, but there was also a small and unsystematic cache of Aristotle, Plutarch, Demosthenes, and Herodotus. Historical works dominated his Classics. But his basic collection was not markedly different from the courtier Matveev's.[178]

These varied libraries of lay and clerical court culture meshed the traditional religious books with the translated eclectic *miscellanea* coming in through Poland. Whatever was the key to these libraries, it was not secularization: Luppov notes[179] that Vasilii Petrovich Sheremetev bought the infantry manual of 1647, as evidence of a thirst for the secular in "feudal" circles. His elder brother, Ivan Petrovich, however, simultaneously bought twelve books: a Gospel of 1644, Cyril of Jerusalem's sermons, four copies of the Psalter, five of a breviary, and a *Kanonik*. The same records reveal that their uncle, Fedor Ivanovich Sheremetev, bought 23 Gospels, 21 Prologs, 50 breviaries of the edition of 1649, 45 of that of 1645, 70 from 1646, 122 of 1647, and 34 copies of the General Menology, and scores more. This family in a five-year period either sold or distributed over 600 volumes of the printed Church texts of Muscovy, book-hawking religious texts on an extraordinary scale.[180]

The Stroganovs' libraries were largely religious in content, but by mid-century the family possessed the kind of random mixed library typical of court circles.[181] Nor were these eclectic courtiers' libraries limited to the secular elites. Afanasii, archbishop of Kholmogory from 1682 to 1702, whom young Tsar Peter befriended, presided over one of Muscovy's most outward-looking dioceses. His library, overwhelmingly a collection of religious literature, also contained the kind of historical literature now in vogue at court.[182] His own composition

---

[178] Luppov considers his herbals as an interest in "natural science," but by all comparisons the "scientific" collection is meager, and it fails to challenge Cizevskij's studied dictum, "Nature apparently inspired little interest." Luppov, *op. cit.*, p. 106; Cizevskij, *History*, p. 327. East German scholars were more inclined to stress comparisons; see Winter, *Frühaufklärung*, p. 273.

[179] Luppov, *XVII vek*, p. 92.

[180] Barsukov, *Rod Sheremetevykh*, Vol. V, pp. 234–35.

[181] Contrast Luppov, *XVII vek*, pp. 117–118, with Mudrova, "Knizhnoe sobranie G. D. Stroganova," pp. 28–40.

[182] Luppov, *XVII vek*, pp. 140–146; Kukushkina, "Obzor sobraniia redkikh knig . . . iz Arkhangel'ska," pp. 253–267.

on the biblical days of creation dimly reflected the new cosmology of the age.[183]

Most Muscovites were shielded, of course, from this imported book culture. In most Russian parishes the two intrusive worlds of Ukrainian humanism and Polonized court and *prikaz* culture remained alien.[184] Old Belief had been called into existence by a battle of books, and it sustained itself by compiling a small repertoire of traditional texts.[185] One strain of Old Belief remained hostile to the printed book itself. They associated book printing with Antichrist; for them the continued use of the manuscript became a singular mark of opposition to the official Church.[186] That official Church was itself torn: Patriarch Nikon's successor, Ioakim, prohibited icons printed on paper, no matter how Orthodox their execution, since the act of printing was necessarily done by heretics.

As late as a century and a half later, the English clergyman Robert Pinkerton, who prided himself on his first-hand contacts with various Old-Believer communities, said that even then the printed versus the manuscript service book divided Russians. The great accomplishment of the Church Council of 1667, he believed, was the distribution of "correct printed editions, in place of the former manuscript copies," an "important and necessary work . . . in order to have the service uniform throughout the whole empire." For Pinkerton, like the official Church hierarchs he translated, uniformity was the goal; for Old Believers in the seventeenth and the nineteenth centuries, "the ancient manuscript copies" were "the only charter of their hope and inheritance of eternal life,"[187] and uniform printed texts be damned. All of this suggests that the Ukrainian-Lithuanian-Belorussian community was small, isolated, and alien, unable to establish real grammar schools in the atmosphere of the Schism and its aftermath.[188] The Polonized court was similarly alien.

The handful of descriptions of libraries in Muscovy reveal the initial

---

[183] Panich, "Osobennosti 'Shestodneva' Afanasiia," pp. 5–24.

[184] Kopanev, "Knizhnost'."

[185] Bubnov, "Knigotvorichestvo moskovskikh staroobriadtsev"; "Rukopisi iz sobraniia rizhskoi grebenshchikovskoi obshchiny."

[186] Rozov, "O kul'turno-istoricheskom znachenii," pp. 19, 21. For the following, Lahana, "Breaking the Rules," p. 2.

[187] Platon, *The Present State of the Greek Church*, pp. 287–89.

[188] See Kapterev, "O greko-latinskikh shkolakh," and Galkin, *Akademiia v Moskve*, pp. 29ff.

impact of Polish and West-European mercenaries and technicians on the court. There was a second influence, a slow penetration of their adventure-laden texts into the manscript collections, *sborniki*, that formed the core of popular reading in the eighteenth century. We will return to that theme in good time.

C. *Peter Tolstoi, Polonized Courtier*

One of the most articulate representatives of Polonized court and *prikaz* culture was Peter Tolstoi. He revealed his tastes in a lengthy account of his voyage to Western Europe in 1697–98.[189] Descended from the court elite—his grandfather and father had achieved the rank of *okol'nichii* and served as *voevody*—Peter Tolstoi was like his father allied with the Miloslavskii faction in court politics. In the 1690s he was *voevoda* of Velikii Ustiug, administering the area linking northern Archangel with Muscovy. There that he met young Tsar Peter who subsequently shipped Tolstoi abroad for study prior to his own Grand Embassy, lest he remain at home to again join a rebellion.

Educated traditionally and raised a child of the *prikaz* and court, Tolstoi was assigned at age fifty-two to study navigation in Venice, an echo of a long-established practice in which foreign expertise in everything from languages to weaponry and silver-smithing was assembled in the *prikazy* and passed on to the bureaucratic ranks. Tolstoi's technical training constituted an adult supplement to his religious upbringing.[190] Tolstoi's assignment was to study navigation but his education had been in traditional Orthodoxy, and necessarily his diary was permeated with religiosity and the new interests of the court.

His diary is a medieval knight's literary quest for the Holy Grail and a typical piece of the new *prikaz* literature, written in a language influenced by Polish. On the one hand Tolstoi had courtly interests in military technology, fortifications, and the hydraulics of a Western

---

[189] Okenfuss, trans., *The Travel Diary of Peter Tolstoi*; page references here are to this edition. Since the appearance of the translation, a new Russian edition has appeared: Ol'shevskaia & Travnikov, *Puteshestvie stol'nika*. On the transformation of old courtiers into new diplomats see Altbauer, "The Diplomats of Peter the Great"; see also Kliuchevskii, "Zapadnoe vliianie v Rossii." The old study of Tolstoi was Pavlov-Silvan'skii, "Graf Petr Andreevich Tolstoi"; it is not replaced by Pavlenko, "P. A. Tolstoi"; in English, see Tolstoy, *The Tolstoys*, pp. 20–88.

[190] See my "Technical Training"; "Russian Students in Europe."

Civilization.[191] On the other hand, he was a fantastic Christian voyage, with winds calmed by prayer (p. 120), pursuit by infidel pirates (pp. 218–24), temptations of the flesh (p. 159), miraculous icons "not made by human hands," (p. 117), icons visibly displeased by heretical Catholic ownership (pp. 23–25, 338), vipers turned to stone (p. 232), and punctuated by the amassing of the thorns from Christ's crown (pp. 180, 235–36), wood from His Cross (pp. 167–68, 180, 235–36), straw from His manger (p. 290), and hair from His mother's head (p. 180). Tolstoi's diary is comfortably shelved with the travels and *skazki* about prodigal sons, saints' lives, lives of Alexander the Great, the chief reading materials of *prikaz* culture under Tsar Aleksei after 1655.[192]

Crucial to his inquiry was the efficacy of Western Catholicism, the Greek Orthodox rite, and his own Muscovite Orthodoxy: did Catholic relics work miracles? Was the Greek faith that had accepted union with Catholicism at Florence-Ferrara, whose patriarchs in 1667 had approved Nikon's changes in Muscovite Orthodoxy, the true religion? Tolstoi observed church architecture, examined holy relics, and investigated miracles everywhere.

Tolstoi wrote autobiography, recounted adventures, sought the One True Faith, and did so in a book chronologically arranged. When one recalls that the three major genres of seventeenth-century Muscovite manuscripts were saints' lives, *povesti* ranging from the exploits of the Turks to the miraculous appearance of icons, chronicles and *skazaniia* about individuals saintly and profane, and when one recalls that this popular reading was typically hung from the skeleton of the Church's annual calendar, one can talk about Tolstoi's own diary as a semi-sacred, semi-secular attempt to pour his journey into an old Muscovite mold.[193] Tolstoi's diary is a morality tale, the kind of religious adventure tale that had gained popularity at Tsar Aleksei's court.

---

[191] See my "The Cultural Transformation of Peter Tolstoi," and "Peter Tolstoi in Rome."

[192] See Cizevskij, *History*, pp. 327, 331ff.; Fennell & Stokes, pp. 250ff.; Ziolkowski, *Hagiography*; and also V. D. Kuzmina, *Rytsarskii roman na Rusi*. On linguistic borrowing see, in addition to the Soviet work cited in *Diary*, pp. xxvi–xxvii, Otten, "Reiseberichte der Petrinischen Zeit," and his *Untersuchungen zu den Fremd- und Lehnwörter bei Peter dem Grossen*.

[193] See the *Slovar' knizhnikov*, Vyp. I, 237–345, 195–294, 344–98; There are also interesting parallels between the content of Tolstoi's diary and the tale of Alexis the Man of God, a story Tolstoi obviously knew. See *Diary*, pp. 266, and V. P. Adrianova, *Zhitie Alekseia cheloveka Bozhiia*.

Tolstoi's quest was medieval, but his mind was modern. He approached the miraculous with a skeptical and inquiring mind which sharpened with contact with the West. Early in his journey he encountered the icon of Borysow, to revisit it two years later on his return. Still in Catholic captivity, a dark spot on the Virgin's face was even more pronounced than it had been previously (p. 338). The Catholics said that the hair on an image of Christ Crucified in the cathedral in Warsaw would grow long if not cut, but Tolstoi carefully reported this with skepticism (p. 33). North of Vienna he reported a small Orthodox icon which miraculously returned to a tree every time the Jesuits removed it (p. 51–2). Near Korcula he was puzzled by a "Greek" icon which swam to a Catholic church to work its miracles (p. 117). Some of the Catholics' miracle-working icons Tolstoi could accept as such because they had been made in antiquity. Both the famous Black Madonna of Czestochowa and the Venetian La Nicopeia of San Marco could work miracles because they had been wrought by St. Luke himself (pp. 41, 121). Tolstoi's mind was a place where rational inquiry and the peasant's faith coexisted.

In Russia a few years later the humanist Teofan Prokopovych expressed a Protestant skepticism concerning "Fables [that] seduce Men from the way of Salvation," "Unprofitable and mischievous Ceremonies," and "unbelievable heaps of Holy Relics." The Petrine Church would investigate these superstitions, since "where these or the idle Practices prevail, the People are led into manifest and gross Idolatry."[194] Teofan demanded a re-examination of Russia's precious collection of relics:

> To enquire concerning holy Relicks, where some seem to be doubtful, there is great Roguery in this pretence; to Instance, in some foreign Stories, the Body of the Proto-Martyr St. *Stephen*, lies interr'd in the Suburbs of *Venice*, in the Monastery of the *Benedictines*; in the Church of St. *George*, and at *Rome*, in St. *Laurence*, at the Back of the City. Also innumerable are the Nails of the Cross of Christ, and an immense Quantity of Milk from the most holy Mother of God, in *Italy*, and

---

[194] For this and the quote following, the Ecclesiastical Regulation in the contemporary translation by Consett, *For God and Peter the Great*, Cracraft, ed., facsimile, pp. 26–29 and *passim*. Note also the modern translation by Muller, *The Spiritual Regulation*, p. 15. Bushkovitch makes the point that Nikon was an opponent of the popular cult of saints and miracles; Teofan was thus his successor; *Religion and Society*, 90–91, 107, 125, and *passim*.

infinite number of such like Fables. We are to examine whether there
are not with us any such idle Tales.

Teofan may in fact have read the diary of Peter Tolstoi, in which all
of these relics are mentioned. Indeed Tolstoi stooped and crawled
through the churches of the West, candle in hand, inquiring assiduously whether Greek and Catholic saints' relics were miraculously
preserved, and whether they or individual icons actually worked
miracles. Like Peter the Great, he knew his prayers could calm a
storm (p. 120),[195] but with Avvakum, he was unprepared to question
icons in general. It took a humanist to do that.

Tolstoi shared religious values with Avvakum, although he was
more open to the Polish literary culture. His values fell short of those
of the invading Ukrainians' Classical education. John Evelyn's Classical
education had alerted him to Monte Testaccio and the pyramid of
Gaius Cestius in Rome, but Tolstoi lacked it; Evelyn came prepared
to sacrifice a dog in the *Grotta dei Cane* "or Charons Cave," but not
Tolstoi; Evelyn had read Martial, Tolstoi had not; Evelyn knew of
the death of Pliny on Vesuvius, Tolstoi did not; Evelyn could identify the temple of Fausta, Tolstoi not (pp. 191, 194–95, 289, 294).
Tolstoi, in fact, stands as evidence of the ignorance of the Classical
world at the pinnacle of seventeenth-century Muscovite society.[196]

The story of Tolstoi and of Muscovite *prikaz* culture is not the
story of "feudal elites" eating forbidden fruits and reading banned
secular books denied the "democratic" masses, but rather of some in
a thoroughly religious Muscovite society exhibiting a cautious curiosity
about other religious worlds, without losing their immortal souls.
Tolstoi's religious quest was the same quest as Avvakum's: The
archpriest knew his one Holy Orthodox Faith would save him if
only he were not tempted by Western novelties. Sent abroad by his
Divinely-ordained tsar, Tolstoi dared to test his Faith with the profane
and with every available species of foreign Christianity, because he
knew with equal conviction that the One True Faith would reveal
itself miraculously and save him. Both were lettered Muscovites, as
both an outward-looking *prikaz* culture and an introspective faithful
had been around since Moscow emerged in the mid-fifteenth century.[197]

---

[195] Peter the Great prayed under similar circumstances in 1694; see Lewitter,
"Peter the Great's Attitude," p. 62.

[196] See Kazakova, *Zapadnaia Evropa v russkoi pis'mennosti*, for the paucity of information about Classical Rome and Greece in Muscovite letters.

[197] Edward Keenan has long insisted upon the necessity of understanding that

5. *Conclusion*

The Petrine "revolution" is typically portrayed as a sudden break with the Muscovite past. But Ukrainian humanism and Polonized court culture had already transformed parts of the clerical and lay elites of Muscovy, and heralded the arrival of modern Russia. The bridge betweeen old and new can be seen in one of the most famous books of the early Petrine age was the *Arithmetika* of Leontii Magnitskii (1703). It became the definition of technical training in the Moscow School of Mathematics and Navigation, in the St. Petersburg Naval Academy, in the ciphering schools imposed on Russian dioceses, and in wharf—and garrison-schools opened by Admiralty and Army. In print and manuscript copies it remained the definition of mathematics in Russia for half a century.[198] It was, however, the culmination of the impact of the foreign on seventeenth-century Muscovy.

Magnitskii was a pupil of the Lichud brothers' short-lived college of the 1680s;[199] he then studied abroad and knew Latin, Greek, and some German and Italian when he reemerged in Moscow in 1701. He wrote as a humanist, concerned above all with the place of mathematics in the mind of an educated man. His book opened with an illustration and a versified discussion of Pythagoras and Archimedes, "the great ancient philosopher." His preface sermonized the point that the Biblical Days of Creation had called forth a world made for rational man's use, and thus religion did not reject reason or secular wisdom. Peter, Magnitskii announced, had now dedicated himself to the improvement of the nation, and required the services of those who knew several languages, who had studied their way up the curriculum to rhetoric and the arts of philosophy, and even to medicine and theology. Thus, he concluded, not only is arithmetic essential to education in the liberal arts, but the practical skills of measuring and counting were needed by a dynamic society as well.[200]

These sentiments had begun to creep into the Muscovite court's

---

Muscovy produced two distinct voices of two separate cultures; see his "Muscovy and Kazan," pp. 550 and *passim*.

[198] Okenfuss, "Technical Training," 330–332. On the teaching of mathematics see too the works of Iushkevich, "Matematika i ee prepodavanie," pp. 11–21, on Magnitskii; note also his *Istoriia matematiki v Rossii*.

[199] The modern biography is Denisov, *Leontii Filippovich Magnitskii*, here pp. 20–33, 141; on mathematics in Muscovy see Bobynin, *Ocherki istorii razvitiia fiziko-matematicheskikh znanii*.

[200] Magnitskii, *Arithmetika*, M, 1704, frontispiece, *predislovie*, *passim*.

manuscript tradition in the second half of the seventeenth century, where one began to encounter "the fundamentals of philosophy, rhetoric, and the other sciences belonging to geometry."[201] Peter sought the geometry needed to calculate the ladder required to scale a fortress wall, the number of soldiers in a formation, the number of revolutions in a gear, and the capacity of various containers. Magnitskii's text provided examples, but the utilitarian was harmoniously blended with the philosophic in introductory syllabic verses on the Roman coat-of-arms, in the naming of the winds in Slavonic, Latin, and Italian, and in a defence of the liberal arts, all of which were the excess baggage of a college education.

Religion was not divorced from mathematics. Magnitskii provided a gloss on the book of Genesis, buttressed by the testimony of Basil the Great, to the effect that there was no perdition in heeding Tsar Peter's injunction to study the things of this world.[202] Early in the text Magnitskii attempted to convey just how large a number might be. He devoted a page to a table which began

1
10
100
1 000
10 000

and which concluded with

1 000 000 000 000 000 000 000 000

and with the verse,

> Numbers are without end,
> Our minds cannot grasp them.
> No one knows their end
> Except God the Creator of all. . . .[203]

To the extent that Magnitskii's *Arithmetika* was "a kind of brief encyclopedia, presenting the bases of the natural science of that day,"[204] natural science was regarded as part of theology.

---

[201] Simonov, "Predystoriia rukopisnoi i pechatnoi russkoi matematicheskoi knigi," pp. 205–212.

[202] Magnitskii, *Arithmetika*, preface, p. 11 recto, and ff.

[203] *Ibid.*, p. 3.

[204] [L. A. Petrov], *Obshchestvenno-politicheskaia i filosofskaia mysl' Rossii*, p. 27.

In Europe it was the age of science. The *Arithmetika* taught the "geometrical harmony" of practical skills, service to Peter, syllabic verses, religion, and the liberal arts of the academy. Harmony defined the age. Between 1650 and about 1715, the age of Vauban in France, the fortifications of old Europe were abandoned after the lessons of artillery in the Thirty Years War, or they were rebuilt on elaborate geometrical principles. Peter Tolstoi travelling about Europe recorded those constructed "in the new style." Philosophers like Leibniz and Christian Wolff would talk of a *mathematica militaris* and of fortifications as applied geometry; the art of fencing would become stylized, as would the drill of massed troops, and one wrote of "the geometrically regulated equestrian"; military parades became stylized non-lethal combat, and court life itself, the graceful *Ballet de Cour*, drew upon dance, music, poetry, and geometry. Contemporaries found court life itself analogous to the movements of the planets around fixed stars. Behind all of this stood the Classics, a revived neo-Platonism, and the metaphysical idea of the unity of man, God, and the world in mathematical orderliness.

In the Baroque, mathematics, astrology, astronomy, even soldiering, diplomacy ("a just equilibrium"), politics, and the life of the royal servitor, were to be governed by geometry, by the Baroque virtues of regularity, proportion, and harmony. These European values too were imported and propagandized by Magnitskii, scion of Latin humanism, and they became part of the culture of the book in Petrine Russia.[205]

It was the spirit of the age. Daniel Defoe, opportunistic journalist, discussed Peter's reforms and attributed his military success to the fact that all was "carry'd on with great Regularity.... Every thing [was] done as it ought to be done." His new navy was carefully planned, and "the Event soon discover'd the Sagacity of the Design."[206]

---

[205] An old statement of these values is the introductory sections of Nussbaum, *The Triumph of Science*. Here I have followed a insightful essay, Eichberg, "Geometrie als barocke Verhaltensnorm." I owe the reference to the best recent continental study of absolutism, Kunisch, *Absolutismus*. One place to see the introduction of European mathematics into Russia as an exercise in the Baroque is in borrowed book illustrations. Note for example, the designs for the 1647 *Uchenie i khitrost'*, Varenius' *Geografiia general'naia* (1718), Buchner's *Uchenie i praktika artilerii* (1711), and Braun's *Noveishee osnovanie i praktika artilerii* (1710), all available in Adariukov & Sidorov, eds., *Kniga v Rossii*, Vol. I, pp. 121, 149, 155, 167.

[206] [Defoe], *Impartial History*, pp. 12, 15.

This far-reaching Baroque ideal was best seen in the new Russia in the complex but harmonious *Arithmetika* of Leontii Magnitskii.

The Baroque in Russian literature, on the other hand, was not a Russian literary movement at all but an alien import: "all baroque [was] *inorodnyi* (foreign)," and Polockij specifically was "almost completely devoid of specific native [Russian] traits."[207] Ukrainian humanism, however, became a Petrine cultural movement, one which blossomed into the Moscow Slavo-Greco-Latin Academy, and eventually into the world of Trediakovskii and Lomonosov, into the definition of the new Russia's architecture, and into a vision of human knowledge represented by Christian Wolff and his mathematically-minded proteges in the St. Petersburg Academy of Sciences. Foreign clerics, Polockij, the Lichuds, and their pupils like Magnitskii founded the new Russia every bit as much as did the courtiers who were transformed into the commanders of Emperor Peter the Great's army and navy.

Several symbolic dates mark the beginning of Peter's active reign and Muscovy's *perestroika* into "Russia": the Azov campaigns, Peter's Grand Embassy, his conversation with Patriarch Adrian about importing Kievan learning, or his refusal to name a new Patriarch. In the context of book ownership, another comes to mind. In the early 1690s the conservative Muscovite clergy had regained their church from the ilk of Patriarchs Nikon and Ioakim. They expelled the Lichud brothers who had just begun teaching Latin, forced the Metropolitan of Kiev to submit to the Muscovite Patriarchate, and to declare agreement with its teachings, and placed the works of the Ukrainian clergy, Hizel', Baranovych, Galjatov'skyj, and even Simeon Polockij himself, on a list of forbidden books. Truly in the 1690s, "the Patriarch's triumph was complete."

Just five years later, however, in 1696, the conservative Patriarch Adrian attempted to extend his grasp over major libraries in Moscow, specifically to have the books of the Foreign Office, which he did not control, transferred to the Printing Court, which he did. On July 29, 1696, young Peter refused, and thus signalled a new world of

---

[207] Bucsela, "The Problems of Baroque," pp. 260–261; Segel, "Baroque and Rococo," pp. 551–558. On the poverty of Russian verse, Smith, "The Most Proximate West," pp. 360–70. On architecture, see Hughes, "The West Comes to Russian Architecture," and her definitive summary of the Moscow Baroque, *Sophia*, pp. 150–161.

access to books in Russia, rather than the Church's sequestering of them in Muscovy.[208]

A new century would dawn, heralded by Peter's travels to the West, and upon his return, by a confrontation with that Patriarch. Soon Ukrainian teachers and pupils would be moving to Russia, commissioned to re-create the Kievan Academy in Moscow. At a glance, it would appear that the pioneering humanists of Tsar Peter's father's day had finally won offical acceptance. What were their activities and opportunities in the new Russia?

---

[208] On the conservative victory, Lewitter, "Poland, the Ukraine and Russia," pp. 424–428. On Peter's emergence, Slukhovskii, *Bibliotechnoe delo*, pp. 122–124; In 1968 he used the word *perestroika* to describe Peter's transformation, long before it was an "official" historiographic convention; *Ibid.*, p. 128. See my review of *Ocherki russkoi kul'tury*, in *JfGO*, Vol. 37 (1989), here pp. 433–34, for the overuse of the term recently to describe Peter.

CHAPTER TWO

RUSSIAN BOOK CULTURE IN THE FIRST HALF
OF THE EIGHTEENTH CENTURY

1. *European Book Culture in the Pre-Enlightenment*

Between the 1680s and the death of Louis XIV the target moved rapidly. So dramatic was the European cultural and intellectual revolution of the lifetime of Peter the Great that Paul Hazard opened his magnificent study of it declaring,

> Never was there a greater contrast, never a more sudden transition than this! An hierarchical system ensured by authority; life firmly based on dogmatic principle—such were the things held dear by the people of the seventeenth century, but these—controls, authority, dogmas and the like—were the very things that their immediate successors of the eighteenth held in cordial detestation.[1]

This was the moment when Newton announced the principles of a new science, as his countryman John Locke proclaimed a new education, a new psychology, and a new political vision. Part and parcel of this intellectual revolution, as Hazard noted, was the dethroning of the Classical mind and a contest between the spirit of enquiry and Holy Writ.

This "Crisis of the European Conscience" was the culmination of a larger intellectual revolution of modernity. It was arguably unprecedented in world history:

> Transformation from a pre-secular to a secular worldview has occurred only once in the history of mankind, and that was in West European, Renaissance Catholic civilization. Its precondition was the readiness of Romano-Germanic barbarians to learn and then to absorb Roman intellectual concepts, first in their Christianized version (the Carolingian Renaissance of the ninth century, the scholasticism of the twelfth to the fourteenth century), and then, with the rediscovery of the ancient Greek concept of humanism, in their civic and political form (*Civitas, libertas, res publica, consules, patria, senatus, natio,* etc). The transformation eventually resulted in the replacement of feudal and patrimonial political

---

[1] Paul Hazard, *The European Mind*, p. xv.

orders by polities of estates. The Italian Renaissance stimulated intellectual commitment and gave rise to a spirit of limitless discovery; the Reformation, with its concept of man's immediate relation to God, fostered the development of vernaculars. There followed the clear separation of church and state and the birth of secular national cultures based on their respective vernaculars, which through the translation of the Holy Writ acquired the *dignitas* needed to embrace an entire nation.[2]

This radical revolution, this dynamo, was the moving target sighted by Peter the Great.

His and his contemporaries' perception of it, however, differed from ours, formed in retrospect. Peter Tolstoi was unaware of it. Walking the streets of Italy he was more likely to note what remained from the Renaissance than what presaged the eighteenth century. Much remained invisible to contemporaries.[3] For Russians in Europe, old continuities were generally more visible and memorable than novelties.

One continuity was the private library. In catalogues of scientists' libraries one could expect to find the newest ideas.[4] One early collection was that of Elias Ashmole (1617–92). Trained as a lawyer, founder-member of the Royal Society, champion of the new science, Ashmole also cultivated a "prime interest in the occult sciences, particularly astrology and alchemy." Robert Hooke (1635–1702) was "one of the greatest geniuses the world has ever known."[5] About half of his books were in Latin, about a third in English, and the vast majority were "scientific and medical," including all the great figures of the Scientific Revolution, "as complete as one could possibly wish." But Hooke also held the great books of architecture, rare cartography and Americana, and the giants of the European age of humanism in English, as well as French, Spanish, and Italian letters. His collection of the ancient authors was complete, most in the original and many in translation. He collected "relatively little theology," but his incidental reading did include a dozen Bibles with further editions of Old and New Testaments, Psalters and Proverbs, much biblical exegesis in English, many volumes of sermons, and much on

---

[2] Pritsak, "The Kiev Mohyla Academy in Ukrainian History," p. 6.

[3] Valentin Boss, *Newton and Russia*, reminds us that awareness of the Newtonian revolution did not dictate acceptance.

[4] The following section is based largely on Munby, ed., *Sale Catalogues*; here, Vol. 11, *Scientists*, Feisenberger, ed., pp. 2–4, 13–37. Since scientists tended to donate their books to institutions, catalogues are relatively rare; of 300 known English book auctions of the late seventeenth century, only about 20 belonged to scientists.

[5] *Ibid.*, pp. 4–7, 37–116.

the Jesuits.[6] He also collected the moral literature of humanism, Erasmus, Gracian, Bellegarde, Castiglione, and the *Reflexions, Prudentes Penseés Morales, Maximes Stociennes* (Amsterdam, 1671). Such libraries remind us of how easily the old co-existed with the new, the spiritual with science.

His contemporary, John Ray, the "English Linnaeus,"[7] the father of natural history in England, held not a "collector's library" but a "working collection" of some 1,350 items, eight hundred of them in Latin, chiefly natural history and botany. He was a scientist but he owned all the Classical authors; as a sideline, he was a Hebrew scholar, and "Christian theology forms the other important section of the library." He had a full range of editions of the Church Fathers, a good Reformation collection, and a "great many other theological works." The library of Edmund Halley (1656–1742) cannot be extricated from another with which it was sold, but the combined collection of a scientist and a lawyer contained over thirty complete Bibles, and over forty-five titles of Cicero.[8] Pagan antiquity and religion were complementary. We should expect as much: Hazard had concluded his study pointing out that through the Western pre-Enlightenment the proofs for God's existence were improved rather than neglected: "Do not the wonders of Nature reveal His existence, His power, His living foresight?"[9]

Of names which defined the age, few shone in the same firmament as John Locke. Kliuchevskii despised him as an educational revolutionary who could sweep away centuries of Christian wisdom and tradition with the irreverent stroke of a pen.[10] He might have been less critical had he seen Locke's library in which the category "Politics and Law," "a collection of political ephemera," comprised only 10.7% of his books. By contrast his holdings of Theology, 23.8% of the library, "shelf upon shelf of lengthy treatises," was the most substantial of his many areas of interest. For the man who perhaps did more than any other to end the reign of Latin in the schools, and even though "Locke was no lover of old books for the sake of their age," "Tully [Cicero] was Locke's favourite Latin author, perhaps

---

[6] *Ibid.*, pp. 101–102, 105, 111–112, and *passim.*
[7] *Ibid.*, pp., 7–10, 117–148.
[8] *Ibid.*, pp. 10–12, 149–296.
[9] Hazard, *op. cit.*, pp. 415, 417.
[10] Okenfuss, "V. O. Kliuchevskii on Childhood," p. 420. For the following, Harrison & Laslett, *The Library of John Locke*, pp. 18–21 and *passim.*

his favourite author altogether"; there are twenty-nine entries under *Cicero* in his library. In all his vast collection of the Classics—twenty editions of Horace, three of Lucretius, ten of Ovid, ten of Tacitus, etc.—only his copy of Cicero's *Letters to Friends* contains his own notations.[11] Locke's name is associated with the rise of the English language to literary and learned preeminence, but only a third of his own library was in English. Of course, only at the end of the eighteenth century did Latin begin to fade as the language of European schoolboys.[12] Trained in medicine, Locke's collection of science comprised only about eighteen per cent of his books, one of the great gentlemen's libraries. But the ratios compare to those of a quite ordinary London doctor.[13] The universal education in religion and the Classics defined these libraries.

Nor did the private library change much in the eighteenth century. Christopher Wren's (d. 1723) collection boasted a vast array of Classical authors, with multiple editions of Cicero, the historians, Ovid, Horace, and others, often with English and French redactions as well. He collected a significant amount of contemporary religious debate, Clarke's *Paraphrase of the Evangelists* and *Scripture Doctrine of Trinity*, Sleiden and Burnet on the Reformation, compendia of sermons by Snape, Littleton, Carleton, Young, and others.[14] In 1740 the effects of the interpreter of classical architecture, Nicholas Hawksmoor, were sold at auction. Here were Dawson's *Lexicon Novi Testamenti*, Allen's *Defence of Purgatory*, Stillingfleet's sermons, a French Bible, among others. Caesar's *Commentaries*, Plutarch's *Lives*, Pliny's *Natural History*, Juvenal, Tacitus—numerically insignificant, but educationally telling.[15]

The poet James Thomson's books were dispersed in 1749, and the sale catalogue informed readers that he had bought the most modern books, "far the largest proportion being less than thirty years old."[16] Still his Classics numbered Tacitus, Lucretius, Terence, Sallust, Horace, Caesar, Virgil, Juvenal, Cicero, and Homer in the original languages, and far more in translation. His interest in religion was minimal, but it did extend to Baxter's *On the Soul*, Millar's *History of*

---

[11] Harrison & Laslett, *Library*, p. 281.
[12] Clark, *Classical Education*, pp. 47ff.
[13] See for example, Bishop, "Le Dr. W. Salmon (1644–1713) et sa bibliothèque," pp. 79–83.
[14] Munby, ed., *Sale Catalogues*, Vol. 4, *Architects*, pp. 1–44.
[15] *Ibid.*, 45–106.
[16] Munby, *Sale Catalogues*, Vol. I, *Poets and Men of Letters*, pp. 45–66.

Christianity, Travels of the Jesuits, Wollaston's *Religion of Nature,* Bower's *History of the Popes*—but this was remarkably skimpy, and one detects the arrival of new values for a few readers.

Much recent scholarship has been devoted to a reevaluation of some preliminary work on private French libraries done by Daniel Mornet in 1910, and incorporated into his classic *La pensée française au XVIIIe siècle* (1926). Mornet's sample of private libraries led him to underestimate the role of theology French libraries at mid-century, his figure of 7% now being abandoned in favor of the 12.4% recently established.[17] The libraries of nobles in France were more numerous, were far larger in size, and contained more religious material, than scholars knew a generation ago.[18] One provincial magistrate's library had an astonishing 37.34% theology at the end of the century, although many of his books had been inherited. The vast size and number of nobles' libraries underscore the differences between Europe and Russia in the eighteenth century.

For Germany the period 1680–1750 was the golden age of book collecting. Most impressive was the size of libraries.[19] The Lübeck scholar and pastor Otto Friedrich Butendach (1730–98) had about 7,500 volumes. "Not particularly large" was the collection of the well-known Christian Thomasius, 8,766 works in 1739; his younger brother, Gottfried Thomasius, held 27,000 volumes, requiring a 2,300-page catalogue! In Hamburg the Lutheran theologian Friedrich Mayer (1650–1712) had 18,000 books, his pupil Johan Albert Fabricius (1668–1736) 32,000 titles, and a third Hamburg gymnasium teacher owned 25,000 volumes. Although the most impressive libraries tended to be those of Protestants, communities of Catholic monks in southern German lands also had vast libraries, rivaling those of the universities.[20]

In Protestant Franconia down to 1750, there existed scant difference between the libraries of nobles and clergy. "The private libraries of the prince-bishops do not differ in any way from other book collections of their contemporaries. Not once do theological works predominate." One of the most magnificent "secular" libraries of the

---

[17] Beckmann, "Französische Privatbibliotheken." This remarkable study is based on 840 sale catalogues, 1700–1799.

[18] See Roche, "Noblesses et culture dans la France," pp. 9–28, and Chaussinand-Nogaret, *The French Nobility,* Chapter 4.

[19] For the investigation of some two thousand catalogues and for the following, Raabe, "Gelehrtenbibliotheken im Zeitalter der Aufklärung," pp. 107, 109, 112–14.

[20] Heilingsetzer, "Wissenschaftspflege und Aufklärung in Klöstern," pp. 83–101.

age belonged to Lothar Franz von Schönborn (1655–1727), Bishop of Bamberg and Archbishop of Mainz, whose 4,000 volumes were a treasure of law and politics, natural science and medicine, Classical literature, and of the courtly manuals of etiquette. Most nobles' libraries ranged from a few dozen volumes to three hundred or so, and those who, like the Grafen von Schönborn, who held thousands of volumes, were exceptions. Every noble's library was stocked with confessional theology but no library was purely of one's own faith: in terms of libraries "the "pure" Pietist or enlightener seldom existed."[21] Protestants bought Catholic authors, and vice-versa.

The patterns of seventeenth-century noble libraries, religion, the Classics, the Italian authors of the Renaissance, and the courtly and moral literature of Erasmus and his followers continued to characterize the new age.[22] Cicero was the ubiquitous author who taught politics, the idea of the state, the relationship between law and force, the godly social order, and rule by an educated elite; who taught rhetoric, and insisted that the public speaker must master history, jurisprudence, and philosophy; and who taught philosophy, self-mastery of the ego, and practical ethics. So significant was Cicero in the libraries of German nobles,[23] that almost alone he defined the educated man. Already in the sixteenth century Ciceronia "had become the generally accepted language of moral and political discourse," and in 1700, joined by Tacitus and other Classical sages, his sway was undiminished.[24]

One new phenomenon of the first half of the eighteenth century was the noble woman's library. An earlier *Frauenzimmerbibliothek*, for example, that of Dorothea Frederica Marschalk von Ebnet (d. 1718), was a collection of theological and edifying works in the vernacular. It contained the Pietist Arndt's *True Christianity*, Thomas à Kempis, Bibles, prayer-books, sermons, plus some sprinkling of literary works, a few in Spanish or French.[25] By mid-century, women's libraries were changing: A library catalogued in the 1750s revealed a both the older

---

[21] Pleticha, *Adel und Buch*, pp. 69–70; for Bishop Lothar below, pp. 164–180, and for the following, her Conclusion, pp. 223–242, appendices, and *passim*.

[22] A handy guide to this literature of civility is Ariès, *Centuries of Childhood*, pp. 375–390. See holdings in specific libraries in Pleticha, pp. 32–33, 44–47, and *passim*.

[23] Pleticha, *op. cit.*, p. 236.

[24] Tuck, "Humanism and Political Thought," pp. 63–5.

[25] Pleticha, p. 99, and also the collection of Amalie Veronica von Seckendorff (1687), p. 82.

German piety and a new more secular but equally moralistic culture, often in French. One sees the Classics, especially ethical texts
in French translation in the library of the Markgräfin von Ansbach
who died in 1729, but the one who died in 1758, Wilhelmine von
Bayreuth, boasted a collection replete with the moderns, Bacon to
the *Encyclopédie*, a vast array of modern history, travel, and mores,
almost all in French, and indeed she had only three German books.[26]
The same pattern could be seen among the Casteller Gräfinnen, from
the religious collection of Dorothea Renata (1669–1743), to that of
Frederika, born Countess zu Ortenburg (1712–1758), whose three
hundred and fifty volumes included Arndt and the stalwarts of Pietism,
but also Grotius and Pufendorf, Gellert, Young, and Rousseau,
Bellegarde's *Reflexions* and Fénelon's *Télémaque*.[27] By the 1740s and
1750s German Pietism was more influential in the profane world
than in the religious as it absorbed a Ciceronian concept of the active
life.[28] Accordingly, in the libraries of female readers in Lutheran
Germany one can see religious movements like Pietism forming a
bridge between the devotional readings of an earlier age, and the
moralistic and moralizing literature of the eighteenth century.

Russia lagged far behind. In 1759 the first Russian private periodical was founded.[29] By 1750 in Britain in addition to many newspapers in London, some twenty-eight towns had their own periodical
presses, and soon one could count thirty more.[30] The late seventeenth century and the first half of the eighteenth century was the
great age of the periodical press in the German-speaking lands. The
standard bibliography lists over sixty-five hundred serials prior to
1800.[31] In broadest terms, the general press appeared between 1670
and 1720, the "moralizing periodicals" dominated the period 1720–
1740, and more specialized periodicals began to appear about mid-
century.[32] But reading the news daily was already an established
routine. From 1695 we read that,

> Newspapers are the foundation, the direction, and the guiding prin-
> ciple of all cleverness, and he who does not attend to the newspapers

[26] *Ibid.*, pp. 72–76.
[27] *Ibid.*, pp. 125–126.
[28] Vierhaus, "Kulturelles Leben im Zeitalter des Absolutismus," pp. 26–27.
[29] Khoteev, *Kniga v Rossii v seredine XVIII v.*, p. 4.
[30] Alston, "The Eighteenth-Century Non-Book," p. 346.
[31] Kirchner, *Bibliographie der Zeitschriften des deutschen Sprachgebietes bis 1900*.
[32] Kirchner, *Das deutsche Zeitschriftenwesen*, employs these categories.

must remain ever and eternally a wretched *Prülker* and bungler in the Sciences of the World and its ways, and he who would be clever nowadays must immediately after his business rush out to pick up another bit of cleverness, which he will then put down and condemn.[33]

If guaranteed delivery on one's lawn was not yet a reality, a daily addiction to news-reading had already manifested itself.

In Germany there were about a hundred moral weeklies, the kind of publication pioneered in Russia by Novikov, in the eighteenth century; many more contained regular moral content while serving other interests.[34] These scores of successful periodicals were the medium by which the Classics reached circles of readers beyond the minority in the Old Regime who were formally educated in Latin. It was early a convention to begin each item with a moralizing headnote from Horace, Virgil, Cicero, Ovid, Seneca, Martial, Juvenal, Lucian, Lucretius, Terence, or if a modern were required, Erasmus. The inexhaustible alternate source, the Bible, was almost completely ignored.[35] In addition to acclimating readers to Classical citations, the moral weeklies enlisted the ancients to explain the universe. According to the moral periodicals the Stoics Marcus Aurelius and Cicero understood the wisdom of the *Werkmeister der Welt*, and the beauty of the world testified to the rule of God in nature. That all was well in this realm could be affirmed by citations of Plato, Thales, and Cicero.[36] The moral weeklies also popularized the idea of a utilitarian science to replace Christian scholasticism. "*Alles, was die Alten gesagt haben, ist Autorität.*"[37]

In the moral weeklies the Classics prepared the way for noble savages, as they constantly idealized a bucolic life. Images were formed by Virgil, Cicero, and Epicurus; mottoes by Horace or Virgil on *Landleben* were ubiquitous. The image of death itself was reshaped by the pagan ancients. Plato and Seneca, Cicero and Horace, taught that death was but a passage to be viewed calmly, as it was nought but transport to a different condition of perfection.[38] The moral weeklies did not destroy religion with pagan authorities; rather

---

[33] von Stieler, *Zeitungs Lust und Nutz*, 1695, cited in Lindemann, *Deutsche Presse bis 1815*, pp. 13, 89.
[34] For the following Martens, *Die Botschaft der Tugend*.
[35] *Ibid.*, pp. 105–06.
[36] *Ibid.*, p. 221.
[37] *Ibid.*, pp. 424, 429.
[38] *Ibid.*, pp. 280, 396.

Classically educated writers, many of them clerical to their souls, employed pagans to reaffirm the principles of Christian morality. In so doing they emphasized the absolute compatibility of the pagan and the Christian, even as they criticized the superstitions of the Middle Ages. "In the moral weeklies, the wisdom and the virtue of the ancient philosophers served Christ in His attempt to find the best path to a righteous life."[39]

In the era of Locke and Newton, the European "target" moved. In the massive libraries of nobles and bourgeoisie, religious works and Latin texts remained ubiquitous, and Cicero led all pagan authors. Translations and periodicals brought them to new readers, including women. How sensitive was Peter to the blend of Christian and pagan in early-modern Western libraries?

2. The Classics in the Petrine Age and Beyond

A. The Classics in Print in Russia

The great cultural divide in late Muscovy was between traditional Orthodox believers, an eclectically Polonized court, and a small community of foreign humanists. Since these Ukrainian humanists were characterized by Latin reading, the circulation of Latin books in Russia assumes significance.

The question here is the nature and scope of the Petrine transformation. If one examines the recent non-specialized literature, one encounters such generalizations as, Peter "wrought fundamental changes in the way that Russia's ruler viewed himself and his domains," "transformed not only the technology, government, and culture of Russia, but also the role of the autocracy," and "forced the Russians into military uniforms and administrative offices styled on Western models." Is it equally certain, however, that "Peter the Great had shattered the precepts that had ruled life in Muscovite Russia?"[40] New *precepts that rule life* implied a new education, and the most visible Western schooling in 1700 was Classical humanism. Did Peter intend humanism to replace older Muscovite "precepts of life?"

Soviet scholars of book history argued that the early eighteenth

---

[39] *Ibid.*, p. 228.
[40] Lincoln, *The Great Reforms*, pp. 5–6, 159.

century accelerated seventeenth-century patterns. The secular book became the center of attention under Peter. Book publishing was transferred from Church to government. More practical books appeared, even "serious scientific literature" such as the works of Pufendorf. Works from Poland were replaced by translations directly from West-European languages.[41] The production of books grew after Peter's death, and secular books circulated to ever larger portions of the population.[42]

Over twenty years ago Peter Gay published the first volume of his influential *Enlightenment*. It offered the interpretation of the philosophes' thought as the "Rise of Modern Paganism" that paralleled dialectically and consciously a Roman Enlightenment of the age of Lucretius and Cicero. While defining the Enlightenment as a wholly modern and "vastly ambitious program, a program of secularism, humanity, cosmopolitanism, and freedom, above all, freedom in its many forms,"[43] Gay was equally eloquent concerning the philosophes' "conscious appeal to pagan antiquity." "As cultivated men in a cultivated age, the philosophes loved classical antiquity and took pure pleasure in it; as reformers, they did not hesitate to exploit, shrewdly and unscrupulously, the classics they loved."[44]

A critical group of five ancient authors contributed to "Modern Paganism."[45] For the philosophes, Tacitus was the philosophical historian who would not flatter tyrants; Seneca was both scientist and public servant who saw an orderly universe which mirrored rational intelligence itself; Lucian's *Dialogues* persecuted "metaphysicians, social climbers and religious believers with impartiality." "Urbane, satirical, he [was] the nemesis of fanaticism." Cicero was philosopher, poet, friend, orator, and public servant, "the thinker in action, the Stoic

---

[41] Luppov, *Kniga v Rossii v pervoi chetverti XVIII veka*, Conclusion, pp. 359–361. (Hereafter, Luppov, *pervoi*).

[42] S. P. Luppov, *Kniga v Rossii v poslepetrovskoe vremia*, Conclusion, pp. 364–65 (Hereafter Luppov, *poslepetrovskoe*). The most favorable review was that of R. Lucas, *Study Group on Eighteenth-Century Russia Newsletter*, No. 5 (1977), 86–94. See also Luppov's retrospective "Russkii chitatel' XVII—pervoi poloviny XVIII veka," pp. 83–95. For the following, T. A. Afanas'eva, "Izdaniia kirillicheskoi pechati XVIII veka svetskogo soderzhaniia," pp. 183–199.

[43] Gay, *The Enlightenment*, I, pp. 3, 31.

[44] Porter and Teich, *The Enlightenment in National Context*, seems the foundation of the recent trend to refer to enlightenments in the plural, united by the Classics.

[45] For the following, Gay, *op. cit.*, pp. 98–108, 116–17, 120, 124, 159, 172, 188, 305; see also Curtius, *Europäische Literatur-geschichte*, pp. 52–62, for another perspective; articles include Montesquieu's debt to Ovid and Virgil, and Diderot's to Horace.

who taught modesty, self-control, meekness, beneficence, practicality, generosity, rationality, tolerance, and obedience to the dictates of nature, but above all the voice of *humanitas* and virtue." Lucretius denounced superstition and tried "to loosen the hold of religion on men's minds." The very idea of light-bringing, *Lumières, Aufklärung, illuminismo*, was borrowed from Lucretius. Renaissance humanists like Lipsius had rescued them and provided the printed critical editions which the philosophes possessed, treasured, and imitated.[46]

The philosophes' love of the Classics united them with their intellectual forebears in the Renaissance. The printing press was the vehicle of a cultural revolution. "Between 1465 and 1470, in the first few years of bookmaking, most of Cicero and all of Horace were made available; Vergil, Ovid, Seneca were printed in dozens of cities and dozens of editions before 1500." "By the middle of the sixteenth century, the educated man who had no Greek, and even the ordinary literate man who had no Latin, found most of Livy and Tacitus, Plato and Aristotle, accessible to him. Machiavelli relied on Latin translations of Polybius, Montaigne on Jacques Amyot's French version of Plutarch's *Lives*; the labors of Amyot, Sir Thomas North who Englished Plutarch, and other translators, opened new windows to the ancients."[47]

The Western Renaissance was synonymous with translations. France led, then Britain and Germany, then Italy and Spain, but the "north and east were still sunk in medieval darkness."[48] One might consider Cicero in translation:

> Cicero's little dialogues *On Friendship (Laelius)* and *On Old Age (Cato Maior)* were widely popular. Laurent Premierfait, who died in 1418, turned them into French. The former was translated into English before 1460 by John Tiptoft, earl of Worcester, whose version was printed by Caxton

---

[46] The indebtedness of Western thought, Christian and secular, individualist and statist, to the ancients, is a story which has been told many times, but one interesting retelling out of the ashes of WWII is Schw. Honorata, "Die antike Philosophie als Grundlage abendländischen Denkens."

[47] Gay, *op. cit.*, pp. 280–81; sixteenth-century France was particularly vigorous in translating the pagans; see Eisenstein, *The Printing Press as an Agent of Change*, pp. 127–28. On editions from this era which eventually ended up in the Soviet Union, see Savel'eva, "Izdatel'stvo Plantena v XVI–XVII vv."

[48] For this paragraph, Highet, *The Classical Tradition*, pp. 113–126, and the quote below, pp. 119–20; this is perhaps the wisest survey of translations of all genres in all European languages. The more recent discussions of the impact of antiquity on the modern are best sampled in the three volumes edited by Bolgar, *Classical Influences on European Culture*.

in 1481 along with a translation of *On Old Age* made from Premierfait's French version (probably by Botoner). They were both included in a collection of translations called *The German Cicero*, by Johann, Freiherr zu Schwarzenberg (1534), which also contained the *Tusculan Discussions*; Jean Colin turned them into French again in 1537–9; John Harrington (father of the poet) translated *On Friendship* from the French version in 1550; R. Whittington *On Old Age* about 1535; and Thomas Newton did both in 1577. Cicero's big treatise *On Duties* had been anonymously translated into German as early as 1488, and again in 1531 by Schwarzenberg. Whittington made a poor English version of it in 1540, and Nicolas Grimald a good one in 1553. The *Tusculan Discussions* were put into French by Étienne Dolet (1–3, 1542) and into English by John Dolman in 1561. Schaidenreisser turned the *Paradoxes* into German in 1538, Whittington into English in 1540, and Thomas Newton again in 1569, together with one of Cicero's finest works, the fragmentary *Dream of Scipio*.

Without this effort Lincoln's Gettysburg Address would have sounded different.[49] The Renaissance merger of Horace' *Art of Poetry* and Aristotle's *Poetics*—no less than six such efforts were made between 1531 and 1555—defined literary and poetic practice in Latin and the vernaculars in the West until the age of Romanticism.

Not in Muscovy.[50] Muscovy missed the print revolution, the wave of translations, and the Classical revival, not only in the fifteenth century, but also in the sixteenth, and the seventeenth century.

Given Peter's infatuation with other things Western, to what extent in Petrine and post-Petrine Russia were the Classics published in the original Greek or Latin, or in Russian translation? Later Falconet's statue of Peter would recall Marcus Aurelius on the Capitoline hill, and an anonymous speech would call St. Petersburg "the Northern Rome."[51] Did Peter welcome the pagan Romans into Russia?

We know that the repertoire of Petrine printed books emphasized regulations and official pronouncements, an undiminished flow of devotional and liturgical books, the Petrine newspaper *Vedomosti*, and technical books.[52] Among school books one found "Pufendorf's *Introduction to European History*, which was used in courses in the Naval Academy, [and] Quintius [sic] Curtius' *Life of Alexander the Great*, [which] taught students about the traditions of the European world in which

---

[49] Highet, *op. cit.*, p. 112.
[50] See Brink, "Horatian Poetry," p. 9.
[51] Baehr, *The Paradise Myth*, pp. 50–51. The story of Falconet is lovingly told in Wes, *Classics in Russia*, pp. 52–59.
[52] Marker, *Publishing, Printing, and the Origins of Intellectual Life*, pp. 24–31.

they were now expected to function and [which] presented heroic examples which they were expected to emulate."[53]

The most enduring "network" of schools established by Peter the Great were classical Latin academies, with curricula drawn in imitation of Western colleges, based not on mastery of Orthodox dogmatics, but on a "Jesuit" hard grounding in religion and the Classics of the ancient world.[54] Founded by Ukrainian humanists, they were ordered spread to the Russian dioceses by the Ecclesiastical Regulation of 1721. They were by law *vse-soslovnyi*, open to all the free orders of society, nobles, clerical sons, and urban dwellers. There was virtually no difference between their Latin curriculum and that of the supposedly "secular" gymnasium of the Academy of Sciences, founded by German Protestant teachers after 1724.[55] Ukrainian humanists also came to dominate the Church's hierarchy.[56] To what extent did the Latin educational values of these Ukrainians and Germans influence "Peter's command-based approach to publishing?"[57]

One asks Peter Gay's question *à la russe*: was there a common grounding in the Classics shared by the Western and the Russian *Frühaufklärer*? Russia, of course, could never reproduce or relive the culture of Western Europe. To what extent were ancient authors were available in Russia? Were they owned or read? To the extent that the Classicist preconditions for modern thought in Russia were absent, her "Enlightenment" would be formed in other intellectual conditions, written in other dialects, and would address concerns other than those of the West's several Enlightenments.

The printing presses of the new Russia, foreign,[58] Cyrillic/Slavonic, and Petrine Civil-Script, contributed little toward opening the Russian mind to the ancients. Peter could distinguish between the education of the Latin colleges and technical training,[59] but his mental outlook scarcely extended to the world of pagan antiquity: Three times he

---

[53] *Ibid.*, pp. 29–30. In Marker's index there is but one reference to Cicero and none to Lucian, Lucretius, Seneca, or Tacitus.

[54] Okenfuss, "The Jesuit Origins, pp. 106–130. For the acceptance of this idea see Nichols, "Orthodoxy and Russia's Enlightenment," pp. 66–67; and Bryner, *Der geistliche Stand*, pp. 14–15.

[55] Okenfuss, "Jesuit," p. 126, and Chapter III below.

[56] Kharlampovich, *Malorossiiskoe vliianie*, is the classic listing.

[57] Marker, *op. cit.*, p. 29.

[58] Peter's attempt to found his presses abroad has received scant attention. See Bykova, "Knigoizdatel'skaia deiatel'nost' Il'ia Kopievskogo," pp. 318–41; see also Pekarskii, *Nauka i literatura*, pp. 10–25.

[59] See my "Russian Student in Europe," pp. 130–145.

would name, in goodly Christian fashion, successive pairs of his short-lived sons, Peter and Paul; only after a century of Western education, and with the meddling of Catherine II, would Russian Grand Dukes be Classically named Alexander and Constantine.[60]

During Peter's reign the only traces of antiquity to see print were works which fit the reading habits of Muscovite court culture. These included Aesop's *Fables* (Amsterdam, 1700, St. Petersburg 1712, 1713, 1717), which echoed the "collections" of the seventeenth century, and Quintus Curtius' demonic retelling of *Alexander the Great* (1709, 1711, 1717, 1723, 1724), which also mirrored the *skazaniia* and *povesti* of court culture.[61] At the same time that Peter was transporting Kievan humanists and their students to Moscow to populate the new Slavo-Greco-Latin Academy, and approving similar schools throughout the Russian empire, he was, by denying them access to the printing press, rooting those tender institutions in sterile sand.[62]

One "Classical" publication was the tri-lingual Slavic-Greek-Latin primer issued by Fedor Polikarpovich Polikarpov-Orlov in Moscow in 1701, addressed to those who would save their souls.[63] It was not a welcoming gift to the arriving Kievan humanists but a belated echo of the chastised Lichuds' Grecophile experiment of the 1680s—Polikarpov had been one of their pupils. It was an illustrated religious primer wholly within the oldest Orthodox traditions, containing reading texts by Gregory of Nazianzus, Basil the Great, John Chrysostom, and the *Stoslov*-catechism of Gennadius of Constantinople (d. 471), which had been in the Slavic religious convoy as far back as the eleventh-century *Izbornik* of Sviatoslav. It devoted so much more emphasis to mastering Greek than Latin that Polikarpov has been called a linguistic Grecophile.[64]

Polikarpov assured his young readers that their precious faith was

---

[60] On Catherine's Greek Project and the "new Constantine," see Baehr, *op. cit.*, pp. 48–49.

[61] See for example Fennell and Stokes, *Early Russian Literature*, pp. 208–263.

[62] One rare Soviet perception of the problem in these terms is Panchenko, "Nachalo petrovskoi reformy," pp. 112–28, a superb piece of *perestroika* historiography, which discusses Peter's cultural reforms as a continuation of the Grecophile-Latinizer debates of the 1680s.

[63] [Polikarpov], *Bukvar' slavenskimi, grecheskimi, rimskimi pismeni ouchitsia khotiashchym i liubomudrie v polzu dushe spasitelnuiu obresti tshchashchymsia*, M. 1701; copies in Helsinki, Uppsala, and Leningrad. In 1725 a Latin dictionary was published by Ioann Maksimovich, Metropolitan of Tobol'sk; he was a Kievan, and his language shows Ukrainianisms; see Pekarskii, *Nauka i literatura*, I, pp. 191–97.

[64] Zhivov, *Kul'turnye konflikty*, p. 181.

not imperiled by reading Greek and Latin, that the Greek Fathers in
ancient times had known them and "dialectical wisdom" as well. With
Faith, *cum vere*, it was possible to study the liberal arts (*nauki svobodnye*)
and read books in several languages. Morality consisted of following
the teachings of the Greek Orthodox Church and the laws given to
Moses on two tablets; 'the laws' did not extend to those of Solon or
Lycurgus, nor to those from Cicero or Socrates. In terms of literature, the reader was assured that the texts here were reverently
Orthodox, and not those of Ovid or of Virgil, or even of Aesop.[65]
The ironic message of the first published invitation to Classical letters in Russian history was a stinging warning that they be used to
advance the inherited Greco-Russian Faith, not to introduce the cursed
pagan authors.

At the moment of the founding of the first permanent institution
of Latin humanism in Moscow, Russia's first Latin book condemned
its learning. With such limitations, the 1703 report in *Europäische Fama*
that Latin was making progress *als eine allgemeine Sprache* on the basis
of the opening of the Slavo-Greco-Latin Academy, would seem premature.[66] More accurate was the report of Christian Stieff, who recorded the arrival of Kievan scholars who had studied in Rome and
Padua, and the publication of Polikarpov's *Leksikon*, but who concluded cautiously, "*Die cultivirung einer gantzen nation ist nicht ein Werck
von einem jahre. . . .*"[67]

Between 1701 and the beginning of Catherine II's reign, under
the rotating rectorship, the Latin Academy in Moscow had twenty-
one rectors teaching the upper forms. Eighteen of them were schooled
in Kiev, and of twenty-five prefects teaching the humanities, twenty-
three came from Kiev.[68] It was a Ukrainian school. To what extent
were their efforts supported by the Russian press after the death of
Peter when the diocesan Latin schools were built? Peter Gay counted
five essential pagan authors, Cicero, Lucian, Lucretius, Seneca, and
Tacitus. None were published in Latin before Catherine's reign (1762–
1796).[69] Nor were they translated into Russian between the begin-

[65] Polikarpov, *op. cit.*, Introduction, pp. 4 recto–6 verso. See on this text Iakimovich,
Deiateli russkoi kul'tury, p. 25, who cites the rejection of the pagans for the style of the
Greek theologians.
[66] Cited in Grabosch, *Studien zur deutschen Russlandkunde*, p. 33.
[67] Stieff, "Relation von dem gegenwärtigen Zustande," pp. 96–98.
[68] Nichik, "Sobranie kursov ritoriki," p. 80; see also generally. Khizhniak, *Kievo-
Mogilianskaia Akademiia*, pp. 211ff.
[69] *Svodnyi katalog knig na inostrannykh iazykakh*, 3 vols. to date.

nings of Russian Westernization and 1760. These are stunning facts.

Only in 1761 was a translation of Cicero's *De officiis* published in 2400 copies by the Academy of Sciences. With *On Duties*, addressed to Cicero's son "who was then a student at the university of Athens and about to embark on life," Russia finally acquired the "prime textbook [read] by generations of university students in England, and France and Germany who were similarly about to embark upon life," and "a sincere and valuable contribution to the ethical literature of the race."[70] It appeared very late in Russia. In the West it had long been otherwise. Cicero's letters had been rendered for schoolboys as early as 1543, and a Latin/English edition of *De officiis*, "done chiefly for the good of Schooles," was available in 1631.

With the exception of Aesop's *Fables*, the Classics made no impact in Russia on publishing for schools or children.[71] It is sometimes still said that Peter built colleges before there were elementary schools. Compared to such propositions it is more remarkable still that Russia should have decreed a Latin college in each diocese, with no superstructure in publishing. The Kievans may have been, in Donald Treadgold's apt phrase, a Trojan Horse,[72] but without access to the press, the concealed soldiers were armed with blunted toothpicks. To own the Classics one had to buy foreign.

Beyond Gay's critical short list of Enlightened Romans, was anything Classical published in Russia after Peter's death? Aesop appeared in an edition of 1200 copies in 1747, reprinted in 1760. So did Quintus Curtius' *Alexander of Macedonia*, in a new translation by Krasheninnikov in 1750, with four additional editions to 1800. Cicero's friend Cornelius Nepos wrote *De viris illustribus* originally in sixteen books in eight pairs of Roman and non-Roman persona. His heroic *Lives of Generals* was translated by the Academy of Sciences in 1748, and there was a Latin version of other *vitae* for students of the gymnasium of Moscow University in 1762. Among other historians the *Breviarum ab urbe condita* of Eutropius (d. ca. 370), a eulogy to the

---

[70] Hadas, *Roman Literature*, p. 135.

[71] Babushkina, *Istoriia russkoi detskoi literatury*, noted that an edition of Aesop for youth did not appear until 1747. On the general poverty of children's literature in Russia see also Setin, *Russkaia detskaia literatura*, and Ternovskii, *Detskaia literatura*, as well as the exaggerated Gregor, "Aufklärerische Tendenzen in russischen Schriften . . . für junge Leute," pp. 64–71.

[72] Treadgold, *The West in Russia. I.*, p. 62; "Kiev was a Trojan horse which the Roman Catholic Poles had left for the Orthodox Muscovites to drag inside their gates."

Emperor Valens (364–378), was put into Russian in 1759.[73]

Special mention must be made of the cult of Marcus Aurelius.[74] His biography and *Meditations* appeared in 1727, 1740, and 1760, with three more editions to the end of the century; by any standard they were "popular."[75] "Popularity" did not mean the triumph of pagan values in Russia, since no ancient philosophical school was more "Christian" in the Muscovite sense than the Stoicism of Aurelius: many parts of his *Meditations* were virtually interchangeable with the text of *Domostroi*. Although Muscovite Christianity lacked the Roman sense of eternal mutation, it could appreciate the fatalistic first clause of passages like this:[76]

> Soon the earth will cover us all; then the earth, too, will change, and the things which result from change will continue to change forever, and these again forever.

Stoicism shared with Muscovy's *Domostroi* a contempt for the things of this world:

> You see how few the things are which a man needs to lay hold of in order to live a life which flows in quiet, and is like the life of the Gods.

Both disparaged the opinions of this world:

> The lover of fame relies on other men's activities for his own good; the lover of pleasure on his sensations; but the man of understanding, knows that his own acts are his good.

Both preached denial, since acquisitiveness could lead to perdition:

> Adorn yourself with simplicity and modesty and with indifference towards the things which are neither good nor bad. Love mankind. Follow God. Receive wealth or prosperity without arrogance; and be ready to let it go cheerfully.

---

[73] The edition of Aesop was the *Ezopy basni s nravoucheniem i premechaniiami*, St. Petersburg, 1747, published by the Academy of Sciences at the same time that a useful dictionary finally appeared, that of Christoph Cellarius, a Latin-German edition which now acquired a Russian text too. Tsellarii, *Kratkoi latinskoi leksikon s Rossiiskim i Nemetskim perevodom dlia upotrebleniia Sanktpeterburgskoi gimnazii*, St. Petersburg, 1746. The full range of history, eight titles, translated under Peter is surveyed in Savel'eva, "Perevodnye istoricheskie trudy v Rossii," pp. 118–30.

[74] Marker, *Publishing*, pp. 201–02, 208.

[75] He and Caesar had a major impact on biography in the West, but no such link has been found for Russia. See Elizavetina, "Stanovlenie zhanrov avtobiografii," pp. 235–263.

[76] For the following quotations, Marcus Aurelius, *Meditations*, ix:28, v:5, vi:51, vii:31, viii:33, and x:32.

Without insisting that primitive Christianity had Stoic roots—it did—or that eighteenth-century Russians were consciously aware of the similarity between Stoicism and Christianity, both could appreciate the same sentiments, "Let it not be in any man's power to say truly of you that you are not simple and good!" Often in early-modern Russia in form and in substance that which was successfully imported was that which conformed to traditional values, as Old-Muscovite culture continued to impose its dominion over reading habits.

Another introduction to Stoicism, a collection of Epictetus, *The Stoic Philosophy*, appeared in 1759 and was reissued in 1767. This was the famous collection of the "Discourses" of Epictetus, usually regarded as his crudely preserved, unoriginal, and unsystematic lecture notes, as remembered by his devoted pupil Arrian. Through the ages they had helped form the moral code of rulers' respectable subjects attuned to the orderly laws of the universe. They were grounded in such concepts as decency, athletic prowess, and personal cleanliness, modesty and a personal sense of dignity, proportion, and a harmony of man and nature. They praised useful labor and the personal independence it brought, pleasant social intercourse without gossip or slander, without contempt for others, but with self-discipline and self-control. Adaptation to the status-quo characterized the work, accounting for its vast market in Europe, and perhaps in Russia as well.[77] Finally, Aristotle was slightly served. The second book of the *Politics* appeared in an edition of just 100 copies in 1757. As part of the small movement known as Russian literary classicism, Kantemir's translation of Horace' *On Poetry* appeared in 1744, although it was "a lonely austere effort" underscoring the divide between him and Russian society.[78]

This tiny list represents the total of the Classics published in Russia before the age of Catherine. If a graduate of a Kievan school were inclined to read some Latin literature, or ethics, or history, he had

---

[77] Unfortunately detailed sales figures are unavailable for the period when the book was marketed, as they are for the years 1749–52: see Luppov, "Die Nachfrage nach Büchern," pp. 257–299.

[78] See Redston, "Kantemir's Translation of Horace," pp. 7–10. One might also add the appearance in 1745 (and in 1773, 1787, 1791, and 1792) of a translation of the *Disticha de moribus*, an anonymous work of the fifteenth century, which acquired the signature of one Dionysius Cato, the Pseudo-Cato. Likewise the Russians issued a Russian version of a famous set of illustrations to Ovid's Metamorphoses: Johann Ulrich Krauss, *Die Verwandlunger des Ovidii*, Augsburg, ca. 1690, published in St. Petersburg, 1722.

to have access to imported books or turn to the manuscript notebooks from his own schooling, for there alone the pagan Classics
were to be found.[79] A century after the arrival of the Ukrainians the
printing presses of Russia had scarcely acknowledged their existence.

   This enormous silence is the context in which to understand why
in the Petrine age "Classical Antiquity played virtually no role in the
development of Russian culture," and why thereafter there were a
few works with classical motifs, but no "solidly based Russian 'classical'
culture."[80] It also helps to explain the minuscule size of the "Euro-
peanized" literary movement. At the end of the century the English-
man William Coxe and the German Heinrich Storch could look back
and see Latin-wielding Lomonosov and Sumarokov as isolated and
unique.[81] Long before Europe had her *Querelle des anciens et des modernes*,
as moderns determined to dispense with slavish imitation of ancient
models. But even among the most prideful the Classics were not
jettisoned, and the unearthed world of Greek archeology over time
heightened rather than diminished the sway of the ancient world on
the modern mind. Russia was scarcely aware of the debate, and if
the ancients had a supporter, it was the poet Sumarokov alone.[82]

   Earlier scholars knew this. There was a moment in the historiography of Russian literature when "classicism" meant the period after
1760 when the 'classic' genres of epic, elegy, and ode, established
themselves in Russia, although their first isolated appearances could
be documented earlier, usually among non-Russians. The decades
from 1650–1750 fell largely outside its definition.[83] Previously, before
the Soviet nationalistic war on invidious comparisons, it was axio-
matic that Orthodox Russians resisted or had limited access to the
literature of the Latin ancients, and therefore that writers like
Sumarokov relied more on Gellert or La Fontaine for the fable than

---

   [79] See Nichik, "Sobranie"; recently four of the ethics portions of philosophy courses
at Kiev have been translated from Latin into Russian for modern readers: *Pamiatniki
eticheskoi mysli na Ukraine*.
   [80] Segel, "Classicism and Classical Antiquity," pp. 52–4.
   [81] Grabosch, *Studien*, pp. 138–139.
   [82] Fuhrmann, "Die 'Querelle des Anciens et des Moderns'," pp. 107–29; Butler,
The Tyranny of Greece over Germany, pp. 9–10, and for Russia, Rosenberg, "The Quarrel between Ancients and Moderns in Russia," p. 199.
   [83] See for example Sakulin, *Istoriia novoi russkoi literatury. Epokha kassitsizma*. The
best introduction to the versification debates of mid-century is Silbajoris, *Russian
Versification*, and perhaps the best English study of the classical genres is Drage, *Russian
Literature*.

on the Classics themselves.[84] Well into the century Jesuit texts on poetics were more influential than Horace, and only with Derzhavin in 1811 could one talk about a real appreciation of Horace.[85]

Until everything was muddled by the "discovery" of the "Russian Enlightenment" in the 1960s, it was recognized that the Russian would-be author in the first half of the eighteenth-century had no desire to seek out the genuine Classical roots of the West.[86] P. N. Berkov began his study of one Classical author with the conclusion, *"Mit Horaz' Namen kam die russische Literatur sehr spät."*[87] He recognized that literature in the West was reliant on a Latin schooling absent in the East.

Most scholars agree that speaking "of a Russian classicism in any Western sense is hazardous,"[88] and even Soviet scholars of the 'era of classicism' detected modern rather than direct Classical influence.[89] Trediakovskii, for example, sometimes deemed a familiar of the ancients, seems heavily reliant on a French course in rhetoric, and to have been a Baroque Ukrainian-schooled writer, rather than a real classicist.[90] In these circumstances it is hardly surprising that the

---

[84] See the fine older work by Rammelmeyer, *Studien zur Geschichte der russischen Fabel*; see also Sazonova, "Ot basni barokko k basne klassitsizma," pp. 118–48; Note too the absence of the Classics in works like Kroneberg, *Studien zur Geschichte der russischen klassizistschen Elegie.*

[85] Busch, *Horaz in Russland*, pp. 70–86.

[86] Winter, "Euler und die Begegnung," pp. 1–18. Soviet and East German contributions to this period are surveyed in Lehmann, "Russische Literatur der Übergangsperiode 1650–1730," pp. 25–33. On the discovery of the concept, see the Introduction above, and the discussion at the end of Chapter V below.

[87] Berkov, "Frühe russische Horaz-Übersetzer," p. 89; for the next statement, Berkov, "Problemy izucheniia russkogo klassitsizma," pp. 12–15.

[88] Segel, *op. cit.*, p. 53. See also Smith, "The Reform of Russian Versification," and the survey of literature in Burgess, "The Age of Classicism," pp. 111–32. A more recent survey of the literature, and a call to abandon the term classicism, is in Jones' review of Kurilov et al., eds., *Russkii i zapadnoevropeiskii klassitsizm*, in *Study Group on Eighteenth-Century Russia Newsletter*, No. 12 (1984), 54–59.

[89] See Peskov, *Bualo v russkoi literature*, and the splendid work of Serman, *Russkii klassitsizm*. See also Berkov, "Pervye gody literaturnoi deiatel'nosti Antiokha Kantemira," pp. 5–29, and Stennik, *Russkaia satira XVIII veka.* On the satires as Kievan school exercise, see Shkliar, "Formirovanie mirovozzreniia Antiokha Kantemira." Tschizewskij, "Das Barock in der russischen Literatur," showed that the satires added Boileau long after they had been written, had little classical content, and fit best in the context of the Ukrainian Baroque humanists.

[90] See Kibal'nik, "Ob odnom frantsuzskom istochnike." In the end even Berkov conceded he was no classicist; see Tschizewskij, "Das Barock," pp. 22–26. Note, however, the sympathetic treatment by Rayfman, *Vasilii Trediakovskii*, including her interesting discussion of classicism, false-classicism, pseudo-classicism, school-classicism, and the like, pp. 64–69.

sole literary study of the impact of antiquity on Russian poetry should
deal with the eighteenth century in a few thin pages, cite no specialized
bibliography, and that it should move swiftly to Zhukovskii and the
nineteenth century.[91] The root of the problem was in the rarity of
Latin books in Russia, even in translation.

If there was one explanation for the failure of the Ukrainians to
gain access to the printing press, it was Peter's own commitment to
Orthodox education. Tempted by Bishop Burnet's offers of a recon-
ciliation of Faiths in 1698, by Leibniz in 1711, and by the Doctors
of the Sorbonne some years later, the tsar-revolutionary never granted
more than a "polite but vague and uncompromising reply." "There
is absolutely no evidence that Peter ever intended to forsake the faith
of his fathers. . . . So far as Peter was concerned he remained, as he
himself declared in a letter of September 1721 to the Eastern patriarchs, 'a devoted son of our Most Beloved Mother the Orthodox
Church.'"[92] Peter could appreciate the Latin education of the Ukrainian humanists, encourage it as a skill, as one form of secondary
education. He could dispatch young Russians of his own family abroad
to pursue it, but he had no intention of allowing it to become a
competing religion or system of values for the Russian population.
Peter, in a word, never allowed the printing press to challenge, distort, or destroy the Orthodox *Ladder of Literacy*.

Teofan Prokopovych became the Tsar's ecclesiastical advisor, and
numerous Ukrainian and Belorussians were invited to head Russian
dioceses. But judged by the output of Russian presses in the first half
of the eighteenth century, they failed to gain control over the Church's
publishing enterprise, which remained in the hands of more conservative clergy. At the moment when the mind of the Enlightenments
was being shaped by a neo-paganism, available in scores of Latin
and modern-language editions, Russia said no. Whatever the nature
of the Petrine "revolution" in ecclesiastical affairs, it did not extend
to publishing materials that challenged traditional Muscovite Orthodox education of everyman.

---

[91] Savel'eva, *Antichnost' v russkoi poezii*. One has to be careful of negative evidence,
but one has to be struck by the silence of the ancient authors in such fine studies
as Robinson, *Bor'ba idei v russkoi literature XVII veka*, and in Moiseeva, *Drevnerusskaia
literatura*, which mentions ancient historians only in the context of being owned by
Teofan; see p. 30.
[92] Cracraft, *The Church Reform*, pp. 27–49. See also Stupperich, "Die kirchlichen
Beziehungen, pp. 113–130.

The Russians' rejection of Latin books was not inherent in Eastern Orthodoxy's attitude toward the Latin language itself. Religious and lay elites in Muscovy's co-religionist Ukraine, Belorussia, and Lithuania, had long adopted humanism and its books, and raised their sons in Latin schools. The rejection was not grounded in language, but in Peter's limited political intentions, his Orthodox sensitivity to the religious faith of his people, and in the resilience of the older Muscovite clergy.

B. *Modern Thought Without the Classics: Pososhkov*

The Ukrainians failed to gain access to the printing press. This limited the impact of humanism on Russian society. Ivan Pososhkov wrote *Of Poverty and Wealth* late in the Petrine era. It shows the survival of Avvakum's educational values, not the impact of Latin learning. Born in 1652 a crown peasant, an Old Believer associated with the *starets* Avraamii who criticized the young tsar Peter, the autodidact Ivan Tikhonovich Pososhkov wrote at least three memoranda for Peter, was an agriculturalist and a "miscellaneous writer, projector, entrepreneur, [and] self-made capitalist." But he was also "an amateur theologian who liked to move in ecclesiastical circles."[93]

Pososhkov's began his work, usually classified as economics, stating, "I shall treat first of ecclesiastical matters" (p. 155). Although he treated "the Tsar's revenues," Pososhkov announced that taxation was really secondary:

> More than for material riches we must all take thought also for our immaterial riches, that is for righteousness. The Father of Righteousness is God and righteousness greatly multiplies wealth and glory and delivers us from death; whereas the Devil is the father of unrighteousness, and unrighteousness not merely cannot enrich us but even whittles away the wealth that we have, reduces us to penury and brings us to death. The Lord God himself said: 'Seek ye first the Kingdom of God and his righteousness,' and added, saying, 'they all these things shall be added unto you'—that is to say, wealth and glory. (p. 154)

---

[93] Ivan Pososhkov, *The Book of Poverty and Wealth*, Vlasto and Lewitter, eds., pp. 6–10, 135–37; page references in the text here are to this edition. The Soviet biography is Kafengauz, *I. T. Pososhkov*, but note the fuller bibliography in the English edition, pp. 401–30. For an unsuccessful attempt to fit Pososhkov into the "Learned Guard" created by Peter the Great, see [L. A. Petrov], *Obshchestvenno-politicheskaia i filosofskaia mysl' Rossii*, pp. 8–9, 218–260; it is missing from Lewitter's superb bibliography.

An inability to separate moral conduct and economics led Pososhkov to begin his memorandum with the regeneration of the clergy. If it continued to be ruled by ignorance, drunkenness, and misconduct (p. 166), "men will fall away from the ancient unity of our faith into divers sects and all kinds of heretical beliefs," and if they were so dammed, improved state revenues would not matter.

In language echoing *Domostroi*'s suggestion that the village priest was the teacher of heads of households in a school without walls,[94] Pososhkov predicted that

> if the life of the clergy, is [reformed] enlightenment will shine forth among the whole people, for all will as it were awake from under such perfect and loving care of their spiritual guides, seeing that all will fully understand how to know God, how to pray to Him, how to worship God's saints and call on them for help, and how to live a truly Christian life. (p. 173).

At the end of the Petrine era, Pososhkov's worldview naturally recognized no separation of Church and State:

> When a man is appointed by His Imperial Majesty to the magistrature he should request a priest to keep an all-night vigil and to sing a liturgy, and a service of intercession to God our Heavenly Father on his behalf. . . . It would be no bad thing if every day, on rising, he were devoutly to recite the newly-composed hymn to God our Heavenly Father, praying that the business of his court may be regulated according to the will of God. . . . (pp. 205–06).

To Pososhkov religious and civil values were inseparable, and contradictions were evidence that human law was misguided. In this sense Boris Krasnobaev was correct when he said that Pososhkov "decisively opposed the new secular culture."[95]

That Pososhkov should be capable elsewhere in his book of sustained discourse on economic matters, relatively free of religious intrusions, is no more surprising than the fact that Muscovy had serviceable mathematical skills of measurement and calculation long before it had textbooks or translations of mathematical science from the West. Traditional Christian thought, however, provided virtually his only metaphor: The minting of coins must be done with consummate wisdom so that the quality of the coinage may at all times be impeccable. . . . Just as the Christian faith has been preserved in Russia

---

[94] Compare the nearly identical language in Okenfuss, "Kliuchevskii on Childhood."

[95] Krasnobaev, *Ocherki istorii russkoi kul'tury XVIII veka*, p. 14.

in its purest state, without any taint of heresy, so our coinage should also be the purest in the world. . . . (p. 375).

Avvakum could not have said it differently. Pososhkov chose consistently traditional religious metaphors: In discussing correctives to the notorious dishonesty of the Muscovite merchant classes, Pososhkov stated the economic reasons for commercial honesty, but he knew that if merchants did not cheat, "God's grace would shine forth on the merchant estate and His blessing would be upon them and their trade be hollowed" (p. 256).

Pososhkov had a clear rational mind. He noted the economic and ecological stupidity of cutting saplings for firewood, of taking undersized fish, and of harvesting unripe nuts. But he concluded that the righteous husbander of the land and its bounty enjoys "blessings in this world for the righteous judgement no less than in the world to come, forever and ever, Amen" (p. 321).

Pososhkov advocated schooling for the clergy for the purpose of "acquiring Grammar" (p. 168), because those who did so "more diligently care for their flocks so that the wolves of Hell shall not scatter them in terror." He would restore that available to Muscovite clergy and laymen a half-century and more earlier: the Bible, the *Margarit* (Pearls) of John Chrysostom and other patristics, the *Evangelicum* and *Apostol*, saints' lives and the Menologies, together with the Ukrainians' seventeenth-century attacks on Protestantism. In good *Domostroi* fashion, Pososhkov allowed a slightly broader reading list for the exceptionally able, for those pupils who were "seen to have a good memory" (p. 170), and it might even include the chronicles, for history was not a bad thing. But this was no blueprint for the Petrine revolution. He had little awareness that the age of the specialized and the technically-trained soldier was dawning, and that the soldier of the day would need to know something more than keeping one's weapon clean and being attentive in drill (p. 186).

At the end of the Petrine decades a Western Latin education had been mandated for every diocese, but Pososhkov did not mention it. The Ecclesiastical Regulation called for a rational examination of miracle-working relics, but this theologically minded savant discussed only the old ways. A full generation earlier schools of mathematics had been ordered created at every cathedral, and hundreds of youth had been dragooned onto school benches, but arithmetical training went undiscussed. Almost every Petrine administrator's library by 1720 owned Pufendorf's *On Duties* or the works of other natural-law theorists,

and indeed some were already in translation, but Pososhkov looked
back to the *zemskii sobor* and *Ulozhenie*. For over two decades Peter
had been sending many young Russians abroad to learn naval skills
and a few for Latin education as well, but Pososhkov was still preoccupied with Tsar Aleksei's icon-painter Ushakov and the Ukrai-
nian-led attack on the icon tradition a half-century earlier. Pososhkov
at the end of the Petrine age advocated the reversal of the Petrine
system by advocating a return to the religious education and values
of Muscovy before the Ukrainians' *raskol*.

Ivan Pososhkov, entrepreneur and governmental advisor, was un-
touched by the imported Western books of the age. He is evidence
of the failure of humanism to penetrate traditional Muscovite society. Modern revolutions are born of the printing press, and it posed
no threat at the end of the Petrine age.

3. *Eighteenth-Century Russian Humanistic Book Culture*

Soviet positivist historiography proposed a predictable model for the
development of Russian book ownership and readership, based on
and parallel to the patterns of Western Europe. The late B. I.
Krasnobaev, for example, proposed an evolution of Russian readership
in four stages. Seventeenth-century Russia, he said, had seen the *chitatel'*
blagochestivyi (the pious reader) in such figures as Semeon Polockij,
and Karion Istomin. The early eighteenth century witnessed the *chitatel'*
razumnyi, mudroliubivyi, trudoliubivyi (the reasonable, wisdom-loving, and
industrious reader), in Polikarpov, Magnitskii, and Prokopovych. The
third stage was the honorably-inclined reader (*chitatel' blagosklonnyi*) of
the mid-eighteenth century, the sort of person who would read Marcus
Aurelius, the works of Trediakovskii, and translated courtly and aristocratic novels. Only in the last quarter of the century, did one encounter the enlightened reading public, the *chitatel' prosveshchennyi*.[96] In
this section we begin to inquire whether the evidence of private libraries in Russia support such a scheme.

Soviet historians of the book began with class analysis. They separated the libraries of secular servitors from those of merchants, and
these from the collections of church hierarchs. If, as an alternative

---

[96] [Krasnobaev & L. A. Chernaia], "Knizhnoe delo," *Ocherki russkoi kul'tury XVIII
veka*, pp. 317–18.

inquiry, one searches for Latin books in private libraries, what can one say about Russian culture and literate society before the age of Catherine?

A. *Humanistic Libraries in Petrine Russia*

The libraries of the European-educated Ukrainian humanists reflected their schooling. Beginning with the death of Patriarch Adrian, Kievans were regularly appointed to the Russian hierarchy. Among the generation older than Teofan Prokopovych, Latin educations already shaped mentalities visible in personal libraries. Metropolitan Dmytro Tuptalo-Rostovs'kyj, for example, was as much courtier as cleric. He was born in the Ukraine 40 versts from Kiev, and studied at its brotherhood school. He had nearly three hundred books, two-thirds of them in Latin or Greek.[97] Fundamentally a collection of theology—he held Augustine, Aquinas, Luther, and Bonaventure in addition to Chrysostom and Gregory of Nazianzus—his library also had a core of Classics. He quoted with ease other ancient authors not found in his library, as for example in 1707 when he quoted Virgil, Ausonius, and Martial.[98]

His contemporary, Stefan Javors'kyj, who would unhappily head the Russian Church until the founding of the Synod, was also a Ukrainian who had studied at Kiev and in Poland.[99] His collection of six hundred books was three-quarters Latin. The ancients, Valerius Maximus, Josephus Flavius, Plutarch, considerable Aristotle, Seneca, Livy, Pliny, Demosthenes and Homer, stood beside the moderns, Justus Lipsius, Pufendorf, Machiavelli, Baronius, and Erasmus, on his shelves. Although based on a solid Classical education, Javors'kyj's library attested to the mind of an Aristotelian and denominational erudite, not the sort of thing Peter had in mind when he originally opted for *latinskoe uchenie* from Kiev. "The inventory of [his] intellectual equipment" revealed him to be "conservative" and "scholastic" rather than literary, reformist, or even political.[100]

---

[97] Luppov, *pervoi*, 248–9; Shliapkin, *Dmitrii Rostovskii*, Prilozhenie V.

[98] Shliapkin, *Rostovskii*, pp. 433–34. An abbreviated version of his own course of rhetoric, the manuscript *Ruka ritoricheskaia Piatiiu chast'mi*, was published in the *Izdanie Obshchestva Liubitelei Drevnei Pis'mennosti*, Vol. XX (1878) in facsimile.

[99] Luppov, *pervoi*, pp. 249–52; The library is in Maslov, "Biblioteka Stefana Iavorskogo."

[100] I follow the nuanced intellectual portrait of Javors'kyj and his books in Lewitter, "Peter the Great, Poland, and the Westernization of Russia," which emphasizes his

Among other Kievan and Ukrainian humanists with careers in the Church and libraries of the Classics, Teofilakt Lopatins'kyj was born in Volynia about 1680. Like Teofan he studied at Kiev, in L'viv and at the College of St. Athanasius in Rome.[101] Already in 1704 he was teaching at the Slavo-Greco-Latin Academy, just created with imported Kievan faculty and students. He would become Archbishop of Tver' and would bring Kievan Latin studies to that diocese. A theologian whose anti-Lutheran views would lead to his incarceration under the rule of the Germans after 1730, Lopatins'kyj had a 1400-volume library which was rich religious thought, especially Catholic. Although he had books in modern languages, although he had materials in Hebrew, Chaldean, Arabic, and Greek needed for Biblical study, the heart of his collection was its Latin holdings. His list of ancient poets, playwrights, orators, historians, and philosophers was complete, with multiple editions of Ovid and Cicero, among others. His moderns were mostly predictable, Bacon, Descartes, Erasmus, Machiavelli, Comenius, and Christian Wolff.[102] Classical antiquity defined Lopatins'kyj's library, education, interests, and passions.

Lavrentij Horka (Gorka) was Cossack-born and Kievan educated. He would succeed Teofan as a teacher in Kiev, and later would be bishop of Astrakhan (1723), of Velikii Ustiug (1727), and of Riazan' (1731).[103] The bulk of his 350 books were in Latin: Caesar, Suetonius, Sallust, and Quintus Curtius, Polidore Virgil, Cornelius Nepos, and Valerius Maximus, Seneca and Cicero, Homer, Horace, Virgil, Ovid, and Terence.[104] Teodosij Janowski (Ianovskii) was the son of a Smolensk *reitar*. Educated at Kiev, he would become Archbishop of Novgorod. His small library, four hundred volumes, included Tacitus, Terence, Ovid, Horace, and Quintus Curtius.[105] Havryjil Buzyns'kyj

---

Jesuit holdings. On Peter's encouragement of Latin studies in Glück's gymnasium, see Rosenfeld, "Justus Samuel Scharschmid," pp. 898ff.

[101] Luppov, *posle*, pp. 266–74; Lavrovskii, "Fiofilakt Lopatinskii i ego biblioteka," pp. 197–210.

[102] Neither Teofan nor Teofilakt appears to have owned Wolff's *Vernüftige Gedanken von dem gesellschaftlichen Leben der Menschen* (5 eds., 1721–1740), his chief work on the theory of the state. Other works by Wolff linked the Kievans to the civil servitors of Peter. See Kunisch, *Absolutismus*, p. 67, and Morozov, "Christian Wolffs Leser," pp. 411–23.

[103] Luppov, *posle*, pp. 274–81.

[104] He had a copy of Dante's *Divine Comedy*, which was virtually unknown in Russia; see Alekseev, "Pervoe znakomstvo s Dante," and more recently, Asoian, *Dante i russkaia literatura*, pp. 6–7.

[105] Luppov, *pervyi*, 252–57; see also Ikonnikov, *Opyt russkoi istoriografii*, Vol. I, Kn.

was educated in Kiev, taught there and in Moscow; in 1722 he was named abbot of the Troitse-Sergiev monastery. Eighty percent of his books were Latin pagan authors.[106] These Ukrainian churchmen were learned aides of government: Janowski translated the Austrian W. H. Hohberg's *Georgica curiosa* to transform the old Muscovite nobility. Buzyns'kyj, Bishop of Riazan', translated the *Einführung in die allgemeine Geschichte* and *Die Pflichten des Menschen und Bürger* of Pufendorf.[107]

Non-Kievan, that is to say, Russian hierarchs had different libraries. That of Bishop Georgii Dashkov of Rostov (1718–30) was traditional, consisting of more manuscripts than printed books, and all in Russian or Slavonic; he was from an old Muscovite courtly family—his uncle was a *stol'nik*—who came to the clergy late in life, with values hostile to the Latin school. The cultural divide between the Teofan and Dashkov came to light in 1729 when Kantemir's satires began to circulate. Dashkov attacked them, while Teofan defended, coining the phrase "Learned Guard (*uchenaia druzhina*)" in the process.[108]

The clergy, like society at large, was divided in its stance toward the Petrine reforms; they were divided on Latin culture as well. Library-holdings confirm that there were three groups of Petrine hierarchs: Great Russians, almost all of whom opposed the reforms, with largely Slavic libraries. They included Ilarion of Suzdal, Job of Novgorod, Isaiah of Nizhnii Novgorod, and Georgii Dashkov, among others. The Ukrainian humanists were divided into two major camps: those *"Malorus"* who had studied at the Kiev Academy and were inclined to Catholicism (Rostovs'kyj, Javors'kyj, Lopatins'kyj, et al.), generally were indifferent or hostile to Peter's innovations; and finally the overwhelmingly Ukrainian group led by Prokopovych and Teodosij Janowski, which had also studied at Kiev, was inclined toward

---

1–2, 1088; abroad in 1716–17, Fedosii bought twenty-four Latin authors. The old source was Moroshkin, "Feodosii Ianovskii."

[106] Luppov, *pervoi*, pp. 259–61. Pitrim, Bishop of Nizhnii Novgorod, was also Ukrainian, the son of a tradesman, Kievan educated, and the owner of a similar library. See Luppov, *poslepetrovskoe*, pp. 285–6; also Bryner, *Der geistliche Stand*, p. 58. The Greek Kondoidi was educated in Italy and became a corrector at the Moscow Printing House in 1716. He was tonsured, took the name Afanasii, and served as Bishop of Vologda and then of Suzdal. He left behind over nine hundred books, seven hundred in Latin, nine in Russian. Luppov, *poslepetrovskoe*, p. 282.

[107] Winter, *Halle*, pp. 139–42.

[108] See Brown, *18th Century Russian Literature*, pp. 32–33, and Plekhanov, *Social Thought*, pp. 73ff., who tried to separate the learning of the Guard from that of the hierarchs, while treating Feofan as both.

Protestantism, and was generally pro-reform.[109] What united the latter two camps and distinguished them from the Muscovites was the pagan book.

Fedor Polikarpov, author of the tri-lingual primer and the first Slavo-Greco-Latin lexicon,[110] would seem to qualify as that rare Muscovite humanist. He had a modest selection of the Classics, the works of Virgil, Ovid, and Homer, a total of only nine Latin and Greek books among 264 works of "religious literature," forty-five percent of his total collection. His library suggested why he rejected the Classics in favor of the Greek Fathers and Patriarchs. His career was that of an ecclesiastical bureaucrat hostile to pagan culture.

Educated foreigners in Russia—the Ukrainian divines counted as such—and those Russians who were educated abroad, regardless of profession, shared the Classics. Doctor Robert Arescine was a Scot, a graduate of the University of Edinburgh who then studied in Paris, and received his medical degree at Utrecht.[111] He came to Russia in Menshikov's employ, headed the *Aptekarskii prikaz*, and travelled as physician to Peter in 1716–17. His sizeable collection of 2,500 volumes was a professional library of medicine and science. It included a very full set of the Classics.

Petr Mikhailovich Eropkin (1689–1740), of an old Russian noble family, was a student Peter sent abroad specifically for his education in 1717, as opposed to the *stol'niki* sent for narrower technical training.[112] He studied for seven years, and became one of the leading architects in eighteenth-century Russia, playing a major role in the rebuilding of St. Petersburg after the fire of 1737. His "professional library" of draughtsmanship and architecture comprised less than ten

---

[109] Moroshkin *op. cit.*, pp. 2–3. Beginning with the other end of the equation, it has been argued that in the Petrine age, Horace was to be found exclusively among the Kievan-educated; see Busch, *Horaz*, p. 18.

[110] Luppov, *pervoi*, pp. 232–236. Based on its Polish roots, his dictionary would seem to represent court culture rather than a commitment to Classical studies; see Speranskii, "Odin iz istochnikov "Triiazichnogo leksikona." See also Iakimovich, *Deiateli russkoi kul'tury*, pp. 21–38.

[111] Luppov, *pervoi*, 238–240; Lebedeva, "Leib-medik Petra I Robert Areskin"; *Istoriia Biblioteki Akademii nauk SSSR*, pp. 24ff.

[112] Okenfuss, "Russian Students in Europe"; for the following, Luppov, *poslepetrovskoe*, 220–227; Luppov, "Biblioteka P. M. Eropkina." Among others who could be discussed here was Feofil Krolik, a Czech in Russian service as a translator who ended his life (d. 1732) as the archimandrite of the Novospass monastery in Moscow. He owned a rich collection of the ancients. See N. V. Kulikauskene, "Knigi perevodchika . . . Feofila Krolika."

percent of his three hundred titles. Visible was his careful selection of the Classics. Cicero can be identified in three items:

77	*Tuskulany tsitseronovy*	=	Tusculan Disputations
99	*Dolzhnosti Marka Tulliia*	=	De officiis
159	*Dialog aratora Tsitseronova*	=	De oratore

One notes Demosthenes' *Philippic*, Aristotle's *Rhetoric*, Livy, Plutarch, Polybius, Sallust, Caesar, Anacreon, Marcus Aurelius, and L. Annaeus Florus' (Julius Florus) *Roman History*. His education was Classical and European. His library was a striking exception to the rule that the Russian nobility rejected Latin learning.

Classical collections in Russia in the eighteenth century appeared almost exclusively among the imported Ukrainian hierarchy, and their non-noble students. Only in the next generation, and Eropkin was one of them, did Classical libraries occasionally appear among noble laymen. They were unique individuals who had been singled out for European educations.

Europeans, Peter himself, and Prokopovych recognized that the Latin schools should be open to all social strata, a principle reversed after Peter's death in the redistribution of educational assignments between Admiralty and Synod. It was one of Teofan's "favorite tenets—that in Russia as in Europe the clergy must not constitute a state within a state," separated from others by their education. But the availability of Latin schooling did not mean acceptance by the Russian nobility.

In the Ukraine, the Kievan Academy always attracted more sons outside the ecclesiastical establishment than clerical offspring, and the Baltic provinces kept alive their Latin schoolings. Everywhere one looks in Russian public life one finds learned Ukrainians and Germans.[113] In Russian society, resistance to Germanic cultural hegemony produced the anti-foreign frenzy of the early 1740s; Ukrainian humanism created the "Russian Levites," a caste with educations alien to those of nobles, most of the middling estates, and the peasantry.

---

[113] The quotation is from Plekhanov, *Social Thought*, p. 72. See Okenfuss, "Jesuit," Bryner, *Der geistliche Stand*, and for Kiev, Khizhniak, *Kievo-Mogilianskaia Akademiia*, and Florovskii, "Latinskie shkoly v Rossii," and for the following, Freeze, *The Russian Levites*, *passim*. On humanistically learned Ukrainians, the classic remains Kharlampovich, *Malorossiiskoe vliianie*.

B. *Teofan Prokopovych and His Books*

The 3,000 volume library of Teofan Prokopovych stands preeminent among the collections of the Ukrainian humanists. "His library, open to all scientists, surpasses the Imperial Library and the Library of the Troitzky Monastery; in its wealth it has no equal in Russia, a country deficient in books."[114] Teofan was in turn student, teacher, and rector at the Academy in Kiev, before studying at L'viv, and at the Athanasian College in Rome. He came to Russia in 1709. He had unique opportunities to amass books.[115] Teofan had a purchasing agent, a Baltic German Pietist named Peter Müller, who obtained books for him. By European standards of the day, however, it was an average to mediocre collection, less specialized than some clerics' libraries, less diverse than others.

Because of the rotating rectorship at Kiev and Moscow Prokopovych was by definition a teacher of Latin grammar, poetics and rhetoric, and of the three parts of philosophy. His library reflected these areas of knowledge. He was a clergyman and theologian.[116] He was also, after being brought to St. Petersburg by Peter (in much the same way his father had recruited Polockij), a state servitor whose task it was to place the Russian church on the legal footing of other divisions of the government.[117] Thus the professional part of his library had several major components.

As a Latin school teacher Teofan was a reader of the Classics. His library contained the works of over seventy-five Latin and Greek authors of antiquity, and his Roman authors included almost every-one of significance, from the early dawn of Plautus' *Comedies* (d. 184

---

[114] The quote is by a Spanish monk, Ribeyra cited in Plekhanov, *Russian Social Thought*, p. 74. The old standards are Chistovich, *Feofan Prokopovich*, and Morozov, *Feofan Prokopovich*, but see now Cracraft, "Feofan Prokopovich," and his *Church Reform*. The standard edition of his library was published by Verkhovskii, "Biblioteka Feofana Prokopovicha"; Some errors were detected by Cizevskij; they are summarized by Tetzner, "Bücher deutscher Autoren," which was not used by Luppov, *poslepetrovskoe*, pp. 253–65.

[115] On the growth of Teofan's collection via confiscated books, see Winter, *Halle als Ausgangspunkt*, pp. 129–30. On Menshikov's ability to manipulate offices to obtain books, see Saverkina, "K istorii biblioteki A. D. Menshikova," pp. 37–8.

[116] Cracraft, "Feofan Prokopovich and the Kiev Academy"; Florovsky, *Ways of Russian Theology*, pp. 116–130, and Treadgold, *Russia 1472–1917*, pp. 93–8.

[117] The general context of the reform is now best read in Peterson, *Peter the Great's Administrative and Judicial Reforms*, and Feofan's contribution in Muller, trans., *The Spiritual Regulation*, or in the contemporary translation edited by Cracraft, *The Works of Thomas Consett*.

B.C.) to the sunset of Claudianus (d. ca. 405), whose public poems, the *Panegyrics*, Teofan held.[118] Teofan was among the first in Moscow to own the works of Catullus, Tibulius, and Propertius, and to cite them from intimate knowledge.[119] Of Peter Gay's essential pagans, only Lucian was held incompletely, and only Lucretius, long abhorred for his atheism, whose vision it was "to liberate men from fear of gods, from fear of death,"[120] was absent from the bishop's collection. Teofan did not seek out rare editions. His was the working library of an educated European. We know whom Teofan studied in Rome: Demosthenes, Cicero, and Quintilian for rhetoric, Virgil for epic poetry, Ovid for the elegy, Horace and Catullus for the ode, Martial for the epigram, and the mature library reflected the education.[121]

Teofan was a theologian. "Russian and Slavonic books," by definition mostly religious, "comprised a very small part of the collection, less than 1 1/2%."[122] He had an excellent collection of Western patristics: Augustine, Ambrose, Eusebius, Tertullian and Leo, and of the East, with John Chrysostom, John Damascene, Gregory of Nazianzus, Basil, and Cyril represented. Teofan possessed Luther's *Works*, a gift-copy of Arndt's *Wahres Christentum*, the foundation of Pietism, as well as numerous other Pietistic tracts,[123] Callenberg, Freylinghausen, Herrnschmid, and Milde.[124] Teofan's theological interests were catholic and central to his library.

As a state servitor, Church administrator, and author of a major piece of Petrine legislation, Prokopovych had a fine collection of Western history and jurisprudence. He shared with his contemporary, fellow non-Russian, and foreign advisor to the Russian crown,

---

[118] Verkhovskii, *op. cit.*, p. 59 and *passim*. See Hadas, *Latin*, 388–92. The Classical authors which Teofan studied in Rome, are discussed in Pekarskii, *Nauka i Literatura*, I, 483.

[119] Kibal'nik, "Katull v russkoi poezii," pp. 45–50. Only in the last years of the century did Catullus have an impact on Russian letters; *Ibid.*, pp. 53–59.

[120] Hadas, *Latin*, p. 69. In Teofan's *de arte poetica . . . Kioviae 1705*, there is a single 7-line quotation from *On the Nature of Things*. See Prokopovich, *Sochineniia*, pp. 38, 438, 499. See also Luznyi, "'Poetika' Feofana Prokopovicha," pp. 47–53.

[121] Pekarskii, *Nauka i literatura*, I. p. 483.

[122] Luppov, *poslepetrovskoe*, pp. 260, 261.

[123] Winter, *Halle*, pp. 114–15, 118, 128, 129–30; see also Cizevskij, *History*, pp. 364–65.

[124] Tetzner, "Bücher." Luppov minimized Teofan's German collection; see Luppov, *poslepetrovskoi*, p. 260. In 1735 the Pietists published Russian versions of Arndt's *True Christianity*, Francke's *Kleinen Katechisis*, and Fleylinghausen's *Schriftliche Einleitung zu rechten Erkenntniss . . . des Lebens . . . Jesu Christi*, and other works. See Bykova, "Über in Halle gedruckte slawische Bücher."

Leibniz, a contempt for the Muscovite past.[125] Thus it is not surprising to find Jean Bodin's *Republic*, or lots of Grotius and Pufendorf, or even Machiavelli, although Germans were more numerous and important. One can doubt whether "Kievan-Russian scholasticism" led anybody to the "relevant legal and philosophical literature" of the *polizeistaat*,[126] but Teofan had a basic collection.

What is noteworthy about Teofan's library is not its predictable strengths, but its lacunae in West European letters since the Renaissance. As a teacher of literature, Teofan was a Classicist, an eastern-European and not a West-European. He could not have involved himself in the French battle of Ancients and Moderns, for example, for he held no Molière, no Racine, and no Corneille, to say nothing of no Ronsard, Rabelais, Montaigne, and no Fénelon. It is surprising to find no Bossuet, and no Richelieu. His English horizons were even lower. Although Francis Bacon's *Novum organum* was there, as well as Robert Boyle (and Galileo and Kepler), there was no Thomas More, no Hobbes or Harvey, no Shakespeare, Locke, or Newton, and apparently none of the Cambridge Neo-Platonists or deists. Perhaps most surprising, there was nothing of Bishop Gilbert Burnet, the one other clerical name which comes immediately to mind in the context of Peter the Great.[127]

Teofan emerges from his personal library one of the best educated statesman of Peter's circle, and a worthy successor to Polockij. But there were limits to his vision, however much they were circumscribed by the book trade in Russia. Soviet book historians hailed him as "among the most enlightened people of his age." Nearer to the mark was the more circumspect judgement of Eduard Winter: to the extent that he remained a believing Orthodox Christian who didn't care much for Jesuits, who was interested in Socinianism and in anti-Trinitarianism, with a general bent toward German Protestantism, he can be more or less included in a central-European *Frühaufklärung*, seeking an end to the war between Confessions.[128] Indeed Lopatins'kyj, Bishop of Tver', defined the whole Petrine-Prokopovych

---

[125] See Ger'e, *Sbornik pisem i memorialov*, pp. 95, 176, 180, 207, 360, and *passim*; I surveyed the literature in my review of V. I. Chuchmarev, *G.-V. Leibnits i Russkaia kul'tura*, M. 1968, in *Kritika*, Vol. VI, No. 1 (1969), 10–21.

[126] Cracraft, "Nuts and Bolts," p. 631, comment to Marc Raeff, "Seventeenth-Century Europe in Eighteenth-Century Russia". On his philosophy collection, see Tschizewskij, *Skovoroda*, pp. 23–27.

[127] See Cracraft, *Reform*, pp. 28ff.

[128] Vinter, "Feofan Prokopovich i nachalo," pp. 43–6.

cultural revolution as a offshoot of Halle Pietism, dismissed it as such, and took up Stefan Javors'kyj's battle against them in these terms.[129] Teofan loved the Classics, but one can note with Peter Gay in mind, that he was generations removed from most textbook notions of the secular Enlightenments.

To reflect adequately the Teofan visible in his personal library, an anthology would include not only the political and legislative writings of his courtly life in Petersburg, but also his rhetorical and poetic works, and especially his sermons. He is consistently disfigured by historians when portrayed without his essential ecclesiastical dress.

C. *Teofan Prokopovych as Humanist*

Our antennae extend and we are automatically on guard when we hear Wilhelm Richmann, Wilhelm Steller, Heinrich Johann Ostermann, and Georg Eisen deemed "Russians," as they were regularly in Soviet scholarship.[130] Far more successful was the Soviet-Russian expropriation of the culture of the Slavic peoples who fell victim to their inexorable expansionism: the names of alien Ukrainians and Belorussians[131] sound Russian, and in the historical literature they are accepted as "Russian" by all. Their libraries, however, told of cultural separation. The issue here, as noted in the Introduction, is not citizenship or place of birth, but fundamental cultural orientation, defined by education and book habits.

There was a vast cultural divide between Teofan and most Russians of his day, including his soul-mates of the "Learned Retinue."[132] Earlier Simeon Polockij must have felt culturally isolated among most natives of Moscow, "the new city of his adoption."[133] His verse integrated the Classics, Catholic learning, and Orthodoxy, in ways alien to his

---

[129] Winter, *Halle*, pp. 147ff.

[130] Muhlpfordt, "Die Petersburger Aufklärung und Halle."

[131] I rather like the formulation of the literary historian Drage, *Russian Literature*, p. 249, who discusses Polockij, Medvedev, Istomin, Polikarpov, and Prokopovych under the rubric of "Russo-Ukrainian Scholasticism."

[132] Teofan invented the phrase late in his life when the forces of reaction were on the rise. See Brown, *18th Century Russian Literature*, p. 33. Plekhanov, *History of Russian Social Thought*, is the classic study, but note also the virulently Marxist presentation by Petrov, *Obshchestvenno-politicheskaia i filosofskaia mysl' Rossii*; It attempts to widen the concept of the "learned guard" to include Pososhkov, the Volynskii circle, A. M. Cherkasskii and I. Iu. Trubetskoi, on the basis of their proposals in the crisis of 1730.

[133] Hippisley, *The Poetic Style of Simeon Polotsky*, p. 11.

new countrymen. Teofan's Latin Classical culture distinguished him
from most learned Russians, even if politically he and his Ukrainian
colleagues came to accept Petrine rule, and indeed to become its
most eloquent propagandists.

Libraries, metaphors, language, and cultural preoccupations reveal
their alien minds. Rhetoric was an established genre in Western
Civilization but absent in unschooled Muscovy. Only in Teofan's *Poetics*
and *Rhetoric*, courses read in Kiev in 1705–07, does one find a serious use of Homer, Horace, Virgil, Ovid, Martial, and Seneca.[134] While
Teofan and his Ukrainian colleagues insisted on reading "the Greeks
Homer and Hesiod, the Latins Ovid, Virgil, and others," their learned
Russian *druzhiniki*, Kantemir and Trediakovskii regarded the French
as equals of the ancients, and the first "manifesto" of Russian classicism said so.[135]

Teofan's *De Arte Rhetorica* was an alien book in Russia. It regarded
rhetoric as a practical art based on *decorum*, aptness or appropriate-
ness. Speech (*officium*), style (*genus dicendi*), subject matter (*res*), and
language (*verba*) merged in the act of communication.[136] Such ora-
torical thinking was innovative in Kiev, but wholly new for Russians,
although it had long been a feature of the European education of
preachers and politicians. Teofan's *Rhetoric* represented a short-course
in Cicero. His use of Cicero's *Orator* almost equalled his reliance on
all other Classical authors combined, including the sermons of John
Chrysostom and Gregory of Nazianzus. Teofan embodied a hard
grounding in religion and the Classics.

Teofan wrote history. He was not a very good historian. His one
serious work scarcely rose above the chronicle, so narrow was its
military and diplomatic reporting.[137] When he discussed the art of
writing history, however, he cited Ovid, Cicero, Tacitus, Pliny, and
Plutarch.[138] Recent examinations of his texts reveal that he esteemed

---

[134] Kurilov, ed., *Russkii i zapadno-evropeiskii klassitsizm*, pp. 24–25, and Lakhman,
"Dva etapa ritoriki 'prilichiia' (decorum)."

[135] Kurilov, *op. cit.*, pp. 25–26. See also on Teofan and his colleagues who knew
few of the guides to sermon-crafting in Europe, Kochetkova, "Oratorskaia prosa
Feofana."

[136] Lakhman, *op. cit.*, pp. 163–168.

[137] Prokopovich, *Istoriia imperatora Petra Velikago*, St. Petersburg, 1773.

[138] See the interesting essay, Gudzii, "Feofan Prokopovich," in his *Literatura Kievskoi
Rusi*, pp. 280–305; the essay appeared in 1941, there was a Ukrainian edition in
1959, prior to this reprinting. The collection also contains his "Po povodu revizii . . .,"
pp. 224–79, one of Gudzii's attacks on A. Mazon who had denied the authenticity

empirical science, and rejected Avvakum's evocation of older folkish worlds of sympathetic nature; he used satire and irony; he attributed error to superstition and fanaticism, and he was a skeptic.[139] He and other Ukrainian humanists had values alien to the bulk of the literate Russian population, and the cultural divide began with the Classics. When Kievan "missionaries of the Synodal church" misunderstood and purged an Old-Believer sect, and persecuted them as vigorously as had Muscovites in the seventeenth century, it testified to the lack of a common culture between humanists and traditional Muscovite religiosity.[140]

Ukrainian humanists never gained control over the printing press. In his *Spiritual Regulation* Teofan listed a kernel of modern Orthodox theology, specifying the patristics which elucidated "the main dogmas of our Faith."[141] In addition to the Eastern Fathers, Gregory Nazianzus, Basil the Great, and Cyril of Alexandria, Teofan recommended on Christology "one epistle of Leo, pope of Rome, to Flavian, Patriarch of Constantinople." Teofan's undisputed political role notwithstanding, Pope Leo was never made available to Russian readers. The Ukrainians' concept of a gentle Christ the Good Shepherd, as opposed to the stern Christ-judge of the Cyrillian Orthodox tradition, had no print audience in Russia,[142] whatever its impact on iconography after 1650.

Teofan's sermons were not the place where his Classical education showed. One could speculate that his Russian audience was unprepared to hear pagan authors quoted, and he was politic enough not to try. He cited Livy in a sermon celebrating the peace of Nystadt

---

of the Igor Tale. It merited reprint for it included the famous Senkovskii's 1854 pronouncement: "The unknown compiler of *The Lay of Igor's Host* was a man who, having drunk of Horace, Virgil, and Cicero, thought in Latin, and wrote in the Slavo-Russian rhetorical language of the schools." (p. 275).

[139] See Lotman, "Die Frühaufklärung," and Winter, "Zum geistigen Profil Feofan," pp. 24–28.

[140] See Clay, "The Theological Origins of the Christ-Faith," pp. 21–41, pp. 23, 34, 41 and *passim*.

[141] Here I use the translation of the Regulation by Muller, *The Spiritual Regulation*, p. 34; note also Cracraft's edition, *For God and Peter the Great*, used below, and Cracraft's complaint that the Soviets fail to make Kievan theology available to scholars, "Theology at the Kiev Academy," p. 72.

[142] In another context I have speculated on the significance of Fedotov's distinction between Leonine and Cyrillian Christology in my "On Crime and Punishment." There was a sudden output of the works of St. Augustine, eight titles in eleven volumes after 1786, at the very end of the century; see the *Svodnyi katalog*, I, Items 14–21.

and in one commemorating the accession of the Empress Anna, and in the same sermon he cited the ancient wisdom that aristocracies and democracies were suitable for small populations living in close proximity. He could also hail Peter's wife, the Empress Catherine I, as Semiramis of Babylon, Tamira of the Scythians, Penthesilea of the Amazons, and St. Helena.[143] In a 1718 sermon on tsarist power and honor he cleverly wove a rich tapestry of biblical citation in a depiction of authority which owed little to the Classics or the modern political thought in his library.[144] Teofan reconciled his Faith and his beloved pagans, as had educated Europeans for centuries, but the ancients only whispered in his sermons.

Teofan's Classicist values are easily detected in the Ecclesiastical Regulation and in a memoir he co-authored for the education of Peter II. In Teofan's words, schools at their best taught both "the Doctrines of Faith" and the "Duties of all the Orders of Men" (p. 30).[145] Against *Domostroi's* booklessness Teofan thundered, "Learning is good and fundamental, and as it were the Root, the Seed, and first Principle of all that is good and useful in Church and State" (p. 63). Addressing "*Russian Roskolsticks*," Teofan insisted that the early Greek Church had not opposed learning, since "all our primitive Doctors not only taught the Holy Scripture, but the Philosophy of the Gentiles" (pp. 61–2).

Elementary education meant the mastery of Latin. Although the Ecclesiastical Regulation did not contain a reading-list of pagan authors, Latin was synonymous with its education. First-year study meant acquiring the ability to translate from Latin to Russian and Russian to Latin, and in the case of history texts, care should be taken "in the Choice of your Author, that he be a pure Latin Writer, such as *Justin* the Historian" (p. 72).[146]

Teofan's educational innovations, the model studies described in the law he wrote, were broadly parallel to the contemporary movement in the British dissenting academies to incorporate the modern

---

[143] Prokopovich, *Slova i Rechi*, St. Petersburg, 1760–65, II, 78, 106; III, 198. Note however the rich Classical flavor of six of his commemorative orations, printed with those of his Kievan colleagues in *Panegiricheskaia literatura petrovskogo vremeni*, and in *Pamiatniki obshchestvenno-politicheskoi mysli*.

[144] *Ibid.*, I, 237–268; p. 247 contains the summary statement, "*ni Tsaria ni zakona.*"

[145] All page references here are to the contemporary translation of the Spiritual Regulation, Cracraft, ed., *For God and Peter the Great*.

[146] Marcus Junianus Justinus, 2nd century; see Muller, *Spiritual Regulation*, p. 112.

subjects into the old vertical Latin curriculum.[147] While rote-learning and a vertical progression from grammar through the humanities of rhetoric and poetics to philosophy was preserved, history and geography could be taught as the texts for grammar forms, and arithmetic and geometry, along with logic, could be introduced early in the curriculum (p. 73). Instruction continued at the refectory:

> At Table, either Martial or Ecclesiastical History shall be read: and in the beginning of every Month, for two or three Days, shall also be read the Histories of Men eminent for Learning, of the principal Doctors of the Church, and of ancient and modern Philosophers, astronomers, Rhetoricians, Historians, etc. For the Hearing of such Stories is not only entertaining and delightful, but stimulates and excites Youth to an Imitation of those excellent Patterns. . . .
> This will contribute much to that Firmness and Resolution, namely that becoming Audacity and Assurance which a Preacher of God's Word, or an Ambassador ought to have . . . (p. 83).

The reading of pagan as well as Christian authors would produce able and self-assured human personalities, whether destined for the pulpit or the chancellery. In the diocesan colleges and his own school at the Alexander Nevskii monastery, non-clerics were encouraged to study and they could transfer easily to the Academy of Sciences. Academicians, like Theophil Siegfried Bayer, could teach in both schools.[148] Teofan went so far as to specify that teachers in his own academy could not be Russians, *must* be foreigners, certified competent by known academies and civil authorities abroad.[149]

In 1731 academician Georg Bernhard Bilfinger (1693–1750) published the plan he had prepared for the education of the boy-Emperor, Peter II (1715–30), son of Aleksei Petrovich and his Lutheran wife, Charlotte of Brunswick-Wolfenbüttel. The document was approved by Teofan as head of the Church, who appended his own thoughts on the proper spiritual upbringing of well-born youth.[150] The education of the future monarch was based on the *Ritterakademien*

---

[147] Compare, for example, the movement described by Watson, *The Beginnings of the Teaching of Modern Subjects.*

[148] Demkov, *Istoriia*, II, 79, 81.

[149] Pekarskii, *Nauka i Literatura*, I, pp. 561–64.

[150] [Georg Bernhard Bilfinger], *Raspolozhenie uchenii ego imperatorskago velichestva Petra Vtorago*, [St. Petersburg, 1731]. All page references in the text refer to this edition. Sopikov had dated it to 1728, but the *Svodnyi katalog*, item 575, corrects it to 1731. Feofan's text is on pp. 67–82; Cracraft, "Feofan Prokopovich: A Bibliography," item 121, dates it to 1732; he also indicates it was translated from the German, but that apparently applies only to the first text by Bilfinger.

at Halle. Latin was not ignored. "All learning consists in part in the study of languages, and in part in the study of the arts and sciences" (pp. 4–5). It was useful for a monarch to know and to use "the modern, or the so-called living languages." "Without doubt German and French" were the most useful. "Beyond that, however, Latin has always been respected as the mark of the well-educated and learned sovereign. And for this reason, for example, the glorious German Imperial Austrian family, and all the sovereigns under their dominion, hold a knowledge of this language to be wonderful and glorious." The boy could already speak it, Teofan noted, and thus was equipped "to pursue the sciences themselves effortlessly" (p. 6).

His Majesty was to attend instruction three hours a day, five days a week. His 'sciences' included mathematics, fortifications and civil architecture; his 'social sciences' geography, cosmology, politics, and heraldry and genealogy; his 'humanities' centered on history, modern and especially ancient. "History is a mirror of the world in which the conditions of previous times and distant lands may be seen" (p. 30). History instructs us in morality: this is why ancient history is studied. It shows what makes a state strong, what makes a monarch "useful to his people" (pp. 31–2). Greek history is instructive of the relations between "republics," of Philip and of Alexander the Great, and of the "liberation of the Greeks from the onerous power of the Persian state." Roman history instructs us of the way that republics become monarchies. His Majesty might read Titus Livy and other authors and attend to the deeds of the Caesars, Augustus, Trajan, Antoninus, and Marcus Aurelius, as well as the evil example of Nero. Constantine too is worth study. He might use a table listing the Caesars and Kings, available in a book called the "*Bilder-Saal*" (pp. 33–6). What one witnesses in this document is the eighteenth-century private tutor, restructuring the elements of the old humanists' education to prepare an upbringing worthy of a gentleman.

Teofan's personal contribution to Peter III's education was an essay on religious instruction, *Khristianskii zakon*. He offered a vision of God and his works suitable for a monarch and a grandson of Peter. Teofan demonstrated the existence of God from "things visible, heavenly, earthly, watery, and ethereal"; from this he could deduce the attributes of God, all-powerful, all-knowing, all-good, and righteous, without beginning and without end; from these attributes one could understand man and deduce God's plan for him. This was natural theology, *bogosloviia naritsaemaia estestvennaia, ili natural'naia, i prirodnaia.*

Natural theology confirmed the truth of Holy Writ (pp. 67–71, 75–6).

This line of reasoning was similar to that of other divines of the central European *Frühaufklärung*. In Russia it was daring. It was, in a European sense, the inevitable result of the acceptance of an education which included the mastery of the original Roman enlighteners, who had campaigned against superstition and fanaticism. The appropriately melancholy observation, however, is that it was voiced by a Ukrainian humanist who had lost the patronage of his Emperor, whose party never gained access to the printing press, at the moment they were educating few non-clerical sons, in an educational platform for a sickly boy-tsar who would die at age 15.

Daniel Boorstin invites us to think of the historical process as shingling a roof: each new piece is partially covered by a new layer of reality; its fullness never disappears, although only part of it is thereafter visible.[151] The pagan Classics were a more prominent part of the roof laid down by Peter than the one of his father accepted after 1655: Teofan was given opportunities that Polockij never enjoyed. The Classics were essential to his modest educational reforms, but they never obscured the Orthodox upbringing of Muscovy's *Domostroi*, and they were not long fully visible after Peter's passing, except among Ukrainians, other foreigners, and their few under-nourished disciples.

Teofan was an alien humanist. Orator and sermonizing cleric, bishop, classical educator of an heir to the throne and of numerous candidates for the priesthood and the professions, theologian and *Aufklärer*—his many personae were mirrored in his library, and in his educational writing.

4. *Eighteenth-Century Courtly Book Culture*

A. *Courtly and Noble Libraries in Russia*

New forces were unleashed in European education. John Locke explored a new noble education less dependent on Latin. The Dissenting Academies in Britain reshaped university studies with the "modern subjects," German *Ritterakademien* and French naval academies implemented vernacular curricula aimed at creating officers and gentlemen, and to pick but one example, in France Jean Baptiste de la

---

[151] Boorstin, *The Discoverers*, p. xvi.

Salle began to build a network of schools which would bring French
literacy and numeracy to humble urban strata. Out of these new
educations, traces of which were introduced into Russia simultaneously
with Ukrainian humanism,[152] would come new definitions of nobility
and new studies suitable to the technologies of modern armies and
fleets, to the skills of bureaucracies and of new manufactories. The
small portions of society touched by these new schoolings owned the
first gentlemen's libraries.

These new libraries were associated with foreign travel, foreign
study, or with foreigners in Russian service. The best example was
that of Jacob Bruce (1669–1735), whose father William had served
the tsars.[153] Bruce accompanied Peter on the Grand Embassy, would
be General-Fieldmarshal in charge of all artillery by 1704, and President of the College of Mines and Metallurgy by 1717. He retired in
1726 and occupied himself with science. He was well educated, but
the source of schooling seems undocumented. He was the leading
scientist in Russia of the Petrine age, a rare champion of Newton, a
man with serious interests in astronomy, mathematics, and engineering. He was the translator of Huygens on the new world-view, and
at least co-author of the first Russian manual of etiquette.

Although born in Russia of a father in Russian service, the catalogue of his books, manuscripts, and scientific instruments reveals
broad interests that separate him culturally from other Russian servitors. He collected books in the languages he read, first by a wide
margin German, then English, Latin, and Dutch, with significantly
fewer in Slavic, and only a smattering of French, Italian, Swedish,
Polish, and Finnish. Naval studies, militaria, architecture, physical
and natural science, medicine, and geology, comprised over a quarter of his books. His books on alchemy and astrology were not opposed to science, "*antinauchnyi*," as alleged, since Newton and every
other scientist of the age shared his interest.[154]

Bruce was a Lutheran and a scientist, and his collection contained
Bibles or books of the Bible in Dutch, German, Finnish, Latin, Greek,

---

[152] See my "Technical Training."

[153] The new literature is impressive. Based on *ex-libris*, the authoritative source for
800 of his 1500 books is [Savel'eva, comp.], *Biblioteka Ia. V. Briusa*, but see also
Luppov, *pervoi*, pp. 184–204; Savel'eva, "Biblioteka Ia. V. Briusa v sobranii BAN";
Luppov, "Biblioteka Ia. V. Briusa," and Valentin Boss, *Newton and Russia*, Chaps. 3,
6, and *passim*. Fundamental to all was the "Vedomost', chto po opisi iavilos' v dome . . .
Briusa."

[154] Luppov, "Biblioteka Ia. V. Briusa,", p. 271.

and English, works on Reformed religion from Luther to the Halle Pietists. He also had a collection of the British deists, neo-Platonists, and natural-religionists, including George Cheyne, five titles by John Clarke, Toland's *Christianity Not Mysterious*, William Wollaston's *Religion of Nature*, and Thomas Woolston's *Miracles of Our Savior*. His science was very British and very up-to-date, with Hooke, Boyle, Halley, Newton, and Locke's *On Human Understanding* (in German), as well as Boerhaave, Leibniz, and Christian Wolff. Of the political and historical literature of the age he had the basics, Bayle's *Dictionary*, Pufendorf, Machiavelli, and Fénelon's *Telemachus*.

The *Télémaque* enjoyed a phenomenal success in Europe, and it was widely held in Russia. It was "a composite of Greek and Latin epic, Greek romance, Greek tragedy, and much else,"[155] written for the Duke of Burgundy, second heir to Louis XIV, by his tutor. As Mentor guided Telemachus through an ethical labyrinth, they encountered monarchs who resembled the Sun King and other baroque monarchs. Indeed the book's European popularity stemmed from the perception of it as a satire on Louis: many kings were encountered in hell, but few in the Elysian fields. It was probably the most popular "classical" text in eighteenth-century Russia; its voyage of adventure fit nicely into the tastes inherited from the seventeenth-century Polonized Muscovite court circles, and it was among eighteenth-century Russian courtiers that it was found.

Bruce's lighter reading included Rabelais in English, Boccaccio in Dutch, Molière in French and in German, Swift's *Tale of a Tub*, and an English *Don Quixote*. His was one of the first libraries in Russia to include books of European courtly etiquette, a German book on dancing, Gracian's *Courtier*, and others, as Russia's first book of etiquette was his own work: His *Honorable Mirror for Youth*, attached to the Civil-Script Primer in 1717, pioneered a new definition of literacy in Russia, a new concept of childhood, and a new vision of nobility.[156]

Bruce was too sophisticated to neglect the Classics, too haphazardly educated to pursue them only in Latin. He had about forty titles, including three copies of Lucretius, with versions in Dutch and English. Among the ancient historians he had Livy in English, German,

---

[155] For this paragraph, Highet, *Classical Tradition*, pp. 335–39. I have used my own French/English copy of Fénelon, Paris, An IX (1801).
[156] See Okenfuss, *Discovery of Childhood*, pp. 43ff.

and Dutch, Plutarch in German, Flavius Josephus in English, German, and in Old Dutch, Tacitus in Latin, English and German, Aesop in English and German, Virgil in Latin and Dutch, Homer and Ovid in Dutch, Terence's comedies in Latin. He also had Seneca, Democritus, Lucian, Anacreon, and Horace. He apparently lacked Herodotus and Thucydides, and surprisingly Cicero as well, but this was the library of a savant, of a proto-philosophe who could with ease move from science to theology, from ancient comedy to modern politics.

Herodotus, Thucydides, and Cicero were not missing from the fullest gentleman's library of the age, that of Dmitrii Mikhailovich Golitsyn (1663–1737).[157] Descended from the Grand Princes of Lithuania, like Kurbskii nurtured in non-Muscovite educational values, Golitsyn was early a friend of Peter, and by 1694 a captain in his favorite Preobrazhenskii regiment. At age thirty-four he was sent to Venice for naval studies, but his life centered around Kiev and its Academy, "wide open to Latin, Roman, and Catholic influence" until 1654, and the "intellectual capital of Russia" thereafter. As governor of Kiev after 1707 he had students at the Academy do translations from Aristotle's *Politics*, Grotius' *War and Peace*, Pufendorf's *Natural Law*, Richelieu's *Testament*, and Locke's *Second Treatise*. The bulk of his 2,600-book collection was in French, but he held numerous Slavonic religious books.[158] He also held a sizeable collection of Polish history and law, typical of the Muscovite courtier's library for over half a century.

Most notable for contemporary social and political literature in French, Golitsyn's collection had a carefully selected library of some twenty-five ancient authors on history and politics: Herodotus, Plutarch, and Thucydides, and all the major Roman historians, Caesar, Cornelius Nepos, Tacitus, Polybius, Livy, Sallust, Suetonius, Valerius Maximus, Quintus Curtius, as well as Plato's *Republic*, Aristotle's *Politics*, and Cicero in French and Latin.

Similar was the 1,300-volume library of Andrei Artamonovich

---

[157] Luppov, *pervoi*, 204–23; see also Golitsyn, "Novye dannye o biblioteke kn. D. M. Golitsyna." Poresh, "'Kniaz' D. M. Golitsyn (verkhovnik) i frantsuzskie knigi'"; and even better on his French books, de Madariaga, "Portrait of an Eighteenth-Century Statesman." We know too little about the library of V. V. Golitsyn, who was known as a Latin stylist, and owned the books of Polish-influenced court and *prikaz* culture. See Hughes, *Russia and the West*, pp. 87–88, and her *Sophia*, pp. 167, 170–72, 182.

[158] de Madariaga, "Portrait," pp. 40, 45, and *passim*.

Matveev (1666–1728), son of Tsar Aleksei's diplomat.[159] Educated by Nikolai Spatharios, he knew Latin and Polish at a young age, and spent the years 1699–1715 as ambassador to Holland and to the Empire, before returning to offices in the revamped administration at home. Over eighty percent of his nine hundred books were in foreign languages, half in Latin. His books on history included Caesar, Polybius, Plutarch, Flavius Josephus, L. Annaeus Florus, and his other ancients included Aristotle, Demosthenes, Cicero, Virgil, Horace, and Petronius. With his roots in Westward-looking *prikazy*, he also had such seventeenth-century "popular" works as Barlaam and Josaphat, Polockij's rhymed Psalter, and such moderns as Gracian, Bayle, Hugo Grotius, Erasmus, Comenius, and Locke, in addition to a selection of about 150 French titles on government and society. In Golitsyn and Matveev one saw the Petrine new man at his educated best. Among Russian nobles, they were exceptions. Not Kievan educated, they could at least move in the cultural world of those who were.

Other libraries of "gentlemen" of the Petrine age included that of Aleksandr Menshikov, the unscrupulous *pirozhki*-hawker-generalissimo who faced scandals before Peter II ordered him arrested and his property confiscated in 1727. There are reports of illiteracy, and that he owned 13,000 books.[160] The latest discovery lists about one hundred and seventy titles. It is an awkward list to interpret in that someone read the titles aloud, while a second scribe recorded them, accounting for such odd entries as *odna kniga v osmushku na nemetskom iazyke ius bublikom* (one German book in 8° jus publicum). One can see predictable interests in mathematics, artillery, and architecture, militaria broadly defined, in courtly literature, royal biography and the court of Louis XIV, and in the natural-law school. Of the Classics one can only speculate about 'a Latin book in 8° a description of nature,' or 'a Latin book in 8° dialogues about various things,' although 'a Latin book in 4° *prava iustinianskaia*' seems clearer. One notes Quintus Curtius' *Alexander* in French, Aesop as well, Ovid in German, but the newly-discovered list confirms what we already knew,

---

[159] Luppov, *pervoi*, 223–227; more recently see Polonskaia, "Rekonstruktsiia biblioteki A. A. Matveeva."

[160] Luppov, *pervoi*, p. 230; On Menshikov see "The Rise and Fall of Prince Menshikoff," in Consett, *The Present State and Regulations*, London, 1729, pp. xxiii–lxvii; and Pavlenko, *Aleksandr Danilovich Menshikov*. On his library see Dolgova, "O biblioteke A. D. Menshikova"; Saverkina, "K istorii biblioteki A. D. Menshikova"; and now Somov, "Reestr knig A. D. Menshikova."

that Menshikov had no formal education but pretensions to culture.

Slightly more flattering to its owner was the library of Baron P. P. Shafirov (1669–1739).[161] His grandfather was a baptized Jew of foreign origin, and his father a translator for the old *Posol'skii prikaz*. He took part in the Grand Embassy in 1697 and became Peter's leading statesmen; convicted of misconduct, Shafirov saw his books confiscated in 1724. He had the model library of a Russian courtier-gentleman. Its size, about five hundred titles, and its breadth evidenced the new age. Shafirov knew that Peter's reforms were not hostile to inherited religion, and he had half a dozen Bibles in almost as many languages, as well as a Koran—he had served in Constantinople. He had a modest collection of the Pietists' theology, enough to convince him to send his son to Halle to be educated.[162] He amassed a tidy collection of Classics. His "Charactères de Theophraste" were in French, but he had both Latin and French versions of Terence's *Comedies* and Petronius' *Satyrica*. He read Latin and had histories by Josephus, Lucan's *Civil War*, Eutropius' *Breviarum*, Seneca's *Annals* (?), and Sallust. His Quintus Curtius was in Polish, his Cornelius Nepos in German, and his Cicero, *Les Offices*, in French. He had fables, ancient and modern, Phaedra, Aesop, and La Fontaine.

The library also contained the literature of the courtier, Erasmus' *De civilitate morum*, Gracian's *L'uomo di corte*, and the Abbe Bellegarde's *Les règles de la vie civile* long before they became the rage in Petersburg.[163] He knew what one might read of the French, Boileau and the works of Molière, of the Italians, Boccaccio and Machiavelli, and he also had two editions of Don Quixote, Le Sage's *Gil Blas*, and Fénelon's *Telemachus*, to say nothing of Voltaire's early *Oedipe. Tragédie*. He had Grotius and Pufendorf, Comenius and Leibniz' *Théodicée* (in French), Descartes, and the anonymous *Der Adeliche Hofmeister*. With Shafirov one feels that one has encountered the successful marriage of the curiosity of old *prikaz* culture with a second-hand appreciation of the texts of humanism. As Shafirov's own origins merged Muscovite service with the culture of the foreigners, so his own library bridged old and new.

---

[161] See Luppov, *pervoi*, 227–29; Trofimova & Khomeev, "Katalog biblioteki P. P. Shafirova."

[162] Winter, *Halle*, pp. 102–04.

[163] See my "Popular Educational Tracts," pp. 308–11.

Political arrests, disturbing as they are for their victims, are good news for the historian, who profits with an increase in sources, if not in the form of interrogations, then in the inventories of confiscated possessions. It is a melancholy thought that Catherine II's kinder and gentler rule decreased information on private libraries. The preceding era of palace revolutions produced a gold mine.

Heinrich Johann Friedrich Ostermann (1686–1747) was a Lutheran minister's son born in Westphalia. He studied at the University of Jena before a duel forced flight to Holland, where he was recruited into Russian service. His name was synonymous with the Russian government from 1734 to 1740 but Elizabeth's accession meant arrest and exile. His Latin books included the basic texts of antiquity, Homer, Horace, Ovid, Terence, among others. His 'professional' library was rich in history and politics and law, travel and diplomacy.[164] Ostermann emerges as a serious reader, serious about his books which included *Don Quixote, Robinson Crusoe,* and *Gulliver's Travels.*

Andrei Fedorovich Khrushchov (1691–1740) was another member of the 'anti-German' party of Artemii Petrovich Volynskii. Of a Ukrainian noble family, Khrushchov was exposed to a European education. He was a student at Pastor Glück's Classical gymnasium in Moscow in 1705, briefly attended another foreign-mastered school in 1711, before being sent to Holland in 1712 for naval training.[165] He returned home and pursued a career in the Admiralty, which accounted for his professional library of mathematics, natural science, militaria, and fortifications. The other half of his six hundred books were devoted to the humanities, to the French language reading habits of someone permitted to dwell in Berlin, the center of refugee Huguenot culture. Khrushchov was the first translator of Fénelon's *Telemachus.* He also owned More's *Utopia,* Erasmus' *Folly,* Gracian's *L'homme de cour,* Fénelon's *Entretiens sur la religion,* and *De l'education des filles,* Grotius' *War and Peace,* Hobbes' *Elements philosophiques du citoyen,* Locke's *Reasonableness of Christianity,* Gassendi, Spinoza, Descartes, Malebranche, and *Don Quixote,* all in French. His Classics, Aristotle and Plato, Herodotus, Xenephon, Plutarch, and Petronius, were incomplete and mostly in French.

---

[164] Luppov, *poslepetrovskoe,* pp. 180–195.
[165] Luppov, *poslepetrovskoe,* pp. 227–34; Poresh, "Biblioteka A. F. Khrushchova." On the libraries of the Volynskii circle in general, see Khoteev, "Inostrannye knigi v bibliiotekakh uchastnikov kruzhka Volynskogo".

Another of the Volynskii circle, Johann Eichler,[166] was the son of a German-born household servant, and we first hear of him as a servant-flutist; under the patronage of I. A. Dolgorukii, the favorite of young Peter II, he was elevated to the *dvorianstvo*, and Biron made him cabinet-secretary to the Empress Anna. In 1740 he was exiled to Siberia, and his property confiscated. Pardoned by Elizabeth, he lived in Moscow until his death in 1779. His library reflected an unsystematic education. There was a bit of the new cosmology, Fontenelle's *Plurality of Worlds*, a good deal of the natural-law school, and a broad selection of the literature of courtiers, *Abélard et Eloise*, Prevost d'Exiles' *Mémoirs et adventures d'un homme de qualité*, Bellegarde's *Réflexions sur l'élégance et la delicatesse*, and Pufendorf's *Les devoirs de l'homme et du citoyen*, also held in the original Latin. He was more Anglophile than most Russians of the period, with Defoe's *Moll Flanders* and *New Voyage*, Swift's *Tale of a Tub*, some of *Spectator*, Locke on *Human Understanding*, and Voltaire's *English Letters*. His Classical authors were mostly literary and held in French, Italian or English as often as Latin. One gets the sense of a European without formal education but with the aspirations of courtly culture.

Artemii Petrovich Volynskii led the anti-German party.[167] He is the one authentic Russian noble in the circle whose library is known. Of the old nobility, Volynskii's father was a *stol'nik* and later *voevoda* of Kazan; five Volynskiis counted among the boyar elite. He was raised traditionally, educated "unsystematically" in the house of S. A. Saltykov, and entered service at age fifteen. He was the Russian ambassador to Persia in 1715, Governor of Astrakhan (1719–23), and like his father, of Kazan (1725). He owned some 545 books, and reflecting his old-fashioned education, over half were in Slavonic, largely religious literature. He had, a generation after the death of Peter the Great, intact the library of a seventeenth-century servitor, with the Polish history and chronicles, tsarist genealogies and law codes, a manuscript copy of Hizel's *Sinopsis*, and a lot of travel literature. He had Livy, Quintus Curtius and Cornelius Nepos in Latin, but most of his spotty Classical antiquity was in German, and the authors he owned were those which fit best into the reading habits

---

[166] See Luppov, *poslepetrovskoe*, pp. 234–5; Fundamenskii, "Biblioteka kabinet-sekretaria I. Eikhlera." Comparable too was the library of another of the circle; see Luppov, "Fedor Ivanovich Soimonov i ego biblioteka."
[167] Luppov, *poslepetrovskoe*, pp. 169–80.

of old *prikaz* culture. He is the exception that makes the rule: the Russian nobility did not study Latin. Among such servitors one can see the range of Petrine trainings and educations, the resistance to Latin, and the enduring reading habits of the seventeenth-century, scarcely touched by the passing of time and the Petrine revolution.

Finally a word can be said about the libraries of the chief courtiers, the Romanovs. The books of Aleksei Petrovich can be roughly fixed at about four hundred titles.[168] One segment reflected the practical education Peter decreed for his presumed heir: foreign languages, mathematics, fortifications, modern history, and geography. Not surprising was a large collection of Bibles and Concordances, saints' lives, a good deal of German Reformation and post-Reformation theology, and a sizeable collection of singing books.[169] Aleksei Petrovich, whose education was divided between the traditionally religious and the brutally militaristic tendered by Menshikov, did not collect the Classics at all.

He did own a copy of W. H. Hohberg, *Georgica Curiosa, oder adelisches Land- und Feld-leben* (Nürnberg, 1701), which his father subsequently claimed, and which arguably offered a new vision of an old nobility. B. I. Syromiatnikov long ago talked about the Petrine metamorphosis of the old serving classes in terms of *Ritter wird Landwirt*, and if Aleksei or Peter dreamed of such a transformation, Hohberg provided the blueprint. Hohberg, one will recall, effectively transformed Classical economic literature into a practical manual for noble European landlords, easing their transition from born aristocratic status to effective estate management. His work reached Russia, and Peter's law of single inheritance aimed at preserving viable estates. But Petrine publishing did not foster that dream.[170]

Aleksei's personal purchases in Prague, Frankfurt on the Oder,

---

[168] The history of the reconstruction, with all relevant citations is lucidly presented in Lebedeva, "Biblioteka tsarevicha Alekseia Petrovicha." Fifty-seven of his books, plus some manuscripts, were absorbed by the library of his father; they can be located in the standard Bobrova, comp., *Biblioteka Petra I*, although the indices are unreliable.

[169] Murzanova, "K istorii sobraniia knig tsarevicha Alekseia Petrovicha," Vyp. I, 119–42 and 422–27. From his father's library that we learn that Aleksei acquired a collection of religious manuscripts in Novgorod in 1716 from Metropolitan Job and Karion Istomin (who had once designed his boyhood primer).

[170] Syromiatnikov, *"Reguliarnoe" gosudarstvo*, I, p. 128. On von Hohberg, see the discussion in Section One of Chapter I above.

Gdansk, Bamberg, and Braunschweig between 1711 and 1714 were religious and bore titles like *Himmel-Brot der Seelen, Biblishcher Kern und Stern*, and *Christliche Gedanken*.[171] Peter the Great also collected religious literature avidly. The core of Aleksei's purchases were the works of Halle Pietism, including Arnold's *Denkmal des alten Christenthums* (Gosslar, 1702), and Freylinghausen's *Geistreiches Gesangbuch* (Halle, 1704), as well as Jesuit authors like Jeremias Drexel and Nicholas Caussin, and the rabid Attorney-Physician-Theologian, Johann Pistorius. These same books made Teofan an able confederate of the reformer-tsar. Halle Pietism, when it had converted crown-prince Friedrich Wilhelm of Prussia, was responsible for a governmental commitment to the ideal of the bettering the lives of all strata of society, for the spread of mercantilist ideas, and for the rise of modern patriotism as well.[172] Had Aleksei been the person to sight on this particular moving target, Peter might have regarded him as a loyal and reform-minded son after all.

The reign of Peter's daughter, Elizabeth, 1740–61, was marked by court intrigues between a French faction headed by de la Chétardie, and the interests of Vienna, London, and Dresden. Out of those politics came an order in the spring of 1745 to remove all of Elizabeth's French books from the Summer Palace, just completed by Rastrelli. A list suggests reading habits more sophisticated than Pekarskii credited her, when he repeated the charge that she did not know England was an island.[173] Hers was a relatively serious "lady's library" in French, heavily weighted to history. Her ancient historians

---

[171] Aleksei's wife was a princess from Braunschweig who did not convert from Lutheranism.

[172] For the last statement, Pinson, *Pietism as a Factor*, and for the preceding, Deppermann, *Der hallische Pietismus*, pp. 152, 173–4. The texts purchased by Aleksei can be sampled in English in Erb, ed., *Pietists. Selected Writings*. The standard histories in English are by Stoeffler, *The Rise of Evangelical Pietism*, and his *German Pietism*.

[173] Kopanev, "Frantsuzskie knigi v letnem dome," pp. 26–41, here p. 30; a more detailed list is provided in his "Knigi imperatritsy Elizavety," pp. 109–18. One of the great howlers in Russian history concerns Elizabeth's reading habits. In a dreadful biography, Rice, *Elizabeth*, p. 7, reports that she "read and understood the works of Corneille, Racine, Boileau and Rousseau before reaching the age of twelve." Since Elizabeth was born in 1709, and J. J. Rousseau in 1712, she must have been reading the very young Rousseau (J. B. Rousseau is often found in the Russian and European libraries of the day). The new history of the reign is Anisimov, *Rossii v seredine XVIII veka*, with a translation by J. T. Alexander in preparation. Lindsey Hughes has found the library of Peter's favorite sister, Natal'ia Alekseevna; heavily and typically religious, it did contain the tales of the courtiers' libraries, as well as scripts for the plays that were her passion.

included Plutarch, Polybius, Lucian of Samosata, Xenophon, Diodorus Siculus and Eusebius' *Histoire de l'Eglise*, in French and nicely interpreted by Charles Rollin's *Histoire ancienne* and *Histoire Romaine*, found in almost every competent library of the age, Russian and European. Among serious moderns she had Bayle's *Lettres* and *Oeuvres diverses*, Montaigne's *Essais*, Grotius, and Henri Boulainvilliers' *Histoire de l'ancien gouvernement de la France*.[174]

Supporting Elizabeth's image as the monarch under whom genteel culture was brought to the Russians, she had the Jesuit Baltasar Gracian's *Le Héros*, *L'Homme de Cour*, *L'Homme universal*, as well as his *L'Homme de trompé, ou le Criticon*, a basic library of etiquette based ultimately on the Senecan Stoicism:[175] Gracian was never really passé in Europe, for after his unexpected afterlife civilizing Russian courtiers, fops, and dandies, he would be rediscovered by "the philosopher of modern pessimism," Arthur Schopenhauer who would describe Gracian as "my favorite author," and the *Criticon* as "my favorite book in all the world."[176] In this subtle guise, Elizabeth did her small part to spread sublimated bits of Classical ethical values, although she did not confront Latin studies herself.

Peter the Great's own library, lovingly catalogued at 1,663 titles,[177] was as multi-faceted as its owner. It embraced the technical areas of architecture, geography, mathematics, and, militaria including mechanics, fortifications, artillery, and naval affairs. It would be wonderful to be able to contrast its secular content with the religious orientation of Aleksei Petrovich's library, and to reach some dramatic conclusion, as Soviet historians are wont to do.[178] Such simplistic analyses are impossible, however, because Peter's library contained a major portion of his son's books. Peter too had a collection of religion which included St. Augustine and Gregory the Great, a collection of Polockij's work, a mass of devotional, scriptural, and liturgical works (including five manuscript psalters) in several languages, and a collection of Lutheranism. At the same time he held, with

---

[174] See Ellis, *Boulainvilliers*.

[175] Gracian, *Handorakel*, intro. by Veßler, citing F. G. Bell, p. xiv. The standard edition is the *Oráculo Manual y Arte de Prudencia*, Madrid, 1954; its notes reveal its heavy reliance on Seneca, and to a lesser extent, Cicero, Horace, and Ovid, plus other ancients, and moderns like Cervantes and La Rochefoucauld.

[176] *Handorakel*, xv–xviii.

[177] For the following, Bobrova, *Biblioteka Petra I*.

[178] See Lebedeva, "Biblioteka tsarevicha Alekseia Petrovicha," p. 63: "the epoch of the Petrine transformation required a different education."

Hohberg's *Georgica*, Iurii Krizhanich, the Serbian *Alexander*, Flavius Josephus, Amartol's *Chronograph*, the *Great Mirror*, in short, the essentials of the library of a Polonized seventeenth-century courtier of his father's era.

His small collection of the Classics consisted almost exclusively those pieces of antiquities which fed the interests of a seventeenth-century courtier: chronologies of emperors and popes, Quintus Curtius Rufus' *Alexander*, historical collections dealing with Troy and the Argonauts, Baronius' *Annales ecclesiastici i civilis* and his martyrology, Polydore Virgil's *De Rerum Inventoribus*, and Apollodorus Atheniensis' *Bibliotecae*, the histories of Caesar and Tacitus, and Vitruvius' *De architectura*. The only significant additions to the old courtly package would appear to be a solitary Terence's *Comedies* in a French edition, and Ovid's *Metamorphosis*, a private passion with Peter, illustrations for which he saw into print. Peter held the moderns, Grotius, Newton, and Pufendorf, but no Halley or Locke, no Montaigne, Corneille, Racine, or Bayle, no Copernicus or Galileo. His considerable library evinces no sharp break with the past, no abandonment of the Orthodox Faith, no exclusive attachment to the technical and the mathematical, no adoption of the Ukrainian humanists' agenda,—in short, no commitment to values other than to those of his father's court. On the basis of his books, it would seem premature to declare that his rise to power and personal decision-making in the mid-1690s was "in many ways the symbolic moment of death of old Russian culture.[179] Rather his books document its eclectic nature, its resiliency, and its durability.

Russian nobles prior to the age of Catherine did not buy or read Latin books. A few titles, those most compatible with the reading habits of their fathers, did penetrate their collections in translations. Aesop and the lives of Alexander the Great are a case in point. But it is exceedingly difficult to find a Russian noble before Catherine who read the Classics.

B. *V. N. Tatishchev, Orthodox Courtier*

V. N. Tatishchev's books say much about the evolution of the courtier from Muscovy to Russia.[180] He represented the gentry molded

---

[179] Bushkovitch, "The Epiphany Ceremony," p. 15.
[180] For the following, see Luppov, *poslepetrovskoe*, pp. 206–220. Largely replacing

under the direct influence of Peter's reforms,[181] but he was also the successor of the seventeenth-century *Stol'nik*, a new embodiment of Polonized court culture.

Tatishchev's vision owed much to the Hanseatic orientation of Pskov, where he was born the son of a *stol'nik* and sometimes *voevoda*.[182] The Tatishchevs had courtly connections to the Saltykovs, and through them to the wife and entourage of Peter's co-tsar Ivan V. Through these means Vasilii attained entrée to the court in 1693. His early education was overseen by his father, and he had his start in public life as a protegé of Jacob Bruce himself even before he attended Bruce's artillery school in Moscow.[183] His unsystematic studies were interrupted by service. He did spend some few adult months in Sweden preoccupied with history in 1724–26 when he made his first significant purchases of books.[184] The results did not impress contemporaries: "[Tatishchev] had no training, did not know a single word of Latin, and did not even understand any modern language other than German."[185]

Soviets praised Tatishchev as "one of the most enlightened people of his age."[186] Although he owned Machiavelli's *Prince*, Hobbes' *Leviathan*, Locke's *Civil Government*, he was inclined to regard the lot as "useless" or "harmful."[187] It seems appropriate to consider his book habits. Tatishchev was the first to admit that he had not the education of the contemporary colleges, "had not studied to philosophy."[188] He was a passionate historian, but unlike contemporary Western scholars,

---

the old classic, Popov, *V. N. Tatishchev i ego vremia*, are the works of Daniels, *V. N. Tatishchev*, Grau, *Der Wirtschafts-organisator*, Iunkt, *Gosudarstvennaia deiatel'nost' V. N. Tatishchev*, and Kuz'min, *Tatishchev*.

[181] Plekhanov, *Social Thought*, pp. 83–119, here p. 84. Plekhanov dismissed his well-known denial that he had higher education as "unnecessary modesty."

[182] Grau, *op. cit.*, pp. 19–23. Tantalizing, but more difficult to assess was the family's original roots in Smolensk. For a view of Smolensk as an almost foreign city, see Korsakov, "Vasilii Nikitich Tatishchev," pp. 567–68; nineteenth-century historians were more sensitive to the regional origins of servitors than are Soviet nationalists. On Tatishchev's *stol'nik* roots see Kuz'min, *op. cit.*, pp. 5–6, and Crummey, *Aristocrats*, pp. 206–07.

[183] Grau, *op. cit.*, 24, 142–43; they remained patron-client; see Luppov, *poslepetrovskoi*, p. 208, and Kuz'min, *Tatishchev*, pp. 29ff.

[184] Thaden, "V. N. Tatishchev, German Historians," pp. 272–73.

[185] A. L. Schlözer, cited in *Ibid.*, pp. 367–68.

[186] Luppov, *poslepetrovskoe*, p. 211, citing S. N. Valk. See also Grau, "Tatiscev und die Aufklärung," p. 81.

[187] Grau, "Tatiscev und Deutschland," p. 148.

[188] Korsakov, *op. cit.*, p. 574.

he knew Greek and Latin literature and texts only second-hand[189] through his friendship with Teofan, who also made his considerable library available, and through the services of one Kir'iak Andreevich Kondratovych.

This remarkable Ukrainian was Kiev educated, and on Teofan's recommendation he was appointed Latin teacher at Tatishchev's school in the Urals and his personal translator.[190] He made Latin histories and Polish chronicles available to Tatishchev, without which the early parts of his *History* were inconceivable, since they were based on his translations of Pliny, Strabo, and Ptolemy.[191]

Tatishchev's personal library makes it possible to understand something of his intellectual world.[192] In addition to books on astronomy, physical geography, chemistry, medicine, militaria, mathematics, philology, and jurisprudence, Tatishchev also had books on the "general problems of religion." Broadly defined religious matter comprised the largest category after history.[193] Tatishchev's Russian books were made up of both the civil press' output of Petrine and post-Petrine editions (Lomonosov's translation of G. Heinsius on comets, Kantemir's translation of Fontenelle's *Plurality of Worlds*, Polikarpov's translation of Varenius' *Geography*, Trediakovskii's translation of Rollin's *Ancient History*), as well as a very large collection of Bibles, patristics, psalters, catechisms, breviaries, Kievan and Belorussian editions of the seventeenth century, and such polemical works as Dmitro Rostov'skyj on Old Belief, and Patriarch Iosif against the Lutherans.

His few Classics were principally the historians, almost all in

---

[189] Thaden, *op. cit.*, p. 367.

[190] One arena in which Tatishchev did make an original contribution was education; see my *Childhood*, pp. 53–56. There is no evidence the school taught Latin; see the text in Demidova, "Instruktsiia V. N. Tatishcheva," pp. 166–178.

[191] Kondratovych would become a translator for the Academy, would translate some of Cicero's Orations, as well as Russifying Johann Mathais Gesner's 1726 edition of Basilius Fabri, *Thesauras eruditionis scholasticae*, 1571, one of the best guides to the study of Latin in Europe. See Grau, *Der Wirtschaftsorganisator*, pp. 140–41, and Thaden, *op. cit.*, p. 380. A copy of Pliny, *Geografiia* was the only Classical work among Tatishchev's 55 manuscripts. See *Istoricheskii ocherk i obzor fondov rukopisnogo otdela*, pp. 434–41.

[192] Luppov, *poslepetrovskoe*, pp. 212–16 recounts what is known, but see also the basic list published by Pekarskii, "Novaia izvestiia o V. N. Tatishcheva"; Valkina, "K voprosu ob istochnikakh Tatishcheva," is based on that list; see also trivia in Astrakhanskii, "Novoe o knigakh V. N. Tatishcheva," and his manuscripts previously cited, *Istoricheskii obzor*, pp. 434–41. The most recent effort at reconstruction is by Bauman & Salakhutdinova, "Knigi iz biblioteki V. N. Tatishcheva," pp. 127–38.

[193] Luppov, *op. cit.*, pp. 215–16.

German, and he did own the first Russian editions of Quintus Curtius, Marcus Aurelius, and Cornelius Nepos. He owned Pufendorf, Grotius, Johann Hübner's *Geography*, Bayle's *Dictionnaire*, and also the Church History of the Pietist Gottfried Arnold, and the Polish chronicles of Matvej Stryikowsky and Marcin Bielski. His manuscript collection contained Kievan and Muscovite law codes with his annotations, many chronicles, a variety of travel accounts of Russia, Tartary, Siberia, and one Classical title:

54. *Plinii. Geografiia. Perevod s latinskogo iazyka 1738 g.*   On the basis of his library one can see the expanded intellectual horizons of the old Polonized court of pre-Petrine times, but also its outer limits.

What sort of thinker was Tatishchev? The text most often cited as archetypical is his "Conversation between two friends on the utility of science and schools" (1733), which Eduard Winter was inclined to regard as the "*Grundbuch der russischen Aufklärung.*"[194] Its first redaction seems to date from the succession crisis of 1730.[195] Tatishchev wrote the colloquy in the form of the catechism:

13. Of what does man consist:
Answer: Of what man consists is a question on which the philosophers of ancient times were divided, and they were even of contradictory opinions, the chief ones of which I mention here: Although the majority recognized two substances, soul and body, still there were differing opinions, to wit:
1st). The very ancient philosopher Ditsearkh [Dicaerchus], whom Cicero cites,[196] wrote that man's essence was body alone, and that the soul was only an illusion, only an empty designation, signifying nothing; among the moderns, Hobbes and others continue to hold this view.
2nd). Opposed to these are others for whom only the soul of man really exists, and the body, which they call a *nagalishche* or a prison, a dungeon, and among these the Pythagoreans, the Platonists, and the Stoics all agree; among the moderns, Marus is their successor.
3rd). Then there are those who hold there to be three essences in man, that is, soul, spirit, and body; this opinion, it seems, was new

---

[194] Winter, *Frühaufklärung*, p. 310; the authoritative text is in his *Izbrannye proizvedeniia*, pp. 51–133, based on the seven extant manuscripts of the work. See the review by Paul Dukes, *Study Group on Eighteenth-Century Russia Newsletter*, No. 8 (1980), 86–92.

[195] Tatishchev returned to it around 1736 and again during the period of his governorship of Astrakhan, 1741–1745. Tatishchev, *Izbrannye*, pp. 8–15.

[196] Dicaerchus of Messana, 4th Century peripatetic philosopher, pupil of Aristotle; this may be an allusion to Cicero, *De Divinatione*, I, 13: "In fact, the human soul never divines naturally, except when it is so unrestrained and free that it has absolutely no association with the body, as happens in the case of frenzy and dreams. Hence both these kinds of divination have been sanctioned by Dicaerchus...."

with Plato and first revived by Theophrastus Paracelsus, and he was succeeded by many lunatic minds, like the Böhmists [Jakob Böhme] and the Weigelians [Valentin Weigel], even though they cannot stand up to arguments derived from Holy Scripture.

4th). There is the opinion which we can confirm through the indubitable testimony of Holy Scripture; that is, man is composed of two completely different properties, the active and the passive, the eternal and the temporal, the perfect and the imperfect, that is, soul and body, in which his life consists, and from which all activity proceeds: Isaiah 26:9 [*With my soul have I desired thee in the night, yea with my spirit within me will I seek thee early*]; Luke 1:46, 47 [*And Mary said, My soul doth magnify the Lord, and my spirit hath rejoiced in God my Savior*]; I Corinthians 14:15 [*What is it then? I will pray with the spirit, and I will pray with the understanding also*]; I Thessalonians 5:23 [*I pray God your whole spirit and soul and body be preserved blameless unto the coming of our Lord Jesus Christ*]; Hebrews 4:12ff. [*For the word of God is quick and powerful, and sharper than any two-edged sword, piercing even to the dividing asunder of soul and spirit, and of the joints and marrow, and is a discerner of the thoughts and intents of the heart*]; Genesis 2:7 [*And the Lord God formed man of the dust of the ground, and breathed into his nostrils the breath of life; and man became a living soul*].[197]

This is an interesting excursion into the history of philosophy—there are several such in Tatishchev's "Conversation"—and it probably doesn't matter much whether Tatishchev got it right or not. Tatishchev ultimately resolves the issue of human nature on the basis of Scriptural authority. Statesman and historian he may have been, but freethinking would seem to be beyond his Christian vision, even if he had piecemeal somewhere read bits of the ancient philosophers.

Tatishchev emerges a thinker who, through translations, confirmed pagan philosophical insights with Christian Revelation. Certainly nothing else known about Tatishchev suggests freethinking: when he had the opportunity to outline his ideal elementary education, he recommended Teofan Prokopovych's "Lutheran" primer, with its prayers and explanations of the Ten Commandments. As a courtier on provincial assignment he recommended Bruce's civil script primer with the *Zertsalo*, the secular book of etiquette, also be used. For instilling a fear of God—the heart of old *Domostroi*'s instruction—and for teaching them how to lead an honorable life, Tatishchev said the old Psalter worked just as well. But since Peter's civil script had been introduced, the linguistic problems of using old Slavonic books made the new texts by Teofan and Bruce preferable on utilitarian grounds.

---

[197] Tatishchev, *Izbrannye*, p. 53.

For Tatishchev's pupils daily church attendance was still required, and the school day began with reading the *Evangelia* aloud; it continued with the *Apostol* at lunch, with appropriate prayers, and the day closed with the recitation of the Lord's Prayer.[198] Tatishchev conceded that clerics' sons should attend the factory schools, but that the best of them might then be sent on to a Latin academy at the diocesan seat, just as the sons of governmental officials should be sent on to a "German" school, presumably the Land Cadet Corps recently established by Anna. This was no endorsement of Latin humanism but a reaffirmation of the specialized trainings of the Muscovite *prikazy*, for Tatishchev's approach to education was both ecclesiastical and bureaucratic: a school needed the Church's liturgical service books, as well as the *Ulozhenie* and printed *ukazy*, the latter to be read aloud in the schools. Any pupil not attending church daily should be fined. His fundamental concept of schooling remained narrowly utilitarian: reading and writing were "necessary in every trade," as were arithmetic and geometry.[199] The three greatest contributions to the history of mankind, according to Tatishchev, were the invention of writing, the teachings of Christ, and the invention of the printing press,[200] but these were integrally related in that the purpose of human life was preparation for Salvation. Beyond that, this putative "Enlightener" failed to endorse the reading of pagan authors, and failed to conceive of "the education of the whole man" among members of any social class, an idea available among the alien Ukrainians for a century.

Shortly before his death, after a life of administrative service, Tatishchev wrote a little testament to his son. In it he wrote,

> God is calling me to Himself and I, exhausted by the hustle and bustle of this world, with outstretched arms go to the sweet repose of His eternal kingdom. . . .
> Above all, my beloved son, fear God and love Him and faithfully serve your Lord and hold Him with honor and with piety. . . . Read the Bible and the New Testament with Commentaries, with your intellect. From the Bible you will learn true wisdom.[201]

---

[198] For the above and the following, Demidova, *op. cit.*, pp. 169–74; on the German schools which were the models for his ideal institutions in the Urals, see Grau, "Russisch-sächsische Beziehungen," pp. 322ff.

[199] For the above, Pavlenko, "Nakaz shikhmeisteru V. N. Tatishcheva."

[200] Plekhanov, *Social Thought*, pp. 114–15.

[201] Dmitriev, "Predsmertnoe uveshchanie V. N. Tatishcheva synu," pp. 227–37.

Urging his son "to scorn everything of this world, and to strive only for life eternal, Tatishchev commended his own "eternal soul" to the "hands of his Creator," and expired.

One hesitates to make too much of a death-bed testament to one's son, but it seems there were limits to the notion of Tatishchev as Enlightener. This was not the death of a La Mettrie, who cried out in pain, "Jesus!", to be asked by a priest if this were a sign of repentance on the part of the arch-materialist, only to receive the response, "No, it's only a figure of speech." Enthusiastic historian, school director, governor, soldier and technocrat he may have been, but he was also an Old-Muscovite servitor, retaining *Domostroi*'s old Fear-of-the-Lord variety of Orthodox Christianity, unshaken by the humanists' education.

Tolstoi, another Orthodox *stol'nik* with roots in the Polish-Lithuanian provinces, a half-century earlier returned from harrowing adventures and temptations, and "thanked the Most Merciful Lord God and Most Blessed Mother of God and those [saints] pleasing to God, that [he] had, by the will of God, returned from [his] required travels from such distant regions to [his fatherland in good health."[202] Tatishchev had acquired a bookish wisdom far broader than Tolstoi's, including a taste of the pagan philosophers, but his values remained those of the old servitor class. His career and his mind testify to the adaptability of that group's values, already clear in 1650, but also to their survival unscathed beyond the Petrine "Revolution." If this man was the "Guardian of the Petrine Revolution,"[203] one must rethink the concept of revolution, as one must ponder the idea of Tatishchev as "a true 18th century enlightener."[204]

5. *Conclusion*

Soviet scholars consistently postulated a social division between the educated ecclesiastical and lay strata of eighteenth-century Russian society. The content of personal libraries, measured by their receptivity to the pagan ancients, suggests that Marxist, ideologically conceived division was a superficial partition in Russia, as it was in

---

[202] Okenfuss, *Tolstoi*, p. 340.
[203] This is the subtitle of Daniels, *Tatishchev*.
[204] Plekhanov, *op. cit.*, p. 117.

contemporary Europe. Another divide appears more important.

Latin humanism remained the culture of Ukrainians and other foreigners, however well they or their ancestors were otherwise integrated into Russian society, ecclesiastical or civil service. Others, of course, as in the case of Johann Eichler, more resembled the typical Russian gentryman, who remained skeptical of, and overwhelmingly hostile to, pagan texts and to Latin, with very few exceptions. The repertoire of the Russians' printing presses to 1760 gave them no reason to feel out of touch with their government's or their Church's policy. Muscovite religious values were undisturbed in the education of most Russians, and the chief role of the printing presses was to feed this inherited religiosity. The old court culture of the seventeenth century remained receptive to eclectic literary and historical texts in the post-Petrine age, and this constituted the new fare of the presses. Latinate culture failed to penetrate significantly the culture of the nobility, or the repertoire of the printing press in Russia before Catherine the Great.

CHAPTER THREE

RUSSIAN BOOK CULTURE IN THE LATER
EIGHTEENTH CENTURY

1. *European Book Culture in an Enlightened Age*

A few years ago Richard Gummere showed that the American founding fathers were steeped in the Classics, above all in Cicero's *Offices*,
"which subsumed the essence of the moral heritage and humanistic
values of the ancient world." He was attacked by historians who
argued that an antiquarian's collection of every mention of a Classical
author did not prove significance. Gummere has recently been vin-
dicated.[1] If America's debt is clearer, the diverse cultures of Europe
preclude simple generalizations. The recent historiographic tendency
has been to talk of several unique Enlightenments, Scottish, Rosicrucian, German Catholic and German Lutheran, French Liberal and
French Conservative, a pluralism that has replaced Peter Gay's unified synthesis.[2] Faced with this complexity, no brief glimpse at book
habits can do justice to the role of the Classics across the European
continent after 1750.

If Latin began to be questioned in the schools, Classical authors
lost none of their position in British libraries. The books of Adam
Smith, beyond their working strengths in economics, physiocracy,
taxation, and commerce, represented also a complete collection of
over a hundred authors of the ancient world. Since first catalogued
a supplement has appeared[3] which lists six editions of Xenophon—
he had previously appeared to be missing—who had informed every
writer on economics since the Renaissance. The secular continued to

---

[1] Gummere, *The American Colonial Mind and the Classical Tradition*. For the quotation, Reinhold, *Classica America*, p. 150, and for the historiography which follows,
especially Jack Green and Howard Mumford Jones, pp. 286–89 and *passim*. The
newest and best of the genre, which specifies Classical contributions to political thought,
is Carl J. Richard, *The Founders and the Classics*.

[2] Gay, *The Enlightenment*; contrast Porter and Teich, eds., *The Enlightenment in National Context*, and Engel-Janosi, et al., eds., *Formen der europäischen Aufklärung*.

[3] Bonar, *A Catalogue of the Library of Adam Smith*, and Mizuta, *Adam Smith's Library.
A Supplement*.

exist with the religious in the age of Enlightenment. Smith praised the *New Theory of Vision* by George Berkeley as "one of the finest examples of philosophical analysis," from which he had "borrowed almost everything."[4] But Berkeley was also Bishop of Cloyne, and Smith collected his "Address to the Catholic Clergy" and his *Sermons*. His library reflected no sudden break with the past.

Libraries continued to be grounded in the Classics, but a dawning allure of translations can be noted. Nor did religious material decline in laymen's libraries. Francis Grose (ca. 1731–1791), the son of a Swiss jeweler, an independently wealthy and Classically-educated artist and professional soldier, had a large professional library of militaria, gunnery, fortifications, mechanics, and mathematics. He collected almost no Latin books, but he had Virgil, Livy, Ovid, Horace, Martial, Sallust, and Tacitus in translation. A century after Salem he amassed some thirty volumes on witchcraft.[5]

Literati continued to read the Classics. Thomas Day (d. 1792), the eccentric author of *Sandford and Merton* and a disciple of Rousseau, collected over a library noted for its "high seriousness of . . . contents and the absence of almost any form of lighter reading." It held religion: *Sermons* by S. Clarke, Donne, and Waterland, "Religious Tracts" by Allen, Baxter on the soul, and a good deal of ecclesiastical history. He had an excellent selection of about twenty-five Classical authors, many in Greek or Latin, some in translation.[6] The architect William Chambers (d. 1796) had studied in France under Blondel. In his library one can see the explosion of the vernacular late in the century, as his vast collection of travel literature, architecture, mathematics, and engineering was in a patchwork of tongues. His Classics were reduced in number and most were in French translation. He collected little religion, four volumes of saints' lives, a history of the Popes, a *Thesaurus Rerum Ecclesiasticarum*, but the secular began to dominate British libraries only at the turn of the nineteenth century.

In France ownership of the Classical texts commands attention for Mme. Roland proclaimed, "Plutarch had disposed me to become a republican."[7] In relatively few appearances before revolutionary assemblies, Camille Desmoulins cited Cicero no less than forty three

---

[4] Bonar, *op. cit.*, pp. 24–26.
[5] Munby, ed., *Sale Catalogues*, Vol. 7, 463–514.
[6] Munby, ed., *Sale Catalogues*, Vol. 2, 173–192; for the following, *Ibid.*, Vol. 4, 107–134.
[7] Cited in Reinhold, *Classica*, p. 152.

times. A deputy of the clergy in 1789, the Abbé Boisgelin, said that
"when Cicero spoke in the Senate, he was the father of his country
[*père de la patrie*]." The oratory of the revolution was heavily Ciceronian,
and it was Cicero who defined the *"homines novi"*—new men—as those
who rose by virtue of their sound civism and eloquence.[8]

Voltaire's love of the Classics was inspired by his teachers. "Voltaire
himself acknowledged that his [Jesuit] teachers had instilled in him
elegant and sure tastes, solid classical culture, and a well-grounded
knowledge of Greek and Latin masterpieces."[9] His library, held in
the Russia thanks to Catherine II, included some 3867 titles.[10] His
Latin authors were the most numerous in his library; he also held
the Greeks, Homer and Hesiod in Latin translation, but he also owned
French translations of many of his Latin authors, and some in Italian as well. He held a dozen editions of Scripture in whole or part,
five editions of Augustine, six titles by Bossuet, and Thomas Aquinas'
Summa Theologica. Everyone owned Fénelon's pseudo-classical *Télémaque*,
but Voltaire's also held the archbishop of Cambray's *Sermons choisis,
instruction pastorale, Oeuvres spirituelles,* and his *Oeuvres philosophiques. 1–e
partie: Démonstration de l'existence de Dieu.* . . . Voltaire owned Élie
Bertrand's works on fossils and on earthquakes, but also his *Instructions chrétiénnes* of 1756. Voltaire's library was well grounded in religion and the Classics.

The Parisian private library has been the subject of intensive research. Among some four thousand household inventories[11] one notes
that among French clerical libraries Latin books fell from 47% of all
titles in the first third of the century to 27% in the decade before
the Revolution. In the same period theology fell from 38% to 29%
of the books of clergy, still an impressive figure.[12] In the 1750s theology, including Scripture, liturgical works, and religious tracts, but
excluding the history of religion or canon law, represented no less
than 22.29% of the books among all Parisians.[13]

---

[8] Simon Schama, *Citizens*, pp. 169–70.
[9] Wade, *The Intellectual Development of Voltaire*, p. 14.
[10] *Biblioteka Vol'tera. Katalog knig*, pp. 7–67, for the following.
[11] The basic work has been done by Michel Marion, Récherches sur les lectures
des Parisiens d'après leurs inventaires après décès (1750–1759), Paris, 1978, but I
have used his summary, "Quelques aspects sur les bibliothèques privées," as well as
the survey of other recent work, Martin, "Livre et Lumières en France."
[12] Martin, *op. cit.*, p. 40.
[13] Marion, *op. cit.*, p. 89.

Which books appeared most frequently in Parisian libraries? The Bible (the edition by de Sacy had seen 74 printings) was by far the most owned; Fleury's *Histoire ecclésiastique*, the New Testament, the Jesuit *Dictionnaire de Trévoux*, and Baillet's *Vie des Saints* were also among the top ten titles. They were accompanied most often by Mézeray's *Histoire de France*, Rollin's *Histoire romaine*, his *Histoire ancienne*, Moreri's *Le Grand dictionnaire historique*, and Bayle's *Dictionnaire historique et critique*.[14] Religion and antiquity defined the modern Parisian library in the age of the Enlightenments.

Concerning the French nobility, Marion could only exclaim, "*Mais dans cette noblesse que d'inégalités!*" On one end of the scale was the massive library of a great magnate like the Marquis de Courtanvaux, a protector of the sciences and a friend of the philosophes—Condorcet would declaim his *éloge funèbre*—as worldly an individual as one could expect of the *président* of *l'Académie des Sciences*, whose collection included only 3.4% theology. But that seemingly insignificant figure consisted of 122 separate inventory-lots of books, twice as many as his books on law.[15] But diversity is what most marked the French noble library. President Claris of the Court of Aids of Montpellier, who owned over 1500 volumes, had over 37% theology: he inherited much, but "pious reading made up a striking proportion of his purchases." On the other extreme, Louis Bruno de Boisgelin de Cucè, Master of the King's Wardrobe, was "a courtier, a great devourer of novelties, a man of the Court but also of the *salons*." He held the whole of eighteenth-century English literature, all the great works of the French eighteenth century except Rousseau, along with much modern history. He owned several anti-religious books, "but no works of theology or piety."[16] But his irreligiosity was as atypical as Claris' huge collection of devotion.

Although book habits in Poland are ultimately more relevant, particular attention is given here to books in German-speaking Europe, since a vast recent scholarship on the "Russian Enlightenment" suggests German and Russian book cultures were closely comparable. There was, in fact, a vast difference. When Russian publishers numbered at most a few dozen in the entire eighteenth century, Germany boasted hundreds at any one moment. The Leipzig Easter book fair annually

---

[14] Marion, *op. cit.*, pp. 91–92, and below, p. 85.
[15] Garden, "Une grande collection des livres de voyage."
[16] Chaussinand-Nogaret, *The French Nobility*, pp. 74–76.

saw displays by two hundred thirty five firms in the 1770s and 1780s, and by about 325 companies after 1785 when Joseph II relaxed the Imperial censorship.[17] On the basis of the catalogues of the fair, we know that in the 1760s 1500 new titles were offered per annum, in the 1780s that number had doubled; the catalogue for 1787 listed 5,492 titles.[18] This means that in the last quarter of the century, in any three-year period, as many titles appeared in Germany as in Russia in the entire century.[19]

Russia celebrates the founding of her first private periodical in 1759.[20] In the Germanies there were already 752 newspapers by 1750, 2,684 for the period 1751–90. The city of Leipzig alone had 438 newspapers in the eighteenth century, about as many as all periodicals published in Russia in the entire century.[21] In the Germanies between 1741 and 1765 about seven hundred and fifty new journals appeared, over two thousand more between 1766 and 1790, the period when genuinely "professional" journals were founded.[22] At the point when a few isolated issues of journals with polemics between Catherine and Novikov command extraordinary attention, the private periodical press in the German-speaking lands was an enormous enterprise of translation, cultural mediation, distribution, popularization, artistic judgement, and moral instruction, in which by 1791, something like 7,000 living Germans were in print.[23] When one remembers that M. M. Shtrange's entire *demokraticheskaia intelligentsiia*[24] numbered only some fourscore names, the scale of difference is clear.

A familiar name in German publishing in the age of the Enlightenment was Friedrich Nicolai (1733–1811). Friend of Lessing, editor

---

[17] Wittmann, "Soziale und ökonomische Voraussetzungen," p. 15.

[18] Raabe, "Aufklärung durch Bücher," pp. 87–104, and his "Zum Bild des Verlagswesens," p. 67.

[19] *Svodnyi katalog* lists 8,956 editions; Petrine editions numbered 882 in civil script; with new titles in Cyrillic the total number of new titles could not have exceeded 12,000 for the century.

[20] Khoteev, *Kniga v Rossii v seredine XVIII v.*, p. 4.

[21] Koppitz, "Bibliographien als geistes- und kulturgeschichtliche Quellen," pp. 839–40; *Svodnyi katalog*, Vol. IV, *Periodika*.

[22] Lindemann, *Deutsche Presse bis 1815*, updates the classic compilation by Kirchner, *Das deutsche Zeitschriftenwesen*, (first ed., 1941).

[23] See Engelsing, "Die Perioden der Lesergeschichte," p. 984; on the roles of the press, see Martens, "Die Geburt des Journalisten," pp. 90–92; see also Raabe, "Die Zeitschrift als Medium der Aufklärung," pp. 103ff., and Göpfert, "Bemerkungen über Buchhändler und Buchhandel," pp. 69–83 with good bibliography, and in general his essays, *Vom Autor zur Leser*.

[24] Shtrange, *Demokraticheskaia intelligentsiia*.

of the two hundred and fifty volumes of the *Allgemeine deutsche Bibliothek* which appeared 1765–1805, he was set the goal of making German books available everywhere.[25] His individual efforts were almost as extensive as all Russian publishing combined. Equally important was the range of his publications. Among his titles formal theology was in second place, behind only the broad category of novels, tales, and plays.[26] His own shelf-lists as late as the eve of the French Revolution indicate that his two most extensive categories of books were moral and philosophical writings, followed closely by theology.[27] The repertoire of Nicolai's editions is evidence that the German *Aufklärung* was not anti-clerical or anti-theological. Its size suggests Russia's relative booklessness.

Throughout the Germanies Pietism transformed Christian ethics and produced the idea of an active life of useful morally responsible civic work, that was ultimately incorporated into the philosophy of Christian Wolff; this goal of personal well-being and utility to society (*Glückseligkeit und Nützlichkeit*), of personal independence and useful behavior, defined the new citizen. It blurred the distinction between religious and secular.[28] In the Western Europe of Spinoza, Bayle, the English Deists, and the radical Cartesians, and later of Voltaire and the Encyclopedists, a critique of the Christian tradition stood at the center of the Enlightenment. In German-reading lands, especially in the Protestant north, with a tradition stemming rather from Leibniz and Christian Wolff, there was less tension between Reason and Revelation. These Enlightenments were not wholly anti-religious movements.[29]

In central Europe, rather than rejecting Christ, Pietism made Christ "a citizen and a subject." The clergy assumed the role of Christ-like mediation, teaching a revived morality, opposing war and the slave trade, and teaching toleration and freedom of expression.[30] By the age of the Revolution this tradition had produced unorthodox theologian-pamphleteers who could preach that Enlightenment was moral and political. "For man as citizen it is the First Commandment that

---

[25] See Göpfert, "Bemerkungen."

[26] Raabe, "Der Verleger Friedrich Nicolai," p. 151.

[27] Raabe, "Zum Bild," p. 69.

[28] See Vierhaus, "Kulturelles Leben in Zeitalter des Absolutismus," pp. 26–30 and *passim*.

[29] Scholder, "Grundzüge der theologischen Aufklärung," p. 461.

[30] *Ibid.*, pp. 476–484.

Thou shalt hold the Law sacred! This is the foundation of human happiness."[31] It was also economic, calling for the encouragement of manufacturing and factories and the development of towns: without this component, with moral regeneration alone, the countryside would remain miserable, as cities drew everything to them, impoverishing the rural parts of the land: "so it is in most of the Catholic parts of Germany."

In Germany not merely the *Aufklärer* but the enlightened clergyman, Catholic and Lutheran, subjected the Bible to reinterpretation and engaged in the new oriental research. Contrary to popular generalizations, it was an enlightened clergy that spoke in defence of Jews, Negroes, and Indians, and "against the Christian inhumanity of the past." They spread the messages of patriotism and peace, and pioneered a new history which extolled progress and freedom and condemned tyranny.[32] When these clerics built their parish libraries to which all ranks of society had access, they included the giants of the seventeenth-century scientific revolution, rationalism, and natural law, the English, Scottish, and French Enlightenments, a great deal of history, and a vast range of theology and scripture. They collected as well a world library of literature, including the ancients in original languages, as well as Renaissance humanism and the French dramatists of the seventeenth-century, English letters, and of course, German literature.[33] The "clerical" collection, especially in northern Germany, did not vary from that of a nobleman, even at the end of the period.

On the German book market the Latin book represented 27.68% of the trade in 1740 and only 3.97% of the books of 1800. However, in the age of the French Revolution 88% of all university and school writings were still published in Latin; of works dealing with philology, Classical and non-Classical, 44% were in Latin, and in 1770 40% of all books of jurisprudence were still in Latin, as were over twenty-five percent of works dealing with medicine.[34] Furthermore, theology as an area of writing best held its percentage of the overall book trade as readership broadened. The decline in theology

---

[31] For this section, Herrmann, "Die Kodifizierung bürgerlichen Bewußtseins," pp. 321–333.

[32] Schütz, "Die Kanzel als Katheder der Aufklärung."

[33] Tiemann, "Die Butendach-Bibliothek."

[34] Wittmann, "Die frühen Buchhändlerzeitschriften," esp. pp. 837–40; see also on the ubiquitous Jentzsch, Langenbucher, *Der aktuelle Unterhaltungsroman*, pp. 48–53. Jentzsch, *Der deutsch-lateinische Büchermarkt*.

and the revolt against Latin came too late in the century to be much reflected in libraries amassed in the age of the Enlightenments.

A constancy in libraries spanned literate society top to bottom. At the zenith Goethe's[35] was a great Classical library with about a hundred and fifty titles of Greek letters, a hundred more of Latin, including nine editions of Cicero. His theology numbered about a hundred and thirty entries, including Scripture and exegesis, ecclesiastical history and historical theology, the largest segment, and sermons. But he also held thirty titles on Freemasonry and the occult, and while he had a good scientific collection of botany, chemistry, physics, mineralogy, anatomy, medicine and pharmacology, he held also forty titles on balneology, the European cult of curative waters.

In the second half of the century German aristocratic libraries began to show new strengths in contemporary French or English literature, but their traditional cores in the Classics, in sectarian and devotional religious readings, and in Renaissance humanism, showed no significant decline.[36] A working lawyer, Justus Möser (d. 1794), had over seventy-five titles among his *Auctores Classici*,[37] but the same core was to be found in the more typical library of Damian Hugo von Schönborn (1676–1743). He was Cardinal and Bishop of Speyer, whose library of two hundred volumes was one-half theology and about ten percent law. But Rudolf Franz Erwein von Schönborn (1677–1754) became the ruling Graf von Wiesentheid, and his library of 1800 volumes also held some forty percent theology. Only in the next generation, in the case of Hugo Damian Erwein von Schönborn (1738–1817) did the "modern" library appear, one in which Latin declined relatively, while modern history, the new French literature and to a lesser extent the English, all became areas of purchasing.[38]

In the age of the Enlightenments and Revolution there were collections in which older richness in pious, edifying, and liturgical publications expanded to include a wider range of moral literature,

---

[35] Ruppert, *Goethes Bibliothek. Katalog.*

[36] For the following see Pleticha, *Adel und Buch*, pp. 223, 279, 281, 292–96, and *passim.*, unless otherwise noted. See also, in addition to the works of Paul Raabe cited above, Arnold, "Der Fürst als Büchersammler," pp. 41–60, a good summary of the state of the art today.

[37] Meyer, "Bücher im Leben eines Verwaltungsjuristen," pp. 149–58.

[38] See also the library of the noble-divine, who wrote a tract on the religious reasons why the daughter of Caroline of Hessen should or should not enter into a Russian Orthodox marriage; Bräuning-Oktavio, "Zwei Privatbibliotheken."

as often in French as in German. In these libraries the literature of English sentimentalism and deism began to appear along with modern French authors, including the Encyclopedia's little flock and the sentimentalist offspring of J. J. Rousseau; absent were the Latin book and humanism. Who owned such books? These were collections of the devotional and the titillating, of the moral and the entertaining. These were the ladies' libraries.[39]

Surveying women's libraries, especially in northern Germany, one can watch Pietism transform traditional piety into social conscience and civic duty. Reading materials from the Halle divines and their songbooks evolved into a broader cult which grew to embrace Montaigne and Bellegarde, Fontenelle and Mme. Beaumont, Rousseau and Gellert, and among many female readers, also the Classics, especially morals and literature, almost invariably in French translations. Unlike their husbands and brothers, women's reading went almost directly from the medieval to the modern, although modern in this sense did not mean secular.

Among the *Bürger* and the *Bauer* something analogous happened. The age of the Enlightenments did not suddenly create widespread literacy, although figures even for Catholic Germany are quite impressive after 1750.[40] Benevolent German nobles distributed practical advice in millions of copies, for example R. Z. Becker's *Noth- und Hülfsbuchlein* for simple farmers. On the other hand we know that often village newspapers intended for the enlightenment of peasants did not reach them; as many as 80% of subscribers to one did not farm the land.[41] In the towns this was the age of the reading club and circle, the sort of vast pan-European phenomenon which would only touch Russia in the age of the Petrashevtsy, the middle of the nineteenth century.[42] As early as 1765 it was recognized that reading

---

[39] See for example *Ibid.*, "1. Die Bibliothek der Herzogin Caroline von Pfalz-Zweibrücke-Birkenfeld," pp. 686–775; Bräuning-Oktavio, "Die Bibliothek der großen Landgräfin Caroline," pp. 681–876; and Pleticha, *op. cit.*, pp. 125ff., 289, for the libraries of the Casteller Gräfinnen from the 1730s to the 1780s.

[40] Engelsing, *Analphabetentum und Lektüre*, pp. 47–48. 52, 61–63. At marriage the most likely to be illiterate were Jews, then Catholics, then Lutherans, and least likely, Pietists; *Ibid.*, p. 48.

[41] Wittmann, "Der lesende Landmann," pp. 145–9, on literacy, 161–162.

[42] On the reading circles see, for example, Prüsener, "Lesegesellschaften," Sauder, "Die Bücher des *Armen Mannes*," pp. 167–186; the essays in Dann, ed., *Lesegesellschaften und bürgerliche Emanzipation*; and van Dülmen, "Die Aufklärungsgesellschaften," pp. 81–99.

societies permitted an edition of 4000 copies to reach as many as 80,000 readers.[43]

At the lower end of the scale, among retailers in Frankfurt am Main in 1700, for example, 28% owned no books, and another 54% owned only religious books; only 7% owned more than five "worldly" books. By 1752 still 52% owned only religious tracts. As late as 1800 inventories from Frankfurt showed that 64% of shopkeepers owned no books, and only 12% had more than ten non-religious books.[44] But religion was the rule: one popular edition of the Bible, that prepared at the beginning of the century by Freiherr Karl Hildebrand von Canstein (1667–1717), sold 340,000 New Testaments and 480,000 Bibles between 1712 and 1739, and some three million Bibles by the close of the century.[45] Understandably at these levels of society, as in the case of women usually excluded from the universities, the Latin book was rare.

In the late eighteenth century a vast spectrum of personal libraries characterized Europe, from the massive collections of the savants to the solitary prayer-books of the poor. It is fair to say that new re-formed religions had attracted far more new readers than the forces of secularism. Nowhere were libraries void of the religious. The antique Classics reached larger audiences, increasingly in translations. Libraries document the end of the solitary reign of Latin in the schools, but if the Latin language was less universally the mark of an educated reader, a broadening readership of the middling classes and of women were fed a constant diet of Classical authors in translation, epigram, and paraphrase, particularly in a burgeoning periodical press.

2. *The Classics vs. Tradition in Catherine's Russia*

A. *Translating and Publishing the Classics*

Lord Macartney's hostile comment on the Russians' education is dated 1766:

> Our error with regard to [the Russians] is in looking upon this nation as a civilized one and treating them as such. It by no means merits

---

[43] Engelsing, *Analphabetentum*, p. 56.

[44] Engelsing, *Der Bürger als Leser*, pp. 92–100, 172–81, 206; and his *Analphabetentum*, p. 46.

[45] Engelsing, *Analphabetentum*, p. 54.

that title. . . . There is not one of the Ministry here that even understands Latin, and few that can be said to possess the common roots of
literature. . . .[46]

Russian diplomats in Macartney's ken, presumably the nobles employed in the College of Foreign Affairs, could not speak Latin, nor
could they discuss some notion of literature which Macartney thought
that "civilized" men should.[47] What steps did Russia take in the age
of Catherine II to spread the availability of authors of antiquity and
the study of Latin? Had Ukrainian humanism reached the nobility
serving in the College of Foreign Affairs by 1766, or was Macartney
mistaken?

The Latin curriculum was largely undisturbed in the West in the
gymnasium and the university. Even on its frontiers in the New World,
where innovation was prized more than at home, colonial universities were founded on the premise that all "incoming students should
have mastered the Greek and Latin languages. . . . The admissions
requirements included a command of Latin grammar and an ability
to translate Cicero and Virgil from Latin into English, and the New
Testament from Greek into Latin."[48] In colonial society, "solidly classical, the college entrance remained the same for about one hundred
and seventy-five years. The only addition was a dash of arithmetic."[49]
On the horizon loomed the expulsion of the Jesuits from education,
experiments in non-Classical educations, and the French Revolution
itself, but the Enlightenments and Catherine's reign began in the
atmosphere of undisturbed Classical values in the Western world.

At the beginning of her reign, Catherine had no objections to
Latin learning. She encouraged Dr. Daniel Dumaresq, for example,
who envisioned a Russian school system which branched into four
types of specialized higher education after a common elementary core-
curriculum; the first of the higher specialized courses was to be the

---

[46] Dukes, "The Russian Enlightenment," p. 176. He also said the bureaucrats
were uneducated in their craft, being incapable of understanding such standard authors
as Pufendorf or Grotius. The Ambassador de la Neuville had reported that he knew
of only four Latin speakers in Russia in the late seventeenth century: see Pekarskii,
Nauka i literatura, I, p. 186.

[47] One forgets how easily and effortlessly writers of that age conducted an inner
dialogue with Terence, Virgil, Horace, Juvenal and others, even in correspondence;
see, among a host of possible examples, Ischreyt, ed., *Die Beiden Nicolai*, pp. 180–82,
255, 272, 324, 326, 348, 508, and *passim*.

[48] Humphrey, *From King's College*, pp. 162–63.

[49] Gummere, *American Colonial Mind*, p. 56.

academic, based on Latin.[50] The redoubtable "Estimate" Brown was one of a series of foreign advisors of the Russians in early-modern times, from Leibniz to Diderot, who knew little of Russia and therefore dismissed all native institutions:

> The Russian empire is at present in that state of manners, knowledge, and policy, which renders it most susceptible of such a general improvement and civilization as are here pointed out. I will add, that I know of no other that is so. For most other nations are either too much sunk in barbarism, or too deeply tinctured with prior institutions, or they want the great connecting Imperial Power, which alone can bind the whole together. But the Russian empire hath (in many parts of it) so far emerged from barbarism as to be sensible of its own defects; and yet hath not so strongly, or universally, received any discordant institutions or impressions, which may not be gradually rooted out, or melted into the general plan of civilization; while the great fountain of power, her Imperial Majesty, leads the way in this grand and unequalled undertaking.[51]

Brown recommended that Russia annually export twenty-five to thirty youths for a proper education at Cambridge or Oxford, for which Latin was a prerequisite. A start was made in the 1760s, and by the mid-1770s several future teachers of Latin in Russian had indeed completed their studies in England.

Catherine thus began her reign with no hostility to Latin education. She sponsored some measures to encourage that definition of education and perpetuated the mixed pattern of the preceding decades in which diocesan Latin studies coexisted with nobles' academies and a variety of technical institutions. The experimental non-Latin institutions of her first educational advisor, Betskoi, did not disturb the diverse inherited networks.

She did encourage reading the Latin Classics. The one systematic and well-funded effort to produce translations of the Classical authors was the "Society Striving for the Translation of Foreign Books." If successful, this enterprise would have answered Macartney's call for the "common root" of literature at least for those not reading Latin.[52] The Translation Society came into existence in the fall of

---

[50] Hans, "Dumaresq, Brown, and some early educational projects," pp. 229–30.

[51] *Ibid.*, pp. 232–33, and below, pp. 234–35.

[52] Semennikov, *Sobranie staraiushcheesia*; Marker, *Publishing, Printing, and the Origins*, pp. 91–94; de Madariaga, *Russia in the Age of Catherine*, p. 330, devotes one paragraph to the topic. The Society for Translation has been studied only by V. P. Semennikov. Marker's argues that through the Society, "Classicism retained the

1768 when Catherine designated 5,000 rubles of her personal funds per annum for paying translators, some of whom eventually were very well paid indeed. The idea for the society arose the previous year during her famous barge-trip down the Volga, when her courtly assembly had begun to translate collectively Marmontel's *Bélisaire*.[53] Included in that polite company had been V. G. Orlov, youthful Director of the Academy of Sciences, and A. P. Shuvalov, correspondent of Voltaire, and the initial proposal for a Society was to render a translation of Diderot's *Encyclopédie*. The last volumes of the Paris Folio Edition had just appeared.

Adding the Classics to the *Encyclopedia* was apparently the proposal of the Ukrainian Hryhorij Koznyc'kyj (Gregorii Vasilevich Koznitskii). He, with Orlov and Shuvalov, became the third director of the Translation Society, but he was intellectually light-years away from Catherine's dashing young favorites. He was an erudite humanist, Kievan born in 1724, and Kievan-Academy educated in languages ancient and modern, who had subsequently studied in Breslau and Leipzig; he had himself already done translations of Lucian, Sappho, Livy, Ovid, and Jonathan Swift, before he translated Chapter 15 of *Bélisaire*, and before the Society was formed.[54] Later secretary to Catherine, in 1759 he had written an article "On the Use of Mythology," in which he had argued "There is no history closer to our age than that of ancient Rome."[55] If Orlov and Shuvalov guaranteed the Society Catherine's favor and fashionable contemporary French tastes, Koznyc'kyj gave it substance in the Classics.

The enterprise began with high expectations. "In its day it was probably the leading voice of the French Enlightenment," especially because "print runs of most of the Translation Society's early publications were high—normally 1,200 copies per book."[56] Among the

---

preeminence in Catherinian Russia which it had held since Peter's day." Marker, *op. cit*, pp. 92, 208.

[53] Potboiler novels are similarly written; see the scandalous "Penelope Ashe," *Naked Came the Stranger. Bélisaire* subsequently saw seven editions, 1768–96. See Marker, *op. cit.*, p. 206, and especially Alexander, *Catherine the Great*, pp. 107–12. Twenty years earlier Tatishchev had proposed such a society without success. See Iukht, "Sviazi V. N. Tatishchev," pp. 364–65.

[54] Kuliabko, *Zamechatel'nye pitomtsy*, pp. 95–103; Semennikov, *op. cit.*, p. 8; Novikov, *Opyt' istoricheskago Slovaria*, pp. 101–02. Koznyc'kyj was also a Synodal censor; see Tiulichev, "Tsensura izdanii Akademii nauk," p. 105.

[55] Baehr, *The Paradise Myth*, pp. 51–52.

[56] Marker, *op cit.*, pp. 91–92. The standard works on translating the Enlightenment are Shtrange, "'Entsiklopediia' Didro," Svetlov, "Russkie perevody proizvedenii,"

publications of the Society was the first Russian rendering of the *Iliad* by Petr Ekimov, Koznyc'kyj's own *Metamorphosis* of Ovid, and the only eighteenth-century printing of some of Terence' *Comedies*. The Society also issued the *Memorable Deeds and Sayings* of Valerius Maximus, the only edition in Russia for this popular writer who has been harshly judged as one who "himself has nothing to say worth hearing." It was also responsible for the only edition of Claudius Claudianus, "the last poet of classical Rome."[57]

The Society for Translation did reasonably well by the ancient historians, although glaring omissions remained to the end of the century. It was responsible for the only translation of Caesar's *Gallic Wars* and a version of Suetonius' *De vita Caesarum (On the Life of the Caesars)*. Tacitus was poorly served by eighteenth-century Russia, and the Translation Society did little to correct the neglect, publishing only the short geographic and ethnologic *Germania, (On the Origin, Geography, Institutions, and Tribes of the Germans)*. Also translated was the *Bibliotheca* of Diodorus Siculus, a Stoic, a contemporary of Livy, whose Greek-based work related the early history of the Assyrians, Medes, Persians, Syrians, Greeks, and early Romans. The Translation Society also published from the Greek the only editions of the *History of the Roman State* by Herodianus (170–241), and of the Greek and Roman history of the non-professional Velleius Paterculus.[58] These were interesting additions to the small corpus of ancient history available in Russia, but lacking Thucydides, for example,[59] they were so unsystematic that one senses the influence of the reading habits of the old *prikazy* which preferred the good yarn to a systematic education in the Classics. The Society did successfully market a new translation

---

and Berkov, "Histoire de l'Encyclopédie." The Ukrainian, Kievan-educated, Skovoroda did translations of Cicero and Plutarch, but they did not see print. See Tschizewskij, *Skovoroda*, p. 22.

[57] The editions in this paragraph can be located in the *Svodnyi katalog* and in Semennikov respectively under the following item numbers: Homer, 1544 and 85 (see also Egunov, *Gomer*, pp. 49–107); Ovid, 4834 and 35; Terence, 7195 and 54; Valerius Maximus, 828 and 31 (see also Hadas, *Roman Literature*, New York, 1952, p. 238); Claudianus, 2927 and 111 (Hadas, *op. cit.*, p. 388).

[58] These editions can be located in the *Svodnyi katalog* and in Semennikov respectively under item numbers: Caesar, 8090 and 58; Suetonius 6333 and 86; Tacitus, 7166 and 42; Diodorus 1899 and 58 (see Hadas, *op. cit.*, p. 233); Herodianus 1401 and 65; and Velleius, 894 and 64 (Hadas, 236).

[59] Herodotus had been published by the Academy of Sciences in 1763–64 in an edition of 600 copies. *Svodnyi katalog*, item 1402. The translation was done by the prolific Andrei Andreevich Nartov, son of the well-known Petrine mechanic, one of the successful new families of the Petrine revolution; see Danilevskii, *Nartov*.

of Flavius Josephus' *Jewish Antiquities*, widely available for over a century; it saw three editions.[60]

In terms of ancient philosophy, the Translation Society was remarkably random. It did publish three works by Cicero, On Good and Evil, On Comfort, and On the Nature of the Gods *(De finibus bonorum et malorum, De consolatione,*[61] *De natura deorum)*.[62] But this was a small part of his opus, great deficiencies being the orations and the letters. The Society produced the only edition of Plato in eighteenth-century Russia, an impressive four-volume set which included the *Republic* and the *Laws*, as well as twenty-three of the thirty-six dialogues, including the *Apology, Crito, Phaedo, Alcibiades I & II, Laches, Meno, Ion, Phaedrus, Georgias, Hippias Major* and *Minor*, and the *Symposium*. Translated by the priest Ioann Sidorovskii and the servitor Matfei Pakhomov, and issued in just 300 copies for the young ladies of Smolnyi, this was a significant addition to the philosophic literature in Russia.[63] These were the major successes of the Translation Society, and they constituted the major effort at making the Classics available to Russian readers.

The Translation Society's Classical list, however, faced many problems. The highest priority remained the French Enlightenment rather than the cultural values of the ancients. The first publication of the Society in 1769 was Voltaire's *Candide* in 1200 copies, a successful endeavor followed by further editions in 1779 and 1789. A series of topical selections from the *Encyclopédie* and Montesquieu's *Considerations on the Causes of the Greatness of the Romans and their Decline* appeared, followed by La Chalotais' plan for national education in the absence of the Jesuits,[64] and Baron Dimsdale on inoculations. In fact, it was not until the Society's thirty-first publication that an ancient author appeared.[65]

Furthermore, the large editions envisioned by the founders of the

---

[60] The *Jewish Antiquities* was published in 1779–83, again in 1787, and again in 1795; an edition of his *Jewish War* appeared in 1786–87; see the *Svodnyi katalog*, items 2647–50, and Semennikov, item 105.

[61] Hadas, *op. cit.*, p. 128, says it is lost.

[62] For these editions, see the *Svodnyi katalog*, and Semennikov respectively: for Cicero, items 8116 and 66, 8117 and 77, 8119 and 104 (this text, *De natura deorum*, alone had a second edition, 1793, 410 copies); for Plato below, 5351 and 109.

[63] *Svodnyi katalog*, item 5351, published 1780–85, three volumes in four parts.

[64] La Shalote, *Opyt narodnago vospitaniia*, St. Petersburg, 1770; *Svodnyi katalog*, item 3485.

[65] Semennikov, *op. cit.*, p. 40.

Society were soon replaced by smaller ones. Among early publications of the Classics, only Koznyc'kyj's prose translation of Ovid—a text already available in Petrine times—saw the impressive press-run of 1200 copies;[66] editions of 600 were common in the first half of the 1770s, and printings of only 300 copies usual thereafter. "A buying public for serious works in Russian was not yet in existence."[67] Not only did the Classics appear later than the moderns, they represented only about twenty percent of the Society's offerings, and most were found among the later editions of a few hundred copies.

A short list of editions that sold well or were reprinted included only Flavius Josephus of the Classics, already a favorite in Muscovy. Other successful editions included the naughty *Candide*, *Gulliver's Travels*, Comenius' *Orbis Pictus*, "Chinese Thoughts" translated from the Manchurian, L. Euler's popularizing "Letters on various physical and philosophical matters," an unidentified little French pamphlet on studying science.[68] This list, void of the serious Classics, with its emphasis on traditional genres of the *conte*, the popularization, the foreign and fantastic voyage, seems to attest to the survival of old courtly tastes into Catherine's reign. It evidences the failure of humanism to create a new reading public even in the Russian language.[69]

That conclusion is reinforced when one considers the sad demise of the Translation Society. In 1783 it found itself burdened with debts which smaller editions could not erase, debts that neither Novikov in Moscow nor the Academy of Sciences could absorb, and faced with new leadership in the person of Catherine's confident,

---

[66] It was followed by V. I. Maikov's verse translation, not a Society publication, and then by a new edition, translated from the French of A. Banier, which appeared in 1794–95; his elegy "Tristia" appeared in 1795; *Svodnyi katalog*, items 4829–37.

[67] Jones, *Nikolai Novikov*, pp. 93–4.

[68] Semennikov, *op. cit.*, pp. 20–21. According to Semennikov the Society published "Sul'tser," *O poleznom s iunoshestvom chtenii drevnikh klassicheskikh pisatelei*, St. Petersburg, 1774, 2nd ed., Moscow, 1787, to encourage sales of its Classical authors. Neither title nor author appear in the *Svodnyi katalog*. The author was probably Johann Georg Sulzer (1729–79), a popular moralist, and the book may have been his *Kurzer Begriff aller Wißenschaften*, 2nd ed., Leipzig, 1759. It was a remarkable survey of learning, notable for its graceful and harmonious evocation of ancient pagan authors with their modern Christian counterparts. In discussing Philosophy he could move from Socrates, Plato, and Aristotle to Thomas Aquinas, Descartes, Leibniz, and Christian Wolff, and Morals from Aristotle and Cicero to Grotius and Wolff. For his 1773 memorandum on school for Russia, see Rozhdestvenskii, *Ocherki po istorii sistem*, p. 321, appendix, pp. 43–48.

[69] See the analogous conclusion suggested in Levin, "Translations of Henry Fielding's Works."

E. R. Dashkova. She had just returned from abroad, overseeing the
education of her son, and writing a memoir that would establish her
enlightened reputation. The trip had produced meetings with Voltaire
and Diderot, and with Adam Smith and Robertson. She assumed
the duties of directing the Academy of Sciences when a damning
financial reckoning for the Translation Society had just been made.
Not surprisingly, her enlightened reputation notwithstanding, within
six months she decisively brought subsidized translating and publishing to an abrupt end.[70] Bits and pieces of work underway would
trickle out for years, but systematic support for publishing the Classics
in Russian, modest and short-lived as it had been, came to a close.[71]

A bit more of Plutarch appeared, a further edition of Flavius
Josephus, and Aulus Gellius' (ca. 123–ca. 165) *Attic Nights*, "a well-
stuffed rag bag."[72] Prepared but unpublished were the *Odessey* by
P. Ekimov, selections from Lucan's *Pharsalia*, and Strabo's *Geography*.
They represented a fading world. By the end of the period, just before
the formal closing of the Society, orders for new translations came
from not from humanists, but from the newly established Commission on National Schools. Its first two requests were for the *Life of
Jesus Christ* and *Moral Tales from Biblical Events*, translations of works
of Jacob Friedrich Fedderson.[73] The age of the Classics in translation,
and of the *Encyclopédie* in Russia, was passing. These new requests for
translations in the early 1780s were part of a major redirection of
Russian education to a single goal, and it was away from the pagan

---

[70] Neither Dashkova's memoirs, nor her correspondence with Catherine for the
period 1783–84, reveal reasons other than financial for the decision to close the
Translation Society. The former notes the Academy's debts, but little else. See
Dashkova, *Zapiski*, pp. 143, 148, and *passim*, and Pekarskii, "Materialy dlia istorii
zhurnal'noi i literaturnoi deiatel'nosti," Prilozhenie 6, 74–87. On her time in England with her son, Cross, *"By the Banks of the Thames"*, pp. 131–34, and for a survey
of the literature on her, his review in the *Study Group on Eighteenth-Century Russia
Newsletter*, No. 6 (1978), 71–76.

[71] Semennikov, *op. cit.*, pp. 21–23, 65–77. Twenty-nine works remained unpublished in 1783. At the time the Society closed Novikov attempted to found a "Translating Seminar" at Moscow University, using its students, but it seems to have failed.
See Svetlov, *Izdatel'skaia deiatel'nost' N. I. Novikova*, pp. 46–59.

[72] Hadas, *Latin Literature*, p. 351.

[73] Semennikov, *op. cit.*, p. 77. Fedderson (1736–88) was a Pietist moralist, and
requested were translations of his *Das Leben Jesu für Kinder*, 4th ed., Frankfurt, 1782,
and *Lehrreiche Erzählungen aus der biblischen Geschichte für Kinder*, Frankfurt, 1778. A Russian
version of his *Beyspiele der Weisheit und Tugend aus der Geschichte mit Erinnerungen für
Kinder*, Halle, 1780, did appear in Moscow, 1787. Nor did he neglect tender audiences other than children. See his *Lehren der Weisheit für das Frauenzimmer*, Flensburg,
1760.

Classics in any language.[74] Dashkova believed the Academy's role was the advancement of native Russian scholarship, and the closure of the Translation Society reflected the Russianist revival.[75]

Early projections of sales for the translated Classics were overly optimistic. In the 1790s century-old favorites still sold briskly. A new edition of Aesop sold 359 of its 900 copies at 65 kopecks each; all of the available Marcus Aurelius sold at 65 kopecks, and Quintus Curtius Rufus, known in seventeenth-century collections and published under Peter, still sold 284 of its 442 copies at an expensive 1 ruble, 50 kopecks. Cheaper editions of the Classics, newly made available by the Translation Society, however would not sell: only

55 of 510	copies of	Epictetus	sold at	25	kopecks,
2 of 43	"	Hesiod	"	30	" ,
1 of 299	"	Tacitus	"	15	" ,
12 of 251	"	Horace	"	20	" ;

At the same time expensive editions of familiar reading materials did sell. Flavius Josephus' *Jewish War*, available in one form or another for a century and a half, sold 65 copies at 2 rubles 20 kopecks the set.[76] New translations did not sell. The history of translating and of publishing was far removed from actual reading. The new translations had created little new demand.

Much suggests the survival of the reading habits of the Muscovite court. A third of a century earlier Quintus Curtius' *Life of Alexander*, Aesop and other fabulists, had sold well in Moscow, but the first edition of new and important titles like Cicero's *Duties (De officiis)*, did not. Only 49 copies of 210 available sold in three years. Only 26 copies of Cornelius Nepos *Lives of Illustrious Generals* sold, although the little book of Stoic philosophy did sell well in the first decade of Moscow University's classes; this seemed to be an exception.[77]

Nor did European and Latin language presss ever establish them-

---

[74] See Chapter IV below. The following sentence was suggested by Ms. Sherri Raney, who has begun her dissertation on Dashkova at Oklahoma State University.

[75] On the Muscovite clerical revival, see Chapter IV below.

[76] For the above, Zaitseva, "Assortment knizhnoi lavki," pp. 140–67.

[77] For the above, Tiulichev, "Prodazha v Moskve izdanii." On Stoicism at Moscow University, see Gleason, *Moral Idealists, Bureaucracy*, pp. 87ff. A total of nine catalogues of books for sale between 1731 and 1752 exist, and they allow one to say something about the availability of books in Latin, German, French, Dutch, and Italian in St. Petersburg, but not about sales. The summarizing techniques of Soviet historians also make it difficult to identify Classical authors on the shelves. See Kopanev, "Rasprostranenie inostrannoi knigi."

selves as a vehicle for the Classics in Russia.[78] In the age of the
Translation Society l'Abbé d'Olivet's French edition of Cicero's selected
Pensées for youth was published (1767). Latin editions included Pliny's
Letters (St. Petersburg, 1774), to accompany a Russian edition,
Plutarch's *Demosthenes* and his *oratio funebris* (Moscow, 1777, 1778), and
Ovid's *Metamorphosis* (St. Petersburg, 1777). Also issued was a German
edition of Terence, *Lehrbuch für Schauspieldichter* with Donatus' com-
mentary. They had been preceded only by an edition of Cornelius
Nepos (1762), and were followed late in the century by partial editions
of Virgil's *Aeneid* and *Georgics* (1786, 1791, 1796), of fifteen pages of
Xenophon (1788), and by an edition of Horace, *Epistolae* (Mitau, 1798).
These were chiefly instructional editions for the gymnasia of the
Academy in Petersburg and of Moscow University, and did not mirror
changed tastes in reading.

Meanwhile, where permitted, the Classical authors enjoyed ongoing publication in Russia's western borderlands. In Vil'nius Latin
culture continued to flourish, as between 1739 and 1793 no fewer
than twenty-two editions of the old Jesuit grammar text by Alvarez
appeared. Likewise there were fourteen editions of Cicero, some for
school use, some bilingual, Polish and Latin. Vil'nius also saw five
Polish editions of Seneca, and Latin editions of Catullus, Horace,
Cornelius Nepos' *Trojan War*, Virgil, and Sallust.[79] A variety of presses,
Polish, Slavonic, and Latin existed in the reg;on of Belorussia.[80] One
decidedly Polish press was that of the Radziwills in Niasviz, which
published Latin editions of Cicero and others in the 1760s. Likewise
in the 1780s and 1790s the Jesuit press in Polock produced Alvarez'
textbook, as well as Cicero, Horace, and others. The Dominicans in
Slonim also kept Alvarez in print. When one recalls that the Baltic
areas also remained centers of German book distribution throughout
the eighteenth century,[81] and recalls that foreigners and especially
Germans dominated the production and especially the distribution
of books in Moscow and in St. Petersburg even in the late eighteenth

---

[78] *Svodnyi katalog knig na inostrannykh iazykakh, izdannykh v Rossii v XVIII veka*, 3vv. [to
date], L, 1984–86.
[79] Cepiene & Petrauskiene, *Vilniaus Akademijos Spaustuves Leidiniai 1576–1805.
Bibliografija.*
[80] Mal'dzis, "Knigadrukavanne Belarusi"; see also Doroshevich, "Prosveshchenie
v Belorussii." A fine study of the vigorous Jesuit educational effort in the area in the
age of the Translation Society, and of the Partitions, is Litak, "Wandlungen im
polnischen Schulwesen."
[81] Latsis, "Knizhnoe delo v Latvii."

century, one begins to suspect how limited were the changes since the days of Simeon Polockij.[82]

Catherine had offered the Classics in Russian, but few partook. Russia enthusiastically absorbed territories westward, but timidly in matters of culture.

B. *Book Consumption in an Enlightened Age*

Soviet and Western historians infatuated with the statistics of books printed in eighteenth-century Russia forget that we know a great deal about what most Russians read well into Catherine's reign. The Latin book did not find a niche in Russian cultural life. The story of reading in early-modern Russia is that of the resiliency of seventeenth-century book habits, in both religious and secular tastes. It is *not* the story of a culture that crumbled with the first appearance of the West.

Before, and long after the age of Peter, the only really popular reading material in Russia were manuscript *sborniki*, or collections.[83] These traditional collections, roughly equivalent to *The Old Farmer's Almanac*, existed in huge numbers. Their readership ranged from court circles and upper nobility to the bureaucracy, provincial gentry, merchants and urban classes, the clergy and even serfs. From owners' marks and signatures we know that the manuscript reading materials of the eighteenth century were not class-divided, that identical works were consumed at all levels of society.[84] Peasants and Old Believers naturally tended to own and presumably to read the most traditional collections which contained tales like Woe and Misfortune, St. George and the Dragon, the Fall of Jerusalem, on David and Solomon, On the Kingdom of Babylon, Il'ia Muromets, or Shemiaka's Judgement.[85]

---

[82] Marker, *op. cit.*, pp. 158–165, is very good, but also see the German literature on J. F. Hartknoch, Russia's first private commercial book publisher, by Ischreyt, "Die königsberger Freimauererloge"; Amburger, "Buckdruck, Buchhandel und Verlage"; as well as Kondakova, "K voprosu o formirovanii professii," and Zaitseva, "Inostrannye knigotorgovtsy," and on Russian dealers, Zaitseva, "Novye materialy o russkikh knizhnykh lavkakh."

[83] Speranskii, *Rukopisnye sborniki XVIII veka*, posthumously published. A bibliography of his works was included, pp. 226–255, covering the years 1889–1963. The manuscript of the book is dated 1934–36. *Ibid.*, pp. 26, 174–80; p. 14 Speranskii talked (in 1934) of the *perestroika* of the "Marxist-Leninist methodology of literary study."

[84] *Ibid.*, pp. 18, 86–99.

[85] *Ibid.*, pp. 23–31, 99, 115–22.

The manuscripts read by the clergy were virtually identical. All showed incremental change over time.

This Muscovite reading culture survived the brutally enforced Petrine educational transformations. Indeed for the eighteenth century, the number of surviving copies grew steadily. Copied and recopied, cheaper than printed books, they consistently absorbed those bits and pieces of Peter's print revolution which fit their preconceived parameters.

Manuscripts did not disappear with the printed book, but fed on it. For example, by mid-century manuscript miscellanies contained a wider repertoire of tales and adventures, translated treaties, fictitious "conversations" between Peter and other monarchs, works of Teofan, tales from Aesop, and descriptions of Sweden, all borrowed from printed books of the Petrine era.[86] Occasionally these adoptions from printed materials touched on the Classics, as in the case of Aesop, or a satire of Horace which appeared in a single manuscript. A few Latin manuscripts are known to have circulated. They had contents similar to those in Russian; they can be identified with owners at diocesan schools. These Latin *sborniki* contained the tales, religious polemics, Latin moral adages, and apocrypha of the more numerous Russian collections.[87] This is remarkable. It indicates that a few Russians who had been Latin educated, presumably at the Academy of Sciences or a diocesan academy, reverted to traditional reading materials, even when they read in Latin!

These monuments of Russian "popular reading" long survived the print revolution. They evidenced the less than revolutionary elementary-educational changes of the Petrine era. The testify not only to the survival of Muscovite reading patterns well into Russian times, but to the active involvement of Russians in choosing their own reading material. Peter's state-operated publishing enterprise decided what would and would not be printed. Ordinary Russians decided what would be read.

Most historians accept Peter Burke's observation that as Europe approached the Romantic age, many nations' urban, educated, monied elites involved themselves in a relatively sudden "Rediscovery of the Volk."[88] Elite and popular cultures that had been separating since

---

[86] *Ibid.*, pp. 32–42.

[87] *Ibid.*, pp. 39–41, 100–114.

[88] I refer to Burke, *Popular Culture*. See *Ibid.*, 48–78.

the rise of Humanism now began to coalesce as intellectuals began to study fold culture. In Russia the separation of cultures had never been as great. The survival of popular-reading *sborniki* at all levels of society made for an easier transition to mass culture. Educated elite Russian writers like N. G. Kurganov (1726–96) in his *Pis'movnik* of 1769, and M. D. Chulkov (1738–1792), in his *Sobranie raznykh pesen*, turned to these manuscript *sborniki* for "folk" wisdom, which they put into print. The process in Europe appears abrupt because of centuries of separate cultures.

Russia was quite different, as European elite educations had touched so few. Every European literati knew Horace. In the east, he belonged only to "foreigners in Russia and Ukrainian bishops in Russian dioceses." Full stop. The most popular printed book in Russia in the eighteenth century was the Psalter. It flourished in well over two hundred editions, and the size of these editions grew steadily with time.

The magnificent catalogues of Russian printed books do not mirror Russian reading. Only "the myth of a new Russia" in the Petrine era, and the myth of a Russian Enlightenment, emphasize the secular editions of his press. Manuscripts remained cheaper and more accessible than the printed book well into the century.[89] Most Russians continued to read the manuscript *sborniki*, the old Orthodox *Volksliteratur* of saints' lives and historical legends, now supplemented by a bit of Ovid, newer Christian literature ranging from Thomas à Kempis to the Pietist Arndt, lore from the herbals, and the spotty appearance of a few lines from Plato and Horace.[90]

The secular, civil-script, printed book was less read than the old manuscript.[91] The Petrine age produced scant formal literature of "relatively little interest" because this older "chaotic and literarily immature" culture was undisturbed, just as its reforms did not disturb the old *Ladder of Literacy* which culminated in the Psalter. Thanks to the vitality of the hand-written *sborniki*, which survived in far greater numbers than the printed books of the age, Muscovite reading habits survived. The new century in Russian literature was

---

[89] Rothe, *Religion und Kultur*, pp. 7–8, 14, 34–38, 110.

[90] *Ibid.*, pp. 38, 58, 59, 78, 80, 85, 89–90, 110–112, and *passim*.

[91] Rothe, *op. cit.*, pp. 34–38; see also Derzhavina, *Fatsetsii*, p. 40; Derzhavina, 'Velikoe Zertsalo', pp. 155–174. Blium, "Massovoe chtenie v russkoi provintsii," pp. 37–57, remarks that 99% of all peasant reading well into the nineteenth century was of this type, and all of it was in manuscript.

"by no means separated from the native traditions of form by a sharp discontinuity."[92]

Indeed, to some extent, the public determined what the press offered. The government's forced publication of militaria dropped off sharply after the death of Peter, to be replaced by the kinds of literature which the seventeenth-century had accepted, above all by calendars and traditional religious literature.[93] Published catalogues of eighteenth-century ecclesiastical books generally show only 70% of the actual number of Books of Hours published, only 83% of the teaching Psalters, 60% of the primers, and for other traditional church liturgical books the figures are even more dramatic: recent research has indicated that in some cases 90 or 95% of editions of religious service books remain uncatalogued. Thus here too there was continuity. Among civil-script books calendars and other popular reading materials were the most published and the most bought.[94] The *Svodnyi katalog* of civil-script publications is not even a first approximation of eighteenth-century Russian reading.[95]

Book sales show that what sold best in mid-century was what had entered the literary canon of the courtiers in the age of manuscripts, works like Aesop's Fables and adventure tales.[96] Religious literature sold massively to all levels of society in 1739, but no clergyman bought Pufendorf's *On Duties*; such books reached only a tiny readership. A wide spectrum of bought Quintus Curtius' adventurous *Alexander*.[97] The Latin book failed to penetrate that old culture. When Russians tried to learn languages, they typically progressed little beyond the ABCs. In the bookstore of the Academy of Sciences in Petersburg between 1749 and 1753 primers made up a full 30% of all Latin books sold, over 50% of the German, and over 80% of the French, although the cult of French was still in its infancy. The image of the Academy of Sciences and of its European staff as an island in a sea of traditional Slavic Orthodoxy is nowhere more obvious.[98]

When one is inclined to regard three hundred copies of Plato as

---

[92] Brown, *18th Century Russian Literature*, pp. 4, 14, 16.
[93] Luppov, "Pechatnaia i rukopisnaia kniga v Rossii."
[94] Luppov, "K voprosu ob utochnenii repetuara russkoi knigi."
[95] See Afanas'eva, "Rasprostranenie kirillicheskoi knigi," and Baklanova, "O sostave bibliotek moskovskikh kuptsov," pp. 644–49, who discusses the books of 14 wine merchants prosecuted in 1738.
[96] Luppov, "Die Nachfrage nach Büchern," p. 263.
[97] Luppov, "Kto pokupal knigi v Peterburge."
[98] Tiulichev, "Knizhnaia torgovlia," p. 23.

significant, one must remember that pagan sales were wholly eclipsed by the consumption of traditional religious primers in the old Cyrillic script, in scores of printings of hundreds of copies.[99] The Latin Classics were not published in Russia to any substantial degree. There had been a flurry of translations between 1768 and 1783, but these initial editions found no market. The Latin translations were minor in comparison to the fashionable French, and the effort was already much reduced in scale when the Society and its definition of "Enlightenment" were axed by Dashkova. The consumption of traditional readers of religion and adventure tales constituted the only real book market in the age.

Theoretically, of course, the Russians need not have actually done the publishing themselves—they could have imported Latin books. Identifying who might have bought such books entails understanding who actually learned and used Latin in the middle of the eighteenth-century.

3. *Learning Latin in Post-Petrine Russia*

Who studied Latin? Recent collective biographical studies have revealed the links between Latin education and career in the middle of the eighteenth century.[100] Some patterns have emerged. It is generally recognized that only a minute number of Russians actually born in Petrine times, the famous universal scientist Lomonosov and the geographer S. P. Krasheninnikov among them, subsequently contributed to Russian book culture.

Thereafter, however, the numbers grew. Of thirty-eight students who attended the Academic University by mid-century, about half were born between 1725 and 1734. This small "generation" comprised the first offspring of Teofan and the Kievan humanists. Russian nobles were absent. These Academic students were chiefly the sons of the ecclesiastical estate, those most easily coerced to Latin studies by the newly-appointed Ukrainian humanist bishops. A small minority included one son of a *raznochinets*, a Cossack's son born in the Ukraine, and a couple of soldiers' sons. Before coming to Petersburg, they

---

[99] Afanas'eva, "Izdanie azbuki i bukvarei."

[100] Kuliabko, *Zamechatel'nye pitomtsy*; *M. V. Lomonosov i uchebnaia deiatel'nost'*; Shtrange, *Demokraticheskaia intelligentsiia*.

had been Latin schooled.[101] Most had attended the Slavo-Greco-Latin
Academy in Moscow, and the remainder were schooled in Kiev, in
Teofan's academy in the Alexander-Nevskii monastery, or in the Latin
school in Novgorod, which owed its quality to the second career of
the Lichud brothers, resurrected from the exile imposed by the last
Patriarch.

After humanistic educations, they were recruited to the Germans'
Academic University, and they subsequently became the backbone
of non-noble, European-educated, Russian society. They translated
the Classics, Sallust and Horace, Cicero, Ovid, as well as the moderns,
Jakob Bielfeld's *Institutions politiques*, Pufendorf, Erasmus, Locke, Pope,
and the *Encyclopédia*.[102]

Typical was Hryhorij Poletika (Gregorii Andreevich Poletika, 1725–
1784). Born in the Ukraine and educated at Kiev, he did not attend
the Academic University: he participated in the Nakaz Commission,
translated part of Aristotle's *Politics*, part of Xenophon, the Stoic
Enchiridion of Epictetus, lost one personal library to a fire, amassed
another, and wrote one of the first histories of Ukraine. His brother
Ivan (1722–1783) received a medical degree abroad after his Kievan
Latin education, and was the first "Russian" to become a professor
at a foreign university, at Kiel. Many of this "generation" were born-
Ukrainians; some studied in Britain, including Semen Desnic'kyj
(Desnitskii), the translator of Blackstone, son of a Ukrainian artisan,
who was in Glasgow, or in Germany, like Koznyc'kyj of the Translation Society, or N. N. Motonis, translator of Erasmus' *Colloquies*,
both of whom studied in Breslau and Leipzig. Indeed, so many were
Ukrainians that Muscovy seems not to have adopted Latin studies
at all.[103]

---

[101] The most recent survey of figures for ecclesiastical and lay attendance at the
schools is Bryner, *Der geistliche Stand*, pp. 116ff. They show that Kiev consistently
educated non-clerics, Moscow and Teofan's own school slightly less, and the new
schools established after 1721 less still. See on priests's sons who studied in England,
Cross, "*By the Banks of the Thames*," pp. 99–112. See Kharlampovich, *Malorossiiskoe
vliianie*, pp. 781–91, on the Kievans' translations.

[102] See the section on the Translation Society above. Of 1685 books published by
the Academy's Press, 573 were translations, and the Moscow Academy was the
most important source of translators. See Istrina, "Akademicheskie perevodchiki,"
pp. 105, 107, and *passim*.

[103] See Kaganov, "G. A. Poletika i ego knizhnye interesy"; Cross, "*By the Banks*,"
pp. 122ff.; and on the 134 Ukrainians who studied in Germany, P. Kirchner,
"Studenten aus der Linksufrigen Ukraine," pp. 367–75. The standard work is
Amburger, "Die russischen Studenten an deutschen Universitäten," in his *Beiträge*,
pp. 214–232.

In 1748 Trediakovskii was still recruiting priests' sons from the clerical academies for the Academy of Sciences' higher classes.[104] From Moscow's Ecclesiastical Academy he selected Anton Barsov, who would later translate eleven works, Boris Volkov (1732–62) who would render Cicero's *On Duties* and Pufendorf, Nikolai Popovskii, who would Russify Locke's *On Education*, and Pope's *Essay on Man*. In Teofan's Nevskii school he found Ivan Barkov (1732–1768) who would translate Sallust, Horace, and Marcus Aurelius, and the Ukrainian Stefan Razumovskii (1734–1812), who would render Tacitus.[105] In Novgorod's seminary he found Mikhail Sofronov (1729–1760)[106] who would in his brief life become an Adjunct of the Academy and a translator of science, and Filipp Iaremskii (b. 1729), who would become the first teacher of Latin at Moscow University. Such was the first group, the priests' sons who would serve the short-lived Translation Society.

This clerical first "generation" was the educational and social infrastructure for the reading, translating, and owning the Classics in eighteenth-century Russia. In maturity, it would be synonymous with Catherine's Society Striving to Translate. Nobles excluded themselves.

A critical moment separated them from a second "generation." It came in the early 1750s. Suddenly the Academy of Sciences' benches were filled with youths who were born between 1735 and about 1750. They were almost without exception the sons of soldiers and a few other *raznochintsy*, and no sons of priests, and of course, no nobles. All had their preparatory schooling not in the Ukrainian humanists' schools, but in the Academy of Sciences' own Gymnasium, now firmly established as a Latin grammar school. Education there was not markedly different than in the Kievans' colleges; it too consisted in a grounding in Latin grammar, rhetoric, and poetics, but there the teachers were German humanists.[107] The elimination of priests' sons

---

[104] Biographical information is derived from the sketches in Kuliabko, *Pitomtsy*. On Trediakovskii's own "most uncommon youth" and Latin education, see Brown, *18th Century Russian Literature*, pp. 54ff., and Florovskii, "Latinskie shkoly v Rossii."

[105] See in addition to Kuliabko, Artem'ev, "Biblioteka Imperatorskago Kazanskago Universiteta," pp. 93–95.

[106] See Smirnov & Kuliabko, *Mikhail Sofronov*. In 1749 his work earned him a prize from the University's staff, a 1618 edition of Virgil, from the duplicates of the Academy's library. See Khoteev, "Episod iz istorii dubletnogo fonda," pp. 52–54. Another example was the classicist Vasilii Petrovich Petrov, (b. 1736), who attended the Moscow Clerical Academy 1752–60, and then taught Latin grammar at the Academy of Sciences gymnasium. See Andrew Kahn, "Readings of Imperial Rome," pp. 752–56.

[107] See D. Tolstoi, *Akademicheskaia gimnasiia*; Vladimirskii-Budanov, "Iz istorii nashego prosveshcheniia," pp. 97–110; and Kuliabko, *Lomonosov i uchebnaia deiatel'nost'*.

as candidates for the Academic University was so sudden that it appears to have been policy.

With the exception of several dispatched to study abroad,[108] this group generally contributed less significantly to Classical translations and education than had the Kievan-educated sons of the clergy. This is not surprising, for after the Ukrainian interlude, these Latin studies were again reduced to the status of a skill, imparted to potential state servitors. No one in the entire century had challenged the *Domostroi*'s assumption that the clergy comprised the natural elementary teachings for the people.

These German-nurtured Latin pupils would contribute most to the sciences in Russia. Vasilii Prokof'evich Svetlov (1744–83),[109] the son of a sergeant, would spend three years in Göttingen. The original prognosis was unfavorable: "bis ins 18. Jahr in wilder Ignoranz aufgewachsen." He would translate Tacitus' *Germania*, as well as textbooks for the Public Schools. Aleksei Iakovlevich Polenev (b. 1738), the son of a regimental musician, attended Strasbourg and Göttingen, and rendered Montesquieu's *Grandeur of the Romans*, and Theophrastus' "On Morality," sketches from the *Characters*. They were exceptions. More typical were Gerasim Andreevich Shpynev (b. 1741), who studied science, served in the medical college, but produced no publications, or Ivan Iudin (1742–1768), son of a Preobrazhenskii grenadier, who studied in Göttingen and translated Euler's *Universal Arithmetic*. Vasilii Fedorovich Zuev (1752–1794) was the son of a Tver' peasant-soldier in the Semenovskii regiment; he attended the Academic Gymnasium, accompanied Pallas to Siberia, and studied at Leiden. He became a natural scientist and the translator of Buffon's *Natural History*. Roots in the peasantry and an initial education in the Academy led many of this generation to pursue careers in the sciences.[110]

---

[108] The Göttingen connection is explored by Mohrman, *Studien über russisch-deutsche Begegnungen*; the historian Schlözer worried about the Latin preparation of his Russian pupils, and recorded high praise for a young Ukrainian; see Winter, ed., *August Ludwig v. Schlözer und Russland*, pp. 33–36, 160–61, 307. See also Winter et al., eds., *Lomonosov, Schlözer, Pallas*, pp. 107–246. Recent work on him, with full bibliography, is available in the commemorative issue of the *Zeitschrift für Slawistik*, Vol. 30, No. 4 (1985). Schlözer as educator emerges in his solicitude for his daughter's schooling. See the account, including her examination-translation of Horace, in Kern, *Madame Doctorin Schlözer*. I owe this reference to I. Koppe of Göttingen. The source for Göttingen is Selle, ed., *Die Matrikel der Georg-August-Universität*.

[109] For the following, Kuliabko, *Pitomtsy*, biographies, but for Svetlov, Winter, ed., *August Ludwig v. Schlözer und Russland*, pp. 159–66, 219.

[110] It was in this sense that "science "arose against the Church" in the person of

Students from the Latin colleges at Kiev, Moscow, St. Petersburg, and Novgorod at mid-century ceased to be channeled into the Academy of Sciences, as they had been in the 1740s. Lomonosov and Trediakovskii effected a major reorientation by ignoring Ukrainian clerical sons and by recruiting Russian soldiers' sons directly into the Academic Gymnasium. This contributed to the social insularity of the Russian "Levites," the clerical estate.[111] It left the Academy's Latin learning in the hands of the declassé, sons of soldiers even less honorable than the sons of priests.

It was in this context in 1755 the Gymnasia of Moscow University opened, initially filled with priests's sons "who knew Latin and were versed in the classical authors,"[112] who were unwelcome in the Academy.

The Germans in the Academy of Sciences recognized their institution as "*unsere Insel.*" Johann Heinrich Merck in 1773 said they "live as if in a zoo.... They remain a rare species in this land." They had failed to lure the Russian gentry to their school. The German curriculum of the Land Cadet Corps for young nobles had been abandoned after the death of the Empress Anna.[113] German academicians had tried to market a Russian edition of their *Commentarii Academiae Petropoli*, but no one bought it.[114] In the mid-1740s they had accepted Lomonosov and larger numbers of Russian students to rebuild an institution sorely threatened by the anti-foreign frenzy of Elizabeth's early reign.[115]

Those Russians, Lomonosov and Trediakovskii among them, when they advanced to positions of authority in the Academy, created a very different kind of school. In fifteen years they recruited almost six hundred students, mostly the sons of soldiers (132), of the lower bureaucracy (80), or of artisans of the admiralty or the Academy itself (50), with some landless nobles (80) and foreigners (93). By

---

Lomonosov." Krasnobaev, *Ocherki istorii russkoi kul'tury XVIII veka*, p. 22. This was also the moment when Trediakovskii and Lomonosov were united in literary debate against the one noble-born poet of the era, Sumarokov. See Reyfman, *Trediakovsky*, pp. 59–60.

[111] On Trediakovskii's role, see the individual biographies in Kuliabko, *Pitomtsy*; Freeze, *The Russian Levites*.

[112] Shtrange, *Intelligentsiia*, p. 52.

[113] Cited in Scharf, "Deutschlandbild," p. 310; Rozhdestvenskii, *Ocherki po istorii*, pp. 15, 40–41.

[114] Kopanev, "Pochemu bylo prekrashcheno."

[115] See now Anisimov, *Rossiia v seredine XVIII veka*, Chap. I.

comparison, the group which had dominated enrollment before 1750, the sons of the clergy, in this period stood at thirteen.[116] Ukrainians and their pupils had been purged. In the 1750s most Russian nobles steadfastly avoided scientific education and Latin. Only the landless noble had been lured to Latin, and only in the Baltic and Ukraine was the generally dismal picture brighter.[117]

Moscow University was founded at the moment when Russia again decided to what extent its national educational effort would be based on mastery of Latin, and to whom pagan learning was to be offered. The 1755 decision was again to offer Latin education to the noble elite and the clergy, in two separate preparatory gymnasia.

The beginnings were humble. In the earliest days of Moscow University, faculty and a handful of well-born and clerical-born students found it exhilarating to confront the Classics.[118] Nobles were there. But so small was this first generation of noble-born pupils that they almost outnumbered their professors, who were almost all Germans, Schaden from Tübingen, Dilthey, a "student of Pufendorf," Reichel and Kellner from Leipzig, Rost from Göttingen, and Fromen from Stuttgart. As teachers, they represented the German natural-law theories which were absorbed by the young Novikov, Bogdanov, and Fonvizin.[119] They taught a doctrine of duty that was born of neo-Stoicism, and their most important author was Justus Lipsius and his works, *Manuductio ad Stoicam Philosophiam* (1604) and *Physiologia Stoicorum* (1610).[120]

The new Nobles' Pension of Moscow University in 1755 was simply another effort in a long sequence of attempts to ground the Latin-based college securely among the Russian gentry. That effort had begun in the seventeenth century with Polockij, had been renewed in 1701 with the Moscow Slavo-Greco-Latin Academy, and renewed twice more with the Ecclesiastical Regulation's diocesan Latin colleges, and with the founding of the Academic Gymnasium. There had even been a short-lived experiment in 1736–37 to forcefully enroll young nobles in the Slavo-Greco-Latin Academy.[121] All had failed.

That the Gymnasium of the Moscow University was to be a

---

[116] Shtrange, *Demokraticheskaia intelligentsiia*, pp. 32–3.
[117] Dukes, *Catherine the Great*, pp. 196–210, makes the point and surveys the literature.
[118] Gleason, *Moral Idealists, Bureaucracy, and Catherine the Great*.
[119] Gleason, *Moral Idealists*, 54–59 and *passim*.
[120] *Ibid.*, pp. 59ff.
[121] Rozhdestvenskii, *Ocherki po istorii*, p. 50.

Classical Latin college is best testified by a document from 1765, a decade after its opening, which noted the fact that in ten years no "undergraduate" library (*uchebnaia biblioteka*) had been built. *Magister* Johannes Urbanski, the Polish Latin teacher in the non-noble gymnasium, was given the task of compiling the list of books required and recommending in what quantities they should be held. The basic undergraduate books of 1765 were listed in a grand *Catalogus librorum pro stipendiariis studiosis et discipulis Universitatis et Gymnasii Moscuensis*.[122]

At the top of the list, for daily reading aloud, stood the Bible, in Russian, Latin, French, and German, the latter *von Hallischer Ausgabe*. Next came history, and although Curtius Rufus, Livy, Sallust, Suetonius, Tacitus and others were to be purchased, it was Caesar alone who should be purchased in multiple copies for students. The class for *Oratores et rhetores* was dominated by Cicero; three sets of his complete works were to be purchased, and for the classroom, sufficient copies for each student to have his *Epistolae ad familiares*, *Selectae orationes*, and of course, *Officia*. Students in the Poetry form would study the ancients exclusively, chiefly Virgil, Horace, Ovid, and Prudentius (348–405), one of the two "true creators of Christian lyrical poetry in the west."[123] Greek would be taught, but apart from linguistic materials, the only texts for reading were to be the Bible, and Xenophon. Such was the undergraduate program at Moscow University.

Only in the higher form of philosophy did the modern authors begin to make their appearance. They were, predictably, German: multiple copies for students were to be purchased of Winkler's *Institutiones philosophicae*, Baumeister's works, and Heinecius' *Elementa philosophiae rationalis et moralis*. Likewise German scholars dominated the list of mathematics texts. Urbanski included linguistic materials and readings for the modern languages, French, German, and Italian. He did list a few modern works of history, genealogy, and

---

[122] Single copies represented reference items, multiple copies were used in classes. See the "Catalogus librorum pro stipendiariis studiosis et discipulis universitatis," *Dokumenty i materialy po istorii moskovskogo universiteta*, Vol. II, pp. 25–35; on Urbanski, *Ibid.*, I, 378, III, 289, 471; see also Penchko, *Biblioteka moskovskogo universiteta*, pp. 55–56, 121–127. On the identical curricula of Kiev, the Academy, and Moscow, see Mühlpfordt, "Zur Rolle der Universitäten," pp. 110–11; and on contemporary perception that Moscow University and the Academy of Sciences were designed to diminish Ukrainian influence, see his "Ein deutscher Rußlandkenner," esp. pp. 54–5.

[123] Hadas, *Latin Literature*, p. 427.

geography, including Voltaire's historical works, but the core curriculum in Classical Latin was never out of sight: the modern-history
list concluded with a request for fifteen copies of *Selectae e profanis*
Scriptoribus historiae tractantur in classibus syntacticis latinis. Lighter reading
pour s'exercer dans la langue françoise included Aesop's fables, Fontenelle's
and Fenelon's *Dialogues des morts*, and of course, *Telemaque*. German
practice favored Gottsched.

What defined education at the Gymnasia of Moscow University?
It was the same hard grounding in religion and the Classics of
Harvard, Paris, and Kiev a century earlier. One began with daily
reading from the Bible, and with immersion in Latin grammar. Once
the fundamentals of the language were acquired, one began to live
and breathe the Latin pagan Classics, above all Caesar and Cicero.
Next one read Virgil and Ovid, followed by Prudentius. Greek was
chiefly studied for Scripture. Those student who continued to advanced study, philosophy, would by the second half of the century
encounter the Germans, some them pupils of the Christian Wolff
who had dominated instruction at the Academy of Sciences' higher
classes a generation earlier.

Did this very German institution vary from what an educated native
Russian would have established? In 1755 Lomonosov wrote his own
version of a curriculum for the gymnasia of Moscow University, as
in 1758 he wrote a proposal to reform the Gymnasium of the Academy of Sciences, to teach the "first fundamentals of all the liberal
arts and sciences." In both instances he proposed a traditional grounding in Latin; he would have followed Cicero and Virgil with Quintus
Horatius Flaccus, Livy, Tacitus, and Erasmus, rather than with Ovid
or Prudentius. He omitted Greek, recommended Molière, Racine,
and Voltaire's dramas for French, Gottsched and Johann Christian
Günther for German, and the French Jesuit Pomey for rhetoric.
Christian Wolff and his pupils would have dominated philosophy,
even as Lomonosov's personal relations with the Germans at the
Academy were at an all-time low.[124] But Lomonosov could have lived

---

[124] See Heller, "Kooperation und Konfrontation," pp. 17–18; The Germans did
not appreciate Lomonosov's efforts. G. F. Müller wrote to the Secretary of the
Academy in 1761 that "Lomonosov is a madman with a knife in his hand," who
would ruin the institution. See Bucholtz, *Die Göttinger Rußlandsammlung*, p. 39. The
proposals are now conveniently available in Lomonosov, *O vospitanii*, pp. 152–61,
162–69, 194–95, 200–03, 215–20.

with Urbanski's booklists. The differences were matters of taste, not of substance.

Lomonosov, hailed in Soviet scholarship as a man of the people, it should be noted, would ban peasants, who were admissible only if their owners freed them "in perpetuity," and so certified legally. "The sciences," Lomonosov wrote,

"are a path to nobility, and all entering [the Gymnasium] should look upon themselves as on those entering a nobility. Therefore all accepted [for study] and not already belonging to the nobility should in their relations with others, and even in the clothes they wear, assume a posture as if they belonged to the nobility."[125]

Scarcely the populist of his reputation, Lomonosov's European years had served him well, as he recognized the ennobling power of the humanists' educational values.

In 1755 the Latin curriculum was flourishing in the Academic Gymnasium, in several diocesan schools, Kiev and Moscow among them. Why then was the Gymnasium of Moscow University founded?

The first answer was social. The revitalized Academic gymnasium was almost entirely stocked by *raznochintsy*, the sons of soldiers. Nobles had never shown any interest in studying under Germans, or with their lowly-born countrymen.[126] An English visitor said so:

There is an academy of sciences in Petersburg, the professors are usually foreigners, and paid by government, and some valuable papers have been published, but the Russians themselves make but little progress in literature, not having the opportunity of a previous education, there being no school or college established. The gentry have indeed, generally a French tutor or a tutoress for their children, who are often as illiterate as the pupils.[127]

This view, penned after a visit in 1776, suggests the gentry's continuing resistance to the Germans' education.

The second answer was ecclesiastical. The old Petrine injunction that the diocesan colleges be Latin schools, offering Slavonic literacy only in their preparatory forms, proved difficult to establish. Seven years after the law was published progress had been made only in the Ukraine, in Kiev, Chernihiv, and Belgorod; there success would

---

[125] Lomonosov, *O vospitanii*, p. 217.
[126] See my "Technical Training," and "The Impact of Technical Training." Note also Kimerling, "Soldiers' Children 1719–1856."
[127] John Richard, *A Tour from London to Petersburgh*, 1780, p. 31.

continue throughout the century. In Russia only Moscow and St. Petersburg really boasted a Latin curriculum. Twenty other dioceses reported attempts, failures, and closings "due to poverty." Only after decades of effort, was "the Latin curriculum . . . firmly rooted in the seminary by 1760."[128] At that point there were some 28 schools in operation, with some 5,500 pupils,[129] some having passed through Slavonic literacy into the Latin classes.

Except in the Ukraine it had been a slow process. In Tobol'sk, for example, the arrival in 1703 of a graduate of Kiev as the new bishop led to the opening of a diocesan school. He began from scratch, as a fire in 1701 had consumed the hundred and thirty books and manuscripts of his predecessor. The new bishop wrote to Kiev for "church books and grammars" and received a package of 206 volumes. But only in the 1740s were Latin studies firmly established with help of "Latin books" purchased in Kiev; St. Petersburg could provide directives but no Latin books.[130] This was not atypical, as even the Muscovite clergy successfully avoided Latin studies.

At the beginning of Catherine's reign, only in this limited sense did a "Latin yoke still lay heavily upon the seminary."[131] But the tiny clientele for Latin education in Russia had changed since 1721.[132] The diocesan schools served almost exclusively the children of the clerical estate. Provincial schools never attracted non-clergy. In the more hospitable Ukraine, Chernihiv, Belgorod, and Kharkhiv, initially drew the sons of non-clerics: in Kiev in 1737 263 of 367 pupils were non-clerical; in 1744 two-thirds were not clerical. In Moscow in 1728 360 of 474 were of lay parentage. Kiev's non-clerical sons would decline to 11% by 1811, largely the result of direct Muscovite

---

[128] Freeze, *Levites*, p. 94; the dioceses' efforts to establish the Latin curriculum of the Ecclesiastical Regulation, based on a survey of the late 1720s, was printed in P. Pekarskii, *Nauka i literatura v Rossii*, pp. 109–124. On the intellectual life of Jesuit colleges in Belorussia and Lithuania, sponsored by the Sapieha and Radziwill families, and centered on the great Classicist Martin Matushevich (1714–73), but ending with Russian acquisitions in the partitions of Poland, see Biralo, *Filosofskaia i obshchestvennaia mysl' v Belorussii i Litve*.

[129] Bryner, *Der geistliche Stand*, pp. 102–03.

[130] Church authorities could provide only primers and psalters; see Guzner, "Biblioteki uchebnykh zavedenii Sibirii" pp. 64–77; the fate of the books can be traced in Sitnikov, "Zapadnoevropeiskaia kniga v Sibirii," pp. 78–98.

[131] Freeze, *Ibid.*, p. 95.

[132] For this and the next paragraph see Rozhdestvenskii, *Ocherki po istorii*, pp. 44–46; Freeze, *Levites*, pp. 34–37, 200–04, and Bryner, *geistliche Stand*, pp. 116–35, and Shtrange, *demokraticheskaia intelligentsiia*, p. 27, and *passim*.

intervention in the 1780s, in the era of the Public School Reform.[133] In Moscow the number of non-clerical sons declined to just 13% as early as 1744. The formation of the caste of Russian Levites began with the rejection of Latin study by the nobilities, confirmed by law and policy after the death of Peter.

The third factor in the founding of Moscow University was the decline of Ukrainians in the hierarchy. Peter the Great had named Belorussians or Ukrainians to 39% of his appointments as bishops in Great-Russian dioceses. Between 1725 and 1741 51.5% of all appointments to Great-Russian Sees were from the Ukraine, and an additional five were Greek, Serb, Rumanian, or Georgian, with Classical educations. Under Elizabeth, 1741–62, and her Cossack paramour Aleksei Razumovskii, of forty-nine appointments, thirty-seven or 76% were White Russians or Ukrainians. The Ukrainians were at the peak of their influence in the Church when Moscow University was founded.

In short, Moscow University was founded in the mid-1750s for Novikov's generation of young nobles, with a Latin curriculum similar to that available across town in the Academy, in St. Petersburg both at the Academy of Sciences and at Teofan's old Seminary, in Kiev, Belgorod, Chernihiv and Kharkhiv, and in some diocesan seats as well. Trediakovskii and Lomonosov had transformed the Gymnasium of the Academy into a haven for Russian non-priestly *raznochintsy*, diminishing what little attraction it held for Russia's nobles. Simultaneously Ukrainian hierarchs, at the height of their influence in the Russian Church, had finally spread modest Latin schools throughout the Empire, although almost exclusively for the clergy. The age of Elizabeth also witnessed Russia's mini-Renaissance in printing when a precious few of the Classics finally appeared in academic editions.[134]

Latin learning at last found roots among a few of Russia's nobles, but alas, it occurred at the moment when the Western cult of Latin was being broken, when the influential D'Alembert was denouncing the humanists who had forged the European curriculum:

> the sixteenth century [produced] a multitude of Latin poets, orators, and historians who works, we must confess, too often draw their principal merit from a latinity which we can hardly evaluate.

---

[133] Those changes are described in Chapter Four below. A first-hand portrait of these schools in the early 19th century is available in Platon, *The Present State*, pp. 6–13.

[134] See above, Chapter II, Section 2A.

> Little by little men of letters at last recovered from this kind of mania. . . . Men began to understand that beauty lost none of its advantages for being expressed in the common tongue, that it even gained by becoming more accessible to the generality of men, and that there was no merit in saying common or ridiculous things in any language whatever, especially in those languages which of necessity were spoken the worst. Therefore, men of letters turned their thoughts to perfecting the vulgar tongues. They tried first to say in these languages what the anceints had said in theirs.[135]

This hostile vision of humanist Europe would affect the education of Europeans only in the years ahead. But Russia's social elite, after a century of nay-saying, showed tentative signs of accepting the Latin humanism at the moment European intellectuals were beginning to question it seriously. The target had moved again, and Russia misfired.

Visitors remained unimpressed with Moscow University. Two decades after its opening a hostile visitor commented,

> The sciences flourish much less at Moscow than at Petersburgh. Astronomy, mathematics and painting, the Russians have no taste for, and indeed there is no possibility of learning those sciences here.[136]

John Richard found the problem in the Russians' hostility to foreigners and to their learning. Peter the Great had established schools, he noted, but

> his successors took as much pains to remain ignorant, as he had taken to improve them. The great epocha of obstancy, in this respect, was the reign of Elizabeth, for at the revolution which brought her in, foreigners were looked on with a jealous eye, and every means taken to get rid of them.

Fragile Latin studies especially suffered in the anti-foreign frenzy of Elizabeth's reign.

In the 1750s an institutional basis for the European Enlightenments for some of Russia's gentry came into being. After the opening of the Nobles' Pension of Moscow University more and more Russian nobles of various political persuasions appeared, for whom the ancient European Enlightenments were accessible and intelligible because they had Latin. Only a few actually studied there; most chose the French gymnasium over the classical; but a barrier had been broken, and those at Moscow were joined by others who pursued a

---

[135] D'Alembert, *Preliminary Discourse*, pp. 65–66.
[136] Richard, *A Tour from London*, p. 60, and for the following, pp. 31–2.

university education in Europe: they were to be found in Göttingen, in British universities, and elsewhere.

The process had its ambiguities. No sooner was a humanist education available in an institution acceptable to the gentry, when Catherine authorized and funded a translation project to bring the ancient authors to the Russians in the vernacular. That effort too would be short-lived and incomplete, but it reflected the lack of commitment that had characterized Russia's flirtation with Latinate culture for over a century.

4. Book Culture in Catherine's Russia

A. The Problem of Sources (I)

In twenty years of effort, Soviet scholars of the book collected, analyzed, and often published, all available descriptions of libraries in eighteenth-century Russia. They concluded that at mid-century and beyond more books of secular content appeared, and that collections became more professional for all, but especially for academicians. Russian libraries began to show "cultural links" with Western Europe, and commercial publishers, rather than governmental decrees, began to determine tastes in books. The manuscript faded from the scene. In general terms, a Russian Enlightenment was possible, because of the secular nature of libraries of these professionals. It is regrettable, they also concluded, that almost nothing is known about the book among the "democratic levels of society," in the hands of peasants, town dwellers, and merchants late in the century. Years of archival research had failed to unearth traces of their libraries.

B. The Library of the Humanistically Educated: Lomonosov

Lomonosov has been sainted by the Soviet establishment as the most learned, the most enlightened, and the most Russian of all cultural representatives of the age. Extraordinary efforts have been made to establish the progressiveness of his thought, and the extent of his private library.[137] The "classic" reconstruction of his books was done

---

[137] Kuliabko & Beshenkovskii, *Sud'ba biblioteki i arkhiva M. V. Lomonosova*. Lomonosov's canonization is not my invention. See the remarkable story of how a single holy portrait became the source of icons; Glinka, *M. V. Lomonosov (Opyt ikonografii)*. After

thirty years ago by G. M. Korovin.[138] It says much about Lomonosov, and about Soviet scholarship. Normally a posthumous inventory is deflated, known after family or friends took what they wanted or were given. In Lomonosov's case, the reconstruction is the most generous attribution of ownership possible.

Lomonosov's humble origins, his teenage walk to Moscow, and the poverty and shame of his student days at the Kievans' Slavo-Greco-Latin Academy (1731–34) are as legendary as Lincoln's log cabin, and Korovin concluded that he could not have afforded books, although the lectures of the Kievan P. Krajs'kyj introduced him to the reading materials of the Latin grammar school and college, to Homer, Cicero, Ovid, Horace, and Seneca. His introduction to poetics was provided by Fedor Kvetnickij, a graduate of the Academy who based his Latin course on the Jesuit Soarez, as well as on masters of the Polish Renaissance.[139] After a year at the Kiev Academy, his stay at the Gymnasium of the Academy of Sciences in St. Petersburg was brief (January to September, 1736), and then he was abroad for five years, chiefly at Marburg with Christian Wolff, but also in Freiburg. Some of his purchases abroad for 1738 are known: a bit of contemporary literature, Fénelon's *Telemachus* and a German *Gulliver*, a collection of literary Classics (Anacreon and Sappho in French, Martial's *Epigrams*, Cicero, Virgil's *Works*, Seneca's *Tragedies*, Pliny's *Letters*, Ovid's *Works*), and a good deal of science, including chemistry, some works of Boerhaave, and an embarrassing amount of the writings of his teacher-mentor Christian Wolff.[140] Lomonosov's early library reflected both Classical education and his German-rooted scientific interests.

One should note that Korovin was at least a silent victim of the norms of Soviet Stalinist scholarship. In order to avoid the inconvenience of having an unscientific category like "theology" in Lomo-

---

his death in 1765 his books were subsumed into the collection of G. G. Orlov, and in 1832 they arrived in Helsinki.

[138] *Ibid.*, pp. 29–30; Korovin, *Biblioteka Lomonosova*. Recent scholarship has been less helpful. See my review of *Lomonosov i kniga*, *Jahrbücher für Geschichte Osteuropas*, Vol. 38, No. 4 (1990), 581–83.

[139] Kvetnickij, *Clavis Poetica*. His biography and literary career are best read in Serman, *Mikhail Lomonosov*, here pp. 17ff.

[140] *Ibid.*, pp. 7–9, 60–64, 373–75, 407–08. Perhaps the best introduction now is Gerlach et al., eds. *Christian Wolff als Philosoph*, but see also Mühlpfordt, "Christian Wolff, ein Enzyklopädist." He shared Wolff with the Classically-educated clerics, Teofan, Buzyns'kyj, and Lopatins'kyj, among others. See Morozov, "Christian Wolffs Leser."

nosov's library, he did some artful and downright Jesuitical categorizing. Theological debates and the Scripture needed to resolve them were within the interests of every scholar, and religious literature formed a significant part of every library. Korovin did Soviet scholarship no service when he catalogued under the rubric *Eloquence* the Bible in whole and in parts, the works of Basil the Great, Gregory of Nazianzus, John of Damascus, John Chrysostom, St. Ambrose [recorded un-canonized and de-sanctified simply as "Ambrosius Mediolanus (340–397)"], and St. Augustine ["Augustinus Aurelius 354–430)"].[141] And while these Western Church Fathers themselves would not be displeased to be grouped with the company of Pliny, Aristotle, Demosthenes, and Cicero, it was deceitful for Korovin to situate them so. Also catalogued under "eloquence" was Tertullian's *Apology*, which ill-suited Korovin's deception. On one hand it defended the believing Christian who could behave "as other men in social and political life," and on the other, Tertullian was not known for eloquence, "one of the most difficult Latin authors to read. . . .—a "barbarizing Tacitus." Likewise under rhetoric one finds the *Letters* of Cyprian, Bishop of Carthage, and works of Lactantius (250–330), "the Christian Cicero," and modern works like Johan Ernst Schubert, *Compendium theologiae dogmaticae* (Halle, 1760). Having catalogued it there, Korovin proceeded to argue unconvincingly that Lomonosov must have been interested in its oratory.[142]

Korovin also listed under rhetoric Johann Lorenz Mosheim, *Heilige Reden über wichtige Wahrheiten der Lehre Jesu Christi*, and Simeon Polockij's *Psalter* was placed under *belles-lettres*. Lomonosov's Biblical Concordance was listed under linguistics. By contrast, Teofan Prokopovych's library had been catalogued in a nineteenth-century editor unintimidated by theology, and it had a category for "Patristics and Writers of the Church." The purportedly materialistic Lomonosov, who categorically owned no theology, held almost 40% of the Church Fathers owned by the head of Peter's Church.[143]

When his religious books are restored, Lomonosov becomes less

---

[141] For this paragraph, Korovin, *op. cit.*, pp. 345–364; see Hadas, *Roman Literature*, 414, 418.

[142] Hadas, *op. cit.*, p. 423; Korovin, *op. cit.*, p. 363. If *glasnost'* ever touches the writing of history in Russia, it might begin by insisting that every scholar read Palmer's *Catholics and Unbelievers*; relevant here is Palmer's second chapter which demonstrated why every theologian was interested in nature and adept at natural science.

[143] The authors listed in Verkhovskoi, "Biblioteka Feofana Prokopovicha," pp. 58–9 were compared to those in Korovin.

the freak that Soviet scholarship has made him. One can understand how, on the eve of his studies in Marburg, when he was still a good seminarist, he could have piously, even willingly, accepted the idea of becoming a priest: it was, after all, the ordinary outcome of his Kievan humanist education.[144] He was a scholar of Psalms and an enemy of "atheists and their teacher Epicurus," thundering, "arise and pay attention, consider that He can . . . dispose you alive into Hell. . . . He can strike with lightning. The One who throws thunder, that One exists: godless, tremble."[145] Thus there was no contradiction between his library and the fact that Lomonosov recognized that the Church Fathers had been "scientific in their times," or that he could admit the possibility of miracles.[146] There was no contradiction between those honorable convictions, his education in religion and the Classics, or his library, once Soviet atheist-seeking subterfuge is removed.

Lomonosov had a powerful collection of the ancients. A core of about twenty-five major Classical authors were held by both Lomonosov and by Teofan a generation earlier; Teofan had a far better collection of the Greeks (in Greek and in Latin translation) than did Lomonosov. One appreciates Harold Segel's remark that in the age after Winckelmann "Hellenism . . . never took hold of the Russian consciousness in the way it did the Germans,"[147] and a luminary like Lomonosov seems to bear this out.

The scientist Lomonosov owned Lucretius, De rerum, which Prokopovych lacked, but which the age read not only for a vision of nature, but of history.[148] Teofan had a better collection of the ancient historians, as Lomonosov lacked Caesar, Livy, Polybius, Sallust, and Thucydides, to mention only the titans. This helps to explain the Germans' notorious disdain for Lomonosov's historical work, and for the fact that one typically mentions Lomonosov's historical writings

[144] Belokurov, "O namerenii Lomonosova priniat' sviashchenstvo."

[145] Serman, Lomonosov, pp. 129–30.

[146] See respectively, A. Popov, "Nauka i religiia," pp. 1–12, and Tukalevskii, "Glavnyia cherty mirosozertsaniia Lomonosova."

[147] Segel, "Classicism and Classical Antiquity," p. 60. Lomonosov, on the other hand, was the first to deal with Homer as an epic stylist, in his Rhetoric of 1748. See Egunov, Gomer, pp. 29–39; but see the qualifications on his originality below. Parts of his Ancient Russian History have recently been reprinted, and one notes his familiarity with the historians; see Lomonosov, Dlia pol'zy obshchestva . . . , esp. pp. 202–06.

[148] On Lucretius' vision of universal historical change, see Mullett, "Lucretius in Clio's Chariot."

as an example of his nationalism and his breadth of interests. Thus Stählin could rightfully regard Lomonosov as a "*rußischen Virgil und Cicero*," as a poetic and rhetorical stylist, but not a historian.[149] Radishchev too was unimpressed, and Pushkin a generation later concurred.[150] Nineteenth-century Russians were generally unappreciative of Lomonosov's style. N. I. Grech regarded him as barbarous, someone who destroyed good Russian word order on the basis of "foreign models, chiefly Latin and German," even to the point of placing verbs at the ends of sentences.[151]

Lomonosov's ownership of the Classics was not tantamount to a habit of using them. He, like his peers, showed "little discrimination in the choice of materials [they] quarried. They took everything which was to hand, and which served their purpose." In all their borrowing, "classical antiquity itself was a minor component."[152] Most of the imagery, language, and style of his celebrated succession—and commemoration-odes can be traced directly to the stage productions of the Moscow Slavo-Greco-Latin Academy.[153] He also remained passively wedded to what he learned in Marburg: his courtly poetry mirrored German odes,[154] his "On the Use of Glass" had Pietistic roots,[155] as he almost single-handed "produced a Russian-language equivalent for the works of his German predecessors" in the Academy of Sciences.[156] His *Rhetoric* was reliant on the work of the French Jesuits Caussin and Pomey, and on Johann Christoph Gottsched's

---

[149] See Mühlpfordt, "Leipzig als Brennpunkt," p. 331. The source of the allusion to Cicero and Virgil was apparently an inscription by his friend Popovskii; see Serman, *Lomonosov*, pp. 205–06.

[150] The newest study of Trediakovskii is premised on the fact that he has been neglected due to "exaggerated praise for Lomonosov." See the revisionist Irina Reyfman, *Vasilii Trediakovsky*.

[151] Brown, *18th Century Russian Literature*, p. 558; Trediakovskii's verse too became incomprehensible when he accepted Latin syntax and inverted word order; see *Ibid.*, pp. 70–71.

[152] Jones, "A Trojan Horse," p. 102.

[153] Serman, "Lomonosovs Oden und die Poetik," and his more recent *Lomonosov*; the starting point of modern scholarship is Rezanov, *Iz istorii russkoi dramy*; more recently see Badalich & Kuz'mina, *Pamiatniki russkoi shkol'noi dramy*, *Novye cherty v russkoi literature i iskusstve*, and Moiseeva, "Znachenie moskovskoi Slaviano-greko-latinskoi akademii," pp. 36–41.

[154] Pumpianskii, "Lomonosov i nemetskaia shkola razuma"; Unbegaun, "Lomonosov und Luther"; Lotman, "Ob Ode, vybrannoi iz Iova," which links him to the anti-Lutheran thought of the Ukrainians.

[155] Schamschula, "Zu dem Quellen."

[156] Smith, "The Most Proximate West," p. 367.

Grundriss einer Redekunst (1729),[157] with little added from his own read-ing in the Classics. His political thought was heavily indebted to Christian Wolff; he was uninterested in law, and uninfluenced by his contemporaries: unlike the French flock of philosophes, Russian "enlighteners" showed little evidence of being a community eagerly learning from each other.[158]

From his earliest upbringing Lomonosov made abundant use of the Bible in his poetry, he borrowed language and content from Polockij's Psalter, and his poetry was at one with the literary tradi-tions of the Kiev Academy of his teachers in pagan and religious metaphors. One need not agree with nastiness of Belinskii's verdict, "The so-called poetry of Lomonosov grew out of the barbaric scholastic rhetoric of the ecclesiastical schools of the 17th century,"[159] to appre-ciate its solid Kievan content. Lomonosov had respectable religious roots, which included unequal parts of northern Old Belief, Kievan theology, and Protestantism—known first-hand though his wife—to say nothing of the religious content of the German *Frühaufklärung* of the Wolffian school.[160]

Given this religious tradition, one understands why Lomonosov envisioned only traditional parochial schooling. He recognized the faults of the Russian clergy, including its booklessness and legendary drunkenness, and sought its reformation. In seeking change, he wrote, "Let the example be Germany." But in his Germany, the clergy was the sole source of teachers in the village and the town: "Pastors in their ecclesiastical schools which teach children literacy should present the catechism (*zakon bozhii*) with all severity and diligence." He rec-ommended church schooling from the age of five to ten or twelve, but said nothing about Latin, mathematics, or any other addition to the Muscovite *Ladder of Literacy*.[161] Even when discussing the secondary Classical gymnasium, Lomonosov said that all youth were

---

[157] Hart, "Continuity and Change," pp. 46–8, Tschizewskij, "Das Barock in der russischen Literatur," pp. 9–39.

[158] See the debunking of Soviet claims in Gleason, "The Two Faces of the Monarch"; the fundamental survey of his German contacts is Cenekal, "Die wissenschaftlichen Verbindungen Lomonosovs."

[159] Cited in Pokotilova, "Predshestvenniki Lomonosova," pp. 66–92, here p. 92; see also Dorovatovskaia, "O zaimstvovaniiakh Lomonosova iz Biblii."

[160] See the recent essay by Heller, "Kooperation und Konfrontation," pp. 1–12, here especially 8–9, 22–24.

[161] Lomonosov, "Premechaniia [ob obiazannostiakh dukhovenstva]," *Polnoe sobranie sochinenii*, VI, 407–8.

to attain literacy in the customary order of primer, Book of Hours, Psalter, and the Commandments.[162]

Although Soviet scholars endlessly depicted Lomonosov as genuine Russian peasant, from his Ukrainian education he seems to have absorbed some of the haughty elitism of his emigrant teachers. One scholar has noted that he consciously chose a rhetorical style contemptuous of both Church Slavonic, implying a pejorative stance toward the liturgical speech of priest, of that of the peasants, who were like children awaiting enlightenment to remove their coarseness. By contrast the Moldavian prince Kantemir, an *homme de lettres* in France long before he was recognized in Russia, could adopt Horace's idealized rustic motifs and bucolic notions of unspoiled peasants unknown to Lomonosov.[163] Although they were both of humbler origins, Lomonosov and Pososhkov differed fundamentally on two issues. One was modern science, of which "Pososhkov was very suspicious." The other was the peasantry: "Pososhkov devoted a lot of attention to the situation of the enserfed peasantry, about whom Lomonosov was silent, since this was an unfamiliar area for him."[164]

Lomonosov's library was oddly composed. His forte was physical science, but his library lacked the medical works which had crept into every educated gentleman's collection; there was no Hippocrates, no Galen, no Vesalius, and no Harvey.[165] His books on technology, military affairs, architecture, and especially economics, including agriculture and household management, were embarrassingly thin, suggesting a cultural gap between Lomonosov and most of his noble contemporaries. His political literature lacked Hobbes, Locke, and many others who had become staples.[166]

Most striking was Lomonosov's marked blindness to France and French culture: there was no Corneille or Molière, no Bodin, Pascal, or Montaigne, no Rabelais or Ronsard. Although he lived a generation

---

[162] Lomonosov, *O vospitanii*, p. 159.

[163] Gesemann, *Die Entdeckung der unteren Volksschichten*, pp. 35–39, 50–56. This is a fascinating book; compare to Peter Burke's "Discovery of the People" sections in his *Popular Culture*. Inferior is Soviet work like *Russkaia literatura i fol'klor (XI–XVIII vv.)*.

[164] Serman, *Lomonosov*, p. 182.

[165] Harvey's circulation of the blood had already been adopted as a metaphor by Peter the Great; see my exploration in "V. O. Kliuchevskii on Childhood," pp. 446–47.

[166] One should add that almost no one knew English at the Academy until the 1780s; See Istrina, "Akademicheskie perevodchiki," p. 107; and in general on the retarded receptivity to English, Cross, "'S anglinskago'," and *Russko-angliiskii literaturnye sviazi*.

into the mature French Enlightenment, his Montesquieu was limited to the early *Grandeur of the Romans*. Rousseau was wholly absent, and so was Boulainvilliers, Helvetius, Condillac, Holbach, Mably, and Diderot,[167] all of whom were in the libraries of foreign doctors and scientists in the Russian capital. Even his holdings of Voltaire were thin: the little book on Newtonianism, *Peter the Great*, one comedy, a pamphlet on natural religion, and a poem to the King of Prussia. There are, in short, serious doubts whether Lomonosov knew the works of Voltaire *"recht gut."*[168] His British horizons were almost as low.

There were obvious bibliographic reasons why Lomonosov did not get along with a new French-speaking Empress after 1762, and why his last years were bitter and isolated. He was "a man of fiery temperament," and had been an adversary of the Ukrainian Kiril Razumovskii, President of the Academy, and brother of Elizabeth's intimate counselor, Aleksei Razumovskii.[169] By 1762 he held a deep grudge against the new wave of foreigners and the Francophile culture supplanting the Kievans and the Germans of his youth. At the end of his life he begged I. I. Shuvalov to recommend him to a membership in the Parisian Academy of Sciences. Should they elect a native Russian, a *prirodnyi Rossianin* like himself, Lomonosov wrote, it would honor the Fatherland and serve to recognize the care with which the arts and sciences were cultivated there.[170] However, he knew the new French letters poorly, and his bid fell on deaf ears.

In Catherine's world of French savants and philosophes Lomonosov had limitations. His library gave testimony to his Kievan roots, to his Germanic scientific accomplishments, but it was not a gentleman's library. It was what it had every right to be, the collection of an impoverished provincial professor on the fringes of an eighteenth-century Germanic scholarship, which was being outdazzled by mid-century in natural and "social" sciences, by the French, Scottish, and

---

[167] Korovin, *op. cit.*, pp. 378–9, 424, ascribes a copy of the *Encyclopédie* to Lomonosov, but the identification is so weak and the possibility of another work so great, and Lomonosov's disinterest in France so marked, that I doubt he owned it. He appears never to have cited it. On the perils of identifying books by their short titles in catalogues, see the detective story by Berkov, "Bibliograficheskaia evristika."

[168] Hoffmann, "Lomonosov und Voltaire," p. 420. I am inclined to agree with the more cautious Boss, in his review of Alekseev, *Epokha prosveshcheniia*, in *Kritika*, Vol. V, No. 1 (Fall, 1968), pp. 25–38.

[169] Vucinich, *Science in Russian Culture*, pp. 112–13.

[170] See Grot, "Pis'ma Lomonosova i Sumarokova k I. I. Shuvalov," p. 28, letter of July 11, 1764.

English, mostly beyond Lomonosov's ken. Lomonosov was not an old man when he died in 1765, but in his maturity he had not kept up with authors or cultural trends in Europe which were being discussed and consumed not only in Paris, but also in Potsdam and Petersburg.

Stripped of Soviet hagiography, Lomonosov was a courtier in the tradition of Tolstoi and Tatishchev. His birth was not as humble as Soviet scholars like to depict it, but his library attests to the social mobility possible in the era of the Table of Ranks. His humanistic education gave him visions, historical, scientific, and literary, far beyond those of early servitors, the Muscovite *prikazchiki*. Germanism, much as he learned to hate it, had replaced Polonism in the courtier's intellectual orientation. He was a provincial rustic who remarkably synthesized the culture of the *prikaz*-technician, the courtier, and the Ukrainian cleric-panegyrist. It was no small feat. Porcelain-maker (and serf-holder in that capacity), Orthodox Christian, collegiate bureaucrat, academician, and court-flatterer—it was a difficult persona, but one fully consistent with the irregular texture of Petrine education, and visible in his books.

C. *Other Humanists' Libraries in Russia*

Lomonosov's contemporary was Dr. Antonio Nunez Ribeyro Sanches (1699–1783), a Portuguese in Russian service for sixteen years during the reign of Elizabeth. University-educated, he studied medicine for three years in Leyden with Dr. Boerhaave, who recommended him to Empress Anna. The library which he sold prior to leaving Russia comprised 446 titles in 700 volumes. About two hundred titles were on medicine and another fifty or so on other areas of natural and physical science, and the major names, Hippocrates, Galen, Avicenna, Vesalius, Celsius, were all there, as were Bacon, Euler, Linnaeus, Newton, and of course, Christian Wolff. Sanches' interests were broad, and he had Boileau and a sixteen-volume edition of Voltaire, Bodin's *De Republica*, Frederick II, and Machiavelli, Bayle, and Descartes. One gets the sense of a thoughtful collection of important titles. At its base were the Classics, about fifty titles, including most of the major authors, with lots of Cicero, most of the historians, the best of literature, and Vitruvius on architecture.[171] But

---

[171] Luppov, *Kniga v Rossii v poslepetrovskoe vremia*, pp. 337–39; Khoteev, "Biblioteka

Sanches also owned R. Barclay, *Theologiae vere Christianae apologia*, Fénelon's *Oeuvres spirituelles*, and the works of Th. Morgan, including his *Physico-theology*. It was the serious library of one for whom medicine was but one of the sciences, and for whom ancient authors sat comfortably with new.

Sanches' finely-textured library should not be confused with that of his contemporary, Johann Hermann Lestocq (1692–1767), a self-educated surgeon and personal physician to Empress Elizabeth. Involved in political intrigues, he was arrested in 1748. There seems no record of university study or of formal medical training, and his library reflected its absence: Half of its 300 titles were on medicine, natural history, and physical science including alchemy, but he owned no Classics save an English edition of Cicero's *Epistles*; there were lots of prayer books, much in French and English, some travel literature, romances, and two titles by Pufendorf.[172]

Dmitrii Ivanovich Vinogradov (1720–58) was a metallurgist and the founder of the St. Petersburg porcelain manufactory. A priest's son from Suzdal with a Kievan-directed education, he was dispatched in 1736, with Lomonosov and Gustav Ulrich Raizer, to Marburg to study mining. He also studied chemistry in Freiburg, stayed abroad until 1744, bought books, returned home, and died young. His scientific working library, *Catalogus librorum metallurgicorum*, included Albertus Magnus, Thomas Aquinas, and Robert Boyle. There was also much science and natural history in his "books in various languages on the various arts and sciences," with names like Christian Wolff, Vauban, Gravesande, Boerhaave, but also Cicero, Cornelius Nepos, Homer, Virgil, and Seneca. His modern authors were varied, including Erasmus, Fénelon's *Telemachus*, a rather consistent and serious collection of European *Russica*.[173] Like Lomonosov and other lowly born, he was receptive to humanism.

S. P. Krasheninnikov (1711–1755), famous for his *Description of the Land of Kamchatka*, which was translated into most modern European languages, also died young. Born a soldier's son, educated in the Slavo-Greco-Latin Academy in Moscow and in the gymnasium of the Academy of Sciences, he participated in the second Siberian

---

leib-medika Ribeiro Sanshesa," and "Leib-medik Ribeiro Sanshes i ego biblioteka."

[172] Khoteev, "Biblioteka leib-medika I. G. Lestoka." John Alexander refers to him as Hermann Lestock.

[173] P. I. Khoteev, "Biblioteka sozdatelia russkogo farfora D. I. Vinogradov," as well as his *Kniga v Rossii*, pp. 67–85.

expedition, was named Adjunct of the Academy in 1745, and Academician in 1750. He was the translator of Quintus Curtius' *Alexander*. The core of his tiny library consisted of Valerius Maximus, Velleius Paterculus, Virgil, Horace, Catullus, Cornelius Nepos, Ovid, Persius, Petronius, Pliny, Propertius, Sallust, Suetonius, Eutropius, Seneca, Terence, Tibullus, Caesar, Cicero, Juvenal, and Justin Martyr.[174] Likewise Aleksei Protas'evich Protasov (1724–1796) was a soldier's son who was educated in Teofan's Nevskii Monastery. He studied subsequently under Lomonosov in the Academy of Sciences' gymnasium, was sent abroad in 1751 to Leyden and Strasbourg, and took his MD degree. For decades he was director of the Academy of Sciences' Press. A third of his books were on medicine, another third on related sciences; forty-five percent of his collection was in Latin. In the remaining third the Classics were well represented, both in Latin and in the new Russian translations.[175]

Who owned Cicero in Russia after mid-century? His *On Duties* was held by an exceptional nobleman from Kursk, Ivan Petrovich Annenkov (d. 1784). He was owned by the Ukrainian Gedeon Krinovs'kyj (1726–63), the court preacher, formerly pupil and teacher at Kiev. Cicero was owned by Bishop Simon Todors'kyj (1700–54), Catherine's Kievan-schooled, Ukrainian tutor in Orthodoxy. He was owned by Vinogradov, who had studied at the Moscow Academy before going to Marburg. And Cicero was held by Dr. Sanches, Classically educated prior to his arrival in Russia.[176] Cicero evidenced an education. His existence in a library symbolized the culture which linked a few Latin-educated clergy, a few academics, native and guest, and now an occasional Russian noble.

Ukrainian humanists who owned Cicero, like Todors'kyj with eight hundred volumes in Latin, Greek, and German, and only 29 Slavic books, had more in common with European educated physicians than they did with the unschooled archimandrite of the Savior monastery in Sevsk, one Nektarii, who owned eleven books, all liturgical, and all in Slavic. His contemporary archimandrite in Kiev, Sil'vestr

---

[174] Fundaminskii, "Biblioteka akademika S. P. Krasheninnikova." There is evidence that the published *Sibirica* of the age touched chiefly scholarly circles in Europe. See Robel, "Die Siberienexpeditionen."

[175] Fundaminskii, "Biblioteka russkogo uchenogo XVIII veka A. P. Protasova"; see also the biography by Lukina, *A. P. Protasov*, p. 173, which mentions his copies of Ovid, Virgil, Hippocrates, Tibullus and Propertius, Seneca, Suetonius, Cicero, and Cato.

[176] These libraries are discussed in detail in the section which follows.

Ljaskorons'kyj, by contrast, owned thirty-six books, but two-thirds of them were in Latin. Educations divided the clergy, and divided Russians from Ukrainians and Europeans, at home and abroad. These libraries mirrored the Petrine social revolution effected by education. The *raznochintsy* took to the Ukrainians' and the Germans' Latin schooling far better than did the nobles, on whom Peter allegedly had hoped to build his new society.[177]

It has long been popular to depict this education as filling the heads of pupils with "irrelevant allusions to classical deities," and to talk of students whose thought demonstrated "a Latin and dialectic form devoid of intellectual and religious content."[178] In the historical literature, such criticism of the Ukrainian humanists and their foreign allies has been accepted at face value. Seldom is it acknowledged that scholars are merely repeating the words of the schools' noble and Russian opponents, who, of course, had every reason to reject his particular strain of Europeanization. On the other hand, the repetition of their charges fails to take into account the fine educations visible almost exclusively in the personal libraries of alien Ukrainians and other foreigners in Russian service.

5. *Russian Nobles' Libraries and Culture*

A. *The Problem of Sources (II)*

It is widely recognized that the sources for the history of Russian nobles' libraries in the last third of the century do not exist.[179] A century ago V. S. Ikonnikov, tried to compile these materials with scant success. The Sheremetev family, for example, had a large collection of over four thousand volumes, but it was lost in 1812, and apparently no catalogue survived. V. G. Orlov, brother of the favorite of Catherine, had a large library at his estate near Moscow; rich in manuscripts, it too was lost in 1812, as was the 40,000 volume collection of Dmitrii Petrovich Buturlin.[180] A. S. Stroganov amassed

---

[177] Kliuchevskii, "Zapadnoe vliianie v Rossii posle Petra."

[178] Freeze, *Russian Levites*, p. 92.

[179] Conversation with Dmitrii Zhivov, Spring, 1990, Göttingen. See also, "Pamiati S. P. Luppova," pp. 192–94.

[180] Ikonnikov, *Opyt russkoi istoriografii*, Vol. I, Kn. 1–2, Kiev, 1891, 1091–94, 1098–11. The best account of the Sheremetev collections is Prokof'eva & Sharkova, "O biblioteke Sheremetevykh." This study is concerned with the working library rather

a significant library in his home, designed by Rastrelli on Nevskii Prospekt, but no catalogue seems available. Potemkin had a large library, but its fate is unknown; V. N. Panin had a collection of almost eleven thousand volumes, but Ikonnikov could find no catalogue. Other vast libraries were held by Ia. I. Bulgakov, M. S. Vorontsov (in St. Petersburg, Moscow, on his estates, and in Odessa), and A. B. Kurakin, who collected "mostly French classics."[181] Among the lesser nobility and the "intelligentsia," we know that two thousand of Nikolai Novikov's books went to the Zaikonospass monastery, almost six thousand to Moscow University, and that the total number of his books may have reached eighteen thousand, but no list is yet available.[182] This disappointing observation introduces the discussion of Russian aristocratic book-owning in the age of Enlightenments.

B. *Nikolai Novikov, Courtier*

Historians rightfully look for change. Russian historians have been fixated on changes within the Russian gentry, to the point where they sometimes fail to recognize how little change had occurred. The European transformation of the Russian elite had been a dream as far back as the 1640s when Rtishchev summoned Slavinec'kyj from Kiev, and borrowed a *Kniga Aristotelova* from the tsarist library.[183] Judging by aristocratic libraries and thought, late in the eighteenth century the process was far from complete.

When Nikolai Novikov attended the Gymnasium of Moscow University it consisted of four "schools," Russian, Latin, Science, and Modern Languages (French and German). After his obligatory year

---

than the professional collector, and Buturlin was a world-renowned devotee of the rarest editions by Didot, Baskerville, Bodoni, and Renoir. Ikonnikov, *op. cit.*, 1157–58; Gennadi, "Russkie bibliofily. (Biblioteki grafa D. P. Buturlina)." Catherine's books are poorly known, but resembled the contemporary "lady's library." See Murzakevich, "Kabinet zimniago dvortsa imperatritsy Ekateriny II."

[181] Ikonnikov, *op. cit.*, pp. 1094–97, 1100–05, 1110, 1118–30, 1130–35. The library of N. N. Vorontsov was described in brief in the "Zapiska N. N. Murzakevicha."

[182] *Ibid.*, pp. 1151–53; Marc Raeff reports that E. Beshenkovsky intends to publish a list of books confiscated at the time of Novikov's arrest. See Ikonnikov, *op. cit.*, pp. 1145–51, for the disappointing information on clerical libraries. Another lost library was that of F. V. Karzhavin, who travelled to America in 1782. See Polonskaia, "Knigi iz biblioteki i s avtografami F. F. Karzhavina." On the provincial library of a Kievan teacher see Krestova & Kuz'mina, "Ioil' Bykovskii, propovednik." One awaits, for the early 19th century, the work of Andrew Kahn, recently defended at Oxford.

[183] Zabelin, *Domashnii byt russkikh tsarei*, I, Pt. 2, 592.

in the Russian school, Novikov chose French. It was a logical choice. His university years coincided with Nikolai Popovskii's abandonment of Latin as the language of instruction for the advanced philosophy course.[184] Cicero's *On Duties* was published in Russian translation by the Academy of Sciences in 1761; it came too late for the formal education of Novikov, who attended the Gymnasium between 1757 and 1760. Only in 1765 did Urbanski recommend the acquisition of twenty copies of Tully's *Duties, Orations,* and his *Epistles* for the classes in rhetoric. The Classics thus could form but a small part of his education.

Novikov's reputation, of course, is one of enlightenment, of bold literary combat with his sovereign, and of secular publisher. We lack precise information on Novikov's personal library, but the lists of books he published were neither more secular and modern, nor more religious or obscurantist, than those of contemporary, successful, commercial publishers in England.[185] During the ten years of Novikov's tenure at the Press of Moscow University, the "religious and Free-masonic" portion of his editions, narrowly defined, ranged annually between ten and eighteen percent of his output.[186] Unless at some point archives reveal more precisely just how day-to-day decisions were made concerning the publication or rejection of individual manuscripts, we are unlikely to resolve his role as an "enlightened" distributor of books.

He was, however, no freethinker. His famous literary squabbles with Catherine have been overly politicized in an historical literature determined to make him the true liberal forerunner of the intelligentsia.[187] But his ties to a particularly mystical strain of Masonry were indisputably deep and sincere.[188] Whatever his education, his mind was characterized by a mystical Christian orientation to an "inner enlightenment" based on Revelation:

> Those wishing to see the Supreme Intelligence in its full radiance should set about reading the Holy Scriptures with true diligence and zeal—

---

[184] Jones, *Nikolai Novikov,* pp. 7, 9. On the four schools, and especially the Latin school, see Rozhdestvenskii, *Ocherki po istorii,* pp. 220–24.

[185] Okenfuss, "The Novikov Problem." Semennikov, *Knigoizdatel'skaia deiatel'nost';* Mel'nikova, *Izdaniia napechatannye v tipografii;* Martynov, *Knigoizdatel' Nikolai Novikov.* The best account is Jones, *Novikov,* Chaps. 10 & 11.

[186] Lauer, "Russische Freimauerdictung," p. 288.

[187] See Jones, "The Polemics of the 1769 Journals."

[188] See for example Baehr, "The Masonic Components," and for the following, McArthur, "Freemasonry and Enlightenment," p. 374.

for in them all the secrets of the divinity and of Nature are noted and explained—although in spiritual language.

Novikov was a religious thinker. When his religious beliefs were subjected to a rigorous twelve-point examination in 1786—he was being investigated under suspicion that Masonry represented a new religious movement—Metropolitan Platon declared, "Before the throne of God . . . in the whole world there should be such Christians as Novikov." A contemporary examination of his personal library revealed 22 suspect works among the 461 books reviewed. They were not dangerous for their atheism. All were Masonic tracts translated by his friends.[189]

Once briefly in youth attracted to neo-Stoicism, Novikov was not indifferent to the Classics. When he and his Masonic friends founded their journal *Morning Light* in 1777, like the moral weeklies in Germany, it bristled with Classical allusions, comparing their circle to the Athenian Areopagus, calling for a *vita activa* ("Be useful to men of good sense"), publishing Plutarch on *fortuna*, and comparing their journal's mission to that of Thucydides.[190]

The most typical and well-known of his writings was the essay "On Education," penned during 1783 and 1784, and based on his readings in Locke and Rousseau. At Moscow University his teacher, Nikolai Popovskii, had translated Locke's *On Education*. In the early 1780s Catherine was, in the aftermath of the Pugachev uprising, increasingly inclined toward conservative political views, seeking to achieve the unquestioning loyalty of her "enlightened subjects." Novikov responded with this essay, Catherine became incensed, and began her investigation of Novikov and of his Masonic friends when its final installment appeared in print.[191] On the basis of his own *On Education*, Novikov has been hailed as the "Russian who did the most to popularize enlightened attitudes and notions among his countrymen."[192]

As early as 1721 a very conservative Montesquieu in his *Persian Letters*

---

[189] Jones, *Novikov*, pp. 188–90.

[190] Raeff, *Russian Intellectual History*, pp. 62–67.

[191] Makogonenko, *Nikolai Novikov*, pp. 490–95.

[192] Raeff, *Russian Intellectual History*, p. 61; for the following, the translation by Valentine Snow, pp. 68–86. All page references in the text are to this translation. Raeff and Snow used the text in Malyshev, ed., *N. I. Novikov i ego sovremenniki*, pp. 257–323; It can be sampled in the context of Novikov's related writings in Novikov, *Izbrannye pedagogicheskie sochineniia*, pp. 89–177.

had begun a political discourse by explicitly rejecting revealed religion. In the regency after 1715, when he inquired "whether men were made happier by the pleasures and satisfactions of the senses or by the practice of virtue," he set the tone for the French Enlightenment when he denounced the priest's scriptural answers as unsatisfactory: "I have talked with the mollahs about this, but they drive me to despair with their quotations from the Koran."[193] His rejection of Revelation set the tone for the age.

Novikov began his essay quite differently. He recognized that religion as much as laws or "the arts and learning" guided behavior. "Base carnal desires and the flames of passion" are controlled by one's upbringing in youth, and thereafter by "law, *religion* (my italics—MJO), decorum, learning, and the arts." From its opening paragraph Novikov's essay explicitly endorsed organized religion.

Did Novikov champion the ancient authors in this essay, even in parts untranslated because they were "merely a restatement of the opinions commonly held on these matters in the eighteenth century"?[194] Novikov encouraged parents to use the examples of history to educate the heart "or soul" of youth, and while any philosophe would have had countless examples of Roman virtue and valor to relate, Novikov was silent. He did not cite the Latin adages of the moral weeklies, but preferred the traditional invocations of the *Proverbs* of Solomon, *"The Fear of the Lord is the beginning of wisdom," "for a Fear of God saves one from evil, and this is wisdom."* He urged parents to raise their children in preparation for "eternal bliss" (pp. 145, 147, 156; *Proverbs* 9:10).[195] Novikov wrote repeatedly that it was all important to teach children from their earliest days the truths of revealed Christianity, to teach them from infancy to recognize religion as the best and most sanguine means of attaining virtue and personal well-being, and to remind them of the sermons of Christ and the words of the Apostles: *"He who loves the Lord, keeps his Commandments"* (pp. 158–9, 166). One can overstate Novikov's Christianity. He did devote pages to physical education in Rousseau's ways; he did, in Montesquieu's fashion talk about fulfilling one's duties as a "man, citizen, father of household, and friend," echoing his categories of secular morality and civic virtue. But these were minor chords.

---

[193] Montesquieu, *The Persian Letters*, p. 22.
[194] Raeff, *op. cit*, p. 86.
[195] The citation of Proverbs is in the Russian text in a portion not translated; see Novikov, *Izbrannnye*, p. 156, and my comment below.

Novikov wrote almost exclusively in the metaphor of religion. "We venture to hope that what we have said already and what we still have to say will not be a sermon delivered in the desert but a word of benediction at the appropriate time" (pp. 85–86). Elsewhere Novikov echoed *Domostroi* and pre-Lockean European thought when he declared, "Every household is a miniature government in which the children are offered the example of various relationships [and] various tasks" (p. 78). The comparison is not forced. In passages dictating the use of wine, vodka, coffee, chocolate, cocoa butter, and beer, Novikov sounded very much like the sixteenth-century compiler of that guide to household management in the quest for eternal salvation. In a lengthy section on "Religion and Christianity"[196] in italics Novikov announced boldly, *"Instill in your children or pupils from earliest age a favorable disposition toward the importance and the truths of religion and of Christianity."*[197]

His Christian message was generally protestant: "Tell and show [the children] that deeds are more important than knowledge," and that the best person is not the Christian who knows best what his faith requires, but he whose "thoughts and behavior most resemble the thoughts and deeds of Jesus Christ, the founder of our religion." "Faith without deeds is death."[198] These passages suggest a positive attitude toward revealed religion, and a persistent religious outlook on moral issues.

Novikov's mind was limited by the poverty of his education in Classical radicalism. He lacked an appreciation of the Roman Enlightenment's revolt against the gods. Novikov was incapable of posing the neo-pagan question, "how are we made moral without the threat of eternal damnation?" As Platon noted, his ethical system did not differ markedly from that of Orthodoxy. If the threat of Hell played no major role in his ideal upbringing for children, neither was he capable of escaping the thought that a "Fear of the Lord" could accomplish as much. He jousted with his sovereign, but he resembled her in her conservative, post-Pugachev mask.

Novikov and his youthful friends had been enthralled with Stoicism. Out of that education came an ability to mix pagan and Christian metaphors, a trait previously rare among Russian nobles. But there

---

[196] They were not included in the translation; Novikov, *Izbrannye*, pp. 156–167.
[197] *Ibid.*, pp. 157–58.
[198] These passages were also untranslated. *Ibid.*, p. 166.

seems no reason to think that neo-Classical studies challenged the Orthodox assumptions of his childhood. He was a moderate, pious *Aufklärer* rather than an anti-clerical philosophe. The scholarly discussions of Novikov's satirical journals and of his Masonic agenda miss the most obvious characteristic of his mind. He was an eighteenth-century courtier, in whom the religious preoccupations of his seventeenth-century forebears were scarcely disturbed.

C. *Paul Demidov and A. T. Bolotov, Noble Readers*

One symbol of a belated acceptance of a Latin education by a small portion of Russia's nobility was to be seen in the life and library of Paul Demidov. He belonged to "The Fourth Generation" of the Demidovs who had lost the entrepreneurial drive of their forebears.[199]

Demidov was born in 1738, privately educated "chez le Professeur Sigismundi," mastered Latin, and departed at age thirteen "to study mathematics, physics and mineralogy at Göttingen and Freiburg." He would travel throughout Western Europe for thirteen years, and eventually study natural science with Linnaeus in Upsala. At home during the rest of his life, "*il y passe son temps dans un vrai répos philosphique, partagé entre la lecture et la contemplation de la nature*," working in his gardens, and corresponding with his former teachers, especially Linnaeus. He counted among his publications seven volumes of his *Reisen*, "philosophical" publications even for savants like Pallas and Linnaeus, as well as his notes on his teachers' lectures. He also credited himself with the publication of the *Catalogue* of his library, since for it he produced an elaborate and reasoned "*Système bibliographique*" in which he attempted to classify human knowledge biologically into "*classes ou Genres.*" This was a formidable enterprise which invited comparison with the Encyclopedia's own iconographic Tree of Human Knowledge, and Detailed System of Human Knowledge based on the Lockean categories of memory, reason, and imagination; it anticipated the post-Kantian *Naturphilosophie* of the nineteenth century.

The library was indeed a philosophical accomplishment, a gentleman's library of works so exquisitely selected and arranged that

---

[199] Hudson, *The Rise of the Demidov Family*, pp. 107–114. For the following see [Paul de Demidoff], *Catalog systématique des livres de la bibliothèque de Paul de Demidoff*, M, 1806, not used by Hudson. On the Bergakademie in Freiburg, founded 1765, see Grau, "Russisch-sächsische Beziehungen."

to read its titles is to contemplate the decline of that kind of education since the nineteenth century. To describe it adequately required two hundred and seventy five pages. Four summary statements can be made. First, Demidov was throughout his whole life a working natural scientist with a vast scientific library, on working terms and in correspondence with other leading scientists throughout the Western world. He also owned an enormous library of theology. He owned over twenty editions of Scripture, all the Greek and Latin Fathers, a rich collection of modern theology and of ecclesiastical history, and even a special sub-section of works "*Contre Voltaire.*" His religious collection should not surprise us. In Russia and the West, the age of Enlightenments had not meant the death of religious literature.[200]

Second, Demidov was a thoroughly modern reader, but on the shelf marked "*Pedagogie,*" Comenius' *Orbis Pictus* stood next to Cicero; in the section "*Théâtre*" Plautus accompanied Molière and Shakespeare; under "*Histoire Ecclésiastique*" Eusebius stood next to the works of the Chair of Theology at Göttingen, Mosheim; under moral philosophy Epicurus accompanied Pufendorf and Kant; and under "*Politique, Administration, etc.,*" Aristotle stood with Bielfeld, Machiavelli, Hume, and Kant's *On Eternal Peace.* For Demidov the ancients lived in an intellectual continuum with the present.

Third, Demidov divided his library into two parts, books in the European languages, and books in Russian or Slavonic. He proposed to organize the latter according to the same categories he had devised for his European books. It didn't work. Although he assiduously collected a huge proportion of the books published in eighteenth-century Russia, including almost all of the translations of the Classics, the editions of the Academy, and much in Cyrillic, when he tried to organize them as he had his Western books the system collapsed for lack of titles. Time and again he was forced to combine and compress whole genera of classes into one, for there simply did not exist enough Russian-language books to fill the spaces, so incomparably small was Russian output.

Fourth, Demidov knew what he wanted, and if unavailable in print, he commissioned and acquired it in manuscript: His Western works numbered only about twenty-five, mostly from his school days in

---

[200] Theology was in fact by far the single largest category of books in the supposedly secular Library of the Academy of Sciences in 1793. See *Istoriia Biblioteka Akademii nauk SSSR 1714–1964*, p. 147.

Germany. For Russian, there were over a hundred and fifty, and they were the books of a seventeenth-century courtier: chronicles and chronographs, a Kurbskii letter, liturgical books, Patristics, sermons of the Church Fathers and of the seventeenth-century Ukrainians who had attempted to disrupt Muscovy, and their polemics against the schismatics and against the Lutherans. The Slavic section of Demidov's library—he had a special section of seventeenth-century printed works of theology "*na Beloruskom dialekte*"—with its large proportion of manuscripts, reminds us of the cultural divide between the book cultures of Russia and Western Europe at the beginning of the nineteenth-century. Its rich fund of manuscripts, reminds us of the survival of a reading culture scarcely touched by the Russian print revolution since the age of Peter the Great. It also challenges the notion that printed books ended the older world of manuscripts.

In Paul Demidov one sees the realization of Peter's dream of transforming the old middle service class into a European gentry, Orthodox, university educated, scientifically minded, travelled, and benevolent in spirit. There were few like him. Matveev and Golitsyn had been earlier exceptions.

Few Russian noblemen had accepted the invitation to Latin. The library of the most famous chronicler of his age, A. T. Bolotov (1738–1833) reflected the more common education. He learned to read in Slavonic through the traditional primer method, then passed into the hands of a Baltic-German sergeant, then to the house tutor of a Baltic landowner; at age eleven he entered a small private pension in St. Petersburg and learned French: it was almost a parody of the notorious education of the private tutor in Russia. His first real book was Fénelon's *Telemachus*, which he curiously regarded as "more classical than the classics of ancient authors." He read the *Allgemeine Geschichte* of H. Curas, Quintus Curtius Rufus, and Aesop, and at age fourteen he attempted to translate a French novel. When orphaned at 15, he was reading *Telemachus* and saints' lives; at 17 his "formal" education ended as he entered service, hated it, and read Barclay's *Argenis* in Trediakovskii's Russian translation, Le Sage's *Gil Blas*, and Prevost d'Exile's *Life of Cleveland, an English Philosopher*. Through them he began to "make a philosopher of himself." In Germany during the Seven-Years War he read *Robinson Crusoe*, Pope's *On Man*, and J. G. Sulzer's *Moralische Betrachtungen über die Werke der Natur*, and J. T. Oxenstierna's *Pensées et réflexions morales*. He credited

Gottsched for his introduction to philosophy and enlightened ethics based on reason rather than on Revelation.[201]

Bolotov was a collector, buying a couple of hundred volumes a year later in his life, on topics ranging from agriculture to literature and philosophy, but no complete catalogue survives. From *ex-libris* and numerous works referred to in his autobiographical sketches, it is possible to get a rather complete portrait of his mind.[202] He retained his teenage interest in moral literature, owning such titles as J. H. Campe, *Theophron oder Der erfahrne Ratgeber für die unerfahrne Jugend*, Formey, *Der christliche Philosoph*, and L. Holberg, *Moralische Gedanken*.

He also collected the popular, sentimental, didactic, and just plain trashy literature of the day, including such works as J. J. Dusch, *Der Verlobte Zweier Bräute*, T. B. Durach, *Sara von Uriz, oder das Ruinengespenst*, *Delia, ou Histoire d'une jeune Héritière*, Elisabeth Bennet, *Les imprudences de la jeunesse*, Baronne de Vasse, *Le mariage platonique*, F. G. Ducray-Duminil, *Lolotte et Fanfan, ou les aventures de deux enfants abandonnés dans une ile déserte*, *Amaliens Schöner Morgan*, the *Geschichte der Miss Fanny Wilkes*, or *L'amitié tragie, ou les mémoires d'un négociant*. His known books, his citations, and his reading habits, evidence an absolute indifference to the Classics. He bought literature which stimulated moral behavior, but he was uninterested in the ancient pagan authors.[203] He represents the ability of the Russian gentry to ignore the repeated offering of Latin humanism for over a century, and instead to preserve the voyeuristic reading habits of the outwardly Orthodox Muscovite courtiers. His books most resembled the ladies' libraries of Europe. Omitting the humanists' modern Latin centuries, he and his readers moved directly from piety to pulp. They shared an indifference to religion found among contemporary philosophes, but a taste for cheap literature with the denizens of grub street.

Once Peter the Great, the seventeenth-century courtier par excel-

---

[201] For the above, Shchepkina, "Popularnaia literatura." On the publishing of Le Sage, Prévost, and other popular works, see Blium, "Massovoe chtenie," and LeBlanc, "Making 'Gil Blas' Russian." On Bolotov's forgettable education, see Rice, "The Memoirs of A. T. Bolotov," pp. 27–32.

[202] For this section, Glagoleva, "A. T. Bolotov kak chitatel'"; and her "Biblioteka A. T. Bolotova."

[203] See Neuhäuser, *Toward the Romantic Age*, pp. 27–31, for this side of Russian letters, based on Bolotov's own survey of Western literature in Russian translation. On the reading of cheap Western novels in Russia, to the exclusion of the significant, see Iu. D. Levin, "The English Novel in 18th-Century Russia," in A. G. Cross, ed., *Literature, Lives, and Legality*, 143–67.

lence, had exercised his freedom of choice of available Wests, and had been titillated by the illustrations from Ovid's *Metamorphosis*. Now Bolotov too selected from the available repertoire of Western learnings, and entertained himself with visions of chaste marriages and incest on desert islands. Most Russians of the elite moved directly from Muscovite values to the modern vulgar revolt against the Classics, without ever absorbing the humanist's values. It is by no means certain that "the Russian nobleman of Elizabeth's time . . . bore no resemblance to his grandfather or even father."[204] The sad fate of Latin studies among the nobility in Russia, and the testimony of their libraries, suggest that they were closer in habits of mind and book to their ancestors than has been realized.

A long time ago, Michael Confino challenged, on convincing economic grounds, Marc Raeff's contention that the fabled nineteenth-century Russian intelligentsia had its cultural roots in the Europeanization of the eighteenth-century nobility.[205] What libraries and texts reveal of the reading habits of most Russian nobles confirms his doubts. Books suggest that the *raznochintsy* of priests' and soldiers' sons were far more susceptible to a Latin education than their well-born cohorts.

D. *Alexander Radishchev, the Culmination of Humanism*

After the founding of Moscow University a few Russian nobles began to share the humanists' vision of life. Some studied in Moscow, or abroad, or both. Some forged a common culture, a vision of education and civic virtue with those sons of priests and *raznochintsy*, who were similarly schooled by the clergy. If Western ideas alienated anyone from "the people," it was this but socially heterogenous group, not the Russian nobility alone.[206]

A small aristocratic "moral fraternity" was formed by Moscow University.[207] "I am bound to remember the University with gratitude." said Fonvizin. "It was there that I learnt Latin and was grounded in several branches of knowledge. At the University I picked up quite a lot of German, and above all acquired a taste for literary pursuits."[208] Out of this milieu came a handful of nobles who had Latin. The

---

[204] Raeff, *Origins*, p. 73.
[205] Michael Confino, "Histoire et Psychologie."
[206] Raeff, *Origins*, Chapters 4 and 5.
[207] Gleason, *Moral Idealists*, Chapter 2.
[208] Cited in Lang, *The First Russian Radical*, p. 24.

way was cleared for a noble Karamzin, pupil of Moscow University's Johann Schaden, to produce a hundred and sixty separate bits of translation, including an extraordinarily broad spectrum of French letters, Shakespeare, and German authors, but also Cicero, Sallust, and Tacitus.[209]

This almost invisible attitudinal breakthrough was the background for Alexander Radishchev, also formed by Moscow University, and his mentor-friend, Fedor Vasil'evich Ushakov.[210] His friendship with Ushakov evoked from Radishchev one of the very few quotations by an eighteenth-century Russian which clearly reflected the Roman Enlightenment, with Cicero thundering against Catiline, and the *Satiricon* criticizing Nero. Radishchev wished his biography of Ushakov could approach the quality of Tacitus' "Life of Agricola." Arguably he was the only Russian noble in the century to master the Latin idiom as a cultural norm. He compared his Classically-educated fore-runner Lomonosov, "the creator of Russian letters," to Horace; he too "flattered sovereigns," as Virgil had flattered Augustus. He re-garded Cato as "the Roman hero par excellence." He wondered openly how good and virtuous Romans could have produced such monstrous rulers, a question that many latter-day enlighteners of many stripes would come to ask in the era of the French Revolution.[211]

Radishchev's Ukrainian friend and fellow-student at Leipzig was one R. M. Tsebrikov (1762–1817), a well-educated careerist in the College of Foreign Affairs, who worked on the codification of the Russian laws as well.[212] His professional library held Bentham, Blackstone, Beccaria and Dilthey, in addition to monuments of Russian law, but he also read Cicero, Virgil, Ovid, Horace, and Homer, as well as Shakespeare, Milton, Defoe, and, one might add, Henry Fielding.

To read Fielding properly required a Classical education. Over a hundred and fifty Classical allusions or Latin citations appear in *Tom Jones* alone. Latin held its sway even as the modern novel was being born in the West, and Fielding was fully aware of the transition. In

---

[209] Kafanova, "Bibliografiia perevodov N. I. Karamzina." The Cicero consisted of short selections from *De natura deorum*.

[210] For the following, McConnell, "Radishchev and Classical Antiquity."

[211] The life of Ushakov is available in Radishchev, *Izbrannye filosofskie i obshchestvenno-politicheskie proizvedeniia*, pp. 220–77. On the mixture of French and of Classical sources in Radishchev's writings, see Page, "A Radiscev Monstrology."

[212] Tatarintsev, "Biblioteka R. M. Tsebrikova."

his pages, the widow Hunt displayed the reading habits of the ladies' library, "dividing her times between her devotions and novels, of which she was always extremely fond," while the very proper and aristocratic Mrs. Western had read the ancients. She reflected, "I am a little altered. Kingdoms and states, as Tully Cicero says in his epistles, undergo alterations, and so must the human form." Fielding confessed his free-wheeling use of Classical quotations:

> The ancients may be considered as a rich common, which every person who hath the smallest tenement in Parnassus hath a free right to fatten his muse. . . . The ancients, such as Homer, Virgil, Horace, Cicero, and the rest, [are] to be esteemed among us writers as so many wealthy squires, from whom we, the poor of Parnassus, claim an immemorial custom of taking whatever we can come at.[213]

Until Russians recognized the universal dependence on Latin, their comprehension of Europe's books would be limited, and access to its Enlightenments as well. Small wonder that the end of the eighteenth century witnessed an explosion of translations of English novels, but almost all by forgotten minor writers whose Classical educations were far inferior to Fielding's.[214]

Radishchev and Tsebrikov, although they were raised on the *Ladder* of Psalter and Book of Hours, came by their solid Classical educations under the sway in Leipzig of a faculty shaped by J. A. Ernesti (1707–1781), Professor of Ancient Literature, after 1759 Professor of Theology, and the "German Cicero."[215] The publisher of Cicero, Tacitus, and Homer, a man famous for his course of rhetoric and for his own orations, Ernesti seems the best source of the Radishchev who could exclaim over "the expressive strength of Demosthenes, the sweetness of Cicero's orations."[216]

Radishchev therefore could care personally about Cicero. His "Brief Account of the Origin of Censorship" asked what would the world have lost if Cicero's books had been burned, as works of Titus Labienus had been by Caesar Augustus?[217] He cared about the study

---

[213] Henry Fielding, *Tom Jones*, [1749], pp. 537–38, 732, 796.
[214] Levin, "The English Novel."
[215] See Lang, *Radishchev*, pp. 20, 47–48, as well as McConnell, *A Russian Philosophe*, p. 11; Kochetkova, "Radishchev i problema krasnorechiia." The role of Ernesti has been suggested since the appearance of Startsev, *Universitetskie gody Radishcheva*, pp. 24–30, which gives their study plan and mentions other faculty, including Gellert.
[216] Radishchev, *A Journey from St. Petersburg to Moscow*, p. 234.
[217] *Ibid.*, p. 173, and for the following, pp. 78, 193.

of Latin. He described a meeting with a student of Latin from Novgorod who deplored his pedantic studies, as they could not "satisfy a mind hungry for learning." Although he could quote Virgil, Horace, Livy, and Tacitus "almost by heart," he felt he knew nothing. Facing the eternal problem encountered in teaching a "dead" language, Radishchev suggested that the ancient authors were being taught badly for mastery of the syntax rather than for the relevance of the text, and thus the Russian diocesan college "belongs to a bygone age." His own faith in the Latin curriculum was unshaken. Re-energized with modern Classics, it could prevail: "Homer, Virgil, Milton, Racine, Voltaire, Shakespeare, Tasso, and many others will be read until the human race is destroyed."

In the nineteenth century, when Classical studies had been reintroduced, Radishchev would find his clandestine readership. Nobles would begin to collect and read the pagan authors. In the meantime, the same Catherine who condemned his book, had abruptly curtailed the study of Latin in Russia.

CHAPTER FOUR

EPILOGUE: THE FATE OF LATIN CULTURE IN RUSSIA IN THE LATE EIGHTEENTH CENTURY

1. *Catherine's Public Schools and the End of Latin*

A. *Introduction: Catherine's School Reform*

Catherine II successfully created a network of two-year schools in the 1780s. It was the educational component of her Provincial Reform of 1775, and the ideological heart of the school system was a book of civics, *On the Duties of Man and Citizen*.[1] The Reform represented her response to Pugachev's uprising. The well-intentioned monarch, whose non-Classical education gave her no reason to appreciate Ukrainian humanism, built a school system antithetic to its ideals. This school system—it was Russia's first and grew to three hundred schools with seventeen thousand pupils by Catherine's death—was an aspect of provincial governance. It was the pedagogical underpinning of crowd-control in a rebellious multinational empire. Its ideological message was timid, statist, and conservative. The textbooks for Catherine's nationwide network of schools were decreed to be uniformly applied to all new institutions, to the old humanist Latin academies, to nobles' institutes, and even to private tutors and pensions, in short, to all schools in Russia and its borderlands alike.[2]

---

[1] The text has been Englished by Elizabeth Gorky and published in Black, *Citizens for the Fatherland*, pp. 209–66, but note the reservations below.

[2] Max J. Okenfuss, "Education and Empire"; see also de Madariaga, "The Foundation of the Russian Educational System," and her *Russia in the Age of Catherine*, pp. 495–502; Matl', "F. Ia. Iankovich i avstro-serbsko-russkie sviazi"; Polz, "Theodor Jankovich und die Schulreform," and his "Die Volksaufklärung"; the anniversary publication was Nikolskii, "Shkol'naia reforma," but see also D. A. Tolstoi, "Gorodskie uchilishcha," and the still incomparable Demkov, *Istoriia russkoi pedagogiia*, Vol. II, and Rozhdestvenskii, *Ocherki po istorii sistem*. The newest study of the financing of the schools is Hartley, "The Boards of Social Welfare." De Madariaga laments the lack of studies of the institutions set up as part of the Provincial Reform of 1775; de Madariaga, "Catherine the Great," in Scott, ed., *Enlightened Absolutism*, p. 298.

The schools created and transformed by Catherine's Commission on Public Schools in the 1780s were modern. If one imagines a continuum from the rough and tumble neglect of students in medieval times to the endless lesson-plans of the present-day teacher, with a seventeenth-century discovery of childhood as a midpoint, the detailed bureaucratic procedures imported from Prussia via the Empire by Iankovich de Mirievo were modern. Those translated from the German and introduced in the 1780s were more detailed than the regulations of the Belorussian Lutsk Brotherhood School (1624), those for the diocesan colleges in Teofan's Ecclesiastical Regulation (1721), and those written in French by Ivan Betskoi for his boarding schools early in Catherine's reign (1764) combined.[3]

The writings of the Prussian Johann Ignatz von Felbiger, as transmitted from conquered Silesia via the Empire to the Russians, were models of modern *Ordnung*. His plan for a school building had chapters on calculating the number and size of classrooms required for a given number of pupils, on building fire-proof ovens in the *Schulmeister*'s quarters, on the proper arrangement of desks and benches, and it contained as well lists of stone, lumber, plaster, nails, doors, locks, and shingles required for construction.[4] It was all very competent, but reading it already one can sense Locke's gentlemanly tutorials fading into the woodwork as the modern professional school administrator was being born: the reform in Europe and in Russia occasioned the first real teacher-training colleges in history.

Regulations governed the students. The German original assigned each student a "diligence catalogue (*Fleisskatalog*)" and regulated their lives by the hourglass. Pupils were to appear with books, notebooks, pens, and abacus at the ready, punctually at 8:00 in winter (7:00 in summer), having already dutifully attended to their biological needs, ready to respond *zdes'*! when their names were called alphabetically, and ready to raise their left (not their right) hands when they knew the correct answer. When the village priest entered the classroom, all knew they must immediately stand and bow, and that at the end of the day all were to file out, two abreast, going straight home, without playing in the streets. Behavior at school and away was regulated; students were to abstain from wine, vodka, and other intoxicating

---

[3] Ivan Betzky, *Les Plans et les statuts*.
[4] Johann Ignaz von Felbiger, *Anleitung Schulgebäude auf dem Lande*, Leipzig, 1783.

drinks; play was permitted at specified times, but it was to be decorous, seemly, and proper.[5]

Bureaucratic procedure was equally the rule for teachers. Their manual contained instructions on how to use the notorious Alphabetic-*Buchstabieren* method and its concomitant *Tabellen*[6] guides to organizing instructional material, information on the benefits of an orderly classroom, on the proper way to hold a pen, specific instructions for the correct prayers to begin and to end the school day, and a prohibition against using any book or text not decreed by the Commission for the Public Schools.[7] Appendices provided detailed hourly lesson plans, as well as the outlines for students' records (name, *sostoianie*, age, date entered school, number of times tardy, number of unexcused absences, etc.).

The texts of the Felbiger-Mirievo schools dictated orderliness, punctuality, and fidelity to prescribed methods. Petty method seemed to overwhelm content entirely, as Felbiger specified how to hang the Tables of Abbreviated Words, how to use the blackboard, how to keep lines straight, how many times to repeat a lesson, and when to use a *tablitsa* vertically and when horizontally.[8] These regulations are the place where one can locate the early-modern separation of grammar school from college, and the origins of the modern antipathy between professors who know, but cannot teach, and teachers who know how, but not what, to teach.

These schools were modern in their separation of pupils by age (Lomonosov could not have attended) and by level of achievement; in their attempt to involve all the senses in an active learning process to replace passive rote-memorization; in the abandonment of the old letter names which contributed nothing to spelling or phonetics; in their injunctions to teachers to impart civic responsibility, religious morality and practical skills; and in their outright ban on flogging,

---

[5] Iankovich, *Pravila dlia uchashchikhsia v narodnykh uchilishchakh*, St. Petersburg, 1782, pp. 10–14, 18–20, 21, 23.

[6] I treated the pedagogy in my "Education and Empire." For this paragraph, Felbiger, *Eigenschaften, Wissenschaften und Beziegen rechtschaffener Schulleute*, Bamberg, 1772; the Russian text was an abridgement: [Felbiger], *Rukovodstvo uchiteliam pervago i vtorago klassa narodnykh uchilishch*, St. Petersburg, 1783, pp. 5–17, 51ff., 94–95, and appendices, which is cited except as noted.

[7] The list of required texts have been outlined by Joseph Mattl, I. Matl', "F. Ia. Iankovich," who made the one attempt to identify the Serbian models for Russian translation; I have been able to identify several others on the basis of the German originals; see also Peter Polz, "Theodore Jankovich," pp. 139–46.

[8] *Rukovodstvo uchiteliam*, pp. 12–47, *passim*.

caning, physical punishment, and bodily injury.[9] Punishment, Felbiger insisted, was a corrective to the child's behavior, not a form of retribution. This was humane learning, and quite ambitious for a two or three-year curriculum.

What were the sources of this educational modernity? Contemporary Europe no longer offered a single definition of education. The educational views of the Abbé de Condillac's *Traité raisonné du sensations* (1754), those of Rousseau in *Émile* (1762), of René de la Chalotais' *Plan d'éducation nationale* (1763), or Diderot's in his *Plan for a University* (1775–76), varied enormously and no one was recognized as the spirit of the age. There was no Iron Curtain: the full extent of contemporary educational debate was known and largely in print in Russia.[10] Catherine's national school system borrowed consciously from the fluid package of educational texts developed over the previous forty years in Prussian Silesia and the Austrian Empire, in both instances, efforts to govern multi-lingual, multi-ethnic, multi-religious, multi-national empires.

B. *Elementary Textbooks and Ideals*

The essential texts for elementary education were outlined in a teachers' manual: needed were a wall-chart showing the alphabet, the primer, the book of rules for pupils, the short catechism, and the book *On the Duties of Man and Citizen*.[11] The primer issued for these schools, an exclusively religious variant, was in form and content an archaic regression from those previously circulating in Russia, including one Catherine herself had prepared earlier in her reign.[12] Over the decades the new text was published in over a hundred thousand copies and became the standard text for all schools. By 1784 the Synod published an identical edition.[13]

Catherine's conservative Church could accept this particular primer because it reverted to a full seventeenth-century Cyrillic primer

---

[9] *Rukovodstvo uchiteliam*, pp. 3, 8, 30–31, 75, 104; on the old mixing of ages and its passing in Europe, see Ariès, *Centuries*, pp. 189–240.

[10] Okenfuss, "Popular Educational Tracts."

[11] *Rukovodstvo uchiteliam*, p. vi.

[12] *The Discovery of Childhood.*

[13] See Demkov, *Istoriia*, Vol. II, 392, 404; on the Synod's edition, see the *Svodnyi katalog, Dopolnenie*, pp. 46–47. The publication and distribution of textbooks for the schools is covered in Martynova and Martynov, "Peterburgskii knigoizdatel' i knigotorgovets," and Smagina, "Iz istorii sozdaniia i rasprostraneniia uchebnykh knig."

interlaced with the civil alphabet. It contained the vocabulary of the
old Slavonic liturgical language broken into syllables, and a selection
of daily prayers in Cyrillic from the breviary, both staples since the
sixteenth-century. It reverted to the hell-and-damnation motif for its
moral sentiments, reversing Catherine's own previous emphasis on
health and happiness in this world.[14] The primer concluded with a
few fables. Tales of the eagle and the raven, the bear and bee, and
the youth and the old man, were included, with one notable alter-
ation: their concluding morals, the *nravouchenie*, were Christianized,
with the lesson now coming not from a clever animal or an elderly
sage, but from "the Creator," or the "Heavenly Father." Compared
to eighteenth-century primers, it was a return to the past.

The catechism issued for the public schools, and required in their
initial classes, was published in the old Cyrillic script.[15] It discussed
religious truth under two heads. When the teacher asked his charges,
"Which existence is called God?", they were to respond,

> By *God* is called that Existence which created us and the entire world,
> and all the things in the world.

This, the text explained, was a "natural knowledge of God." It was
affirmed by another knowledge of Him, "Revealed Religion," which
was found in the *Symvol very*, the Nicaeno-Constantinopolitan Creed.
The catechism included the traditional lists of the sacraments, and
the ten commandments, with explanations. The injunction to honor
one's parents meant obeying also kings, spiritual pastors, civil authorities, teachers, benefactors, masters, and the elderly. This was
commonplace, since no primer ever taught disobedience.

The theological content of this catechism was a reversion to traditional Orthodoxy and a rejection of Teofan's compromises with Protestantism. Its basis was not the inoffensive Prussian text, but the
Russian catechism of 1765 of Metropolitan Platon (Levshin), now at
the pinnacle of his powers in the 1780s, shortly before his elevation
to the Metropolitanate. It omitted phrases Prokopovych had borrowed
sixty years earlier from Luther's *Short Catechism*.[16] The author of the

---

[14] Okenfuss, *Discovery*, pp. 59–60, 63, and "Education and Empire," p. 56, for
examples; [Iankovich de Mirievo], *Rossiiskii Bukvar' dlia obucheniia iunoshestva chteniiu*,
St. Petersburg, 1782, pp. 18–21, 21–31.

[15] de Mirievo, *Sokrashchenyi katikhizis dlia obucheniia iunoshestva pravoslavnomy zakonu
khristianskomu*, M. 1797. The teachers' version differed from the students' in that
each page contained a series of pedagogical questions on the text, set in the civil script.

[16] See Hauptmann, *Die Katechismen*, pp. 272–74; on the Protestant paths tested
earlier but abandoned here, see Gessinger, *Sprache und Bürgertum*, pp. 35–51.

EPILOGUE203

reform, Iankovich de Mirievo, was devoutly Orthodox, and the Russian version of reform differed from Prussian and Austrian antecedents in its dedication to Orthodox religious principles, even to the coopting of clergy into its teaching corps, a policy unthinkable in Austria when the Jesuits were being disbanded under a general policy of secularization.[17]

When the public schools opened a privately published guide to penmanship has just appeared.[18] It was a beautiful little booklet with engravings reminiscent of those in the *Encyclopédie*, showing correct posture for writing, and the holding of the pen. Its sample-alphabets were gracefully drawn free-hand. The student's practice texts were secular, humane, and by any standard enlightened: "For the learned, all is light, but for the unlearned, darkness."[19] Christianity was neither scorned nor omitted, but the eighteenth-century tendency to deism was emphasized: "The Law commands one to love his neighbor as himself." It contained the old Hellenistic rule of the seven ages of man ascribed to Solon: "A child is a boy until the age of seven; after seven he is a lad; and after fifteen a youth."[20] This non-dogmatic Christianity was harmonized with Xenocrates of the Old Academy:

> The whole teaching of Xenocrates consists of this:
> First, honor God, and then your parents.
> Preserve the truth;
> God will judge those who choose evil.
> Hold no contempt for the needy.
> Keep yourself clean.

This enlightened blend of Classicism, deism, and traditional religion was not adopted by the Commission for Public Schools. Instead it remained faithful to Felbiger, choosing an adaptation of his German guide to writing.[21]

In it the correct form of letters were rigidly girdled by a staff. The first text for copying, also differed in intellectual content: "Fear God;

---

[17] See Matl', "Epokha prosveshcheniia," pp. 202–06, and his "F. Ia. Iankovich," p. 81; also Okenfuss, "Education and Empire," pp. 47, 58–59.

[18] Aleksandr Rykov, *Rukovodstvo, vedushchee k udobnomu izucheniu Rossiiskago chistopisaniia*, St. Petersburg, 1782.

[19] It is probably not worth a major effort of research to establish the provenance of this sentiment, but it has been found in the writings of Field-Marshal A. V. Suvorov; "Bidlung ist Licht, Nichtbildung Dunkelheit (Ucenie svet, neucenie t'ma)"; see Hoffmann, "Zur Differenzierung der russischen Aufklärung," p. 54.

[20] Rykov, *Rukovodstvo*, p. 14. On the ages of man, see my "The Times of our Lives," [forthcoming].

[21] [Iankovich de Mirievo], *Propisi raspolozhennyia po pravilam rukovodstva k chistopisaniiu*, St. Petersburg, 1782; compare to Felbiger, *Eigenschaften*, pp. 160–167, and *passim*.

Honor your Lord and keep His commandments." Prescriptions echoing
Proverbs were revived: "He who does not study in youth will be
bored in old age." "Honor thy parents at every age of your life."
"Children owe their parents gratitude, obedience, and respect."
"Honor all elderly and noble persons, and be the cause of no impu-
dence, offence, or annoyance." A general prescription for good health
to be copied by pupils varied from the theme of earthly health and
happiness taught by the humanists: without prayer and God's intervention, doctors and medicines were doomed to be ineffective. If
God is not inclined to grant one health, no physician and no rem-
edy could help.[22]

To prepare the young for letter writing, the official guide to penmanship provided correct forms of address. A bishop should be addressed as

> *Ego Preosviashchenstvu Arkhiepiskomu Kievskomu i*
> *Chernigovskomu N. N: milostivomu moemu*
> *Arkhipasteriu . . .,*

while to a general, this form was appropriate:

> *Ego Vysokoprevoskhoditel'stva Gospodinu Generalu*
> *Anshefu i Ordena Sviatago velikomuchenika i*
> *pobedonostsa Georgiia Kaveleru N. N: milostivomu moemu*
> *Gosudariu. . . .*

The originals for such forms were found in Felbiger's original German
instructions to address a *Graf* as *Euer hochgräfliche Excellenz*, an ordinary noble as *Euer hochwohlgebohrne Gnaden*, and even a *Bürger* as *Euer
Hochedelgebohrner Herr*.[23] Here is where significant numbers of Russian
non-enserfed pupils learned the prerogatives of the God-given hierarchy of authority, abject submission to one's betters, and the divine
injunctions to obedience, subservience, and social immobility.[24]

The elementary arithmetic decreed for the public schools was a
translation from German.[25] It introduced the four functions and one

---

[22] *Propisi*, pp. iv, vi, ix.

[23] Felbiger, *Eigenschaften*, pp. 273–75, 322–404, for letter writing. It has been argued that these style-books replaced the more aristocratic manuals for the courtier
and their exclusive *style de l'honnête homme* of mid-century; this argument ignores their
religious content. See Dmitrieva, "Russkie pis'movniki," pp. 543–52.

[24] Here I question an old theme in historiography. See Bissonnette, "Peter the
Great and the Church," and in general, Black, *Citizens for the Fatherland*, passim.

[25] I compared for the following [Felbiger] *Anleitung zur Rechenkunst. Zum Gebrauche*

can judge the sophistication of the mathematics from its final problems:

> A certain tower is built in water; 1/4 of its height is in the excavation, 1/3 is in the water, and 10 sazhens are above the water. How many sazhens tall is the tower? Someone leaves a place travelling 6 miles every day, and on the fourth day later another traveller departs, and he covers 10 miles a day. The question is, on which day will the latter meet the former?[26]

The Russian version in places varied from its source, which had been designed for the polyglot Austrian Empire. The original had introduced pupils to several coinages, *Goldmünzen, ein Souverain d'or, ein Kremnitser Dukaten*, but also *ein Kaiserlichen, Hollander, Florentiner* and *ein Salzburger Dukaten*, reflecting the diverse monetary reality of the Empire. All were faithfully rendered into Serbian in the bilingual edition for the Banat. The Russian text, however, omitted the potential lesson in geopolitics, and settled for a list of Russian coins only. Where the original differentiated necessarily between the Austrian and the Hungarian weights and measures, and those used in the *"ottomannischen Gebietye"* of the realm, the Russian version simply omitted such lessons, and gave Russian standards only.[27]

When selecting a textbook for cosmology, of all the possible European books available a century after Newton, the one translated was Johann Heinrich Lambert, *Système du monde*.[28] It declared in a language reminiscent of Creationists a century after Darwin, "The system of Copernicus is, in fact, only a theory; but we have seen that astronomy can come at truth only by carefully bringing under review every possible hypothesis. . . . Upon the whole, we may draw this conclusion, that the heavens are made to endure, but the things of this earth to pass away." Although the advanced textbook of physics gave a fuller version of the scientific revolution, it too remained noncommittal. Under the title, "the theoretical part of astronomy," it mentioned the system of Ptolemy, the mid-sixteenth-century publication of Copernicus, the late sixteenth-century appearance of the

---

der in den Trivialschulen/Rukovodstvie ko Arithmetik, Wien, 1777, with the [Felbiger] *Rukovodstvo k arifmetika*, St. Petersburg, 1783.

[26] Answers: 24 sazhens; on the 6th day.

[27] The literary equivalent of such wallowing in the narrowly nationalistic theme is discussed by W. Gareth Jones, "A Trojan Horse."

[28] 2nd edition, Berlin, 1784; the Russian edition is dated 1797. There is an English edition, *The System of the World*, London, 1800, from which the quotations are taken, pp. 160, 161.

Danish astronomer Tycho Brahe, and concluded with Kepler's laws. But the well documented Russian resistance to the Newtonian world view persisted, even at the end of the eighteenth century.[29] Now it was dictated to young learners throughout the Russian empire.

The public schools fostered an attitude toward organized religion and religious values. The tone for the institutions was set by the first words on the first page of the *Rules for Students*, the first book read after the liturgically based primer itself:

> *The beginning of wisdom is the Fear of God* [Psalms 111:10]; above all else this fear must be instilled in students.

Attendance in the public schools meant regularly attending the Holy Liturgy with one's schoolmates. During the service pupils were to be attentive and pious, recalling constantly to themselves "the eternal love of our Savior who bled on the cross to atone for our sins."[30] Beyond the revival of Cyrillic, the purging of Teofan's rational Protestantism, and the Christianization of Aesop, the heart of the public schools was the revival of Orthodox religiosity.

C. *On the Duties of Man and Citizen*

Nowhere was religion more apparent than in the most famous of Catherine's educational publications, the textbook of civics, *On the Duties of Man and Citizen*. This text has been seen as fundamental to Catherine's enlightened reputation. On it more than anything else hinges the question whether the school reform was really a "turning point for the better," the claim when the text was translated as the premiere educational document of the century.[31] It became a standard text with nine printings between 1783 and 1796, totalling about 47,000 copies.[32] It has received surprisingly little analysis.

The Prussian antecedent had attempted to create a new kind of person and a new social behavior, a *Sozialdisziplinierung*, and to redefine acceptable cultural norms. It aspired to an internal *Kolonisierung*, designed to produce a modern citizen divorced from parental super-

---

[29] See Petr Gilorovskii, *Rukovodstvo k fizike...*, St. Petersburg, 1793, pp. 401–10.

[30] Iankovich, *Pravila dlia uchashchikhsia v narodnykh uchilishchakh*, St. Petersburg, 1782, pp. 5, 8–9.

[31] Black, *Citizens*, p. 130, and the translation by Elizabeth Gorky, pp. 209–66.

[32] Demkov, *Istoriia*, Vol. II, 382–91. The English translation was made from a tenth edition of 1811, and Demkov worked from an eleventh of 1817.

stitions.[33] The Russian text was generally faithful to the German/ Serbian edition. It contained sentiments which went back to Felbiger's general handbook for teachers, chiefly those of a religious instruction based on "catechizing" the Gospels, and those devoted to freezing the divinely inspired social hierarchy.[34]

Every document consists of form and substance. It is one of the tragedies of Russian history in the English language that the translation of *On the Duties of Man and Citizen* so mangles the form that the substance is distorted. In the translation one finds paragraphs on the family as the basis of civil society:

On marital union.
1. The first union is the marital union. This union is the oldest because God himself established it in Heaven. The purpose and the end of it is the continuation of the human race.
2. Only one husband and one wife form this union. They must love each other and be faithful to each other. [They must] be together until death do them part.
3. The husband is the head of the family and the wife is his helper; she has to honour and obey him, be subordinate to him and help him in the home building.
4. The husband should not treat his wife strictly, nor use his power over her maliciously, but should treat her with love; he is obliged to try his utmost to provide food and other necessities. . . .

On Union of parents and children.
From the first or marital union when children are born begins another, namely: *the union between parents and children.*
   Parents, generally speaking, should care for their children. As long as the children are small and still incapable of helping themselves, parents should feed them, bring them up and point out what they should do, because children do not know yet what is good and what is really useful for them and because they would be subjected to want and great harm without the parent's care and guidance since children are helpless. This care of children by their parents should be in the upbringing and upbringing is the guidance of children towards good; [upbringing is] teaching them . . . everything that is necessary in their situation especially the scriptures, providing good examples to deter the evil in them at its inception, and when admonition does not help,

---

[33] See Gessinger, *Sprache und Bürgertum*, pp. 28–30.
[34] The original was [Felbiger], *Rukovodstvo k chestnosti i pravosti/Anleitung zur Rechtschaffenheit*, Wien, 1777, and the Russian, [Felbiger], *O dolzhnostiakh cheloveka i grazhdanina*, St. Petersburg, 1783. A general source was Felbiger, *Eigenschaften*, pp. 6ff., 72ff., and 535ff.; See also a separate but similar work, Felbiger, *Christliche Grundsätze und Lebensregeln zum Unterrichte den Jugend*, Frankenthal, 1773.

not missing the opportunity to punish them without doing them any harm, so that they might not become irritable and embittered from excessive strictness. Parents must also make an effort to acquire and pass on to their children some inheritance. Negligence by the parents in anything mentioned here is a serious violation of their duties.[35]

From these passages one could conclude that while the institution of matrimony was divinely established, it was built on mutual love and on the procreation and nurture of children; that while the husband was the head of the household, he had an obligation to treat his partner-spouse and to raise his children lovingly.

What challenged this notion, however, was the intellectual apparatus published at the bottom of the Russian page and omitted from the English translation. Its message is quite contrary: It is restored here:

Genesis 2:22. *Be fruitful and multiply.* 1 Genesis 1:27, 28. *Male and female created he them. And God blessed them and God said unto them, be fruitful and multiply.*

Genesis 2:24. *A man shall leave his father and his mother, and shall cleave unto his wife.*

Hebrews 13:4. *Marriage is honourable in all, and the bed undefiled: but whore mongers and adulterers God will judge.* I Corinthians 7:39. *The wife is bound by the law as long as her husband liveth.* I Corinthians 7:27. *Art thou bound to a wife? Seek not to be loosed.*

Genesis 3:16. *Unto woman he said . . . thy desire shall be to thy husband, and he shall rule over thee.* Ephesians 5:22. *Wives, submit yourselves unto your own husbands, as unto the Lord.* Ephesians 5:23. *And the wife see that she reverence her husband.* Genesis 2:18. *It is not good that man should be alone: I will make him a help meet for him.*

Colossians 3:19. *Husbands, love your wives and be not bitter against them.* I Peter 3:7. *Ye husbands, dwell with them according to knowledge, giving honour unto the wife, as unto the weaker vessel.* Ephesians 5:28, 29. *So ought men to love their wives as their own bodies. He that loveth his wife loveth himself. For no man every yet hated his own flesh.*

Ephesians 6:4. *Bring them up in the nurture and admonitions of the Lord.* Deuteronomy 4:9. *Teach them thy sons and thy sons' sons.* Deuteronomy 6:5, 6, 7. *Love the Lord thy God with all thine heart . . . and these words . . . thou shalt teach them diligently unto thy children.*

Proverbs 23:13. *Withhold not correction from the child: for if thou beatest him with the rod, he shall not die.* Proverbs 13:25 (24). *He that spareth his rod hateth his soul but he that loveth him chasteneth him betimes.* Proverbs 19:18. *Chasten thy son while there is hope and let not thy soul spare for his crying.* Ephesians 6:4. *Ye fathers provoke not your children to wrath.*

II Corinthians 12:14. *Children ought not to lay up for the parents, but parents*

---

[35] Black, *Citizens*, pp. 235–36.

for the children. I Timothy 5:8. *But if any provide not for his own . . . [he] is worse than an infidel.*

The primary text of Catherine's public schools was intellectually based on a reaffirmation of Holy Scripture as the sole fount of knowledge in social and familial relations.

Likewise one might get the impression from the book's description of authority that the text was a secular assertion of the obligations of temporal power, compatible with Montesquieu's views, and not terribly different from the statements which opened Catherine's *Nakaz* twenty years earlier.

> *On the title and authority of The Ruler.*
> 1. For the well-being and security of their subjects, Rulers have the duty and authority to make *laws and regulations, and to take care that they are enforced; to preserve and administer justice and jurisprudence, to punish criminals and wrongdoers, to protect the life and possessions of citizens against unjust offense and resist attacks by a foreign enemy. . . .*
>
> *On the obligations of subjects in general.*
> 4. All subjects, or members of society, must honour their rulers for their good deeds and the protection they provide. [All subjects must] pray to God for them, obey their laws and regulations, willingly and diligently, give taxes and services without which the rulers can not maintain the general well-being and safety. [One must do this] not out of fear of punishment but because it is their moral obligation before God. Every subject must show honour, love, obedience and loyalty not only to the Sovereign but also to those lesser authorities who are appointed and designated by Him.[36]

The message becomes quite different, however, when the sub-text is restored, that is, when the original medium is considered:

> Romans 13:4. *Put ye on the Lord Jesus Christ. . . .*
> Romans 13:3. *For rulers are not a terror to good works, but to the evil.* Romans 3:4, 5. *. . . as it is written, That thou mightest be justified in thy sayings, and mightest overcome when thou art judges. But if our unrighteousness commend the righteousness of God, what shall we say? Is God righteous who taketh vengeance?* I Peter 2:17. *Love the brotherhood. Fear God. Honour the King.* I Timothy 2:1. *. . . supplications, prayers . . . be made . . . for kings and for all that are in authority.* Romans 13:1, 2. *Let every soul be subject unto the higher power.* Romans 13:6, 7. *Whoever . . . resisteth the power, resisteth the ordinance of God. . . . for they are God's ministers.* I Peter 2:13, 14, 15. *. . . render therefore to all their dues. Submit yourself to every ordinance of man . . . be it to the king or unto governors . . . For so is the will of God.*

---

[36] Black, *Citizens*, pp. 239, 241.

When Felbiger's texts were introduced elsewhere in both Protestant and Catholic Europe, teachers applauded the disappearance of "metaphysical statements, dogmatic beliefs, [and] piles of Biblical quotations that had guided the teachers and students of past generations."[37] In the second half of Catherine's reign it was a tacit conspiracy between Felbiger's pupil Iankovich, and his Russian clerical disciples to reassert voluminous citations of Holy Scripture.

The private reading of the Bible had virtually no tradition in Russia, so these texts can be interpreted as a Protestant and likely a Pietistic incursion. Richard Pipes has popularized the idea that the Russian Church abdicated its moral role and opened the floodgates to secular ideologies.[38] That may have come later, but in Catherine's Russia the School Reform was a reaffirmation of ecclesiastical morality, scripturally affirmed.

O Dolzhnosti with Biblical citations stayed in print as the official text of Russian schools well into the nineteenth century. It is thus hazardous to talk about a national school reform which "practically ignored religion as a subject to be taught in school,"[39] as does one modern scholar. Catherine's schools did indeed repeat themes "emphasized by Tatishchev in his Testament of the 1730s," since both ultimately derived their arguments from the revealed truths of Holy Scripture. A single fleeting reference to Cicero in Felbiger's book, derived from his own book on duties, *De Officiis*, on the subject of proper decorum, was but a vestige of a humanism now abandoned in Russian educational history.

The Russian version of Felbiger's *On Duties* was even more scripturally based than the original Imperial Austrian text. The Russian text alone contained a Biblically supported section which argued that without prayer no medicine and no doctor was effective against illness, and indeed that illness itself was a sign that God was warning us to seek forgiveness for our sins. Youth were taught that one should "seek help and advice from a skilled physician," and obey his instructions exactly, not because his skill cured, but because "God acts through people [the doctors—MJO] he has created," and "when we

---

[37] Ingrao, "The Smaller German States," p. 240.
[38] Pipes, *Russia under the Old Regime*, pp. 244–45 and *passim*. On the failure to the Russian, as opposed to the Ukrainian, Church to produce moral literature, see Platon, *The Present State*, p. 19.
[39] Black, *Citizens*, p. 134, and for the following, p. 135.

are ill He wants us to appeal to Him," for "God Himself guides physicians to a cure."[40]

> Isaiah 38:9, 10, 12, 13, 14. *The writing of Hezekiah king of Judah, when he had been sick, and was recovering of his sickness: I said in the cutting off of my days, I shall go to the gates of the grave: I am deprived of the residue of my years. Mine age is departed, and is removed from me as a shepherd's tent: I have cut off like a weaver my life: he will cut me off with pining sickness: from day even to night wilt thou make an end of me. I reckoned till morning, that as a lion, so will he break all my bones: from day even to night wilt thou make an end of me. Like a crane or a swallow, so did I chatter: I did mourn as a dove: mine eyes fail with looking upward: O Lord, I am oppressed; undertake for me.*

Catherine had herself bravely inoculated against smallpox by Dr. Thomas Dimsdale in 1768. By the 1780s mystical denials of medicine permeated the book of civics and the copybook for penmanship,[41] to be rewritten by each young student attending the schools; the reform was consciously structured on a reaffirmation of revealed religion.

The Russian text of *O Dolzhnosti* was not only fortified with citations of Scripture not present in the German-Serbian text, it also omitted passages from the original. The most significant treated rural folk, "*Vom Bauernstände.*" That section taught that to the ranks of the farmers belonged not only the owners of large fields and of farmsteads, the German *Bauernhof,* but also those "gardeners" who owned smaller arable lands, those who possessed fenced garden-plots, and even those petty rural folk whose labor was essential to those who actually owned extensive fields. This total *Bauernstand* was important: all others lived off their labor, even princes and kings; the farmers fed the cities; they provided the soldiers for the army; their ranks also provided the artisans and all those who worked with their hands; they produced all of the raw materials which laborers, artisans, and craftsmen needed and used to ply their trades; and their excess children also provided the servants and apprentices to all of the other strata of society. Since, therefore, they were the most necessary of all the social strata, they should be treasured as such, and it was essential in every society that they be prosperous, fully contented (*glückselig*), and thoroughly satisfied with their condition in life.

That such a description of peasant life should quietly disappear

---

[40] *O Dolzhnosti*, pp. 59–60. See Black, *Citizens*, pp. 230–31, which omits the Biblical text which follows.

[41] [Iankovich], *Propisi*, p. ix.

from the Russian version of a reader published in the aftermath of the Pugachev uprising, and designed to quiet the provinces, is not surprising.[42] Rural Russia was not likely to be less restive if these inflammatory sentiments against serfdom circulated among the middling orders, now invited into the classrooms of the empire.

Felbiger's educational reforms in Prussia had been based on the ancient and hollowed principle of *Ständesmässigkeit*, the idea that studies should always correspond to a pupil's social position. Peasants should not study Latin since it "only stimulates a desire to enter the priesthood, thereby destroying their natural inclination to practice the occupation of their fathers." Other Prussian officials concurred: "Those peasants who have learned Latin ... are in all respects the most disobedient."[43] "Enlightened" education in central Europe was to preserve the unequal social fabric.

The Russian version of *On Duties* concurred. The social message of the public school reform was encapsulated in the concluding sentence from the omitted paragraphs "On the Farmers," preserved in the Russian text. It prescribed satisfaction with one's born social status, however lowly. The Russian text, like its European model, preached the idea that kings were meant to be and ought to be kings, and peasants peasants: *Fear God. Honour the King. Let every soul be subject to the higher power ... for they are God's ministers. ... Render therefore to all their dues. ... Submit yourself to every ordinance of man ... be it to the king or unto governors. ... For so is the Will of God.* I Peter 2:13–17; Romans 13:1–7.[44] All were commanded by the Lord to recognize the status to which they were born, to accept it cheerfully and willingly, and to renounce any dream of altering or bettering that status.[45] *I therefore, the prisoner of the Lord, beseech you that you walk worthy of the vocation where with ye are called, With all lowliness and meekness, with long suffering; Brethren let every man wherein he is called, therein abide. No man,*

---

[42] See the fine essay by Neuschäffer, "Der livländische Pastor," and now Bartlett, "Russia's First Abolitionist." Johann Georg Eisen, at the first meeting of the Free Economic Society, declared his to be not an age of moral reform, but an *"ökonomisches Jahrhundert."* A graduate in theology from Jena, he was already writing about abolishing serfdom when recommended to Peter III. Catherine too knew his ideas on emancipation but found them dangerous. He was still advocating emancipation in the Baltic provinces in the early-1770s to Prince Peter von Biron, but such thoughts were risky in the age of Pugachev.

[43] Melton, *Absolutism*, p. 188.

[44] *O Dolzhnosti*, p. 99.

[45] *Ibid.*, p. 158; see my summary in "Education and Empire," pp. 55–60.

*having put his hand to the plough, and looking back, is fit for the kingdom of
God.* Ephesians 4:1–2; I Corinthians 7:24; Luke 9:62. Such was the
static social message of the Catherine's public schools, and the Scriptural authority, on which it was dogmatically based.

Based on Imperial precedents, the Russian public schools taught
duties: *die Pflichten der Frau, die Pflichten des Mannes, die Pflichten der Eltern,
der Kinder, der Herren, der Diener und Knechte, die Pflichten der Befehlenden,
der Unterthanen, der Pfarrern, und der Pfarrkinder.*[46] Russia's first national
school system meant the reestablishment of the Orthodox bonds of
Russian society, uniformly imposed on noble and lowly-born alike,
on Russian and Ukrainian, on Baltic nobles and peasants, and on
the Islamic peoples of Russian Asia.

D. *The Fate of Latin*

In the expansionist Prussia that produced Felbiger and the school
reform, it was essential to learn to read and spell in German and
also in Latin. Although his were pioneering schools of mass education aimed at audiences beneath the traditional elites, and although
he recognized that the vernacular languages were increasingly important, Felbiger knew that Latin was encountered everywhere, and
anyone who had been exposed to schooling should be able to read
it. The French language was also becoming popular, and he advised
teachers to collect old copies of French newspapers to introduce it to
children. But he assumed his teachers would have Latin: if their accents
were poor, he said, they might enlist the neighborhood pastor to
help with pronunciation.

Later in Austria recovering from Jesuit control of education, Latin
was de-emphasized, but not eliminated for German-speaking youth.[47]
The Austrian General Regulation offered Latin to all who left the
village and attended secondary schools. In the Banat Felbiger assured the government his schools would not make students discon-
tent with "the station into which they are born." In practice this

---

[46] [Felbiger], *Rukovodstvo/Anleitung*, pp. 104–18.

[47] Felbiger, *Eigenschaften*, pp. 100, 127, 128. For the following see Melton, *Absolutism*, pp. 16–17. On Austria generally, see O'Brien, "Maria Theresa's Attempt,"
p. 550. The Slavs of the Empire were to learn to read in both German and Serbian
at the elementary level, hence their bi-lingual texts, and Latin was delayed to the
secondary schools, the institutions omitted from the Russian reform. See Adler,
"Hapsburg School Reform," pp. 41, 45.

meant discouraging peasants from Latin, but offering it routinely and universally to "the children of noble persons, councilors, and clerks."

Felbiger's guidebooks for teachers in Russia purged every such reference, even to the modern languages. F. U. T. Aepinus of the School Commission said that Latin should be replaced entirely by modern languages; the only choice was between French or German: the Empress must, he wrote, decide whether Russians should acquire the features "*vom deutschen oder französischen National-Character.*"

Catherine decided that Latin would be treated as other languages: as French should be part of "domestic education" (for those nobles able to hire a tutor), as Greek was appropriate for schools in Kiev, New Russia, and Azov in the South, as Arabic might be added to the curriculum in Central Asia or Chinese in Irkutsk, so Latin should be taught only in a few urban district schools, essentially the secondary schools of the Reform. There it was to be confined to those pupils who had already been selected "to continue their educations in the higher schools or universities."[48] Solely in this narrowly utilitarian sense, an echo of Muscovite *prikaz* attitudes, did Latin language study survive in Catherine's School Reform. She now regarded Latin as a skill, needed by a select few. The general invitation to Latin humanist culture died.

Iankovich de Mirievo did prepare an edition of the *Orbis Pictus* of Jan Comenius in *Latin*, Russian, and German. It had been available since the days of Aleksei Mikhailovich, and Moscow University had issued it in 1768 (Latin, Russian, German, Italian, and French) for students; Novikov would reissue it in 1788. But elementary textbooks for the Commission regularly appeared in editions of over a hundred thousand copies; this edition of Comenius in four printings totalled 15,500 copies. Its preface mimicked Catherine's decision: it specified that the fundamentals of Latin and of modern foreign languages were required by students who studied in a gymnasium or a university. This book thus was published not for student generally, but for those pupils selected from the higher class of the district secondary schools to continue their studies.[49]

Russia's European borderlands, it should be noted, successfully evaded this attack on Latin. They used Comenius. A year after the

---

[48] Rozhdestvenskii, *Ocherki po istorii*, p. 574.
[49] Ian Amos Komenskii, *Zrelishche vselennyia, na latinskom, rossiiskom i nemetskom iazykakh*, St. Petersburg, 1788.

promulgation of the uniform Russian school reform, a special statute was issued for the Empire's German-speaking youth, whose parents had pointed out the absurdity of their using Russian texts which had been translated from German originally, through a Serbian intermediary. Thereafter the Petersburg publishers Breitkopf and Schnor began to issue their own editions of the original German textbooks. These, unlike the prescribed Russian variants, included the old guides to penmanship and reading in German *and Latin*, and invited youth to master Latin fully, the language the Reform was denying to Russians.[50]

The Reform attempted to jettison traditional rote-learning through the infamous Alphabetic/*Buchstabieren* method. When Felbiger had explained to teachers how to use it, he had used the Table of Contents of his own guidebook as an example of how to compile a chart. The Russian version substituted such formulas as "*V. v. e. B. O.*," *Veruiu vo edinago Boga Ottsa*, "I believe in one God the Father."[51] When a list of words was required to teach children which required capitalization, the Russian adapters included, in addition to geographical terms borrowed from the original, a Russian litany of authorities, God, Lord, Savior, Creator, Jesus Christ, followed by *Imperator, Tsar', Kniaz', Korol', Graf, Siiatel'stvo, Svetlost', Prevoskhoditel'stvo, Namestnik*. Thus in every way possible the Russian school reform aimed at provinciality, the revival of traditional Orthodox religious values, and the Scriptural assertion of authority. Thus could each school day end with a prayer:

> We thank You, Oh Creator! for keeping us in Your grace in our studies. May the good words of those in authority, our parents and our teachers, lead us to a recognition of the Good, and may they grant us the strength and the fortitude to continue our studies.[52]

As the Kievan Academy, like all other diocesan schools in the empire, abandoned their Classical roots and submitted to the new regime of religiosity, the seventeenth- and eighteenth-century flirtation with Latin paganism had ended.

The Public Schools' Orthodox revival, the purging of Latin, and the abandonment of the ancient authors by the printing presses, suggest

---

[50] Smiagina, "Iz istorii sozdaniia i rasprostraneniia," manages to tell the story without mentioning the German origins of the texts and the schools themselves. See the *Svodnyi katalog knig na inostrannykh iazykakh*, Vol. I, p. 278.

[51] [Felbiger], *Rukovodstvo uchiteliam*, p. 9, and below, pp. 13–4.

[52] [Felbiger], *Rukovodstvo uchiteliam*, p. 34.

that the School Reform consciously undid the deistic Love of the Lord that had characterized Catherine's early reign.

E. *The Context: A Religious Revival*

Catherine the Great's Public School Reform took place in the context of a religious revival. Simultaneously with its publications, the Translation Society abandoned French philosophy and the Classics; the Commission on Schools itself requested Russian editions of Fedderson's *Life of Christ*. The Western Church Fathers appeared in Russian. This may have been related to Catherine's harboring of former Jesuits invited to teach in her Public Schools, but between 1786 and 1795 seven editions of St. Augustine appeared, including the *City of God, The Confessions*, and other works. Titles of a pseudo-Augustine, were also published by the Synod, by Novikov, and by private presses. The *Ecclesiastical History* of Eusebius (264–340), the *Divine Institutions* of Lactantius (d. 325), Boethius' (484–524) *Consolations* and the writings of the second-century Christian Justinus, all appeared. To them can be added the thoughts on the Resurrection of Athenagoras Atheniensis, the second-century Christian philosopher.

Simultaneously in the 1780s the Greek Fathers made their debut in civil-script translations, including works of John Chrysostom, Dionysius the Areopagite, Gregory of Nazianzus, and St. Basil the Great. In several cases the first edition was issued by Novikov at Moscow University, with subsequent printings by the Synod. The School Reform occurred in the context of a general revival of religion on the presses.

The era also witnessed a flood of religious texts aimed specifically at youth, especially in the old Cyrillic script. They included the primer and catechism for the public schools. Iankovich de Mirievo also prepared an *Prostrannyi katikhizis*, which saw at least six editions between 1786 and the turn of the century. Meanwhile older religious texts remained in print. Teofan's old primer, the *Pervoe uchenie otrokom*, appeared in nine separate printings between 1758 and 1794. Its more conservative competitor in the early part of Catherine's reign, the *Nachal'no uchenie chelovekom, khotiashchym uchitisia knig bozhestvennago pisaniia* (Elementary reading for he who would read the books of Holy Scripture), by Metropolitan Platon (Levshin), appeared in 1772, again in 1775 (2 printings totalling 1440 copies), 1778, 1782 and 1798. His *Pravoslavnoe uchenie*, an eighty-page catechism first written for the young future-Emperor Paul, saw editions in 1766, 1768, 1773, 1779, and 1782; temporarily eclipsed by the editions of the School Reform, it would reappear in 1800. The number and size of editions of breviaries, saints' lives, and especially of psalters, increased dramatically in latter half of Catherine's reign, making traditional texts available to new generations of readers.[53]

The implementation of the Public School Reform and this religious revival were two faces of a single national policy. In 1785 officials of the School Commission, led by Archimandrite Apollos, rector of the transformed Moscow Clerical Academy, visited eleven private schools looking for pedagogical deficiencies.[54] By that date all schools were required by law to have been restructured in texts and pedagogy into uniform Reformed Schools. The report on the pension of a Catholic Frenchman, one Franz von Eisen, noted that many of his young charges did "not know the Ten Commandments." He and other directors of pensions were ordered to teach the catechism, and to use either learned Orthodox priests or teachers certified in Orthodoxy by the Moscow Academy as teachers of religion exclusively. The school of the Frenchman Bordenau was told to replace its teacher of religion. The Prussian Horn was told to segregate his male and female students. The school at the old Lutheran Church in Moscow was told either to teach the Greco-Russian Confession of Faith and to hire a certified Russian teacher, or to eject its six Russian children. The report revealed wide variations among the private schools— some were deemed excellent, some dreadful like that of the Frenchman de Forsh, in which catechism was not studied, in which the Credo and the Ten Commandments were not memorized, and in which the teaching of French, geography, history, German, Russian, arithmetic, and geometry was judged poor. But everywhere the first question and chief concern of the Commission's agents was the Orthodoxy of religious instruction. This was the religious revival in education.

Behind this religious revival, the School Reform, and the drive for religious conformity, stood Metropolitan Platon, the symbol of a

---

[53] Editions from the *Svodnyi katalog*, and from Afanas'eva, *Katalog izdanii kirillicheskoi pechati.* There are indications that still more editions have not been counted in these lists.

[54] For this paragraph, see Sivkov, "Chastnye pansiony"; Papmehl, "The Empress," seems unaware of these documents, and thus does not comment on the link between the purge of the Masons and the implementation of the School Reform.

resurgent Muscovite clergy. In the aftermath of Pugachev's rebellion, he had begun to preach a moral revival. In 1777 he had delivered a sermon that called for putting Christ back into the educational institutions of the empire, and in 1779 he preached a sermon on child-rearing, insisting that "God, the Church, and the Gospel" be its basis. Indeed an early sermon on child-rearing of 1765 had said that parents' goal was the production of "a good Christian, an honest citizen, a prudent house-holder, a true friend, a trustworthy neighbor, and an agreeable comrade." Enlightenment, *Prosveshchenie*, he insisted, consisted not in speaking several languages, but in a true knowledge of God. Historians have generally accepted his self-definition as enlightened, but have overlooked his personal definition of the term.

In 1780, on the eve of the meeting between Joseph II and Catherine at Mohylev, Platon's sermons were collected and printed, as were his several catechisms. They were designed to wrest the Muscovite clergy from the grasp of Ukrainian humanism, and their sentiments were shortly incorporated into the School Reform.[55] Who was this "enlightened" reformer?

Platon Levshin, born in 1737 near Moscow, had attended the Moscow-Slavo-Greco-Latin Academy, and studied to philosophy and theology with Genadii Dranitsyn, completing the Latin curriculum in 1757. But he became an ardent Grecophile who soon gained a reputation as a "second Chrysostom" and the "Apostle of Moscow." He was also one of those masters of self-advertisement who successfully managed his own career. When Catherine asked him why he became a monk, he replied, "for a love of enlightenment." With that response he became the tutor to her heir Paul, was named archbishop of Moscow in 1775, the protector of his *alma mater*, and in 1787, Metropolitan of Moscow; he died in 1812.[56]

Although his control of clerical education may be termed "benevolent paternalism," in essence his activities consisted of purging Ukrainian humanism. The appointment of Ukrainians as bishops of

---

[55] Platon, *Pouchitel'nyia slova*, Vol. 4, M. 1780, pp. 160–67, 298–305, for the sermons, and for the catechisms, Platon, *Raznye sochineniia*, Vol. 6, M. 1780, pp. 152–214. The famous sermon of 1765 is discussed in Demkov, *Istoriia russkoi pedagogii*, Vol. II, M. 1910, 314–17. It is one of the deceits of modern Russian history writing that his influential educational writings have been purged from the anthologies of Russian thought, while those of Novikov survive.

[56] *Russkii biograficheskii slovar'*, XIV, 48–54; Demkov, *op. cit.*, 307–317, and Papmehl, *Metropolitan Platon*, esp. pp. 61–66, for the following.

the Russian church ceased; the number fell to only thirty-three percent of appointments during Catherine's entire reign, but the purge
intensified in the 1780s with the ascendancy of Platon.[57] "Platon put
an end to 'the Ukrainian influence' at the Academy. Under his administration ethnic Ukrainians were no longer appointed to teaching
positions and the Russian language was everywhere given prominence
over Latin."[58] Only the name "Slavo-Greco-Latin Academy" would
linger for a few years: instruction and the disputations were now
exclusively in Russian. Classical Greek became the chief language to
be studied (Hebrew was proposed), and Latin was reduced to an
"elective" class for the minority of students who continued studies to
philosophy and theology. A knowledge of Latin was now deemed
the equivalent of "theology on stilts."[59] The old humanistic curriculum, once synonymous with education throughout Europe, was now
seen in Moscow as "only a course in Latin literature."[60]

Platon rebuilt and expanded the school, but it was his school. While
he strengthened the library, introduced modern languages, and increased enrollment, Platon ended its eighty-year Latin epoch. At the
expense of Latin he introduced the literary models of Haller, Lessing,
Klopstock, Fénelon, and Bossuet. Platon had gained notoriety by
reading the school's first theology course in Russian as early as 1765,
and as Archbishop of Moscow he saw to it that all elementary studies were in Russian, and that the famous courses in poetics and
rhetoric, the old humanities, were also taught in Russian.[61] At this
point the once proud Moscow Academy was prepared for its next
tasks, submissively supplying Orthodox teachers for the Public Schools,
and Great-Russian graduates who could sermonize in Russian in the
parishes of the empire.

Catherine's well-known campaign against the Moscow Masons arose
from this religious revival. In 1779 Novikov and Platon had cooper-
ated when the publisher asked the Archbishop for funds to allow
seminarians to study at Moscow University.[62] By 1784, however,
Catherine mistrusted their ties, and indeed she charged Platon with

---

[57] Bryner, *Der geistliche Stand*, pp. 32–3.

[58] Papmehl, *Platon*, p. 63, citing the nineteenth-century historians Smirnov and
Znamenskii. See also Bryner, *op. cit.*, pp. 134–5.

[59] Nichols, "Orthodoxy and Russia's Enlightenment," p. 78.

[60] Zhivov, *Kul'turnye konfliktov*, p. 148, citing the clerical historian of ecclesiastical
writers, Evgenii Bolkhovitinov.

[61] Papmehl, *Platon*, p. 63; Demkov, *op. cit.*, pp. 395, 400–01.

[62] For the following, Papmehl, "The Empress and 'Un fanatique'."

the investigation of his friend. When the government inspected Moscow's private schools in October, 1785, Platon and two professors were both to insure use of the uniform texts of the Public Schools, and to ferret out any links between schools, private pensions and the Masonic movement. Platon was personally to investigate Novikov's religious beliefs, to identify "any possible deviation from Orthodoxy," and to inspect the output of private presses for heretical materials.

Catherine's constant preoccupation in the mid-1780s was the purging of "works filled with the new schism" of Rosicrucianism, but also of other "nonsense, and all sorts of absurd philosophizing."[63] She feared they contained the roots of a new *Raskol* that, like Pugachev, could divide the empire when the Public School Reform was attempting to bind it together. Novikov, the Freemasons, and the Martinists were potentially such "a new sect" that had "fallen into all the depths of error contained in the metaphysical and airy dreams of Swedenborg, Boehme, Martin, Eckhartshausen, and other such mystical writers." According to Catherine, for all their pretensions to learning, they differed little from "the poor and ignorant peasants" who had been deluded by sectarian thought back in the seventeenth century.[64]

Platon did his job and was rewarded. He exonerated Novikov, declaring "in the whole world one could not find a better Christian than Novikov."[65] There is no reason to think subterfuge was involved. In the summer of 1787 two years before the French Revolution, Catherine toured her newly acquired southern Ukraine, and on that tour she elevated the anti-Ukrainian Platon to the Metropolitanate. Upon her return to St. Petersburg she banned all private presses and book-shops from dealing in books of religious content.[66] She and Platon had allayed suspicions of Novikov and the Masons, purged dissonance from Russian Orthodoxy, reassumed control of the press, and implemented a uniform religious-based School Reform to re-secure her Empire.

In the Hapsburg Empire, which provided Catherine with textbooks and her director of schools, "the Orthodox *pop* was specifically ex-

---

[63] Papmehl, "The Empress," pp. 674–76.

[64] Platon, *Present State*, pp. 336–38.

[65] Florinsky, *Russia. A History*, I, 601; this is a different, and more emphatic, translation of the line cited in Chapter Three above.

[66] Papmehl, "The Empress," p. 478.

cluded from the teaching post."[67] In 1772, under very different circumstances, the Hapsburgs went so far as to propose the total secularization of education. In Russia, on the contrary, native sons of the clerical estate were removed from their classrooms in Moscow and the diocesan academies—Latin had been purged by Platon—and conscripted into the new teachers' institutes. More efficient was the second step. Soon the clerical academies themselves were transformed with the texts and methods of the uniform school system.

The results were dramatic. In 1784 the Kievan Academy had just begun experimenting in the "modern subjects," when it was forced to conform totally to the standards of the School Reform. That decree arrived on December 27, 1785, and immediately its teachers were dispatched to St. Petersburg for retraining in Felbiger's method.[68] The old Kievan Academy died, and Moscow's acquisition of Ukraine was finally complete.

In Austria the Felbiger system was introduced as the basis of a national state-operated school system in the aftermath of the dissolution of the Jesuits. In Russia Catherine protected the Jesuit order and gave former Jesuits positions of authority in education.[69] According to the report of the Sicilian Serracapriola, the education of Belorussia was simply given to the Jesuits, sixteen in number, after their retraining in the Felbiger method in St. Petersburg. Their base was the old Jesuit college in Polock.[70] The Public Schools spread the Orthodox religion and the Russian language to non-Christian parts of the empire, reversing policies of educational pluralism, toleration and respect for native traditions which characterized Catherine's earlier reign.[71]

From humble beginnings, eight schools and five hundred pupils, the system had grown to three hundred schools and almost twenty thousand pupils by 1800, slightly less than ten percent of them girls.[72] This was an impressive achievement, although insignificant when compared to the Empire.[73] These numbers were no barometer of

---

[67] Adler, "Hapsburg School Reform," p. 33; for the following, Scott, "Reform in the Hapsburg Monarchy," p. 175. See also in *Ibid.*, Beales, "Social Forces," pp. 50–1.

[68] Saunders, *The Ukrainian Impact*, p. 47.

[69] See Hans, "Educational Reform in Poland," pp. 302ff.; Hans, "Polish Schools in Russia," pp. 395–96.

[70] Winter, *Russland und das Papsttum*, II, 101–102; and his "Die Jesuiten in Russland."

[71] See Okenfuss, "Education and Empire," pp. 62–63.

[72] The newest edition of Dmytryshyn, *Imperial Russia. A Source Book 1700–1917*, 3rd ed., pp. 118–121, republishes the statistics.

[73] Engelsing, *Analphabetentum und Lektüre*, p. 62. In Bohemia and in Austria proper

Enlightenment. Catherine's schools were a reaffirmation of traditional religious culture. They restored to the traditional Muscovite clergy its traditional role in national education, a role they had shared with others since the days of Peter.

The comparative study of Enlightened Absolutism has produced one generalization:

> To enlarge religious toleration, to reduce the influence of the clergy and churches generally, to exclude it altogether from a growing range of affairs now conceived to be purely secular, to control the study of theology, to attack what was seen as 'superstition' and 'fanaticism'— there were always and everywhere aspects of Enlightened statesmanship. [T]his is almost the only generalization that can validly be made about Enlightened policies across the whole of Europe.[74]

By this bare-bones standard, Catherine's schools were oddly out of step with most of Europe's Enlightenments.

Elsewhere monarchs compromised reluctantly and used some clergy or former Jesuits as teachers, but Russia seems unique in structuring its entire reform on the values of its traditional clergy. Russian schools opposed teaching peasants to read. They affirmed that "the most honest peasant is invariably the stupidest and the most ignorant, . . . the most uncouth and ignorant peasant will invariably make the best soldier."[75] The heavy-handed implementation of the reform threatened all existing schools, including those of the German community, arguably the last viable source of Latin learning in the empire, after Platon began his Russification of the Church's schools.[76]

In October, 1782, a brochure appeared from the press of Moscow University inviting new membership to a "Friendly Learned Society."[77] Novikov's group, founded on the model "of other European universities where such groups already aided popular enlightenment (*narodnuiu prosveshcheniiu*)," encouraged the full flowering of the natural sciences and the healing arts, economics, agricultural and industrial management, the full scope of philosophical inquiry from logic and

---

the reform, made available to the peasantry, attracted half of the school-age population into the classroom, figures Russia would not approach until the twentieth century.

[74] Beales, "Social Forces," pp. 41–2.
[75] Epstein, *The Genesis of German Conservatism*, p. 79.
[76] See Amburger, "Die deutschen Schulen in Rußland," pp. 5–6.
[77] Krasnobaev, "Eine Gesellschaft gelehrter Freunde," pp. 257–70.

mathematics to morals, history, geography, statistics, and politics, and good taste. They sponsored the Greek and Roman authors which "all enlightened European peoples" recognized as contributing to good manners.[78] Catherine's conservative Christian School Reform of the 1780s represented instead a return to the Orthodox religion, and to the *Domostroi's* goal of education as indoctrination in quiescent spiritual values of home, caste, clergy, and Biblical authority. The century and a half flirtation of Russia with Latin education came momentarily to an end.

Long ago historians noted the heavy dependence on catechism, Scripture, and Biblical history in the elementary curriculum, the recruitment of students from seminaries to serve as teachers, the religious basis of the myriad duties prescribed in *O dolzhnosti*, and pointed out that the social message of the schools was a strictly conservative doctrine of retaining privilege and preserving the status quo.[79] How is it that these schools came to be the hallmark of the Russian Enlightenment?

2. *Afterword: The Historiographic Context and the Creation of the Russian Enlightenment*

Religious revival is an unfamiliar interpretation of Catherine's School Reform. Most historians would discuss her schools in the context of Enlightened government.

Rudolf Vierhaus, the venerable director of the Max Planck Institute for History in Göttingen, said, "Whoever would write about the history of pedagogy, schooling, and education in the eighteenth century must deal with the idea and the reality of the Enlightenment."[80] It is a little appreciated fact that the concept of a Russian Enlightenment began during the post-Stalinist thaw on October 4, 1956, in East Berlin, when Eduard Winter delivered a little lecture at a Plenary Session of the (East) German Academy of Sciences. Published

---

[78] Svetlov, "'Obshchestvo liubitelei rossiiskoi uchenosti'," pp. 303–22. Their goal was akin to Basedow's ideal of training "the whole man," the notion of broad liberal arts education based on great books from antiquity. Cited in Epstein, *Genesis*, pp. 7–9.

[79] Voronov, *Fedor Iankovich de-Mirievo*, pp. 9, 95–96, 132ff., 140.

[80] Vierhaus, "Aufkläring als Lernprozeß," p. 84.

without footnotes,[81] it constituted a very fragile foundation for the hundreds of publications around the globe which subsequently assumed the reality of a "Russian Enlightenment."

Winter began with a simple observation about the absence of symmetry in literary history: one talked routinely about a "Slavic Baroque," but never of a "Slavic Enlightenment" (*"ist noch niemals von "Slavischen Aufklärung" gesprochen worden"*).[82] In proposing the adoption of the concept, Winter opted for a minimalist program so vague that anything to the left of Avvakum would qualify as "Enlightenment." He said it need consist only of religious toleration (introduced by Peter as early as 1702 but in Austria only in 1781), the encouragement of education and technical schooling (evidenced in Russia with Magnitskii's *Arithmetic* and schools of navigation and engineering), and the nurturing of science (as in the case of the Russian Academy of Sciences). By such standards Petrine Russia practically pioneered the European Enlightenment, although there were to be more spectacular developments in the stages represented by Lomonosov and Radishchev. Such were the humble beginnings of the Russian Enlightenment.

Winter also fed Great-Russian nationalism when he early defined a lesser Ukrainian Enlightenment which was *"subsequent to and independent of"* (my emphasis: MJO) the Russian phenomenon:

> In the eighteenth century a Ukrainian *Aufklärung* also developed, one which previously had been seen almost solely as a moment in the history of [literary] styles, as has been the Baroque. The linguist and philologist Simeon Todor'skyj, who received his stimulus in Halle, and the genius and thinker Skovoroda, who got it in Vienna were, in spite of the Baroque style in which they expressed themselves, significant representatives of the Ukrainian Enlightenment in Russia.[83]

A year later Winter went further, stating that the term Enlightenment was all-embracing and embraced everything from the seven-

---

[81] Winter, "Die Aufklärung bei den slawischen Völkern"; See Grau & Flentije, "Chronologische Bibliografie," pp. 5–27. There is a portrait of the contribution of Eduard Winter and his school in Wiegand, "Rußland im Urteil."

[82] Winter, "Die Aufklärung," p. 152. On Winter and his school, see Hellmann, et al., eds., *Osteuropa in der historischen Forschung der DDR*, Vol. I, 135–141, II, 104–111; these essays by Carsten Goehrke have been kept up to date by the East Germans themselves; see the two reports by Zeil, "Forschungen zur Geschichte der Völker der UdSSR."

[83] Winter, "Die Aufklärung," pp. 154–55.

teenth to the nineteenth century, from Baroque to Romanticism.[84]

In Russian literary historiography such pronouncements were bomb-shells. When official Soviet history was formulated in the 1930s, the concept of a Russian Enlightenment was still regarded as nonsensical. The great scholar of eighteenth-century literature Gukovskii not only did not use the word *prosveshcheniia*, he also evidenced no cult of Lomonosov or of Radishchev.[85] The early works of his illustrious successor P. N. Berkov, were also void of any hint of a "Russian Enlightenment." He even insisted that Russian interest in the *Encyclopédie* had been a one-way street of cultural borrowing, un-matched by any significant French interest in sleepy Russia.[86] In those days Radishchev was seen as the passive receptacle for the French Enlightenment; nowadays all that has changed; it is academically correct to regard him "without a doubt, as the most radical thinker of the 18th century not only among the representatives of Russian thinking, but of socio-political thought throughout the entire world of that age."[87]

In discussing the eighteenth century, early Soviet scholarship tended to follow Kliuchevskii and his pupils. In the *History of Russia* prepared by Paul Miliukov, for example, the educational reforms of Betskoi and of the 1780s were dismissed in a short paragraph. Three cultural directions in educated society under Catherine were identified, Orthodoxy, Masonry, and "Voltaireanism," the latter being the fad of very few.[88] In that bygone era textbooks reflected this inherited wisdom. M. T. Florinsky's *Russia,* the universal "heavy" textbook of the 1950s, never used the phrase "Russian Enlightenment," spoke only of "Enlightened Absolutism," and viewed all educational efforts in the eighteenth century negatively. Florinsky wrote, "According to Pypin the only redeeming features of literature during this period were a certain improvement in style and language, which cleared the way for later writers," but the process began slowly, since

---

[84] Winter, "Die Aufklärung in der Literaturgeschichte."

[85] Gukovskii, "Za izuchenie vosemnadtsatogo veka."

[86] Berkov, "Izuchenie russkoi literatury vo Frantsii," pp. 21–68, esp. 723–28; the opposite view can be sampled in Kopanev, "'Entsiklopediia' i Rossiia"; see also the recent survey by Somov, "Frantsuzskaia 'Rossika' epokhi Prosveshcheniia," pp. 105–20.

[87] Contrast Makashina, "Literaturnye vzaimootnosheniia Rossii i Frantsii," pp. v–lxxxii, esp. p. xix, with *Ocherki russkoi kul'tury XVIII veka,* Vol. III, p. 211.

[88] Miliukov, Seignobos and Eisenmann, *History of Russia,* Vol. II, New York, 1968, pp. 63–72, 122–24, 160–69, and in general his *Ocherki po istorii,* esp. Part 3, Vyp. 2.

"the first quarter of the eighteenth century failed to make any contribution to belles-lettres," and the pattern of the century was solely
"the infiltration of western ideas."[89] Likewise Bernard Pares, who
credited Kliuchevskii for "more brilliant and informing suggestions"
than any other historian, never considered the possibility of a Russian Enlightenment. He devoted a single paragraph to the literary
movement under Catherine.[90]

Among German scholars a similar pattern prevailed. Karl Stahlin
discussed Betskoi and Mirievo, Catherine's educational directors, and
Catherine's relationships with Voltaire and Grimm without a hint of
a "Russian Enlightenment." Günther Stökl discussed Catherine's age
as *aufgeklärte Adelsherrschaft*, contrasted the age's palace revolts with
aufgeklärten Absolutismus, referred to Alexander I's tutor La Harpe's
Aufklärungsphilosophie, and noted that Catherine herself did much *für
die Aufklärung*, but that was a far cry from talking about a Russian
Enlightenment.[91] The reason for this stance was simple: in the 1930s
scholars internationally still read eighteenth-century Russian thought
and culture as fundamentally religious.[92]

Because his theory in the 1950s flattered Russian national pride
while being properly dialectical, Winter's scheme was quickly adopted
by Soviet scholars. P. N. Berkov reversed his youthful position. He
allowed them to escape Lenin's dicta that the "Russian Enlightenment" referred to the age of Belinskii and Herzen, the 1840s to
1860s.[93] A programmatic statement Russified Polockij, Teofan, and
the other Ukrainians, dismissed forever the idea of the "*Europäisierung
Rußlands*," provided ideological flexibility within the Marxist frame-
work, and dismissed the religious content of Russian literature as the
interaction of world literature with the Russian.[94] The heart of Berkov's
argument was his recitation of the names of authors translated into
Russian: "Corneille, Voltaire, Montesquieu, Rousseau, Mably, Swift,
Fielding, Gellert, Sulzer, Marino, Tasso as well as ancient literature:

---

[89] Florinsky, *Russia. A History*, Vol. I, pp. 401–03, 491–92, 597–99, and *passim*.
[90] Pares, *A History of Russia*, pp. vii, 253–54.
[91] Stahlin, *Geschichte Russlands*, pp. 552–593 (reprint of the 1930 edition); Stökl,
Russische Geschichte von den Anfangen, pp. 399, 430, 436, and *passim*.
[92] See for example Lapchine, *La phenoménologie de la conscience religieuse*, pp. 75–79.
[93] Berkov, "Osnovnye voprosy russkogo prosvetitel'stva." See also the overview of
the debate between Berkov and L. I. Kulakova on terminology in Neuhäuser, *Towards the Romantic Age*, pp. ix–xii.
[94] Berkov, "Besonderheiten des literarischen Prozesses," Vol. III, pp. 10–13, 14–
17, 20–23, 28–33.

Hellanicus, Homer, Hesiod, Lucian, Diodorus, Herodian, Velleius Paterculus, Cicero, Virgil, Valerius Maximus, Ovid, and others, and in addition numerous articles from Diderot's and D'Alembert's *Encyclopedia* and Büsching's *Geographie*."[95] With such intellectual companions one could obviously speak of "enlightened monarchy" in Russia.

Still Berkov talked cautiously about how Russian [or better, Ukrainian—MJO] thinkers fit into the *"aufklärerische Gedankenwelt"* —rather than proclaiming outright a Russian Enlightenment.[96] Western scholars with access to Soviet pages in the mid-1960s attempted to stem the tide. Joseph Mattl, for example, showed that the Russian School Reform of the 1780s was limited to elementary education, when in Austria it had touched universities as well, and that enlightened thought could be found among an immeasurably greater portion of the population in central Europe compared to Russia.[97]

Eduard Winter had argued that the rise of the middle class and the Enlightenment were dialectically linked in Europe, and it should have been true for Russia as well. Subsequently East-German scholars backed away from the suggestion that eighteenth-century Russian literature was produced by a "rising middle class," but under the sway of Winter's notion of a *Frühaufklärung* religious toleration and the founding of some schools without clerical tutelage were deemed sufficient grounds for a Russian Pre-Enlightenment. Now it was possible to compare favorably Sumarokov with Corneille and Racine, Fonvizin with Holberg, and Radishchev with Sterne, Rousseau, and Herder.[98] The Enlightenment in Russia had been born.

Once the concept of a Russian Enlightenment had become canon, it was only a matter of time before someone would work out a tidy topology in which precise parallels with Western literature were found. As Germany knew *Frühaufklärung* and *Aufklärung* so Russia moved from

---

[95] *Ibid.*, pp. 49–50. This list indicates the significance Berkov placed on the activities of the Society Striving to Translate Foreign Books; see Chapter III above.

[96] *Ibid.*, pp. 10–13.

[97] Matl', "Epokha prosveshcheniia v Rossii.

[98] For the above, Hoffmann, "Aufklärung, Absolutismus"; Lehmann, "Barock und Aufklärung," p. 325; Winter, *Frühaufklärung*. Graßhoff, "Die Humanitätsideale der russischen Frühaufklärung," pp. 655–56; one notes too continuing East German generosity in such conference reports as Schmidt, "Die russische Literatur der Aufklärung (1650–1825)," pp. 602–608. It should also be noted that East-German scholarship has produced a splendid etymological study of the words for Enlightenment, enlightening, and enlighteners in West European, but especially in Slavic languages. See Günther, "Zur Epoch-beziechnung 'Aufklärung.'"

prosvetitel'stvo to mature *prosveshcheniia*.[99] In Russia the latter embraced Lomonosov and Radishchev, and covered the period 1750–1790,[100] precisely the parameters of the Western Enlightenment. More recent Soviet comment defines Russian reformist *prosvetitel'stvo* as an autonomous, bourgeois, anti-feudal ideology born in the 1760s. In the 1780s it would move to a *prosvetitel'sko-revoliutsionaia pozitsiia* in time for the French Revolution. Radishchev would be replaced by a third *radikal'nye prosvetitel'skie idei*, in the person of the Decembrists.[101] Such were the fruit of seeds planted by Winter in 1956.

These formulations, and the Soviet publications that contained them, found a ready response among Western scholars. Already in his Trevelyan Lectures Franco Venturi regarded catalogues of secular books published as an accurate statement of Russian books tastes. Oblivious to the more voluminous publication of religious texts, he declared, "The *philosophes* became the soul of Russia at that time."[102] Russian participation in the Enlightenment was "firmly rooted." The translated and secular titles in the *Svodnyi katalog* came to represent, for such scholars, what was actually published and read in eighteenth-century Russia.[103] Soon cautious West-German scholars argued that publishing and reading in Russia were fully comparable to Western Europe. Heinz Ischreyt, for example, defined a "north-eastern European cultural zone" of reading Russians and Prussians; grounded in Soviet exaggeration, taking no account of the failure of books to sell, counting the number of provincial bookstores without noting that they sold mostly traditional religious materials, treating plans to translate books as the equivalent of circulating them, and void of quantitative contrasts, it convinces only if one is ideologically committed to finding an Enlightened Russia.[104]

Overlooked in this Soviet and East-German orchestrated panegyric

---

[99] Valitskaia, *Russkaia estetika XVIII veka*, pp. 76–77.

[100] Valitskaia, *op. cit.*, pp. 6 and *passim*. See also Moriakov, "Izuchenie russkogo prosvetitel'stva," pp. 44–5; such Soviet scholars tend to accept the reading habits of one or two individuals as indicative of society.

[101] Moriakov, *op. cit.*, p. 55. For the spread of these concepts among Soviet scholars, see the essay by David Griffiths, "In Search of Enlightenment."

[102] Venturi, *Utopia and Reform*, pp. 127, 134. Venturi began his lectures with comments on Peter Gay and the Classics, pp. 2–7, but did not apply those standards to Russia. See my cautions on the selected contents of the so-called *Svodnyi katalog* in *Kritika*, Vol. VI, No. 2 (1970), 112–123, No. 3, 125–130.

[103] Krasnobaev, "Die Bedeutung der Moskauer Universitäts-typographie."

[104] Ischreyt, "Buchhandel und Buchhändler im nordost-europäischen Kommunikationssystem"; see also his "Zur Aufklärung in Mittel- und Osteuropa."

to the Russian Enlightenment were scholarly voices like Hans Rothe, who investigated the sources used by Russian authors and discovered that *only* in the case of the "Dilettant-Historian" and "political journalist" Shcherbatov were Classical models and metaphors, references to Plato and to Socrates, to Virgil and to Horace—only in Shcherbatov was the Classical tradition to be found in a Russian in the age of the Enlightenments.[105]

Criticizing the Soviet concept of a Russian Enlightenment is not new. A decade ago David Griffiths examined twenty years of tortured Soviet and East-German attempts to squeeze Russian intellectual life into Marxist-Leninist categories, and politely concluded that the rest of the scholarly world was laughing.[106]

The legacy of this Marxist-inspired historiography has been enormous and pernicious. Since dialectically Russia required her own Enlightenment, the pedagogical efforts of Ukrainian humanists and German academicians became Russian efforts. Because that Enlightenment had to be secular, heaps of "secular" books were found in medieval Muscovite libraries. Because simplistic definitions of Enlightenment required the eclipse of religion, the educational contributions of Russia's clergy, including such opposites as the Ukrainian humanists and Platon, were neglected or distorted. Because obscurantist scholasticism crumbled to dust under the glowing rays of Enlightenment, the humanistic education of the Ukrainians went virtually unstudied, except for Lomonosov, who rose above it; hiding his religious roots and espousing science made him the premier man of Enlightenment, his clerical educational roots and interests notwithstanding. Noble forerunners of the intelligentsia, of bourgeoisie, and the revolutionaries, eighteenth-century figures like Novikov were deified. Non-Russian clerical writers and teachers were Russified, secularized, or forgotten.

A century of attempts to root Western Latin culture in Russia had failed. Catherine's major educational reform shared little with the

---

[105] See above, Chapter III, Section 2B. Rothe, "Zur Frage von Einflüssen in der russischen Literatur," pp. 21–68, esp. 25–27. On Shcherbatov's education, see Lentin's introduction in Shcherbatov, *On the Corruption of Morals*, pp. 16–21.

[106] Griffiths, "In Search." Marc Raeff has urged us to distinguish between the *Aufklärung* and *lumières* in Russian thought, and has especially noted the impact of the less individualistic and liberal "Rosicrucian Enlightenment." See his "On the Heterogeneity of the Eighteenth Century."

common Latin and pagan roots of the liberal European French and
Scottish Enlightenments. In the more religious Enlightenments of the
Germanies there were better parallels, but these were seldom what
Soviet historians had in mind when they secularized Teofan and
praised Novikov beyond his merits. A whole generation of scholars
has been misled by questionable ideological assumptions born in
Soviet-occupied East Germany.

CONCLUSION

A 1992 mailing from the Harvard Graduate School Fund announced *"Morale monet gratarium reciprocam retributionem"*: One good turn deserves another. -Aesop. The Bulletin of my own university from the 1860–61 academic year announced that all "Candidates for admission to the Freshman Class will be examined in the following books: LATIN. Caesar's Commentaries; the Bucolics, and the Aeneid of Virgil to Book VII; Cicero's Select Orations, Folsom's or Johnson's edition," as well as in grammar and writing Latin. In the first term the Freshman Class was to begin "Lincoln's Livy"; in the second the "Odes and Epodes of Horace." In provincial St. Louis, at the outset of Civil War, Latin defined an educated man. There were no women among the nine graduates of '64.

Since the days of Erasmus, the mastery of ancient Latin and pagan authors defined the West. In 1792, Thomas Paine could say, "How strangely is antiquity treated! To answer some purposes it is spoken of as the times of darkness and ignorance, and to answer others it is put for the light of the world."[1] But the West defined itself and judged its neighbors by their knowledge of the authors of antiquity. Of Russia, for example, late in the century, it could be complained that

> literature in general not being as yet arrived at that degree of estima-
> tion, which it has attained in other cultivated nations of Europe, it is
> no wonder that authorship and bookselling are in less consideration
> than elsewhere.

William Tooke, chaplain of the English church at Kronstadt in the 1790s, reported most bookstands offered only "spiritual writings, collections of popular ballads, and some old romances which have been long in possession of the public admiration"[2]—a fair description of the readings adopted by the Court and the literati of the reformed *prikazy* in the age of Aleksei Mikhailovich.

In Europe, Latin pagan letters were largely undisturbed as the measure of true education. The Classics continued to shape the literate

---

[1] Cited in Reinhold, "Eighteenth-Century American Political Thought," p. 223.
[2] W. Tooke, *History of Russia*, 2nd ed., Vol. II, London, 1800, p. 413.

population. The Latin reading list of eighteenth-century French colleges was faithfully mirrored in the speeches and pamphlets of the
French Revolution.[3] The most cited authors in the Revolutionary
era were Cicero, followed by Horace, Plutarch, and Tacitus, authors
regularly included in the colleges' curricula. Long would it be so: In
schools for England's nobility,

> Classics dominated the curriculum in 1815 and were still overwhelm-
> ingly pre-eminent a century later: 'In 1884 Eton employed twenty-
> eight classics masters, six mathematics masters, no modern language
> teachers, no scientists and one historian.' The position of classics was
> a pale reflection of Renaissance humanism and of the sense that Greece
> and Rome, together with Christianity, were the pillars of European
> civilisation.[4]

In colonial America, the "founders knew that intellectual independence had been a defining characteristic of their Greek and Roman
heroes, who had formulated the revolutionary theories of popular
sovereignty, . . . and had defended them against the rampant absolutism of the ancient world."[5]

By 1789 the Russian reading public had scarcely been touched by
the Classics. What was available in print was regularly rejected by
Russian book buyers, and Catherine's school system formally shunned
them. One cluster of defenders were *die Herrn Academiciens*, but as late
as 1773 they lived in Petersburg "as in a zoo. . . . They remain a
rare species in this land."[6] The other defenders of the Classics, the
Ukrainian hierarchs, had systematically been replaced. Library holdings attest that a handful of literati and numerous foreigners appreciated Latin letters, but few Russian nobles.

Just before the Great War, the French ambassador to Russia, Maurice Paléologue, inspired by Falconet's equestrian statue of Peter the
Great, denounced the tsar-revolutionary:

> I greet the greatest revolutionary of modern times. . . . All Peter
> Alexeievitch liked was destroying things. that is why he was so essen-
> tially Russian. In his savage despotism he undermined and overturned
> the whole fabric. For nearly thirty years he was in revolt against his
> people; he attacked all our national traditions and customs; he turned
> everything upside down, even our holy orthodox Church.[7]

---

[3] Parker, *The Cult of Antiquity*, pp. 17, 18, and *passim*.
[4] Lieven, *Aristocracy in Europe*, p. 165.
[5] Richard, *Founders and the Classics*, p. 5.
[6] Cited in Claus Scharf, "Deutschlandbild," p. 310.
[7] Cited in Kelly, *St. Petersburg*, p. 28.

Peter was such revolutionary. He did not fundamentally challenge the values of Muscovy with an alien learning.

Most Russians were permitted to remain hostile to Latinate Westernization with the full approval of government. From Aleksei through Catherine, the various regimes' commitment to Latin learning was weak and sporadic. Humanism remained the cult of the foreigner and of new subjects on the Western borders, while literate society's rejection of Latin educations was continuous and wide-spread. The age culminated in an official revival of anti-Ukrainian, anti-Latin religiosity in the 1780s.

Catherine ended the early-modern flirtation with the Classics. In the late eighteenth century, Ukrainian humanists were purged from the Russian Church and Russian schooling. The Germans' bastion of Latin learning, the Academy of Sciences, was Russified. Catherine II's *Frauenzimmerbibliothek* led her to undervalue Classical education, and to see no possibility of expanding the alien learning of the clerical academies to a general system of education. This position, probably unavoidable and certainly popular, simultaneously and fortuitously gave her the support of the long-suffering, anti-Ukrainian, Muscovite clergy, symbolized here by Metropolitan Platon.

While early in her reign she encouraged Betskoi, himself no champion of Latin studies, she presented in her *Nakaz* a fundamentally religious definition of education.

> Every one ought to inculcate the Fear of God into the tender Minds of Children, to encourage every laudable Inclination, and to accustom them to the fundamental Rules, suitable to their respective situations; to incite in them a Desire for Labour, and a Dread of Idleness, as the Root of all Evil, and Error; to train them up to a proper Decorum in their Actions and Conversation, Civility, and Decency in their Behaviour; and to sympathise with the Miseries of poor unhappy Wretches; and to break them of all perverse and forward Humours; to teach them Oeconomy, and whatever is most useful in all Affairs of Life; to guard them against all Prodigality and Extravagance; and particularly to root a proper Love of Cleanliness and Neatness, as well in themselves as in those who belong to them; in a Word, to instill all those virtues and Qualities which join to form a good Education; by which, as they grow up, they may prove real Citizens, useful Members of the Community, and Ornaments to their Country.[8]

---

[8] I cite the contemporary translation by Michael Tatishcheff as given in Dmytryshyn, *Imperial Russia*, p. 90. The modern reading is Paul Dukes, trans., *Catherine the Great's Instruction (Nakaz)*, here p. 90.

To an extent she was unaware, the values of her petulant father and of her fundamentalist Huguenot tutor were her values. It was but a matter of time before she discovered in Europe, in Felbiger's *Realschulen*, an alternative to the Latin college.

Mastery of the Classics had the potential to diminish the provincial, the nativist, and the national specific, the autocratic, and to impart a common culture with Europeans. Numerous Ukrainians and foreigners and a few Russians so educated testified to their potential. But because Muscovite culture proved to be so resilient, because its popular reading survived virtually unchanged, because the government's educational policy only flirted with Latin, because a century of nobles rejected humanism out of hand, Russia entered the post-French-Revolutionary world more provincial, more traditional, more nativist than is usually recognized. Her elites were smaller and culturally less "alienated from the people." Because Classicism was rejected by readers and Ukrainian humanism abandoned in the 1780s, Russia's Church entered the nineteenth century more likely to cite the Bible untempered by Cicero. Arguably it was less able to oppose serfdom, since "the Apostle" stated clearly that "each should remain in the place to which he has been called."[9]

For far-off America, the newest study of the founders' Classical reading shows specifically its contribution to both classical republicanism and liberalism in the colonies, and how Stoic natural law paved the way for egalitarian doctrines of rights, laissez-faire economics, popular sovereignty, and mixed government, other modern sources notwithstanding.[10] Because humanism did not seriously impact eighteenth-century Russia, and especially not its ruling nobility, there one detects only the slightest traces of this tradition, for example, among the foreign-educated participants in the frustrated "constitutional" projects of 1730.

Prince Shcherbatov, that well-educated curmudgeon, knew all this. He railed against the "necessary but, perhaps, excessive reformation wrought by Peter the Great." Echoing Rousseau, Shcherbatov concluded that old Muscovite "Coarseness of morals decreased, but the place left by it was filled by flattery and selfishness." Shcherbatov valued *humanitas*. In 1785 he recommended that young nobles have

---

[9] Paperno, "The Liberation of the Serfs as a Cultural Symbol," p. 419.
[10] Richard, *The Founders*, here introduction, and passim.

a "knowledge of ancient poets in the original," and be required to memorize their verses.[11] But his was a minority voice, already explicitly rejected in the School Reform, to be revived only in the lycees of Alexander I's Russia, and in the Classical schools of his younger brother.[12]

Understanding that Russia's nobility had consistently rejected the humanistic education of the West is essential to understanding nineteenth-century intellectual history. Only when one appreciates that the social elites had rejected the Latin West, are the debates between Chaadaev, Belinskii, and the Slavophiles intelligible, for their explicit message is a road not taken. Chaadaev's famous letter of 1836, for example, is usually discussed for its Catholic religious theme. It is equally eloquent on the potential of humanism. Chaadaev knew it was not merely Roman Christianity that Muscovy had rejected, but also Latin and a moral code that synthesized Stoic pagan and Christian elements. This was the source of the "ideas of duty, justice, right, and order [that were] part and parcel of the social fabric" of the West. Russia was not only outside true Christendom, but lacking Latin pagan authors, cut off as well from this continuum of essential ideas.

Had the Russian eighteenth-century nobility accepted the texts of humanism, had their alienation begun in Latin study, had they culturally been the "origins of the Russian intelligentsia," as is alleged, Chaadaev could not have written as he did. His recommendation for Russia was not only the Catholic faith, but also ancient notions of virtue and law. It was an essential tenet of the subsequent Westernizer-Slavophile debates of the mid-nineteenth century that Russians had failed to accept Latin education and its pagan texts.

"What is the life of man, says Cicero, if memory of earlier events does not relate the present to the past?"[13] The Slavophiles, major historians in the Romantic tradition, in their response to Chaadaev,

---

[11] Lentin, "'The *parole* of Literary Men'," pp. 11–13; on our deficient knowledge of his library and on his educational views, also his "Shcherbatov on Education," pp. 14–15. Note his awareness of the Kievan humanists' efforts and failure in Shcherbatov, *On the Corruption of Morals*, pp. 135–145, and his [The Pace of Russia's Modernization], in Raeff, ed., *Russian Intellectual History*, p. 58.

[12] The best guide to results is now Wes, *Classics in Russia.*

[13] For the above, Chaadaev, "Letters on the Philosophy of History," in Raeff, *Russian Intellectual History*, pp. 164, 165, 167, 169. For the reconstruction of Chaadaev's two libraries and an attempt to judge the influence of books in them, see McNally, *Chaadayev and His Friends*, Chapter 5, pp. 164–98.

applauded the absence of a pagan-informed historical memory in Russia. They knew the Latin foundations of the West had been rejected by their fathers and generations of their aristocratic ancestors. They could begin their analysis of the present celebrating "*the soul, the turn of mind, the whole inner content, so to say, of any Russian who has not yet been transformed by Western education.*" Ivan Kireevskii knew that "Ancient Rome left its imprint on the basic structure of society, on the laws, the language, the ways and customs, the early arts and learning of Europe; it was therefore, bound to impart to every aspect of Western life something of that specific character which had distinguished it from all other peoples; and that specific character was bound to affect the very substance of Western man's existence."[14] Defending Russian traditions, he could conclude that, mercifully, Russia had rejected Rome and Latin learning.

At the outset, a clarification of the discordant views of Professors Raeff and Treadgold was promised. The one suggested that Latinism began in its seventeenth-century importation, and remained, largely the culture of the Church; the latter found that Latin education had been widely accepted as normative by the middle of the eighteenth century, and thus that Peter's was indeed a major cultural revolution. The evidence of printing, book owning, and Latin study, the voices of eighteenth-century writers, and later of Chaadaev, the Slavophiles, and the Westernizers, suggests modification to both positions. Professor Treadgold's generalization simply goes too far, as Latin never took hold to the extent he suggests, and no Russian government envisioned such a frontal attack on Muscovite education. Professor Raeff's view, on the other hand, and especially the central argument of his influential *Origins of the Russian Intelligentsia*, slights the non-noble clerical and soldiers' sons and other *raznochintsy* who did take to Latin, and who struggled unsuccessfully, alongside Ukrainian divines, Germans academics, and other resident Europeans, to bring Russia into the world of humanism. This polyglot coalition, not the native Russian nobility, can be regarded as the seedbed of any subsequent alienated intelligentsia.

By the early nineteenth century, the target would move again, and Russia would again consider Western educations. Those borrowings,

---

[14] Kireevskii, "On the Nature of European Culture," in Raeff, *Russian Intellectual History*, pp. 175ff.

the lycées of Alexander, the odd Grecophilia and especially the intense Classical scholarship of the professorate of Nicholas I, lie beyond
the horizons of the present study.[15] Even during those changes in
elite educations, however, a rejection of Latin culture, and an undisturbed religious upbringing, would continue to shape most Russian
youth. Girls, for example, would continue to read Scripture and saints'
lives. The examples of Brutus, Gracchus, the Horatii might inspire
revolutionaries in the Western world, but in Russia a thirteen-year-
old Vera Zasulich would be inspired by her Bible. Having read, "Leave
thy father and thy mother and follow Me," she would abandon
medical school, and pursue full-time radical activity.[16]

The study of private libraries in Russia affords more specific generalizations. In the period between 1650 and 1700 individuals exposed
to the Western university or to Ukrainian humanism—few were
Russians—had collections which contained the pagan Latin authors,
sometimes to the exclusion of Slavonic books. The libraries of Muscovite court culture also changed with Aleksei's conversion to Western values. They contained the traditional Slavonic liturgical texts of
Orthodoxy and an increasingly eclectic range of Polish letters, tales
of travel, adventure, and history. For the vast majority of Muscovites, exclusively ecclesiastical and liturgical readings remained the
rule, although printed versions began to accompany manuscripts.
Numerous Old-Believers resisted even that compromise.

   After 1700 book habits began to change, although not in ways
consonant with the notion of a sudden, energetic, Westernization
sponsored by Tsar Peter. Everyone, including the few touched by
humanism, continued to own works of religion, often broadened in
scope with Pietism. Formal education became synonymous with
ownership of Classical authors, although they were not published in
Russia, and they were held mostly by Ukrainian clergy and their
pupils. A few individuals of Russian courtly culture, like Peter himself, began to sample ancient authors in translation. They also began
to own modern political, technical, and practical authors. For belles-
lettres Germans began to replace texts from Poland. But there is no

---

[15] Still useful is Hans, *History of Russian Educational Policy*, on the reforms of Alexander
I, but note Flynn, *The University Reform*. On Nicholas see Whittaker, *The Origins of
Modern Russian Education*, here esp. chap. 7, and Wes, cited above.
[16] Engel, *Mothers and Daughters*, pp. 11, 141, 199.

evidence that traditional religious educations had been disturbed, that Russians ceased to own or read traditional liturgical works, or that they abandoned the old manuscript collections, which would remain the definition of reading well into the century. There is no evidence that the Petrine reforms did, or were meant to disrupt the liturgical *Ladder of Literacy* or to touch the pious reading habits of the many.

After 1750 the Russian library became more diverse. Only in this period did any significant number of Russian *raznochintsy*, as opposed to Ukrainian clergy and foreigners in Russian service, begin to acquire the kinds of libraries that characterized intellectual life in Western Europe since 1500. In so far as the Russian gentry was concerned, the evidence suggests that most wealthy enough to own printed books moved directly from works of traditional religiosity to the modern library of romance, travel, and popular science, without the intermediate education in the Classics which characterized European nobilities. When Andrew Kahn recently investigated authors who manipulated the concept of Imperial Rome in eighteenth century Russia, he focused on V. P. Petrov and Lomonosov, both poets of stature, but both decidedly non-noble.[17] Over time, Russian nobles' educations would be mirrored in their book collections. Their evolution did not generally resemble those of educated European nobles, ecclesiastical or lay, but rather those of women.

Late in the era, a small number of Russia's elite were finally attracted to Latin. They included Shcherbatov, Demidov, and Radishchev, and others less well documented. They represented the tiniest portion of the gentry, as indeed book buying itself was reserved to the smallest portion stratified by wealth. The nobles' gymnasium of Moscow University attracted an enthusiastic few, and made Latin learning respectable for the first time, although French ruled. But any chance that the Russian *dvorianstvo* would adopt the humanist education of European nobilities was ended by Catherine's Russophile and religious revival of the 1780s, which temporarily withdrew the invitation to Latin in Moscow, Petersburg, Kiev, and the provinces, in the old clerical academies, in private schools, and in the new institutions of the School Reform.

Neither Soviet Great-Russian nor Western liberal historians have dealt adequately with these themes. Soviet historians exaggerated the secu-

---

[17] Kahn, "Readings of Imperial Rome," pp. 747–756.

lar, denigrated the religious, and dismissed alien humanism as mere "scholasticism." Liberal historiography was in many ways more pernicious. It assumed a gentry-led Russian cultural establishment, and thus it dismissed real Westernizers like Polockij as religious curiosities, relegated to the pre-history of Russian intellectual life. Archbishop Teofan might be studied, but out of his clerical context as "Feofan Prokopovich," a secularized "Russian" writer. He was neither. His voluminous sermons were ignored in favor of commissioned unrepresentative works in which he discussed themes that reflected the subsequent political concerns of the gentry. Tatishchev and Lomonosov were secularized beyond recognition, and made the champions of intellectual movements they detested, or to which they had no access; their libraries mirrored their true religious faces. Influential shapers of modern Russia's revitalized religious education like Metropolitan Platon were slighted in favor of proto-*intelligenty* like Novikov, whose schools educated comparatively few, simply because they were more secular noblemen, and therefore, according to Marxist historiography, the logical *Kulturträger*. Especially pernicious was the effect of the scholarly conviction that Russia had shared in the European Enlightenments.

The dominant cultural patterns of early-modern Russia were created by geography and by education: Russia annexed the Ukraine, but did not embrace Ukrainian humanism. The imported Ukrainian hierarchy had adopted the Latin curriculum of the Western grammar-school and college, but most of their adopted society rejected it. Only dragooned sons of clergy and of the middling classes sat on their school-benches.

Geography and education shaped Psalm-quoting peasant, alien Ukrainian divine, and Radishchev. Most Russians who read in 1750 read pretty much as they had in 1650. No mandated educational reform had ever questioned their Orthodox books, religion, or assumptions about the earthly sojourn. The Church grudgingly accepted Ukrainian hierarchs, but denied them the printing press; elite and popular society denied them an audience.

An attitude toward the Latin Classics, toward Cicero, is a useful tool in measuring degrees and styles of Westernization in early-modern times. Education and the geography of empire produced a complex cultural slope in eighteenth-century Russia. A handful of resident Germans, Ukrainians, and a few others, subscribed to the humanist values that had defined education in Europe since 1500. The Russian government, and a minute portion of the upper and middling classes of Russian society flirted with the Latin culture of the West between 1650 and 1789, through the mediation of their annexed Ukrainian, Lithuanian, and Belorussian co-religionists, or through imported German scholars. It never exceeded a flirtation: it never developed into a love-affair. For nineteenth-century Westernizers that was a tragedy, because Russia remained Orthodox and obscurantist; for better informed Slavophiles, it was her salvation, for exactly the same reasons.

Today Russia and Ukraine, Belorussia, and Lithuania are again disunited. For the new Russian nationalists, the division is wholly desirable and indeed crucial to Russia's identity:

> Russia is something else. From the early Middle Ages, Western societies have experienced a steady accretion of rationalism in their psychology and their institutions. There was the Reformation, the Renaissance, the Enlightenment. We had none of this. . . . Without my getting stereotypical, Russia's psychology is more spontaneous, predictable, artistic, more inclined to extremes of endless patience and explosions of license.[18]

In such words contemporary Russians tacitly applaud the failure of humanism to impact the eighteenth century of their fathers.

Today's new Russian nationalists are equally convinced that their ancestors were not imperialistic, and that other Slavs and other non-Slavic populations were destined to become Russians. Raisa Maksimovna Gorbacheva responded to nationalistic taunts by proclaiming, "Who are they—these Georgians, Armenians, Estonians, Lithuanians, Jews, Kazakhs and Azerbaidzhanians—are they enemies? . . . The strength of the Russian people lies in the fact that we have never exploited anybody."[19] Contemporary Russian authors of the "peasant school" concur: "No nation but Russia had so many other nations unite with it voluntarily—the Armenians, the Georgians, the Ukrainians, and others, too! . . . No one anywhere has treated a Little Russian [Ukrainian—MJO] as a foreigner."[20]

In the first century or so that Ukrainians and Belorussians were

---

[18] David Remnick, quoting Yeltsin's friend Sergei Stankevich, in "Yeltsin's Tightrope," *The New Yorker*, May 10, 1993, p. 82.

[19] Raisa Gorbachev, *I Hope*, David Floyd, trans., NY, 1991, p. 180.

[20] Sergei Pavlovich Zalygin, *The Commission*, David Gordon Wilson, trans., DeKalb, 1993, pp. 289–290.

politically united with the Russians, it is generally held, their cultural influence was enormous, and therefore modern Russian nationalism is justified. "In the seventeenth and early eighteenth century Ukrainian religious culture streamed into Russia, having a profound impact on the intellectual evolution of the northern neighbor. From then on, the Ukraine was increasingly under the influence of the culture of the metropolis, and has remained so to a greater or lesser extent to the present day."[21] The history of humanist education in Russia, the output of the Russian presses, the evidence of the private library, and Russian thought, all suggest that the Ukrainian cultural impact was less than profound, and that it early and consistently succumbed to the pre-established norms of a resilient Muscovite book culture.

---

[21] Paul Bushkovitch, "The Ukraine in Russian Culture 1790–1860: The Evidence of the Journals," *JfGO*, Vol. 39, No. 3 (1991), p. 339.

BIBLIOGRAPHY OF WORKS CONSULTED

Abbreviations:

M.	Moscow
L.	Leningrad
M-L.	Moscow-Leningrad

AGB	Arkhiv für Geschichte Buchwesens
AHR	American Historical Review
CASS	Canadian-American Slavic Studies
CJ	Classical Journal
COidr	Chteniia v Obshchestve istorii i drevnostei rossiikikh pri Moskovskom universiteta
CSP	Canadian Slavonic Papers
FzoG	Forschungen zur osteuropaischen Geschichte
HEQ	History of Education Quarterly
HSS	Harvard Slavic Studies
HUS	Harvard Ukrainian Studies
Ia	Istoricheskii arkhiv
JfGO	Jahrbücher für Geschichte Osteuropas
JfGU	Jahrbuch für Geschichte UdSSR und der volksdemokratischen Länder Europas
JHI	Journal of the History of Ideas
KIm	Kniga. Issledovaniia i materialy
KS	Kievskaia starina
Ln	Literaturnoe nasledstvo
NZSJ	New Zealand Slavonic Journal
OSP	Oxford Slavonic Papers
RH	Russian History/Histoire Russie
RR	Russian Review
Rs	Russkaia starina
SEEJ	Slavic and East European Journal
SEER	Slavonic and East European Review
SGECR	Study Group on Eighteenth-Century Russia. Newsletter.
SR	Slavic Review
Todl	Trudy otdeleniia drevnerusskoi literatury
WSA	Wolfenbüttler Studien zur Aufklärung
ZfHF	Zeitschrift für Historische Forschung
ZIAn	Zapiski Imperatorskoi Akademii nauk
ZMnp	Zhurnal Ministerstva narodnogo prosveshcheniia
ZS	Zeitschrift für Slavistik
ZSP	Zeitschrift für Slavische Philologie

I. *Bibliographic Aids Consulted*

Afanas'eva, T. A., *Katalog izdanii kirillicheskoi pechati Moskovskoi tipografii XVIII veka*, 2vv. L. 1986, 1987.

Aleksandrova, K. V. comp., "Sovetskaia literatura po istorii russkoi knigi do serediny XIX v." in A. A. Sidorov & S. P. Luppov, eds., *Kniga v Rossii do serediny XIX veka*, L. 1978, pp. 300–304.

Andreyev, Nikolay, "Appanage and Muscovite Russia," in Robert Auty & Dmitri Obolensky, eds., *An Introduction to Russian History. Companion to Russian Studies*, I, Cambridge, 1976, pp. 78–120.
——, "Literature in the Muscovite Period (1300–1700)," in Robert Auty & Dmitri Obolensky, eds., *An Introduction to Russian Language and Literature. Companion to Russian Studies*, 2, Cambridge, 1977, pp. 90–110.
Botvinnik, M. B., "Istochniki i literatura o Lavrentii Zizanii Tustanovskom," *Iz istorii knigi, bibliotechnogo dela i bibliografii v Belorussii*, Vyp. II, Minsk, 1972, 200–237.
——, "Istoriografiia izucheniia 'Azbuki' Ivan Fedorova v SSSR," *Kniga, bibliotechnoe delo i bibliografiia v Belorussii*, Minsk, 1974, pp. 93–114.
Burgess, M., "The Age of Classicism (1720–1820)," in Robert Auty & Dmitri Obolenski, eds., *An Introduction to Russian Language and Literature. Companion to Russian Studies*, 2, Cambridge, 1977, pp. 111–132.
Bykova, T. A. & M. M. Gurevich, comps., *Opisanie izdanii grazhdanskoi pechati 1708—ianvar' 1725 g.*, M-L. 1955.
——, *Opisanie izdanii napechatannykh kirillitsei 1689—ianvar' 1725 g.*, M-L. 1958.
Bykova, T. A., M. M. Gurevich, & R. I. Kozintseva, comp., *Opisanie izdanii napechatannykh pri Petre I. Svodnyi katalog. Dopolneniia i prilozheniia*, L. 1972.
Cepiene, K. & I. Petrauskiene, *Vilniaus Akademijos Spaustuves Leidiniai 1576–1805. Bibliografija. (Izdaniia tipografii Vil'niusskoi akademii 1576–1805. Bibliografiia)*, Vilnius, 1979.
Clendenning, Philip & Roger Bartlett, *Eighteenth Century Russia: A Select Bibliography of Works Published Since 1955*, Newtonville, 1981.
Cooke, Olga Muller & Pierre R. Hart, "XVII–XVIII Centuries," *The SEEJ*, Vol. 31 (1987), 31–51.
Cracraft, James, "Feofan Prokopovich: A Bibliography of his Works," *OSP*, N.S. Vol. VIII (1975), 1–36.
Cross, A. G. & G. S. Smith, "A Bibliography of English-Language Scholarship on Eighteenth-Century Russian Literature, Thought, and Culture (1900–1974)," in A. G. Cross, ed., *Russian Literature in the Age of Catherine the Great*, Oxford, 1976. Continued in *SGECR*, No. 5 (1977), 55–65.
——, *Eighteenth Century Russian Literature, Culture and Thought: A Bibliography of English-Language Scholarship and Translations*, Newtonville, 1984.
Dneprov, E. D., *Sovetskaia literatura po istorii shkoly i pedagogiki dorevoliutsionnoi Rossii 1918–1977. Bibliograficheskii ukazatel'*, M. 1979.
Egan, David R. & Melinda A. Egan, *Russian Autocrats from Ivan the Great to the Fall of the Romanov Dynasty: An Annotated Bibliography of English Language Sources to 1985*, Metuchen, N.J./London, 1987.
Fessenko, Tatiana, *Eighteenth Century Russian Publications in the Library of Congress. A Catalogue*, Washington, 1961.
Gorfunkel', A. Kh., *Katalog knig kirillovskoi pechati 16–17 vekov*, L. 1970.
"Greek and Latin Literature in Translation"; "1988 Supplementary Survey," *CJ*, Vol. 82, No. 2 (Dec–Jan, 1987) 164–177; Vol. 83, No. 2 (Dec–Jan, 1988) 176–178.
Grau, C. & I. Flentje, "Chronologische Bibliographie der Veröffentlichungen von Eduard Winter von 1924 bis 1965," in W. Steinitz et al., eds., *Ost und West in der Geschichte des Denkens und der kulturellen Beziehungen. Festschrift für Eduard Winter zum 70. Geburtstag*, Berlin, 1966, pp. 5–27. =Quellen und Studien zur Geschichte Osteuropas. XV.
Hellmann, Manfred et al., eds., *Osteuropa in der historischen Forschung der DDR*, 2vv. Düsseldorf, 1972.
Harvard Ukrainian Studies. Special Issue. The Kiev Mohyla Academy, Vol. VIII, No. 1/2 (June, 1984), 154–250; review articles and bibliographies by Frank E. Sysyn, Matei Cazacu, Paulina Lewin, Omeljan Pritsak & Oksana Procyk.
Istoricheskii ocherk i obzor fondov rukopisnogo otdela Biblioteki Akademii Nauk, Vyp. I. XVIII vek, M-L. 1956.

Kameneva, T. N., "Chernigovskaia tipografiia, ee deiatel'nost' i izdaniia," *Trudy: Biblioteka SSSR imeni V. I. Lenina*, III (1959), 224–384.

[Kameneva, T. N. & A. A. Guseva], *Ukrainskie knigi kirillovskoi pechati XVI–XVIII vv. Katalog izdanii, khraniashchikhsia v Gosudarstvennoi biblioteke SSSR imeni V. I. Lenina*, 3vv. M. 1976ff.

Kapusta, V. I., comp., "Sovetskaia literatura (1976–1981) po istorii russkoi knigi do serediny XIX v.," *Russkie biblioteki i ikh chitatel'*, L. 1983, pp. 235–239.

Kasinec, Edward, comp., "Eighteenth-Century Russian Publications in The New York Public Library: A Preliminary Catalogue," *Bulletin of the New York Public Library*, Vol. 75, No. 9 (Nov. 1971), 474–494.

Katalog izdanii Imperatorskoi Akademii nauk s 1726 goda po 1–e iunia 1912 goda, 3vv. St. Petersburg, 1912, 1915, 1916.

"Khronika," [1957–1962] *Mezhdunarodnye sviazi russkoi literatury. Sbornik statei*, M-L. 1963, pp. 450–456; [1963–1972] *Rossiia i zapad. Iz istorii literaturnykh otnoshenii*, L. 1973, pp. 320–327; [1972–1982] *Vzaimosviazi russkoi i zarubezhnykh literatur*, L. 1983, pp. 316–320.

Kirchner, Joachim, *Bibliographie der Zeitschriften des deutschen Sprachgebietes bis 1900. I. Die Zeitschriften des deutschen Sprachgebietes bis 1830*, Stuttgart, 1969.

Kniga Belarusi 1517–1917. Zvodnyi katalog, Minsk, 1986.

Mel'nikova, N. N., *Izdaniia napechatannye v tipografii moskovskogo universiteta XVIII vek*, M. 1966.

Nemirovskii, E. L., comp., *Nachalo knigopechataniia v Moskve i na Ukraine. Zhizn' i deiatel'nost' pervopechatnika Ivana Fedorova. Ukaz. literatury 1574–1974*, M. 1975.

Nerhood, Harry W., *To Russia and Return: An Annotated Bibliography of Travelers' English-Language Accounts of Russia from the Ninth Century to the Present*, Columbus, Ohio, 1968.

Pekarskii, P., *Nauka i literatura v Rossii pri Petre Velikom. II. Opisanie slaviano-russkikh knig i tipografii 1698–1725 godov*, St. Petersburg, 1862.

Pozdeeva, I. V. et al., comps., *Katalog knig kirillicheskoi pechati XV–XVII v.v. Nauchnoi biblioteki Moskovskogo universiteta*, M. 1980.

Pritsak, Omelian and Oksana Procyk, "A Select Bibliography of Soviet Publications Related to the Kiev Mohyla Academy and its Founder, 1970–1983," *HUS*, Vol. VIII, No. 1/2 (June, 1984), 229–250.

Raeff, Marc, "Imperial Russia. Peter I to Nicholas I," in Robert Auty & Dmitri Obolensky, eds., *An Introduction to Russian History. Companion to Russian Studies*, 1, Cambridge, 1976.

Slavianskie knigi kirillovskoi pechati XV–XVIII vv. Opisanie knig, khraniashchikhsia v Gosudarstvennoi publichnoi biblioteke USSR, Kiev, 1958.

Slovar' knizhnikov i knizhnosti drevnei Rusi. Vyp. 2. (Vtoraia polovina XIV–XVI v.), 2vv. L. 1988–1989.

Stepanov K. P. & Iu. V. Stennik, comps., *Istoriia russkoi literatury XVIII veka. Bibliograficheskii ukazatel'*, L. 1968.

Svodnyi katalog knig na inostrannykh iazykakh, izdannykh v Rossii v XVIII veke 1701–1800, 3vv. to date, L. 1984ff.

Svodnyi katalog russkoi knigi grazhdanskoi pechati XVIII veka 1725–1800, 5vv. M. 1963–1967; *Dopolneniia, razyskivaemye izdaniia, utochneniia*, M. 1975.

"Ukazatel' statei v izdaniiakh Gruppy po izucheniiu russkoi literatury XVIII veka za 1935–1974 gg.," *XVIII vek. Sbornik 10. Russkaia literatura XVIII veka i ee mezhdunarodnye sviazy*, L. 1975, pp. 303–314.

Vierhaus, Rudolf, *Staten und Stände. Vom Westfälischen bis zum Hubertusberger Frieden 1648 bis 1763. Fünfter Band. Propyläen Geschichte Deutschlands*, Berlin, 1984, [bibliography] pp. 357–364.

Zernova, A. S., *Knigi kirillovskoi pechati, izdannye v Moskve v XVI–XVII vekakh. Svodnyi katalog*, M. 1958.

Zernack, Klaus, ed., *Handbuch der Geschichte Russlands. Band 2. 1613–1856*, Stuttgart, 1986.

246 BIBLIOGRAPHY OF WORKS CONSULTED

Zeil, Wilhelm, "Forschungen zur Geschichte der Völker der UdSSR und der deutsch-russischen Beziehungen bis 1917," *Historische Forschungen in der DDR 1960–1970*, Berlin 1970. =Zeitschrift für Geschichtswissenschaft XVIII Jahr. 1970. Sonderband. pp. 660–675; [same title] 1980. Sonderband. pp. 381–392.

II. *Works Cited in the Notes*[1]

Abramov, K. I., *Istoriia bibliotechnogo delo v SSSR*, 3rd ed., M. 1980.
Adariukov V. Ia. & A. A. Sidorov, eds., *Kniga v Rossii. I. Russkaia kniga ot nachala pis'mennosti do 1800 goda*, M. 1924.
Adler, Philip J., "Habsburg School Reform Among the Orthodox Minorities, 1770–1780," *SR*, Vol. 33, No. 1 (Mar, 1974) 23–45.
Adrianova, V. P., *Zhitie Alekseia cheloveka Bozhiia v drevnei russkoi literature i narodnoi slovesnosti*, Petrograd, 1917 (reprint 1969).
Aesop, *Esopy basni s nravoucheniem i primechaniiami*, St. Petersburg, 1747.
Afanas'eva, T. A., "Izdanie azbuki i bukvarei kirillicheskoi pechati v XVIII veke," *Iz istorii rukopisnykh i staropechatnykh sobranii (Issledovaniia. Obzory. Publikatsii)*, L. 1979, pp. 33–60.
——, "Izdaniia kirillicheskoi pechati XVIII veka svetskogo soderzhaniia," *Problemy istochnikovedcheskogo izucheniia rukopisnykh i staropechatnykh fondov*, L. 1979, pp. 183–199.
——, "Rasprostranenie kirillicheskoi knigi v Rossii v XVIII v.," *Rukopisnaia i pechatnaia kniga v Rossii. Problemy sozdaniia i rasprostraneniia*, L. 1988, pp. 131–139.
Alekseev, M. P., "Erazm Roterdamskii v russkom perevode XVII v.," *Slavianskaia filologiia. I. Sbornik statei, posviashchennyi IV Mezhdunarodnumu s'ezdu slavistov*, M. 1958, pp. 275–330.
——, *Iavleniia gumanizma v literature i publitsistike drevnei rusi (XVI–XVII vv.)*, M. 1958.
——, "Pervoe znakomstvo s Dante v Rossii," *Ot klassitsizma k romantizmu. Iz istorii mezhdunarodnykh sviazei russkoi literatury*, L. 1970, pp. 6–62.
——, *Slovari inostrannykh iazykov v russkom azbukovnike XVII veka. Issledovanie, teksty i kommentarii*, L. 1968.
Alexander, John T., *Catherine the Great. Life and Legend*, New York, 1989.
Alston, R. C., "The Eighteenth-Century Non-Book: Observations on Printed Ephemera," in Paul Raabe, ed., *Buch und Buchhandel in Europa im achtzehnten Jahrhundert*, Hamburg, 1981, pp. 343–360. =Wolfenbütteler Schriften zur Geschichte des Buchwesens. Bd. 4.
Altbauer, Dan, "The Diplomats of Peter the Great," *JfGO*, Vol. 28, No. 1 (1980), pp. 1–16.
Amburger, Erik, *Beiträge zur Geschichte der deutsch-russischen kulturellen Beziehungen*, Gießen, 1961.
——, "Buchdruck, Buchhandel und Verlage in St. Petersburg im 18. Jahrhundert," *Buch- und Verlagswesen im 18. und 19. Jh. Beiträge zur Geschichte der Kommunikation in Mittel- und Osteuropa*, Berlin, 1977, pp. 201–216.
——, "Die deutschen Schulen in Rußland mit besonderer Berücksichtigung St. Petersburg," in Friedhelm Berthold Kaiser & Bernhard Stasiewski, eds., *Deutscher Einfluss auf Bildung und Wissenschaft im östlichen Europa*, Köln/Wien, 1984, pp. 1–26.
——, "Die Gründung gelehrten Gesellschaften in Rußland unter Katarina II," in Erik Amburger et al. eds., *Wissenschaftpolitik in Mittel- und Osteuropa*, Berlin, 1976, pp. 259–270.
Amosov, A. A., "Zametki o moskovskom staropechatanii. K voprosu o tirazh izdanii

---

[1] Reviews, sometimes cited in the notes, are generally not included in this bibliography.

XVI—nachala XVII veka," *Russkie knigi i biblioteki v XVI—pervoi polovine XIX veka*, L. 1983, pp. 5–12.

Andreev, V. V., *Raskol i ego znachenie v narodnoi russkoi istorii*, St. Petersburg, 1870 (reprint, 1965).

Andreyev, Niklolay, "Nikon and Avvakum on Icon-Painting," *Studies in Muscovy. Western Influence and Byzantine Inheritance*, London, 1970, pp. 37–44 (orig. 1961).

Anisimov, E. V., *Rossii v seredine XVIII veka. Bor'ba za nasledie Petra*, M. 1986.

Anushkin, A., *Na zare knigopechataniia v Litve*, Vil'nius, 1970.

Appel, Klaus, "Die Anfänge des Buchdrucks im Moskauer Rußland," *AGB*, X. Frankfurt/M., 1970, pp. 1355–1398.

Ariès, Philippe, *Centuries of Childhood. A Social History of Family Life*, New York, 1962 (Fr. orig. 1960).

Arnold, Werner, "Der Fürst als Büchersammler. Die Hofbibliotheken in der Zeit der Aufklärung," in Werner Arnold & Peter Vodosek, eds., *Bibliotheken und Aufklärung*, Wiesbaden, 1988, pp. 41–60. =Wolfenbütteler Schriften zur Geschichte des Buchwesens. Bd. 14.

Artem'ev, K. [A.], "Biblioteka Imperatorskago Kazanskago Universiteta," *ZMnp*, Vol. LXX, No. 6 (Jun, 1851), Otd. III, 83–112, LXXII, No. 11 (Nov., 1851), Otd. III, 1–30.

Aseev, B. N., *Russkii dramaticheskii teatr ot ego istokov do kontsa XVIII veka*, 2nd ed., M. 1977.

Ashworth, E. J., "Changes in Logic Textbooks from 1500 to 1650: The New Aristotelianism," in Eckhard Keßler et al., eds., *Aristotelismus und Renaissance*, Wiesbaden, 1981, pp. 75–87.

Asoian, A. A., *Dante i russkaia literatura*, Sverdlovsk, 1989.

Astrakhanskii, V. S., "Novoe o knigakh V. N. Tatishcheva," *Knizhnoe delo v Rossii v XVI–XIX vekakh*, L. 1980, pp. 76–78.

Avvakum, Archpriest, *The Life written by Himself*, Kenneth N. Brostrom, trans., Ann Arbor, 1979.

Babushkina, A. P., *Istoriia russkoi detskoi literatury*, M. 1948.

Badalich, I. M. & V. D. Kuz'mina, *Pamiatniki russkoi shkol'noi dramy XVIII veka (po zagrebskim spiskam)*, M. 1968.

Baehr, Stephen L., "Regaining Paradise: the "Political Icon" in Seventeenth- and Eighteenth-Century Russia," *RH*, Vol. 11, No. 2–3 (Summer-Fall, 1984), 148–167.

——, "The Masonic Components in Eighteenth-Century Russian Literature," in A. G. Cross, ed., *Russian Literature in the Age of Catherine the Great*, Oxford, 1976, pp. 121–139.

——, *The Paradise Myth in Eighteenth-Century Russia. Utopian Patterns in Early Secular Russian Literature and Culture*, Stanford, 1991.

Baklanova, N. A., "O sostave bibliotek moskovskikh kuptsov vo vtoroi chetverti XVIII v.," *Todl*, Vol. XIV (1958), 644–649.

——, "Russkii chitatel' XVII veka," *Drevnerusskaia literatura i ee sviazy s novym vremenem*, M. 1967, pp. 156–193. =Issledovaniia i materialy po drevnerusskoi literature [2].

——, "'Tetradi' startsa Avraamiia," *Ia*, Vol. VI. (1951), 131–155.

——, "Znachenie vladel'cheskikh zapisei na drevnerusskikh knigakh kak istochnik dlia istorii russkoi kul'tury," *Arkheograficheskii ezhegodnik za 1962 g.*, M. 1963, pp. 197–205.

Barenbaum, Iosif E., *Geschichte des Buchhandels in Russland und der Soujetunion*, Wiesbaden, 1991.

Baron, Samuel H., "The Origins of Seventeenth-Century Moscow's Nemeckaja Sloboda," *Muscovite Russia. Collected Essays*, London, 1980, pp. 1–17 (orig. 1970).

——, trans., *The Travels of Olearius in 17th-Century Russia*, Stanford, 1967.

Barsukov, Alexandr, *Rod Sheremetevykh*, Vol. 5, St. Petersburg, 1888.

Bartlett, R. P., "Culture and Enlightenment: Julius von Canitz and the Kazan' Gimnazii in the Eighteenth Century," *CASS*, Vol. 14, No. 3 (Fall, 1980), 331–360.

Bartlett, Roger, "Russia's First Abolitionist: The Political Philosophy of J. G. Eisen," *JfGO*, Vol. 39, No. 2 (1991), 161–176.

Bauman, V. G. & D. K. Salakhutdinova, "Knigi iz biblioteki V. N. Tatishcheva v Leningradskom gornom institute," *Kniga v Rossii XVI–XIX v. Materialy i issledovaniia*, L. 1990, pp. 127–138.

Beales, Derek, "Social Forces and Enlightened Policies," in H. M. Scott, ed., *Enlightened Absolutism. Reform and Reformers in Later Eighteenth-Century Europe*, London, 1990, pp. 37–54.

Beauplan, Sieur de Guillaume le Vasseur, *Description D'Ukrainie qui sont plusieurs Provinces du Royaume de Pologne*, Paris, 1661. *A Description of Ukraine*, Andrew B. Pernal and Dennis F. Essar, trans., HUS, Cambridge, MA, 1993.

Beckmann, Friedhelm, "Französische Privatbibliotheken. Untersuchungen zu Literatursystematik und Buchsitz im 18. Jahrhundert," *AGB*, Vol. 31 (1988), 1–162.

Belobrova, O. A., ed., *Nikolai Spafarii. Esteticheskie traktaty*, L. 1978.

Belokurov, S. A., *O biblioteke moskovskikh gosudarei v XVI stoletii*, M. 1898.

——, "O namerenii Lomonosova priniat' sviashchenstvo i otpravit'sia s I. K. Kirillovym v Orenburgskuiu ekspeditsiiu 1734 g.," *Lomonosovskii sbornik*, St. Petersburg, 1911, pp. 67–75.

—— & A. N. Zertsalo, *O nemetskikh shkolakh v Moskve v pervoi chetverti XVIII v.*, M. 1907.

Belorusskii prosvetitel' Frantsisk Skorina i nachalo knigopechataniia v Belorussii i Litve, M. 1979. =Fedorovskie chteniia 1977.

Berkov, P. N., "Besonderheiten des literarischen Prozesses in Rußland im 18. Jahrhundert," in Helmut Grasshoff & Ulf Lehmann, eds., *Studien zur Geschichte der russischen Literatur des 18. Jahrhunderts*, Band III, Berlin, 1968, pp. 9–55.

——, "Bibliograficheskaia evristika (K teorii i metodike bibliograficheskikh razyskanii)," *Izbrannoe. Trudy po knigovedeniiu i bibliografovedeniiu*, M. 1978, pp. 112–185.

——, "Biografiia moei biblioteki," *Izbrannoe. Trudy po knigovedeniiu i bibliografovedeniiu*, M. 1978, pp. 220–226.

——, "Frühe russische Horaz-Übersetzer," in his *Literarische Wechselbeziehungen*, Berlin, 1968, pp. 89–106, 235–240.

——, "Histoire de l'Encyclopédie dans la Russie du XVIIIe siècle," *Revue des Études Slaves*, Vol. XLIV, No. 1 (1965), 47–58.

——, "Izuchenie russkoi literatury vo Frantsii, Bibliograficheskie materialy," *Ln*, Vol. 33–34 (1939), 721–768.

——, "Osnovnye voprosy russkogo prosvetitel'stva," *Problemy russkogo prosveshcheniia v literature XVIII veka*, M-L. 1961, pp. 5–27.

——, "Pervye gody literaturnoi deiatel'nosti Antiokha Kantemira (1726–1729)," *Problemy russkogo prosveshcheniia v literature XVIII veka*, M-L. 1961, pp. 190–220.

——, "Problemy izucheniia russkogo klassitsizma," *Russkaia literatura XVIII veka. Epokha klassitsizma*, M-L. 1964, pp. 5–29.

——, *Vvedenie v izuchenie istorii russkoi literatury XVIII veka. Chast' l. Ocherk literaturnoi istoriografii XVIII veka*, L. 1964.

Betzky, [Betskoi, Ivan Ivanovich], *Les Plans et les statuts, des différents éstablissements ordonnés par sa majesté impériale Catherine II. Pour l'éducation de la jeunesse et l'utilité générale de son empire*, 2vv., Amsterdam, 1775.

Bezborod'ko, N. I., "Uchebnaia latyn' na Ukraine," *Voprosy iazykoznaniia*, 1978, No. 6 (Nov–Dec), 85–92.

Biblioteka Vol'tera. Katalog knig, M-L. 1961.

Bilevich, V. V., "Staropechatnye inostrannye knigi estestvennonauchnoi tematiki v fondakh FBAN BSSR," *Knigovedenie v Belorussii (Sbornik statei)*, Minsk, 1977, pp. 108–121.

[Bilfinger, Georg Bernhard], *Raspolozhenie uchenii ego imperatorskago velichestva Petra Vtorago*, [St. Petersburg, 1731].

Biralo, A. A., *Filosofskaia i obshchestvennaia mysl' v Belorussii i Litve v kontse XVII—seredine XVIII vv.*, Minsk, 1971.

Bishop, W. J., "Le Dr. W. Salamon (164–1713) et sa bibliothèque," *Librarium. Zeitschrift der Schweizerischen Bibliophilen*, Vol. II, Heft 2 (Aug, 1959), 79–83.

Bissonnette, Georges, "Peter the Great and the Church as an Educational Institution," in J. S. Curtiss, ed., *Essays in Russian and Soviet History in honor of Geroid Tanquary Robinson*, New York, 1963, pp. 3–19.

Black, J. L., *Citizens for the Fatherland. Education, Educators, and Pedagogical Ideals in Eighteenth Century Russia*, Boulder/New York, 1979.

——, *G.-F. Müller and the Imperial Russian Academy*, Kingston/Montreal, 1986.

Blium, A. V., "Massovoe chtenie v russkoi provintsii kontsa XVIII—pervoi chetverti XIX vv.," *Trudy: Leningradskii gos. institut kul'tury im. N. K. Krupskoi. XXV. Istoriia russkogo chitatelia*, Vyp. 1, L. 1973, pp. 37–57.

Bobrova, I. B., comp., *Bibliotek Petra I. Ukazatel'—spravochnik*, L. 1978.

Bobynin, V. V., *Ocherki istorii razvitiia fiziko-matematicheskikh znanii v Rossii XVII stoletie*, 2 vv. M. 1886, 1893. Continued as "Ocherki razvitiia fiziko-matematicheskikh znanii v Rossii. Epokha gosudarstvennago sodeistviia razvitiiu nauchnykh znanii," *Fiziko-matematicheskiia nauki v ikh nastoiashchem i proshedshem*, Vol. VII (1888), No. 1, 27–55, No. 2, 113–131, No. 3, 192–210, No. 4, 267–308.

Bochkaraev, V. A., *U istokov russkoi istoricheskoi dramaturgii (Posledniaia tret'ia XVII—pervaia polovina XVIII veka)*, Kiubyshev, 1981.

Bogdanov, A. P., "Pamiatnik russkoi pedagogiki XVII veka. (Poeticheskii triptikh Kariona Istomina dlia nachal'noi shkoly)," *Issledovaniia po istochnikovedeniiu istorii SSSR dooktiabr'skogo perioda*, M. 1989, pp. 96–144.

Bolgar, R. R., ed., *Classical Influences on European Culture, A.D. 500–1500*, Cambridge, 1971.

——, ed., *Classical Influences on European Culture, A.D. 1500–1700*, Cambridge, 1976.

——, ed., *Classical Influences on Western Thought, A.D. 1650–1870*, Cambridge, 1979.

Bonar, James, *A Catalogue of the Library of Adam Smith*, 2nd ed., London, 1932.

Boorstin, Daniel J., *The Discoverers*, New York, 1983.

Boss, Valentin, *Newton and Russia. The Early Influence, 1698–1796*, Cambridge, Mass., 1972.

Botvinnik, M. V., "Istoriografiia izucheniia 'Azbuki' Ivan Fedorova v SSSSR," *Kniga, bibliotechnoe delo i bibliografiia v Belorussii*, Minsk, 1974, pp. 93–114.

——, *Otkuda est' poshel bukvar'*, Minsk, 1983.

Braudel, Fernand, *Civilization and Capitalism 15th–18th Century. Vol. I, The Structures of Every-day Life*, New York, 1982.

Bräuning-Oktavio, Hermann, "Die Bibliothek der großen Landgräfin Caroline von Hessen-Darmstadt," *AGB*, VI (1966), 681–876.

——, "Zwei Privatbibliotheken des 18. Jahrhunderts. 1. Die Bibliothek der Herzogin Caroline von Pfalz-Zweibrücken-Birkenfeld, Mutter der "Großen Landgräfin, (gestorben 1774). 2. Die Bibliothek des Freiherrn Louis von Schrautenbach (gestorben 1783)," *AGB*, X (1970), 686–835.

Brink, Charles O., "Horatian Poetry. Thoughts on the Development of Textual Criticism and Interpretation," *Geschichte des Textverständnisses am Beispiel von Pindar & Horaz*, München, 1981, pp. 7–18.

Brown, John H., "The Printed Word in Provincial Russia: The Reading Habits of A. T. Bolotov (1738–1833)," Unpublished paper, AAASS Convention, St. Louis, October 8, 1976.

Brown, William Edward, *A History of 18th Century Russian Literature*, Ann Arbor, 1980.

——, *A History of Seventeenth-Century Russian Literature*, Ann Arbor, 1980.

Brückner, Alexander, *Culturhistorische Studien. Die Russen im Ausland, die Ausländer im Russland*, 2 vv. Riga, 1878.

——, *Die Europäisierung Rußlands. Land und Volk*, Gotha, 1888.

Brunner, Otto, *Adeliges Landleben und europäischer Geist. Leben und Werk Wolf Helmhards von Hohberg 1612–1688*, Salzburg, 1949.

——, "Das 'Ganze Haus' und die alteuropäische 'Ökonomik'," in his *Neue Wege der Sozialgeschichte. Vorträge und Aufsätze*, Göttingen, 1956, pp. 33–61 (Orig. 1950).

——, "Österreichische Adelsbibliotheken des 15. bis 18. Jahrhunderts," in his *Neue Wege der Sozialgeschichte. Vorträge und Aufsaätze*, Göttingen, 1956, pp. 155–167 (Orig. 1949).

Bryner, Erich, *Der geistliche Stand in Rußland. Sozialgeschichtliche Untersuchen zu Episkopat und Gemeindegeistlichkeit der russischen orthodoxen Kirche im 18 Jahrhundert*, Göttingen, 1982. =Kirche im Osten Monographienreihe Band 16.

Bubnov, N. Iu., "Knigotvorchestvo moskovskikh staroobriadtsev XVII veka," *Russkie knigi i biblioteki v XVI—pervoi polovine XIX veka*, L. 1983, pp. 23–37.

——, "Rukopisi iz sobraniia rizhskoi grebenshchikovskoi obshchiny v Biblioteke AN SSSR," *Knizhnoe delo v Rossii v XVI–XIX vekakh*, L. 1980, pp. 97–104.

——, "Rukopisnoe nasledie pustozerskikh uznikov (1667–1682 gg.)," *Knigotorgovoe i bibliotechnoe delo v Rossii v XVII—pervoi polovine XIX v.*, L. 1981, pp. 69–84.

Bucholtz, Arnold, *Die Göttinger Rußlandsammlung Georgs von Asch. Ein Museum des russischen Wissenschaftsgeschichte des 18. Jahrhundert*, Giessen, 1961.

Bucsela, J., "The Problems of Baroque in Russian Literature," *RR*, Vol. 31, No. 3 (1972), 260–272.

Burke, Peter, *Popular Culture in Early Modern Europe*, New York, 1978.

Busch, Wolfgang, *Horaz in Russland*, München, 1964.

——, "Berichte russischer Reisender," in Dagmar Herrmann, ed., *Deutsche und Deutschland aus russischer Sicht. 18. Jahrhundert: Aufklärung*, München, 1992, pp. 341–377.

Bushkovitch, Paul, *Religion and Society in Russia. The Sixteenth and Seventeenth Centuries*, Oxford/New York, 1992.

——, "The Epiphany Ceremony of the Russian Court in the Sixteenth and Seventeenth Centuries," *RR*, Vol. 49, No. 1 (Jan., 1990), 1–17.

——, "The Ukraine in Russian Culture 1790–1860: The Evidence of the Journals," *JfGO*, Vol. 39, No. 3 (1991), 339–363.

Butler, E. M., *The Tyranny of Greece over Germany*, Boston, 1958 (Orig. 1935).

Bykova, T. A., "Über in Halle gedruckte Slawische Bücher," in W. Steinitz, et al. eds., *Ost und West in der Geschichte des Denkens und der kulturellen Beziehungen*, Berlin, 1966, pp. 262–267.

"Catalogus librorum pro stipendiariis studiosis et discipulis universitatis et gymnasii moscuensis," *Dokumenty i materialy po istorii moskovskogo universiteta vtoroi poloviny XVIII veka. II. 1765–1766*, M. 1962, pp. 25–35.

Cellarius, Christoph, *Kratkoi latinskoi leksikon s Rossiiskim i Nemetskim perevodnom dlia upotrebleniia Sanktpeterburgskoi gimnazii*, St. Petersburg, 1746.

Chalotais, Louis-René de Caradeuc de la, *Essay on National Education*, H. R. Clark, trans., London, 1934. Lui Rene La Shalote, *Opyt narodnago vospitaniia ili chertezh nauk*, St. Petersburg, 1770.

Chaussinand-Nogaret, Guy, *The French Nobility in the Eighteenth Century. From Feudalism to Enlightenment*, William Doyle, trans., Cambridge, 1985.

Cenekal, V. L., "Die wissenschaftlichen Verbindungen Lomonosovs mit deutschen Gelehrten," in E. Winter et al., eds., *Lomonosov Schlözer Pallas: Deutsch-russische Wissenschaftsbeziehungen im 18. Jahrhundert*, Berlin, 1962, pp. 3–12.

Chistovich, I. A., *Feofan Prokopovich i ego vremia*, St. Petersburg, 1868.

Chitatel' i kniga. Sbornik nauchnykh trudov, M. 1978. =Fedorovskie chteniia 1976.

Cizevskij, Dmitrij, *History of Russian Literature From the Eleventh Century to the End of the Baroque*, 'S-Gravenhage, 1960. =Slavic Printings and Reprintings XII. [see also Tschizewskij].

Clarke, M. L., *Classical Education in Britain 1500–1900*, Cambridge, 1959.

Clay, Eugene, "The Theological Origins of the Christ-Faith [Khristovshchina]," *RH*, Vol. 15, No. 1 (1988), 21–41.

[Collins, Dr. Samuel], *The Present State of Russia*, London, 1671.

Confino, Michael, "Historie et Psychologie," *Annales: Économies, Sociétés, Civilisations*, November–December, 1967, 1163–1205.

Consett, Tho., *The Present State and Regulations of the Church of Russia*, London, 1729. Note also the facsimile edition, James Cracraft, ed., *For God and Peter the Great. The Works of Thomas Consett 1723–29*, Boulder/New York, 1982.

Cracraft, James, "Feofan Prokopovich," in J. G. Garrard, ed., *The Eighteenth Century in Russia*, Oxford, 1973, pp. 75–105.

——, "Feofan Prokopovich and the Kiev Academy," in R. L. Nichols & T. G. Shaw, eds., *Russian Orthodoxy under the Old Regime*, Minneapolis, 1978, pp. 44–66.

——, *The Church Reform of Peter the Great*, Stanford, 1971.

——, "Theology at the Kiev Academy during its Golden Age," *HUS*, Vol. VIII, No. 1/2 (1984), 71–80.

Cross, A. G., *"By the Banks of the Thames": Russians in Eighteenth Century Britain*, Newtonville, Mass., 1980.

——, "'S angliiskago': Books of English Origin in Russian Translation in Late Eighteenth-Century Russia," *OSP*, N.S. Vol. XIX (1986), pp. 62–87.

Cross, Samuel Hazzard & Olgerd P. Sherbowitz-Wetzor, trans., *The Russian Primary Chronicle. Laurentian Text*, Cambridge, Mass., 1953. =Medieval Academy of American Publication #60.

Crummey, Robert O., *Aristocrats and Servitors. The Boyar Elite in Russia 1613–1689*, Princeton, NJ, 1983.

Curtius, Ernst Robert, *Europäische Literaturgeschichte und lateinisches Mittelalter*, 3rd ed., Bern/München, 1961.

Custine, Marquis de, *Empire of the Czar, A Journey Through Eternal Russia*, New York, 1989.

D'Alembert, Jean Le Rond, *Preliminary Discourse to the Encyclopedia of Diderot*, Indianapolis, 1963.

Daniels, Rudolf, *V. N. Tatishchev. Guardian of the Petrine Revolution*, Philadelphia, 1973.

Danilevskii, V., *Nartov*, M. 1960.

Dann, Otto, ed., *Lesegesellschaften und bürgerliche Emanzipation, Ein europäischer Vergleich*, München, 1981.

Dashkova, Princess, *The Memoirs of Princess Dashkov*, K. Fitzlyon, ed., London, 1958; Dashkova, Ekaterina, *Zapiski 1743–1810*, G. I. Moiseeva, ed., L. 1985.

[Defoe, Daniel], *An Impartial History of the Life and Actions of Peter Alexowitz, The Present Czar of Muscovy*, London, 1723.

[Demidoff, Paul de], *Catalogue systématique des livres de la bibliothèque de Paul de Demidoff*, M. 1806.

Demidova, N. F., "Instruktsiia V. N. Tatishchev o poriadke prepodavaniia v shkolakh pri uralskikh kazennykh zavodakh," *Ia*, Vol. V (1950), 166–178.

Demin, A. S., *Pisatel' i obshchestvo v Rossii XVI–XVIII vekov*, M. 1985.

——, *Russkaia literatura vtoroi poloviny XVII—nachala XVIII veka. Novye khudozhestvennye predstavleniia o mire, prirode, cheloveke*, M. 1977.

——, ed., *Russkaia staropechatnaia literatura (XVI—pervaia chetvert' XVIII v). Literaturnyi sbornik XVII veka. Prolog*, M. 1978.

Demkov, M. I., *Istoriia russkoi pedagogii. Chast' I. Drevne-Russkaia pedagogiia (X–XVII vv.). Chast' II. Novaia russkaia pedagogiia (XVIII–i vek.)*, 2nd ed., M./St. Petersburg, 1899, 1910.

——, "Vliianie zapadno-evropeiskoi pedagogiiki na russkuiu pedagogiku," *ZMnp*, Vol. XXVII N. S. (May, 1910), Otd. IV, 28–60.

Denisov, A. P., *Leontii Filippovich Magnitskii, 1669–1739*, M. 1967.

Deppermann, Klaus, *Der hallische Pietismus und der preußische Staat unter Friedrich III*, Göttingen, 1961.

Derzhavina, O. A., *Fatsetsii. Perevodnaia novella v russkoi literature XVII veka*, M. 1962.

——, "Simeon Polotskii v rabote nad 'Psaltyr'iu rifmotvornoi,'" in A. N. Robinson,

ed., *Simeon Polotskii i ego knigoizdatel'skaia deiatel'nost'*, M. 1982, pp. 116–133.
——, *'Velikoe Zertsalo' i ego sud'ba na russkoi pochve*, M. 1965.
Dmitriev, Al., "Predsmertnoe uveshchanie V. N. Tatishcheva synu," *ZMnp*, Vol. CCXLIV (Apr. 1886), Otd. 2, 227–237.
Dmitrieva, E. E., "Russkie pis'movniki serediny XVII—pervoi treti XIX v. i evoliutsiia russkogo epistoliarnogo etiketa," *Izvestiia Akademii nauk SSSR. Seriia literatury i iazyka*, Vol. 45, No. 6 (1986), 543–552.
Dmitrieva, R. P., "Svetskaia literatura v sostave monastyrskikh bibliotek XV i XVI vv. (Kirillo-Belozerskogo, Volokolamskogo monastyrei i Troitse-Sergievoi lavry)," *TOdl*, Vol. 23 (1968), 143–170.
Dmytryshyn, Basil, *Imperial Russia. A Source Book, 1700–1917*, 3rd ed., Fort Worth, 1990.
Dneprov, E. D., "'Relentlessly Running in Place': The Historiography of Schools and Pedagogical Thought in Medieval Russia (Some Conclusions, Problems, and Perspectives)," *HEQ*, Vol. 26, No. 4 (Winter, 1986), 537–551.
Dokumenty i materialy po istorii Moskovskogo universiteta vtoroi poloviny XVIII veka, 3 vv. M. 1960–62.
Dolgova, S. R., "O biblioteke A. D. Menshikova," *Russkie biblioteki i ikh chitatel'*, L. 1983, pp. 87–98.
Domostroi, V. V. Kolesova, ed., M. 1991; *Domostroi*, Ryan, W. F., ed., Letchworth, 1971 (Reprint of ed. of Moscow, 1882. =Rarity Reprints, No. 18; "Domostroi," *Pamiatniki literatury drevnei Rusi. Seredina XVI veka*, D. S. Likhachev, ed., M. 1985, pp. 70–173, 580–86; [Müller, Klaus, ed.,], *Altrussisches Hausbuch "Domostroi"*, Leipzig & Weimar, 1987. (reprint, Darmstadt, 1989); Orlov, A., ed., *Domostroi po konshinskomu spiska i podobnym*, 2 vv. M. 1908/1910. (reprint, The Hague, 1967). Carolyn Johnston Pouncy, trans., *The Domostroi. Rules for Russian Households in the Time of Ivan the Terrible*, Ithaca, 1994.
Donnert, Erich, *Peter der Grosse*, Göttingen/Zürich, 1987.
——, *Politische Ideologie der russischen Gesellschaft zu Beginn der Regierungszeit Katharinas II*, Berlin, 1976.
——, *Russland im Zeitalter der Aufklärung*, Wien/Köln, 1985.
Doroshevich, E. K., "Prosveshchenie v Belorussii (Otrozhdenie obshchestvennogo soznaniia v literaturnykh istochnikakh)," *Knigovedenie v Belorussii (sbornik statei)*, Minsk, 1977, pp. 54–64.
Dorovatovskaia, Vera, "O zaimstvovaniiakh Lomonosova iz Biblii," in V. V. Sipovskii, ed., *1711–1911. M. V. Lomonosov. Sbornik statei*, St. Petersburg, 1911, pp. 33–65.
Drage, C. L., *Russian Literature in the Eighteenth Century*, London, 1978.
Dülmen, Richard van, "Die Aufklärungsgesellschaften in Deutschland als Forschungsprobleme," in Ulrich Herrmann, ed., *"Die Bildung des Bürgers." Die Formierung der bürgerlichen Gesellschaft und die Gebildeten im 18. Jahrhundert*, Weinheim/Basel, 1982, pp. 81–99.
Dukes, Paul, *Catherine the Great and the Russian Nobility. A Study based on the materials of the Legislative Commission of 1767*, Cambridge, 1967.
——, trans., *Catherine the Great's Instruction (NAKAZ) to the Legislative Commission, 1767*, Vol. II, *Russia under Catherine the Great*, Newtonville, Mass., 1977.
——, "Russia and the 'General Crisis' of the Seventeenth Century," *NZSJ*, 1974, No. 2, 1–17.
——, "The Russian Enlightenment," in Roy Porter & Mikulas Teich, eds., *The Enlightenment in National Context*, Cambridge, 1981, pp. 176–191.
Dvoichenko-Markova, I. A., "Iz istorii russko-rumynskikh kul'turnykh vziamosviazei XVII veka," *Russkaia literatura na rubezhe dvukh epokh (XVII—nachalo XVIII v.)*, M. 1971, pp. 264–276.
Egunov, A. N., *Gomer v russkikh perevodakh XVII–XIX vekov*, M-L. 1964.
Eichberg, Henning, "Geometrie als barocke Verhaltensnorm. Fortifikation und Exerzitien," *ZfHF*, Vol. 4 (1977), 17–50.

Eisenstein, Elizabeth L., *The Printing Press as an Agent of Change. Communications and Cultural Transformations in early-modern Europe*, 2 vv. in 1, Cambridge, 1980.
Eleonskaia A. S., *Russkaia oratorskaia prosa v literaturnom protsesse XVII veka*, M. 1990.
——, *Russkaia publitsistika vtoroi poloviny XVII veka*, M. 1978.
Elizavetina, G. G., "Stanovlenie zhanrov avtobiografii i memuarov," *Russkii i zapadno-evropeiskii klassitsizm. Proza*, M. 1982, pp. 235–263.
Ellis, Harold A., *Boulainvilliers and the French Monarchy: Aristocratic Politics in Early-Modern France*, Ithaca, 1988.
Engel, Barbara Alpern, *Mothers and Daughters. Women of the Intelligentsia in Nineteenth-Century Russia*, Cambridge, 1983.
Engel-Janosi, Friedrich, Grete Klingenstein & Heinrich Lutz, eds., *Formen der europäischen Aufklärung. Untersuchungen zur Situation von Christentum, Bildung und Wissenschaft im 18. Jahrhundert*, München, 1976. =Wiener Beiträge zur Geschichte der Neuzeit, Band 3.
Engelsing, Rolf, *Analphabetentum und Lektüre. Zur Sozialgeschichte des Lesens in Deutschland zwischen feudaler und industrieller Gesellschaft*, Stuttgart, 1973.
——, *Der Bürger als Leser. Lesergeschichte in Deutschland 1500–1800*, Stuttgart, 1974.
——, "Die Perioden der Lesergeschichte in der Neuzeit. Das statistische Ausmaß und die soziokulturelle Bedeutung der Lektüre," *AGB*, X (1970), 945–1002.
Epstein, Klaus, *The Genesis of German Conservatism*, Princeton, 1966.
Erb, Peter C., ed., *Pietists, Selected Writings*, New York, 1983.
Fedosov, I. A., *Iz istorii russkoi obshchestvennoi mysli XVIII stoletiia*. M. M. Shcherbatov, M. 1967.
Felbiger, Johann Ignaz von, *Anleitung Schulgebäude auf dem Lande wohl abzutheilen, wohlfeil, dauerhaft und Feuersicher aufzuführen*, Leipzig, 1783.
——, *Anleitung zur Rechenkunst. Zum Gebrauche der in den Trivialschulen lernenden nicht unirten Illyrischen Jugend./Rukovodstvie ko Arithmetiki. Za oupotreblenie Illyricheskiia neunitskiia v malykh ouchilishchakh ouchashchiiasia iunosti*, Wien/Vienne, 1777.
——, *Christliche Grundsätze und Lebensregeln zum Unterrichte den Jugend*, Frankenthal, 1773.
——, *Eigenschaften, Wissenschaften und Beziegen rechtschaffener Schulleute, um nach dem in Schlesien für die Römischkatholischen bekannt gemachtem Königl. General-Landschul-reglement in den trivialschulen der Städte, und auf dem Lande der Jugend nützlichen Unterrich zu geben*, Bamberg/Wirzburg, 1772.
——, *O dolzhnostiakh cheloveka i grazhdanina, kniga, k chteniiu opredelennaia v narodnykh gorodskikh uchilishchakh Rossiiskoi imperii*, St. Petersburg, 1783.
——, *Rukovodstvo k arifmetike dlia upotrebleniia v narodnykh uchilishchakh Rossiiskoi imperii*, St. Petersburg, 1783.
——, *Rukovodstvo k chestnosti i pravosti, to est': v malykh ouchilishchakh ouchashchei sia Slavennoserbskoi Neunitskoi iunosti na chtenie opredelennaia Kniga./Anleitung zur Rechtschaffenheit oder das für die in den Trivialschulen lernende slavonisch-servische nicht unirte Jugend bestimmte Lesebuch*, Wien, 1777.
——, *Rukovodstvo uchiteliam pervago i vtorago klassa narodnykh uchilishch Rossiiskoi imperii*, St. Petersburg, 1783.
Fénelon, François de Salignac de la Motte, *Les Aventures de Télémaque, fils d' Ulysse*, 2vv. Paris, An IX (1801), French-English ed. by Mr. des Maiseaux.
Fennell, John & Antony Stokes, *Early Russian Literature*, London, 1974.
Fielding, Henry, *Tom Jones*, New York, 1950 (orig. 1749).
Flickinger, Roy C., "The Classics in Russia, Germany, Turkey and America," (continuation of his) "Horace's First Bimillennium," *CJ*, Vol. XXXII, No. 2 (Nov, 1936), 65–91, and No. 7 (Apr, 1937), 424–427.
Florinsky, Michael T., *Russia. A History and an Interpretation*, 2vv., New York, 1957.
Florovskii, A. V., "Latinskie shkoly v Rossii v epokhu Petra I," *XVIII vek, Sbornik 5*, M-L. 1962, 316–335.
——, *Le conflict de deux traditions—la latine et la byzantine—dans la vie intellectuelle de l'Europe Orientale aux XVI–XVII siècles*, Prague, 1937. =Bulletin de l'Association Russe pour les Recherches scientifiques, Vol. V, No. 31 (1937), 171–192.

Florovsky, Georges, *Ways of Russian Theology*, Part One, Robert L. Nichols, trans., Belmont, Mass., 1979.

Flynn, James T., *The University Reform of Tsar Alexander I*, Washington, 1988.

Fonkich, B. L., *Grechesko-russkie kul'turnye sviazi v XV–XVII vv. (Grecheskie rukopisi v Rossii)*, M. 1977.

Franklin, Simon, "Booklearning and Bookmen in Kievan Rus': A Survey of an Idea," *HUS*, Vol. XII–XIII (1988–89), 830–848. =Proceedings of the International Congress Commemorating the Millennium of Christianity in Rus'-Ukraine.

Frantsisk Skorina—Belorusskii gumanist, prosvetitel', pervopechatnik, Minsk, 1989.

Freeze, Gregory L., *The Russian Levites. Parish Clergy in the Eighteenth Century*, Cambridge, Mass., 1977.

Freis, Richard, "The Classics and a Contemporary Liberal Education," *CJ*, Vol. 77, No. 4 (Apr–May, 1982), 349–358.

Freydank, D., "A. M. Kurbskijs Rezeption der humanistischen Bildung," *ZS*, Vol. 33, No. 6 (1988), 806–815.

From Kievan Rus' to Modern Ukraine: Formation of the Ukrainian Nation, Cambridge, Mass., 1984.

Fuhrmann, Joseph T., *Tsar Alexis. His Reign and His Russia*, Gulf Breeze, Fl., 1981.

Fuhrmann, Manfred, "Die 'Querelle des Anciens et des Modernes', der Nationalismus und die deutsche Klassik," in R. R. Bolgar, ed., *Classical Influences on Western Thought A.D. 1650–1870*, Cambridge, 1979, pp. 107–129.

Fundaminskii, M. I., "Biblioteka akademika S. P. Krasheninnikova," *Russkie biblioteki i ikh chitatel'*, L. 1983, pp. 142–149.

———, "Biblioteka kabinet-sekretaria I. Eikhlera," *Knizhnoe delo v Rossii v XVI–XIX vekakh*, L. 1980, pp. 43–65.

———, "Biblioteka russkogo uchenogo XVIII veka A. P. Protasova," *Kniga i biblioteki v Rossii v XIV—pervoi polovine XIX v.*, L. 1982, pp. 56–67.

Garden, Maurice, "Une grande collection de livres de voyage au XVIIIème siècle: La bibliothèque de marquis de Courtanvaux," *Buch und Sammler. Private und öffentliche Bibliotheken im 18. Jahrhundert*, Heidelberg, 1979, pp. 29–42.

Gay, Peter, *The Enlightenment: An Interpretation. [I] The Rise of Modern Paganism. II. The Science of Freedom*, New York, 1967, 1969.

Gennadi, G. [N.], "Russkie bibliofily. (Biblioteki grafa D. P. Buturlina i ikh katalogi)," *ZMnp*, Vol. XC, No. 4 (Apr, 1856), Otd. III, 1–10.

Ger'e, V. [Guerrier], *Sbornik pisem i memorialov Leibnitsa otnosiashchikhsia k Rossii i Petru Velikomu*, Spb. 1873.

Gerlach, Hans-Martin, et al., eds., *Christian Wolff als Philosoph der Aufklärung in Deutschland*, Halle, 1980.

Gesemann, Wolfgang, *Die Entdeckung der unteren Volksschichten durch die russische Literatur. Zur Dialektik eines literarischen Motivs von Kantemir bis Belinskij*, Wiesbaden, 1972. =Veröffentlichungen des Osteuropa-Instituts München, Nr. 39.

Gessinger, Joachim, *Sprache und Bürgertum. Zur Sozialgeschichte sprachlicher Verkehrsformen im Deutschland des 18. Jahrhunderts*, Stuttgart, 1980.

Geyer, Dietrich, "Der Aufgeklärte Absolutismus in Rußland. Bemerkungen zur Forschungslage," *JfGO*, Vol. 30, No. 2 (1982), 176–189.

Gilorovskii, Petr, *Rukovodstvo k fizike . . .*, St. Petersburg, 1793.

Gizel', Innokentii, *Synopsis*, Kiev, 1681, Hans Rothe, ed., Köln/Böhlau, 1983, =Bausteine zur Geschichte der Literatur bei den Slaven. 17. Also, *Sinopsis' ili kratkoe opisanie otrazlichnykh letopistsev o nachale slavenskago naroda . . .*, 5th ed., St. Petersburg, 1762.

Glagoleva, O. E., "A. T. Bolotov kak chitatel'," *Rukopisnaia i pechatnaia kniga v Rossii. Problemy sozdaniia i rasprostraneniia*, L. 1988, pp. 140–158.

———, "Biblioteka A. T. Bolotova," *Kniga v Rossii XVI—seredina XIX v. Knigorasprostranenie, biblioteki, chitatel'*, L. 1987, pp. 79–95.

Gleason, Walter J., *Moral Idealists, Bureaucracy, and Catherine the Great*, New Brunswick, 1981.

——, "The Two Faces of the Monarch: Legal and Mythical Fictions in Lomonosov's Ruler Imagery," *CASS*, Vol. 16, Nos. 3–4 (Fall-Winter, 1982), 388–409.

Glinka, M. E., *M. V. Lomonosov (Opyt ikonografii)*, M-L. 1961.

Glukhov, Aleksei, *Rus' knizhnaia*, M. 1979.

Göpfert, Herbert G., "Bemerkungen über Buchhändler und Buchhandel zur Zeit der Aufklärung in Deutschland," *WSA*, Vol. I (1974), 69–83.

——, *Vom autor zum Leser. Beiträge zur Geschichte des Buchwesens*, München/Wien, 1977.

Goldstein, Thomas, *Dawn of Modern Science*, Boston, 1980.

Golenishchev-Kutuzov, I. N., *Gumanizm u vostochnykh Slavian (Ukraina i Belorussiia)*, M. 1963.

Golitsyn, N. V., "Novye dannye o biblioteke kn. D. M. Golitsyna (verkhovnika)," *COidr*, 1900, Kn. 4, Otd. 4, Smes' 1–16.

Goodman, Anthony and Angus Mackay, eds., *The Impact of Humanism on Western Europe*, London & New York, 1990.

Gorfunkel', A. Kh. & N. I. Nikolaev, *Nachalo universitetskoi biblioteki (1783 g.). Sobranie P. F. Zhukova—pamiatnik russkoi kul'tury XVIII veka*, L. 1980.

Grabosch, Ulrich, *Studien zur deutschen Russlandkunde im 18. Jahrhundert*, Halle/Wittenberg, 1985.

Gracian, Baltasar, *Oráculo Manual Y Arte de Prudencia*, Madrid, 1954. =Revista de filologia espanola, Anejo LXII. Also, Gracian, *Handorakel und Kunst der Welt klugheit*, Arthur Schopenhauer, trans., Stuttgart, 1948 (orig. Oráculo manual, 1647).

Graßhoff, H., "Der Fortschrittsgedanke in der russischen Literatur der Aufklärung," *ZS*, Vol. 14 (1969), 444–452.

——, "Die Humanitätsideale der russischen Frühaufklärung. Das humanistische Weltbild des Aufklärer und Satirikers A. D. Kantemir," in Helmut Grasshoff & Ulf Lehmann, eds., *Studien zur Geschichte der russischen Literatur des 18. Jahrhunderts*, Vol. III, Berlin, 1968, pp. 206–230.

——, Annelies Lauch, & Ulf Lehman, eds., *Humanistische Traditionen der russischen Aufklärung*, Berlin, 1974.

Grau, Conrad, *Der Wirtschaftsorganisator, Staatsmann und Wissenschaftler Vasilij N. Tatiscev (1686–1750)*, Berlin, 1963. =Quellen und Studien zur Geschichte Osteuropas. XIII.

——, "Russisch-sächsische Beziehungen auf dem Gebiet des Berg- und Hüttenwesens in der ersten Häfte des 18. Jh.," *JfGU*, Vol. 4 (1960), 302–330.

——, "Tatiscev und Deutschland," in E. Winter, ed., *Die deutsche-russische Begegnung und Leonhard Euler*, Berlin, 1958, pp. 143–149.

——, "Tatiscev und die Aufklärung in Rußland, in Helmut Grasshoff & Ulf Lehmann, eds., *Studien zur Geschichte der russischen Literatur des 18. Jahrhunderts*, [I], Berlin, 1963, pp. 78–85. =Veröffentlichungen des Instituts für Slawistik, No. 28.

Grebeniuk, V. P., "Evoliutsiia poeticheskikh simvolov rossiiskogo absoliutizma (ot Simeon Polotskogo do M. V. Lomonosova)," *Razvitie Barokko i zarozhdenie Klassitsizma v Rossii XVII—nachala XVIII v.*, M. 1989, pp. 188–200.

Gregor, Rudolf, "Aufklärerische Tendenzen in russischen Schriften und internationaler Lektüre für junge Leute," in Horst Schmidt, ed., *Die Literatur der Aufklärung (1650–1825)*, Halle, 1985, pp. 64–71.

Grendler, Paul F., *Schooling in Renaissance Italy: Literacy and Learning 1300–1600*, Baltimore, 1989.

Griffiths, David M., "In Search of Enlightenment: Recent Soviet Interpretations of Eighteenth-Century Russian Intellectual History," *CASS*, Vol. 16, No. 3–4 (Fall-Winter, 1982), 317–356.

Grot, Ia. K., "Pis'ma Lomonosova i Sumarokova k I. I. Shuvalov. Materialy dlia istorii russkago obrazovaniia," *ZIAn*, Vol. I (1861), Prilozhenie I, 1–47.

Grunebaum, G. E. von, "The Concept of Cultural Classicism," in his *Modern Islam. The Search for Cultural Identity*, New York, 1964, pp. 98–128.

Gudzii, N. K., *Istoriia drevnei russkoi literatury*, 5th ed., M. 1953. Gudzy, *History of Early Russian Literature*, Susan Wilbur Jones, trans., New York, 1970.

——, *Literatura Kievskoi Rusi i ukrainsko-russkoe literaturnoe edinenie XVII–XVIII vekov*, Kiev, 1989.

Günther, K., "Zur Epochbeziechnung 'Aufklärung,' speziell im Deutschen und Russischen: Eine wortgeschichtliche Studie," in Helmut Grasshoff & Ulf Lehmann, eds., *Studien zur Geschichte der russischen Literatur des 18. Jahrhunderts*, Vol. III, Berlin, 1968, pp. 56–92.

Gukovskii, G., "Za izuchenie vosemnadtsatogo veka," *Ln*, Vol. 9–10 (1933), 295–326.

Gummere, Richard M., *The American Colonial Mind and the Classical Tradition*, Cambridge, Mass., 1963.

Guseva, A. A., "Vzaimosviazi ukrainskikh tipografii kontsa XVI—pervoi poloviny XVII vv. (Problema migratsii tipografskikh materialov)," *400 letie knigopechataniia na Ukraine*, M. 1976, pp. 78–100. =Fedorovskie chteniia. 1973.

Guzner, I. A., "Biblioteki uchebnykh zavedenii Sibirii v pervoi polovine XVIII veka," *Kniga v Sibirii XVII—nachala XX vv.*, Novosibirsk, 1980, pp. 64–77.

Hadas, Moses, *A History of Greek Literature*, New York, 1950.

——, *A History of Roman Literature*, New York, 1952.

Hans, Nicholas, "Dumaresq, Brown, and some early educational projects of Catherine II," *SEER*, Vol. 40, No. 94 (1961), 229–235.

——, "Educational Reform in Poland in the Eighteenth Century," *Journal of Central European Affairs*, Vol. XIII, No. 4 (Jan., 1954), 301–310.

——, *History of Russian Educational Policy*, London, 1931.

——, "Polish Schools in Russia," *SEER*, XXXVIII, No. 91 (June, 1960), 394–414.

Harrison, John & Peter Laslett, *The Library of John Locke*, Oxford, 1965.

Hart, Pierre R., "Continuity and Change in the Russian Ode," in A. G. Cross, ed., *Russian Literature in the Age of Catherine the Great*, Oxford, 1976, pp. 45–65.

Hartley, Janet, "The Boards of Social Welfare and the Financing of Catherine II's State Schools," *SEER*, Vol. 67, No. 2 (Apr, 1989), 211–227.

Harwood, Natalie, "Latin for All Americans," *CJ*, Vol. 84, No. 4 (Apr–May, 1988), 358–362.

Hauptmann, Peter, *Altrussischen Glaube. Der Kampf des Protopopen Avvakum gegen die Kirchenreformen des 17. Jahrhunderts*, Göttingen, 1963. =Kirche im Osten. Monographienreihe Band 4.

——, *Die Katechismen der russische-orthodoxen Kirche. Entstehungsgeschichte und Lehrgehalt*, Göttingen, 1971. =Kirche im Osten. Monographienreihe Band 9.

Hazard, Paul, *The European Mind, 1680–1715*, Cleveland, 1963.

Hecker, Hans, "Aus welchem Grunde sie evangelisch genant werden, weiß ich nicht." Symon Todorskyj und Ivan Pososkov über die deutschen," in Dagmar Herrmann, ed., *Deutsche und Deurschland aus russischer Sicht. 18. Jahrhundert: Aufklärung*, München, 1992, pp. 114–138.

Heilingsetzer, Georg, "Wissenschaftspflege und Aufklärung in Klöstern der Augustiner Chorherren und Benediktiner im bayerisch-österreichischen Raum," in Werner Arnold & Peter Vodosek, eds., *Bibliotheken und Aufklärung*, Wiesbaden, 1988, pp. 83–101. =Wolfenbütteler Schriften zur Geschichte des Buchwesens. 14.

Heller, Wolfgang, "Kooperation und Konfrontation. M. V. Lomonosov und die russische Wissenschaft im 18. Jahrhundert," *JfGO*, Vol. 38, No. 1 (1990), 1–24.

Hellie, Richard, *Enserfment and Military Change in Muscovy*, Chicago, 1971.

Hermann, Ulrich, "Die kodifizierung bürgerlichen Bewußtseins in der deutschen Spätaufklärung—Carl Friedrich Bahrdts "Handbuch der Moral für den Bürgerstand" aus dem Jahre 1789," in Rudolf Vierhaus, ed., *Bürger und Bürgerlichkeit im Zeitalter der Aufklärung*, Heidelberg, 1981, pp. 321–333.

Hexter, J. H., "The Education of the Aristocracy in the Renaissance," in his *Reappraisals in History*, New York, 1961 (orig. 1950).

Highet, Gilbert, *The Classical Tradition: Greek and Roman Influences on Western Literature*, New York, 1957.

Hippisley, Anthony R., "Simeon Polotsky's Library," *OSP*, NS Vol. XXI (1983), 52–61.

——, "The Emblem in the Writings of Simeon Polockij," *SEEJ*, Vol. XV, No. 2 (1971), 167–183.

——, *The Poetic Style of Simeon Polotsky*, Birmingham, [1985]. =Birmingham Slavonic Monographs No. 16.

Hoffmann, Peter, "Aufklärung, Absolutismus, aufgeklärter Absolutismus in Rußland," in Helmut Grasshoff & Ulf Lehmann, eds., *Studien zur Geschichte der russischen Literatur des 18. Jahrhunderts*, Band IV, Berlin, 1970, pp. 9–40.

——, "Lomonosov und Voltaire," in Helmut Grasshoff & Ulf Lehmann, eds., *Studien zur Geschichte der russischen Literatur des 18. Jahrhunderts*, Band III, Berlin, 1968, pp. 417–425, 600–603.

——, "Zur Differenzierung der russischen Aufklärung in der zweiten Hälfte des 18. Jahrhunderts," *Die russische Literatur der Aufklärung (1650–1825)*, Halle, 1985.

Honorata, Schw., "Die antike Philosophie als Grundlage abendländischen Denkens," in Joseph Schnippenkotter, ed., *Bildungsfragen der Gegenwart*, Heft 13, Bonn, 1947.

Houston, R. A., *Literacy in Early Modern Europe: Culture and Education 1500–1800*, New York, 1988.

Howatson, M. C., ed., *The Oxford Companion to Classical Literature*, 2nd. ed., Oxford, 1989.

Hudson, Hugh D. Jr., *The Rise of the Demidov Family and the Russian Iron Industry in the Eighteenth Century*, Newtonville, Mass., 1986.

Hughes, Lindsey A. J., *Russia and the West, the Life of a Seventeenth-Century Westernizer, Prince Vasily Vasil'evich Golitsyn (1643–1714)*, Newtonville, Mass., 1984.

——, *Sophia. Regent of Russia 1657–1704*, New Haven, 1990.

——, "The West Comes to Russian Architecture," *History Today*, Vol. 36 (Sept, 1986), 27–34.

Humphrey, David C., *From King's College to Columbia 1746–1800*, New York, 1976.

Iakimovich, Iu. K., *Deiateli russkoi kul'tury i slovarnoe delo*, M. 1985.

Iankovich de Mirievo, F. I., *Pravila dlia uchashchikhsia v narodnykh uchilishchakh . . .*, St. Petersburg, 1782.

——, *Propisi raspolozhennyia po pravilam rukovodstva k chistopisaniiu izdannago dlia iunoshestva v narodnykh uchilishchakh Rossiiskoi Imperii*, St. Petersburg, 1782.

——, *Rossiiskii bukvar' dlia obucheniia iunoshestva chteniiu izdannyi pri uchrezhdenii narodnykh uchilishch v Rossiiskoi imperii . . .*, St. Petersburg, 1782.

——, *Rukovodstvo k chistopisaniiu dlia iunoshestva v narodnykh uchilishchakh Rossiiskoi imperii . . .*, St. Petersburg, 1782.

——, *Sokrashchennyi katikhizis dlia obucheniia iunoshestva pravoslavnomy zakonu khristianskomu . . .*, M. 1797.

Iavorskii, Stefan, *Ruka ritoricheskaia Piatiiu chast'mi ili piattiiu persty oukreplenaia*, (facsimile edition in), *Izdanie Obshchestva Liubitelei Drevnei Pis'mennosti*, Vol. XX (1878).

Ikonnikov, V. S., *Opyt russkoi istoriografii*, Vol. I, Kn. 1–2, Kiev, 1891–1892.

Ingrao, Charles, "The Smaller German States," in H. M. Scott, ed., *Enlightened Absolutism. Reform and Reformers in Later Eighteenth-Century Europe*, London, 1990, pp. 221–243.

Isaevich, Ia. D., "Krug chitatel'skikh interesov gorodskogo naseleniia Ukrainy v XVI–XVII vv.," *Fedorovskie chteniia 1976*, M. 1978, pp. 65–76.

Ischreyt, Heinz, "Buchhandel und Buchhändler im nordosteuropäischen Kommunikationssystem (1762–1797)," in Paul Raabe, ed., *Buch und Buchhandel in Europa im achtzehnten Jahrhundert*, Hamburg, 1981. =Wolfenbütteler Schriften zur Geschichte des Buchwesens, Band 4.

——, ed., *Die Beiden Nicolai. Briefwechsel zwischen Ludwig Heinrich Nicolay in St. Petersburg und Friedrich Nicolai in Berlin (1776–1811)*, Lüneburg, 1989.

——, "Die königsberger Freimauererloge und die Anfänge des modernen

Verlagswesen in Rußland (1760–1763)," in Uwe Liszkovski, ed., *Rußland und Deutschland*, Stuttgart, 1974, pp. 108–119. =Kieler Historische Studien. Band 22.
——, "Zur Aufklärung in Mittel- und Osteuropa. Probleme und Tendenzen," in Paul Raabe & Wilhelm Schmidt-Biggemann, eds., *Aufklärung in Deutschland*, Bonn, 1979.
Istoki russkoi bellestristiki. Voznikovenie zhanrov siuzhetnogo povestvovaniia v drevnerusskoi literature, L. 1970.
Istomin, Karion, *Bukvar otpechataia v 1694 godu v Moskve*, [facsimile edition], L. 1981.
Istoriia Biblioteki Akademii nauk SSSR 1714–1964, M-L. 1964.
"Istoriia russkogo chitatelia," *Trudy: Leningradskii gos. institut im. N. K. Krupskoi*, Vyp. 1, XXV (1973), Vyp. 2, XXXII (1976), Vyp. 3, Vol. 42 (1979).
Istrin, V., *Aleksandriia russkikh khronografov. Izsledovanie i tekst*, M. 1893.
Istrina, M. V., "Akademicheskie perevodchiki v XVIII v.," *Knizhnoe delo v Rossii v XVI–XIX vekakh*, L. 1980, pp. 105–115.
Iukht, A. I., *Gosudarstvennaia deiatel'nost' V. N. Tatishchev v 20-kh—nachale 30-kh godov XVIII v.*, M. 1985.
——, "Sviazi V. N. Tatishchev s Akademiei nauk," *Problemy istorii obshchestvennoi mysli i istoriografii. K 75-letiiu akademika M. V. Nechkinoi*, M. 1976, pp. 354–367.
Iushkevich, A. P., *Istoriia matematika v Rossii do 1917 goda*, M. 1968.
——, "Matematika i ee prepodavanie v Rossii XVII–XIX vv.," *Matematika v shkole*, (1947), No. 1, 26–39; No. 2, 11–21; No. 3, 1–13.
Jentzsch, Rudolf, *Der deutsch-lateinische Büchermarkt (nach den Leipziger Ostermeßkatalogen von 1740, 1770, und 1800 in seiner Gliederung und Wandlung)*, Leipzig, 1912.
Jones, W. Gareth, "A Trojan Horse Within the Walls of Classicism: Russian Classicism and the National Specific," in A. G. Cross, ed., *Russian Literature in the Age of Catherine the Great*, Oxford, 1976, pp. 95–120.
——, *Nikolai Novikov. Enlightener of Russia*, Cambridge, 1984.
——, "The Polemics of the 1769 Journals: A Reappraisal," *CASS*, Vol. 16, No. 3–4 (Fall-Winter, 1982), 423–433.
Kämmerer, Jürgen, "Katherina II. im Rahmen hugenottischen Bildungsbemühungen," in Erik Amburger et al., eds., *Wissenschaftspolitik in Mittel- und Osteuropa*, Berlin, 1976, pp. 295–308.
——, *Rußland und die Hugenotten im 18. Jahrhundert 1689–1789*, Wiesbaden, 1978.
Kafanova, O. B., "Bibliografiia perevodov N. I. Karamzina (1783–1800)," *Itogi i problemy izucheniia russkoi literatury XVIII veka*, L. 1989, pp. 319–337. =XVIII vek. Sbornik 16.
Kafengauz, B. B., *I. T. Pososhkov. Zhizn' i deiatel'nost'*, M. 1951.
Kaganov, Ivan Ia., "Der Bibliothekskatalog und die "Instruktion" des Charkover Kollegiums aus dem Jahre 1769," *JfGU*, Vol. 7 (1963), 393–410.
——, "G. A. Poletika i ego knizhnye interesy. (Iz istorii knizhnoi kul'tury XVIII v.)," *Rol' i znachenie literatury XVIII veka v istorii russkoi kul'tury*, M-L. 1966, pp. 138–144. =XVIII vek. Sbornik 7.
——, "Katalog biblioteki Khar'kovskogo kollegiuma 1769 goda (Iz istorii ukrainskoi knizhnoi kul'tury XVIII stoletiia)," *KIm*, VI, M. 1962, pp. 105–122.
Kahn, Andrew, "Readings of Imperial Rome from Lomonosov to Pushkin," *SR*, Vol. 52, No. 4 (Winter, 1993), 745–768.
Kaldor, Ivan L., "The Genesis of the Russian *Grazhdanskii Schrift* or Civil Type," *The Journal of Typographic Research*, III, No. 4 (Oct., 1969), 315–344, IV, No. 2 (Spring, 1970), 111–139.
Kapterev, N., "O greko-latinskikh shkolakh v Moskve v XVII veke do otkrytiia Slaviano-greko-latinskoi Akademii," *Pribavleniia k Tvoreniiam Sviatykh Ottsev*, Vol. XLIV (1889), No. 4, 588–671.
Kashuba, M. V., *Georgii Konisskii*, M. 1979.
——, ed., *Pamiatniki eticheskoi mysli na Ukraine XVII—pervoi poloviny XVIII st.*, Kiev, 1987.

Kasinec, Edward, "P. N. Berkov and the Beginnings of Soviet Russian Book Studies," in his *Slavic Books and Bookmen*, New York, 1984, pp. 35–48 (Orig. 1981).

Kazakova, N. A., *Zapadnaia Evropa v russkoi pis'mennosti XV–XVI vekov. Iz istorii mezhdunarodnykh sviazi Rossii*, L. 1980.

Keenan, Edward L., "Muscovite Perceptions of the Other East Slavs—An Agenda for Historians," in Peter J. Potichnyj et al. eds., *Ukraine and Russia in Their Historical Encounter*, Edmonton, 1992, pp. 20–38.

——, "Muscovy and Kazan: Some Introductory Remarks on the Patterns of Steppe Diplomacy," *SR*, Vol. XXVI, No. 4 (Dec., 1967), 548–558.

——, "Semen Shakhovskoi and the Condition of Orthodoxy," *HUS*, Vol. XII/XIII (1988/1989), 795–815.

Kelly, Laurence, *St. Petersburg. A Travellers' Companion*, New York, 1983.

Kern, Bärbel & Horst Kern, *Madame Doctorin Schlözer. Ein Frauenleben in den Widersprüchen der Aufklärung*, München, 1988.

Kharlampovich, K. V., "Bor'ba shkolnykh vliianii v do-petrovskoi Rusi," *Ks*, LXXVIII (1902), Jul.–Aug., 1–76, Sept., 358–394, LXXIX (1902), Oct. 34–61.

——, *Malorossiiskoe vliianie na velikorusskuiu tserkovnuiu zhizn'*, I, Kazan', 1914 (reprint 1968).

Khizhniak, Z. I., *Kievo-Mogilianskaia Akademiia*, Kiev, 1988.

Khoteev, P. I., "Biblioteka leib-medika I. G. Lestoka," *Kniga i biblioteki v Rossii v XIV—pervoi polovine XIX veke*, L. 1982, pp. 42–55.

——, "Biblioteka leib-medika Ribeiro Sanshesa," *Knigotorgovoe i bibliotechnoe delo v Rossii v XVII—pervoi polovine XIX v.*, L. 1981, pp. 104–118.

——, "Biblioteka sozdatelia russkogo farfora D. I. Vinogradov," *Russkie knigi i biblioteki v XVI—pervoi polovine XIX veka*, L. 1983, pp. 72–84.

——, "Episod iz istorii dubletnogo fonda Biblioteki peterburgskoi Akademii nauk," *Kniga v Rossii XVIII—serediny XIX v. Iz istorii Biblioteki Akademii nauk*, L. 1989, pp. 52–54.

——, "Inostrannye knigi v bibliotekakh uchastnikov kruzhka Volynskogo," *Knizhnoe delo v Rossii v XVI–XIX vekakh*, L. 1980, pp. 67–75.

——, *Kniga v Rossii v seredine XVIII v. Chastnye knizhnye sobraniia*, L. 1989.

——, "Leib-medik Ribeiro Sanshes i ego biblioteka," *Russkie biblioteki i ikh chitatel'*, L. 1983, pp. 134–141.

Kibal'nik, S. A., "Katull v russkoi poezii XVIII—pervoi treti XIX veka," *Vzaimosviazi russkoi i zarubezhnykh literatur*, L. 1983, pp. 45–72.

Kimerling, Elise, "Soldiers' Children 1719–1856: A Study of Social Engineering in Imperial Russia," *FzoG*, Vol. 30 (1982), 61–136.

Kirchner, Joachim, *Das deutsche Zeitschriftenwesen. Seine Geschichte und seine Probleme. Teil I. Von den Anfängen bes zum Zeitalter der Romantik*, 2nd ed., Wiesbaden, 1958.

Kirchner, P., "Studenten aus der Linksufrigen Ukraine an deutschen Universitäten in der zweiten Häfte des 18. Jahrhunderts," in W. Steinitz et al., eds., *Ost und West in der Geschichte des Denkens und der kulturellen Beziehungen*, Berlin, 1966, pp. 367–375.

Kirk, Russell, "What did the Americans Inherit from the Ancients?," *The Intercollegiate Review*, Vol. 24, No. 2 (Spring, 1989), 43–48.

Kliuchevsky, V. O., *A Course in Russian History. The Seventeenth Century*, Natalie Duddington, trans., Chicago, 1968. =Kurs russkoi istorii, Vol. 3.

——, "Zapadnoe vliianie i tserkovnyi raskol v Rossii XVII v.," *Ocherki i rechi. Vtoroi sbornik statei*, St. Petersburg, 1918, pp. 373–453.

——, "Zapadnoe vliianie v Rossii posle Petra," *Neopublikovannye proizvedeniia*, M. 1983, pp. 11–112.

Knight, Isabel F., *The Geometric Spirit. The Abbé Condillac and the French Enlightenment*, New Haven, 1968.

Kochetkova, N. D., "Oratorskaia prosa Feofana Prokopovicha i puti formirovaniia literatury klassitsizma," *Problemy literaturnogo razvitiia v Rossii pervoi treti XVIII veka*, L. 1974, pp. 50–80. =XVIII vek. Sbornik 9.

——, "Radishchev i problema krasnorechiia v teorii XVIII veka," *A. N. Radishchev i literatura ego vremeni*, L. 1977, pp. 8–28. =XVIII Vek. Sbornik 12.

Kolosova, E. V., "'Sozertsanie kratkoe' Sil'vestra Medvedeva i traditsii russkoi istoricheskoi povesti v XVII veke," *Russkaia literatura na rubezhe dvukh epokh (XVII—nachalo XVIII v.)*, M. 1971, pp. 207–229. =Issledovaniia i materialy po drevnerusskoi literature [3].

Komenskii, Ian Amos (Comenius), *Zrelishche vselennyia, na latinskom, rossiiskom i nemetskom iazikakh, izdannoe dlia narodnykh uchilishch Rossiiskoi imperii...*, St. Petersburg, 1788.

Kondakova, T. I., "K voprosu o formirovanii professii izdatel'ia v Rossii v XVIII v.," *Trudy. Biblioteka SSSR imeni V. I. Lenina. 14. Istoriia knigi*, M. 1978, pp. 167–176.

Kondufor, Iu. Iu., R. G. Simonenko & I. S. Khmel', "Kritika sovremenykh burzhuazno-natsionalisticheskikh fal'sifikatsii istorii druzhby i bratstva russkogo i ukrainskogo narodov," *Istoriia SSSR*, 1980, No. 4 (Jul–Aug), 201–211.

Kopanev, N. A., "'Entsiklopediia' i Rossiia. (Novye materialy)," *Kniga v Rossii v epokhu prosveshcheniia. Sbornik nauchnykh trudov*, L. 1988, pp. 169–181.

——, "Frantsuzskie knigi v letnem dome imperatritsy Elizavety Petrovny," *Knigi i biblioteki v Rossii v XIV—pervoi polovine XIX veka*, L. 1982, pp. 26–41.

——, "Knigi imperatritsy Elizavety Petrovny," *Kniga v Rossii XVI—serediny XIX v. Materialy i issledovaniia*, L. 1990, pp. 109–118.

——, "Knizhnost' severnoi volosti XVI–XVII vv.," *Kul'turnoe nasledie drevnei rusi (Istoki. Stanovlenie. Traditsii)*, M. 1976, pp. 394–399.

——, "Pochemu bylo prekrashcheno pervoe nauchnoe periodicheskoe izdanie na russkom iazyke," *Kniga v Rossii XVIII—nachala XIX v. Problemy sozdaniia i rasprostraneniia*, L. 1989, pp. 36–45.

——, "Rasprostranenie inostrannoi knigi v Peterburge v pervoi polovine XVIII veka (Po materialam akademicheskikh knigotorgovykh katalogov)," *Russkie knigi i biblioteki v XVI—pervoi polovine XIX veka*, L. 1983, pp. 38–53.

——, "Volostnye krest'ianskie biblioteki XVI–XVII vv.," *Russkie biblioteki i ikh chitatel'*, L. 1983, pp. 59–70.

Koppitz, Hans-Joachim, "Bibliografien als geistes- und kulturgeschichtliche Quellen im deutschen Sprachgebiet," *AGB*, V (1964), 827–848.

Korb, John George, *Diary of the Journey into Muscovy... in the Year 1698*, London, 1863 (Orig. Latin, Vienna 1700, reprint, New York, 1968).

Korovin, G. M., *Biblioteka Lomonosova. Materialy dlia kharakteristiti literaturi, ispol'zovannoi Lomonosovy v ego trudakh i katalog ego lichnoi biblioteki*, M-L. 1961.

Korsakov, D. A., "Vasilii Nikitich Tatishchev 1686–1750," *Rs*, Vol. LIV (June, 1887), 563–590.

Kosta, Peter, *Eine russische Kosmographie aus dem 17. Jahrhundert. Sprachwissenschaftliche Analyse mit Textedition und Faksimile*, München, 1982. =Specimina Filologiae Slavicae, Band 40.

Krasnobaev, B. I., "Die Bedeutung der Moskauer Universitäts-typographie unter Novikov für die Kulturverbindungen Rußlands mit anderen europäischen Ländern, in Herbert G. Göpfert et al., eds., *Buch- und Verlagswesen im 18. und 19. Jahrhundert*, Berlin, 1977, pp. 217–234.

——, "Eine Gesellschaft gelehrter Freunde am Ende des 18. Jahrhunderts. "Druzeskoe ucenoe obscestvo"," in Éva H. Balázs et al., eds., *Beförderer der Aufklärung im Mittel- und Osteuropa. Freimaurer, Gesellschaften, Clubs*, Berlin, 1979, pp. 257–270.

——, *Ocherki istorii russkoi kul'tury XVIII veka*, M. 1972.

[Krasnobaev, B. I. & L. A. Chernaia], "Knizhnoe delo," *Ocherki russkoi kul'tury XVIII veka*, Vol. II, M. 1987, pp. 294–322.

[Kraus, Johann Ulrich], *Ovidievy figury v 226 izobrazheniiakh*, (Spb., 1722); translation of his Die Verwandlunger des Ovidii.

Krestova, L. V. & V. D. Kuz'mina, "Ioil' Bykovskii, propovednik, izdatel' "Istinny" i pervyi vladelets rukopisi "Slova o polku Igoreve," *Drevnerusskaia literatura i ee sviazy s novym vremenem*, M. 1967, pp. 25–53.

Krizhanich, Iurii, *Politika*, M. N. Tikhomirov, ed., M. 1965. Also John M. Letiche and Basil Dmytryshyn, eds. and trans., *Russian Statecraft. The Politika of Iurii Krizhanich*, Oxford., 1985.

Kroneberg, Bernhard, *Studien zur Geschichte der russischen klassizistschen Elegie*, Wiesbaden, 1972. =Osteuropastudien der Hochschulen des Landes Hessen. Reihe III. Frankfurter Abhandlungen zur Slavistik. Band 20.

Kuchkin, V. A., "Pervye izdaniia russkikh Prologov i rukopisnye istochniki izdaniia 1661–1662 gg.," *Rukopisnaia i pechatnaia kniga*, M. 1975, pp. 139–154.

Kukushkina, M. V., *Monastyrskie biblioteki Russkogo Severa. Ocherki po istorii knizhnoi kul'tury XVI–XVII vekov*, L. 1977.

——, "Obzor sobraniia redkikh knig, postupivshikh v Biblioteku AN SSSR iz Arkhangel'ska," *Sbornik statei i materialov Biblioteki AN SSSR po knigovedeniiu*, II, L. 1970, pp. 253–267.

Kuliabko, E. S., *M. V. Lomonosov i uchebnaia deiatel'nost' Peterburgskoi Akademii nauk*, M. 1962.

—— & E. B. Beshenkovskii, *Sud'ba biblioteki i arkhiva M. V. Lomonosova*, L. 1975.

——, *Zamechatel'nye pitomtsy akademicheskogo universiteta*, L. 1977.

Kulikauskene, N. V., "Knigi perevodchika i obshchestvennogo deiatelia petrovskoi epokhi Feofila Krolika v Irkutske," *Fedorovskie chteniia 1980*, M. 1984, pp. 149–154.

Kunisch, Johannes, *Absolutismus. Europäische Geschichte vom Westfälischen Frieden bis zur Krise des Ancien Régime*, Göttingen, 1986.

Kurilov, A. S., ed., *Russkii i zapadno-evropeiskii klassitsizm. Proza*, M. 1982.

Kuz'min, Apollon, *Tatishchev*, M. 1981.

Kuzmina, V. D., *Rytsarskii roman na Rusi (Bova, Petr Zlatykh Kliuchei)*, M. 1964.

Kvetnickij, Fedor, *Clavis Poetica. Eine Handschrift der Leninbibliothek Moskau aus dem Jahre 1732*, Köln/Wien, 1985.

Lahana, Martha, "Breaking the Rules: The Example of A. S. Matveev," Unpublished paper, Southern Slavic Conference, Savannah, April, 1991.

Lakhman, R. (Lachmann, R), "Dva etapa ritoriki "prilichiia" (decorum)—ritorika Makarii i "Iskusstvo ritorika" Feofana Prokopovicha," *Razvitie Barokko i zarozhdenie Klassitsizma v Rossii XVII—nachala XVIII v.*, M. 1989, pp. 149–169.

Lambert, Iogann Genrikh (Johann Heinrich Lambert), *Sistema mira slavnago Lamberta . . .*, St. Petersburg, 1797. *System du monde*, 2nd ed., Berlin, 1784; *The System of the World*, London, 1800.

Lang, David Marshall, *The First Russian Radical. Alexander Radishchev 1749–1802*, London, 1959.

Langenbucher, Wolfgang, *Der Aktuelle Unterhaltungsroman. Beiträge zu Geschichte und Theorie der Massenhaft verbreiteten Literatur*, Bonn, 1964. =Bonner Beiträge zur Bibliotheks- und Bücherkunde, Bd. 9.

Lapchine, J., *La phenoménologie de la conscience religieuse dans la littérature russe*, I, II. (Bulletin de l'Association russe pour les recherches scientifiques, Vol. V (X), No. 28, Prague, 1937, 69–108, Vol. VI (XI) No. 35).

Latsis, M. A., "Knizhnoe delo v Latvii v XVIII veke," *Knigopechatanie i knizhnye sobraniia v Rossii do serediny XIX v.*, L. 1979, pp. 59–75.

Lauer, Reinhard, "Russische Freimauerdictung im 18. Jahrhundert," in Éva H. Balázs, ed., *Beförderer der Aufklärng in Mittel- und Osteuropa. Freimauer, Gesellschaften, Clubs*, Berlin, 1979, pp. 271–291.

Lavrovskii, A. N., "Feofilakt Lopatinskii i ego biblioteka," *Uchenie zapiski: Kalininskii gosudarstvennii universitet*, Vol. XV (1947), 197–210.

Lebedev, E. N., "Filosofskaia mysl' pisatelei epokhi klassitsizma," *Russkii i zapadno-evropeiskii klassitsizm. Prosa*, M. 1982, pp. 138–176.

Lebedeva, I. N., "Biblioteka tsarevicha Alekseia Petrovicha," *Kniga i knigotorgovlia v Rossii v XVI–XVIII vv.*, L. 1984, pp. 56–64.

——, "Leib-medik Petra I Robert Areskin i ego biblioteka," *Russkie biblioteki i ikh chitatel'*, L. 1983, pp. 98–105.

——, "Lichnaia biblioteka tsaria Fedora Alekseevicha," *Kniga v Rossii XVIII—serediny XIX v. Iz Istorii Biblioteki Akademii nauk*, L. 1989, pp. 84–92.

——, ed., *Povest' o Varlaame i Ioasafe. Pamiatnik drevnerusskoi perevodnoi literatury XI–XII vv.*, L. 1985.

LeBlanc, Ronald, "Making 'Gil Blas' Russian," *SEEJ*, Vol. 30, No. 3 (1986), 340–354.

Lehmann, Ulf, "Barock und Aufklärung. Zum Anwendungsbereich beides Begriffe," *ZS*, Vol. 13 (1968), 319–328.

——, "Russische Literatur der "Übergangsperiode 1650–1730. Probleme ihrer Erforschung und Darstellung" in Horst Schmidt, ed., *Die russische Literatur der Aufklärung (1650–1825)*, Halle, 1985, pp. 25–33.

Lentin, A., "Shcherbatov on Education," *SGECR*, No. 15 (1987), 14–16.

——, "'The *parole* of Literary Men': A Classical quotation in M. M. Shcherbatov?," *SGECR*, No. 16 (1988), 11–13.

Leser und Lesen im 18. Jahrhundert. Colloquium der Arbeitsstelle Achtzehntes Jahrhundert Gesamthochschule Wuppertal. Schloß Lüntenbeck, 24.–26. Oktober 1975, Heidelberg, 1977. =Beiträge zur Geschichte der Literatur und Kunst des 18. Jahrhunderts. Band. 1.

Levin, Iu. D., "The English Novel in 18th-Century Russia," *Literature, Lives, and Legality in Catherine's Russia*, A. G. Cross and G. S. Smith, eds., Nottingham, 1994, pp. 143–167.

——, "Translations of Henry Fielding's Works in Eighteenth-Century Russia," *SEER*, Vol. 68, No. 2 (Apr, 1990), 217–233.

Lewin, Paulina, "Polish-Ukrainian-Russian Literary Relations of the Sixteenth-Eighteenth Centuries: New Approaches," *SEEJ*, Vol. 24, No. 3 (1980), 256–269.

Lewitter, L. R., "Peter the Great, Poland, and the Westernization of Russia," *JHI*, Vol. XIX, No. 4 (Oct., 1958), 493–506.

——, "Peter the Great's Attitude Towards Religion: From Traditional Piety to Rational Theology," in R. P. Bartlett et al., eds., *Russia and the World of the Eighteenth Century*, Columbus, Ohio, 1988, pp. 62–77.

——, "Poland, the Ukraine and Russia in the 17th Century," *SEER*, Vol. 27 (1948–49), 157–171, 414–429.

Lieven, Dominic, *The Aristocracy in Europe 1815–1914*, New York, 1992.

Likhachev, Dmitry, ed., *A History of Russian Literature 11th–17th Centuries*, K. M. Cook-Horujy, trans., M. 1989.

Lincoln, W. Bruce, *The Great Reforms. Autocracy, Bureaucracy and the Politics of Change in Imperial Russia*, Dekalb, Ill., 1990.

Lindemann, Margot, *Deutsche Presse bis 1815. Geschichte der deutschen Presse*, Teil I, Berlin, 1969.

Litak, Stanislaw, "Wandlungen im polnischen Schulwesen im 18. Jahrhundert," in Friedrich Engel-Janosi et al., eds., *Formen der europäischen Aufklärung*, München, 1976, pp. 96–125.

Literaturnyi sbornik XVII veka. Prolog, M. 1978.

Lomonosov, M. V., *Dlia pol'zu obshchestva . . .*, M. 1990.

——, *O vospitanii i obrazovanii*, M. 1991.

——, *Polnoe sobranie sochinenii*, 10 vv., M-L. 1955–59.

——, *Sochineniia*, M-L. 1961.

Longworth, Philip, *Alexis. Tsar of All the Russias*, New York, 1984.

Lotman, Iu. M., "Die Frühaufklärung und die Entwicklung des gesellschaftlichen Denkens in Russland," in Helmut Grasshoff & Ulf Lehmann, eds., *Studien zur Geschichte der russischen Literatur des 18. Jahrhunderts*, Band III, Berlin, 1968, pp. 93–119.

——, "Ob 'Ode, vybrannoi iz Iova,' Lomonosova," *Izvestiia Akademii nauk SSSR, Seriia literatury i iazyka*, Vol. 42, No. 3 (1983), 253–262.

Lukina, T. A., *A. P. Protasov—russkii akademik XVIII veka*, M-L. 1962.
Lupinin, Nickolas, *Religious Revolt in the XVIIth Century: The Schism of the Russian Church*, Princeton, 1984.
Luppov, S. P., "Biblioteka Ia. V. Briusa," *Sbornik statei i materialov Biblioteki AN SSSR po knigovedeniiu*, III, L. 1973, pp. 249–272.
——, "Biblioteka P. M. Eropkina," *Knigopechatanie i knizhnye sobraniia v Rossii do serediny XIX v.*, L. 1979, pp. 142–152.
——, *Chitateli izdanii moskovskoi tipografii v seredine XVII veka*, L. 1983.
——, "Izuchenie istorii bibliotek i kharaktera chitatel'skikh zaprosov razlichnykh sloev obshchestva kak odna iz vazhnykh zadach stoiashchikh pered issledovateliami v oblasti istorii kul'tury (na primere izucheniia istorii russkikh biblioteki epokhi feodalizma)," *Russkie biblioteki i ikh chitatel'*, L. 1983, pp. 20–34.
——, "Die Nachfrage nach Büchern der Akademie der Wissenschaften und nach ausländischen Veröffentlichungen in Petersburg und Moskau in der Mitte des XVIII. Jahrhunderts," *AGB*, Vol. XVII (1981), 257–299.
——, "Fedor Ivanovich Soimonov i ego biblioteka," *Russkie biblioteki i chastnye knizhnye sobraniia XVI–XIX vekov*, L. 1979, pp. 13–28.
——, *Kniga v Rossii v XVII veke. Knigoizdatel'stvo, knigotorgovlie, Rasprostranenie knig sredi razlichnykh sloev naseleniia, Knizhnye sobraniia chastnykh lits, Biblioteki*, L. 1970.
——, *Kniga v Rossii v pervoi chetverti XVIII veka*, L. 1973.
——, *Kniga v Rossii v poslepetrovskoe vremia*, L. 1976.
——, "Kto pokupal knigi v Peterburge vo vtoroi chetverti XVIII veka," *Istoriia knig i izdatel'skogo dela*, L. 1977, pp. 122–155.
——, "K voprosy ob utochnenii repertuara russkoi knigi pervoi poloviny XVIII veka. Novye dannye o nedoshedshikh do nas izdaniiakh," *Knizhnoe delo v Rossii v XVI–XIX vekakh*, L. 1980, pp. 32–42.
——, "Pechatnaia i rukopisnaia kniga v Rossii v pervom sorokaletii XVIII v. (problema sosyshchestvovaniia)," *Rukopisnaia i pechatnaia kniga*, M. 1975, pp. 182–192.
——, comp., *Pokupateli izdanii moskovskoi tipografii v seredine XVII veka. Ukazatel' imen i geograficheskikh nazvanii*, L. 1984.
——, "Russkii chitatel' XVII—pervoi poloviny XVIII veka," *Fedorovskie chteniia 1976*, M. 1978, pp. 83–95.
Luzhnyi, R., "'Poetika' Feofana Prokopovicha i teoriia poezii v Kievo-Mogilianskoi Akademii (Pervaia polovina XVIII v.)," *Rol' i znachenie literatury XVIII veka v istorii russkoi kul'tury*, M-L. 1966, pp. 47–53. =XVIII vek. Sbornik 7.
Madariaga, Isabel de, "Catherine the Great," in H. M. Scott, ed., *Enlightened Absolutism. Reform and Reformers in Later Eighteenth-Century Europe*, London, 1990, pp. 289–311.
——, "Portrait of an Eighteenth-Century Statesman: Prince Dmitry Mikhaylovich Golitsyn," *SEER*, Vol. 62, No. 1 (1984), 36–60.
——, *Russia in the Age of Catherine the Great*, New Haven/London, 1981.
——, "The Foundation of the Russian Educational System by Catherine II," *SEER*, Vol. 57, No. 3 (July, 1979), 369–395.
Magnitskii, Leontii, *Arithmetika sirech nauka chislitelnaia*, M. 1704.
Maier, Lothar, "Deutsche Gelehrte an der St. Petersburger Akademie der Wissenschaften im 18. Jahrhundert," In Friedhelm Berthold Kaiser & Bernhard Stasiewski, eds., *Deutscher Einfluss auf Bildung und Wissenschaft im östlichen Europa*, Köln/Wien, 1984, pp. 27–51.
Makarii, episkop Vinnitskago, *Istoriia russkago raskola izvestnago pod imenem starobriadstva*, St. Petersburg, 1855.
Makarii, Met. of Moscow, *Istoriia russkoi tserkvi*, 3rd ed., St. Petersburg, 1889, 12 vols. (reprint, The Hague, 1968).
Makashina, S., "Literaturnye vzaimootnosheniia Rossii i Frantsii XVIII–XIX vv.," *Ln*, Vol. 29/30 (1937), v–lxxxii.

264   BIBLIOGRAPHY OF WORKS CONSULTED

Makogonenko, G., *Nikolai Novikov i russkoe prosveshchenie XVIII veka*, M-L. 1952.
Mal'dzis, A. I., "Knigadrukavanne Belarusi v XVIII stagoddzi," *Kniga, bibliotechnoe delo i bibliografiia v Belorussii (Sbornik statei)*, Minsk, 1974, pp. 130–150.
Marion, Michel, "Quelques aspects sur les bibliothèques privées à Paris entre 1750 et 1759," *Buch und Sammler. Private und öffentliche Biblioteken im 18. Jahrhundert*, Heidelberg, 1979, pp. 85–98. =Beiträge zur Geschichte der Literatur und Kunst des 18. Jahrhunderts. Band 3.
Marker, Gary, "Literacy and Literacy Texts in Muscovy: A Reconsideration," *SR*, Vol. 49, No. 1 (Spr, 1990), 74–89.
——, "Primers and Literacy in Muscovy" A Taxonomic Investigation," *RR*, Vol. 48, No. 1 (Jan, 1989), 1–20.
——, *Publishing, Printing, and the Origins of Intellectual Life in Russia, 1700–1800*, Princeton, 1985.
Martens, Wolfgang, *Die Botschaft der Tugend. Die Aufklärung im Spiegel der deutschen moralischen Wochenschriften*, Stuttgart, 1968.
——, "Die Geburt des Journalisten in der Aufklärung," *WSA*, I (1974), 84–98.
Martin, Henri-Jean, "Livre et Lumières en France à propos de Travaux Récents," in Paul Raabe, ed., *Buch und Buchhandel in Europa im achtzehnten Jahrhundert*, Hamburg, 1981, pp. 11–52. =Wolfenbütteler Schriften zur Geschichte des Buchwesens, Bd. 4.
Martynov, I. F., "Kniga v russkoi provintsii 1760–1790-kh gg. Zarozhdenie provintsial'noi knizhnoi torgovli," in A. A. Sidorov & S. P. Luppov, eds., *Kniga v Rossii do serediny XIX veka*, L. 1978, pp. 109–125.
——, *Knigoizdatel' Nikolai Novikov*, M. 1961.
—— & I. F. Martynov, "Peterburgskii knigoizdatel' i knigotorgovets XVIII v. E. K. Vil'kovskii i izdanii uchebnykh posobii dlia narodnykh uchilishch," *Istoriia knigi i izdatel'skogo dela. Sbornik nauchnykh trudov*, L. 1977, pp. 62–95.
Maslov, S. I., "Biblioteka Stefana Iavorskogo," *Chteniia v Istoricheskom Obshchestve Nestora Letopistsa*, Vol. XXIV (1914), No. 2, Otd. 2, 91–162, Otd. 3, 17–102.
Matl', I, "Epokha prosveshcheniia v Rossii i ee otlichie ot prosveshcheniia v drugikh slavianskikh stranakh," *Rol' i znachenie literatury XVIII veka v istorii russkoi kul'tury*, M-L. 1966, pp. 199–206. = XVIII vek. Sbornik 7.
——, "F. Ia. Iankovich i avstro-serbsko-russkie sviazi v istorii narodnogo obrazovaniia v Rossii," *Russkaia literatura XVIII veka i ee mezhdunarodnye sviazi*, L. 1975, pp. 76–81. =XVIII vek. Sbornik 10.
Matveev, A. A., "Zapiski Andreia Artamonovicha Grafa Matveeva," *Zapiski russkikh liudei. Sobytiia vremen Petra Velikago*, St. Petersburg, 1841.
McArthur, Gilbert H., "Freemasonry and Enlightenment in Russia: The Views of N. I. Novikov," *CASS*, Vol. 14, No. 3 (Fall, 1980), 361–375.
McConnell, Allen, *A Russian Philosophe. Alexander Radishchev 1749–1802*, The Hague, 1964.
——, "Radishchev and Classical Antiquity," *CASS*, Vol. 16, No. 3/4 (Fall-Winter, 1982), 469–490.
McNally, Raymond T., *Chaadayev and His Friends. An Intellectual History of Peter Chaadayev and His Russian Contemporaries*, Tallahassee, Fla., 1971.
McNeill, William H., *The Pursuit of Power: Technology, Armed Force, and Society since A.D. 1000*, Chicago, 1982.
Medlin, William K. & Christos G. Patrinelis, *Renaissance Influences and Religious Reforms in Russia. Western and Post-Byzantine Impacts on Culture and Education (16th–17th Centuries)*, Genève, 1971.
Melton, James Van Horn, *Absolutism and the eighteenth-century origins of compulsory schooling in Prussia and Austria*, Cambridge, 1988.
Meyer, Horst, "Büchern im Leben eines Verwaltungsjuristen: Justus Möser und seine Bibliothek," *Buch und Sammler. Private und öffentliche Bibliotheken im 18. Jahrhundert*, Heidelberg, 1979, pp. 149–158.

Miliukov, Paul, Charles Seignobos & L. Eisenmann, *History of Russia*, 3 vv. Charles Lam Markmann, trans., New York, 1968.

Miller, David B., "The Velikie Minei Chetii and the Stepennaia Kniga of Metropolitan Makarii and the Origins of Russian National Consciousness," *FzoG*, Vol. 26 (1979), 263–382.

Mizuta, Hiroshi, *Adam Smith's Library. A Supplement to Bonar's Catalogue with a Checklist of the whole Library*, Cambridge, 1967.

Mohrmann, Heinz, *Studien über russisch-deutsche Begegnungen in der Wirtschaftswissenschaft (1750–1825)*, Berlin, 1959.

Moiseeva, G. N., *Drevnerusskaia literatura v khudozhestvennom soznanii i istoricheskoi mysli Rossii XVIII veka*, L. 1980.

——, "Znachenie moskovskoi Slaviano-greko-latinskoi akademii v formirovanii Lomonosova-poeta," *Lomonosov i kniga. Sbornik nauchnykh trudov*, L. 1986, pp. 36–41.

Montesquieu, *The Persian Letters*, George B. Healy, trans., Indianapolis, 1964.

Moore, Cornelia Niekus, *The Maiden's Mirror. Reading Material for German Girls in the Sixteenth and Seventeenth Centuries*, Wiesbaden, 1987. =Wolfenbüttler Forschungen, Band. 36.

Moriakov, V. I., "Izuchenie russkogo prosvetitel'stva XVII—nachala XIX veka v sovetskoi istoriografii," *Istoriia SSSR*, 1986, No. 2 (Mar.–Apr.), 42–55.

Moroshkin, I. Ia., "Fedosii Ianovskii, Arkhiepiskop Novgorodskii. Istoriko-biograficheskii ocherk," *Rs*, LV (1887), Jul., 1–34; LVI (1887), Oct., 31–44.

Morozov, Aleksandr, "Christian Wolffs Leser in Rußland in der ersten Hälfte des 18. Jahrhunderts," *JfGU*, Vol. 7 (1963), 411–423.

Morozov, P. O., *Feofan Prokopovich kak pisatel'*, St. Petersburg, 1880.

Mudrova, N. A., "Knizhnoe sobranie G. D. Stroganova na rubezhe XVII–XVIII vv. (k postanovke problemy)," *Istochniki po istorii russkogo obshchestvennogo soznaniia perioda feodalizma*, Novosibirsk, 1986, pp. 28–40.

Mühlpfordt, Günter, "Christian Wolff, ein Enzyklopädist der deutschen Aufklärung," *Jahrbuch für Geschichte der deutsch-slawischen Beziehungen*, Vol. I (1956), 66–102.

——, "Die Petersburger Aufklärung und Halle," *CASS*, Vol. 13, No. 4 (Winter, 1979), 488–509.

——, "Ein deutscher Rußlankenner des 18. Jahrhunderts. F. Büsching als Herausgeber einer Schrift über die Weidervereinigung der Ukraine mit Rußland. (Halle 1775)," *Zeitschrift für Geschichtswissenschaft*, Beiheft 1 (1954), 40–62.

——, "Leipzig als Brennpunkt der internationalen Wirkung Lomonosovs," in Helmut Grasshoff & Ulf Lehmann, eds., *Studien zur Geschichte der russischen Literatur des 18. Jahrhunderts*, Band III, Berlin, 1968, pp. 271–416.

——, "Zur Rolle der Universitäten Halle und Moskau in den deutsch-russischen Beziehungen seit der Aufklärung," *Jahrbuch für Geschichte der deutsch-slawischen Beziehungen*, Vol. I (1956), 103–123.

Muller, Alexander, trans. & ed., *The Spiritual Regulation of Peter the Great*, Seattle/London, 1972.

Mullett, Charles, "Lucretius in Clio's Chariot," *JHI*, Vol. XIX, No. 3 (June, 1958), 307–322.

Munby, A. N. L., ed., *Sale Catalogues of Libraries of Eminent Persons*, 11 vv. London, 1971ff.

Murzakevich, N. N., "Kabinet zimniago dvortsa imperatritsy Ekateriny II," *ZMnp*, Vol. CLXII, No. 8 (Aug, 1872), Otd. II, 327–341.

——, "Zapiski N. N. Murzakevicha," *Rs*, Vol. LIV, No. 4 (Apr., 1887), 128–144.

Murzanova, M. N., "K istorii sobraniia knig tsarevicha Alekseia Petrovicha," *Istoricheskii ocherk i obzor fondov rukopisnogo otdela Biblioteki Akademii nauk*, M-L. 1956, Vyp. I, 118–142, 422–427.

Nef, John U., *War and Human Progress. An Essay on the Rise of Industrial Civilization*, Cambridge, Mass., 1950.

Nemirovskii, E. L., *Fransisk Skorina. Zhizn' i deiatel'nost' belorusskogo prosvetitelia*, Minsk, 1990.

——, *Ivan Fedorov okolo 1510–1583*, M. 1985.

——, *Ivan Fedorov v Belorussii*, M. 1979.
——, "Izdaniia pervoi pol'skoi tipografii v Gosudarstvennoi biblioteke SSSR imeni V. I. Lenina," *Russko-pol'skie sviazi v oblasti knizhnogo dela*, M. 1980, pp. 5–27.
——, *Nachalo knigopechataniia na Ukraine. Ivan Fedorov*, M. 1974.
——, *Voznikovenie knigopechataniia v Moskve. Ivan Fedorov*, M. 1964.
Neubauer, Helmut, *Car und Selbstherrscher. Beiträge zur Geschichte der Autokratie in Rußland*, Wiesbaden, 1964. =Veröffentlichungen des Osteuropa-Instituts München, Band. 22.
Neuhäuser, Rudolf, *Towards the Romantic Age. Essays on Sentimental and Preromantic Literature in Russia*, The Hague, 1974.
Neuschäffer, Hubertus, "Der livländische Pastor und Kameralist Johann Georg Eisen von Schwarzenberg, Ein deutscher Vertreter der Aufklärung in Rußland zu Beginn der zweiten Hälfe des 18. Jahrhunderts," in Uwe Liszkowski, ed., *Rußland und Deutschland*, Stuttgart, 1974, pp. 120–143.
Neuville, Foy de la, *A Curious and New Account of Muscovy in the Year 1689*, Lindsey Hughes, ed., London, 1994.
Nichik, V. M., *Iz istorii otechestvennoi filosofii kontsa XVII—nachala XVIII v.*, Kiev, 1978.
——, "Sobranie kursov ritoriki i filosofii professorov Kievo-Mogilianskoi akademii v TsNB AN SSSR," *Russkie biblioteki i ikh chitatel'*, L. 1983, pp. 80–87.
Nichols, Robert L., "Orthodoxy and Russia's Enlightenment, 1762–1825," in Robert L. Nichols & Theofanis George Stavrou, eds., *Russian Orthodoxy under the Old Regime*, Minneapolis, 1978, pp. 67–89.
Nikolskii, A., "Shkol'naia reforma imperatritsy Ekateriny II," *ZMnp*, Vol. CLVII, No. 8 (Aug., 1872), Otd. II, 272–318.
Nikol'skii, N. M., *Istoriia russkoi tserkvi*, 3rd ed., M. 1983. (1st ed, 1930).
Nimchuk, V. V., ed., *Leksikon latins'kii E. Slavinets'skogo. Leksikon Sloveno-latins'skii E. Slavinets'skogo ta A. Korets'kogo Satanovs'kogo*, Kiev, 1973.
Novikov, N. I., *Izbrannye pedagogicheskie sochineniia*, N. A. Trushin, comp., M. 1959.
——, *Opyt' istoricheskago Slovaria o rossiiskikh pisateliakh*, St. Petersburg, 1772.
——, "O vospitanii . . .," in *N. I. Novikov i ego sovremenniki. Izbrannye sochineniia*, I. V. Malyshev, ed., M. 1961, pp. 257–323.
Novikov, N. V., *Russkie skazki i rannikh zapisiakh i publikatsiiakh (XVI–XVIII veka)*, L. 1971.
Nussbaum, Frederick L., *The Triumph of Science and Reason 1660–1685*, New York, 1953.
O'Brien, C. Bickford, *Muscovy and the Ukraine. From the Pereiaslavl Agreement to the Truce of Andrusovo, 1654–1667*, Berkeley, 1963.
O'Brien, George M., "Maria Theresa's Attempt to Educate an Empire," *Paedagogica Historica*, Vol. X, No. 3 (1970), 542–565.
Ocherki russkoi kul'tury XVII veka, 2 vv. M. 1979.
Ocherki russkoi kul'tury XVIII veka, 4 vv. M. 1986, 1987, 1988, 1991.
Okenfuss, Max J., "Education and Empire: School Reform in Enlightened Russia," *JfGO*, Vol. 27, No. 1 (1979), 41–68.
——, "From School Class to Social Caste: The Divisiveness of Early Modern Russian Education," *JfGO*, Vol. 33, No. 3 (1986), 321–344.
——, "On Crime and Punishment. The Moral Awakening of Russia in the Age of Peter the Great," *History Today*, September, 1986, pp. 23–27.
——, "Peter Tolstoi in Rome: The Hydraulics of Mystery and Delight," *SGECR*, No. 12 (1984), pp. 35–41.
——, "Popular Educational Tracts in Enlightened Russia: A Preliminary Survey," *CASS*, Vol. 14, No. 3 (Fall, 1980), 307–326.
——, "Russian Students in Europe in the Age of Peter the Great," in John G. Garrard, ed., *The Eighteenth Century in Russia*, Oxford, 1973, pp. 130–145.
——, "Technical Training in Russia under Peter the Great," *HEQ*, Vol. XIII, No. 4 (Winter, 1973), 325–345.
——, "The Ages of Man on the Seventeenth-Century Muscovite Frontier," *The Historian*, Vol. 56, No. 1 (Autumn, 1993), 87–104.

——, "The Cultural Transformation of Peter Tolstoi," in A. G. Cross, ed., *Russia and the West*, Newtonville, Ma., 1983, pp. 228–237.

——, *The Discovery of Childhood in Russia: The Evidence of the Slavic Primer*, Newtonville, Ma., 1980.

——, "The Impact of Technical Training in Eighteenth-Century Russia," in A. G. Cross et al., eds., *Russia and the World in the Eighteenth Century*, Columbus, Ohio, 1988, pp. 113–125.

——, "The Jesuit Origins of Petrine Education," in John G. Garrard, ed., *The Eighteenth Century in Russia*, Oxford, 1973, pp. 106–130.

——, "The Novikov Problem: An English Perspective," in A. G. Cross, ed., *Great Britain and Russia in the Eighteenth Century: Contacts and Comparisons*, Newtonville, Mass., 1979, pp. 97–108.

——, trans., *The Travel Diary of Peter Tolstoi. A Muscovite in Early Modern Europe*, DeKalb, Ill., 1987.

——, "V. O. Kliuchevskii on Childhood and Education in Early Modern Russia," *HEQ*, XVII, No. 4 (1977), 417–447.

Ot klassisizma k romantizmu. Istorii mezhdunarodnykh sviazi russkoi literatury, L. 1970.

Otten, Fred, "Reiseberichte der Petrinischen Zeit als linguistische Quelle ("Dnevnik"—1697/99)," *ZSP*, Vol. XLIV (1984), 354–414.

——, *Untersuchungen zu den Fremd- und Lehnwörter bei Peter dem Grossen*, Köln/Bonn, 1985. =Slavistische Forschungen Band 50.

Page, Tanya, "A Radiscev Monstrology: The *Journey from Petersburg to Moscow* and Later Writings in the Light of French Sources," in Victor Terras, ed., *American Contributions to the Eighth International Congress of Slavists, Vol. 2. Literature*, Columbus, Ohio, 1978, pp. 606–629.

Palmer, R. R., *Catholics and Unbelievers in Eighteenth Century France*, Princeton, 1939. (Reprint, New York, 1961).

"Pamiati S. P. Luppova," *Kniga v Rossii v epokhu prosveshcheniia. Sbornik nauchnykh trudov*, L. 1988, pp. 192–194.

Pamiatniki eticheskoi mysli na Ukraine XVII—pervoi poloviny XVIII st., M. V. Kashuby, trans., Kiev, 1987.

Pamiatniki obshchestvenno-politicheskoi mysli v Rossii kontsa XVIII veka. Literaturnye panegiriki, M. 1983.

Panchenko, A. M., "Nachalo petrovskoi reformy i ideinaia podopleka," *Itogi i problemy izucheniia russkoi literatury XVIII veka*, L. 1989. =XVIII vek. Sbornik 16.

——, "O smena pisatel'skogo tipa v petrovskuiu epokhu," *Problemy literaturnogo razvitiia v Rossii pervoi treti XVIII veka*, L. 1974, pp. 112–128. =XVIII vek. Sbornik 9.

——, *Russkaia stikhotvornaia kul'tura XVII veka*, L. 1973.

Panegiricheskaia literatura petrovskogo vremeni, M. 1979. =Russkaia staropechatnaia literatura (XVI—pervaia chetvert' XVIII) 4.

Panich, T. B., "Osobennosti "Shestodneva" Afanasiia Kholmogorskogo," *Istochniki po istorii russkogo obshchestvennogo soznaniia perioda feodalizma*, Novosibirsk, 1986, pp. 5–24.

Paperno, Irina, "The Liberation of the Serfs as a Cultural Symbol," *RR*, Vol. 50 (Oct. 1991), 417–436.

Papmehl, K. A., *Metropolitan Platon of Moscow (Petr Levshin, 1737–1812). The Enlightened Prelate, Scholar and Educator*, Newtonville, 1983.

——, "The Empress and 'Un Fanatique': A Review of the Circumstances Leading to the Government Action Against Novikov in 1792," *SEER*, Vol. 68, No. 4 (Oct., 1991), 665–91.

Parker, Geoffrey, *The Military Revolution. Military Innovation and the Rise of the West 1500–1800*, Cambridge, 1988.

Parker, Harold T., *The Cult of Antiquity and the French Revolutionaries*, Chicago, 1937 (reprint 1965).

Pavlenko, N. I., *Aleksandr Danilovich Menshikov*, M. 1981.

——, "Nakaz shikhmeisteru V. N. Tatishcheva," *Ia*, Vol. VI (1951), pp. 199–249.
——, *Ptentsy gnezda Petrova*, M. 1984.
Pavlov-Silvan'skii, N. P., "Graf Petr Andreevich Tolstoi (Prashchur grafa L'va Tolstogo," in his *Sochineniia*, I, St. Petersburg, 1910, 1–41. (reprint, 1966).
Payne, Harry G., *The Philosophes and the People*, New Haven/London, 1976.
Pekarskii, P., "Materialy dlia istorii zhurnal'noi i literaturnoi deiatel'nosti Ekateriny II," *ZIAn*, Vol. III (1863), Prilozhenie 6, 1–87.
——, *Nauka i literatura v Rossii pri Petre Velikom. I. Vvedenie v istoriiu prosveshcheniia v Rossii XVIII stoletiia*, St. Petersburg, 1862.
——, "Novaia izvestiia o V. N. Tatishcheve," *ZIAn*, Vol. IV, Knizhka II (1864), Prilozhenie 4, 1–66.
Pelenski, Jaroslaw, "The Contest for the 'Ukrainian Inheritance' in Russian-Ukrainian Relations: The Origins and Early Ramifications," in Peter J. Potichnyj et al. eds., *Ukraine and Russia in Their Historical Encounter*, Edmonton, 1992, pp. 20–38.
——, "The Origins of the Official Muscovite Claims to the 'Kievan Inheritance'," *HUS*, Vol. I, No. 1 (Mar, 1977), 29–52.
Penchko, N. A., *Biblioteka moskovskogo universiteta s osnovaniia do 1812 goda*, [I], M. 1969.
Perkins, Etta L., "Mobility in the Art Profession in Tsarist Russia," *JfGO*, Vol. 39, No. 2 (1991), 225–233.
Perry, John, *The State of Russia Under the Present Czar*, London, 1716. (Reprint, New York, 1967).
Peskov, A. M., *Bualo v russkoi literature XVIII—pervoi treti XIX veka*, M. 1989.
Peterson, Claes, *Peter the Great's Administrative and Judicial Reforms: Swedish Antecedents and the Process of Reception*, Stockholm, 1979.
Peterson, Eleanor K., "Who Killed Cock Robin?," *CJ*, Vol. XXXII, No. 3 (Dec., 1936), 153–161.
[Petrov Lev Aleksandrovich], *Obshchestvenno-politicheskaia i filosofskaia mysl' Rossii pervoi poloviny XVIII veka. Lektsii po spetskurzu "Istoriia russkoi filosofii"*, Irkutsk, 1974.
Petrov, V. A., "Geograficheskie spravochniki XVII v.," *Ia*, Vol. V (1950), 74–165.
Pinson, Koppel, *Pietism as a Factor in the Rise of German Nationalism*, New York, 1934.
Pipes, Richard, *Russia Under the Old Regime*, New York, 1974.
Pis'ma i doneseniia iezuitov o Rossii kontsa XVII i nachala XVIII veka, St. Petersburg, 1904.
Platon (Levshin), *Pouchitel'nyia slova pri Vysochaishem Dvore eia imperatorskago velichestva . . . Ekateriny Alekseevny . . . s 1763 goda po 1780 god . . .*, Vol. 4, M. 1780.
——, *The Present State of the Greek Church in Russia or a Summary of Christian Divinity*, Translated from the Slavonian . . . by Robert Pinkerton, Edinburgh, 1814.
——, *Raznye sochineniia*, Vol. 6, M. 1780.
Platonov, S. F., *Moscow and the West*, Joseph L. Wieczynski, trans., Hattiesburg, Miss., 1972.
Plekhanov, G. V., *History of Russian Social Thought*, Boris M. Bekkar, trans., New York, 1967.
Pleticha, Eva, *Adel und Buch. Studien zur Geisteswelt des fränkischen Adels am Beispiel seiner Bibliotheken vom 15. bis zum 18. Jahrhundert*, Neustadt a. d. Aisch, 1983. =Veröffentlichungen der Gesellschaft für Fränkische Geschichte, Reihe IX, Band 33.
Pokotilova, Ol'ga, "Predshestvenniki Lomonosova v russkoi poezii XVII-go i nachala XVIII-go stoletii," in V. V. Sipovskii, ed., *1711–1911. M. V. Lomonosov. Sbornik statei*, St. Petersburg, 1911, pp. 66–92.
[Polikarpov-Orlov, Fedor Polikarpovich], *Bukvar' slavenskimi, grecheskimi, rimskimi pismeny ouchitsia khotiashchym i liubomudrie v polzu dushe spasitelnuiu obresti tshchashchymsia*, M. 7209 (1701).
Polonskaia I. M., "Knigi iz biblioteki i s avtografami F. V. Karzhavina v sobranii otdela redkikh knig," *Trudy: Biblioteka SSSR imeni V. I. Lenina. 14. Istoriia knigi*, M. 1978, pp. 130–164.
——, "Rekonstruktsiia biblioteki A. A. Matveeva (1666–1728)," *Fedorovskie chteniia 1980*, M. 1984, pp. 126–148.

Polotskii, Simeon, *Izbrannye sochineniia*, I. P. Eremin, ed., M-L. 1953.
——, *Virshi*, Minsk, 1990.
Polz, Peter, "Die Volksaufklärung unter Katharina II," *CASS*, Vol. 14, No. 3 (Fall, 1980), 376–388.
——, "Theodor Jankovic und die Schulreform in Rußland, in Erna Lesky et al., eds., *Die Aufklärung in Ost- und Südosteuropa. Aufsätze, Vorträge, Dokumentationen*, Köln/Wien, 1972, 119–174.
Popesku, T. A., "Osnovnye istochniki XVII veka po istorii biblioteki Troitse-Sergieva monastyria. Opis' 1641 g. i vkladnye knigi 1639 i 1673 gg.," *Knigopechatanie i knizhnye sobraniia v Rossii do serediny XIX veka*, L. 1979, pp. 26–38.
Popov, A., "Nauka i religiia v mirosozertsanii Lomonosova," in V. V. Sipovskii, ed., *1711–1911. M. V. Lomonosov. Sbornik statei*, St. Petersburg, 1911, pp. 1–12.
Popov, Andrei, *Obzor kronografov russkoi redaktsii*, Vyp. I–II, M. 1866–1869. (Reprint, Osnabrück, 1968).
Popov, N. A., *V. N. Tatishchev i ego vremia*, M. 1861.
Poresh, V. Iu., "Biblioteka A. F. Khrushchova (Sobranie preimushchestvenno frantsuzskikh knig)," in A. A. Sidorov & S. P. Luppov, eds., *Kniga v Rossii do serediny XIX veka*, L. 1978, pp. 260–267.
——, "Kniaz' D. M. Golitsyn (verkhovnik) i frantsuzskie knigi ego biblioteki," *Knigopechatanie i knizhnye sobranii v Rossii do serediny XIX v.*, L. 1979, pp. 98–111.
Porter, Roy & Mikulas Teich, eds., *The Enlightenment in National Context*, New York, 1981.
Pososhkov, Ivan, *The Book of Poverty and Wealth*, A. P. Vlasto & L. R. Lewitter, eds., London, 1987.
Pouncy, Carolyn Johnston, "The Origins of the Domostroi. A Study in Manuscript History," *RR*, Vol. 46, No. 4 (Oct., 1987), 357–374.
Preobrazhensky, Alexander, ed., *The Russian Orthodox Church. 10th to 20th Centuries*, M. 1988.
Pritsak, Omeljan, "The Kiev Mohyla Academy in Ukrainian History," *HUS*, Vol. VIII, No. 1/2 (June 1984), 5–8.
Prokof'eva, L. S. & I. S. Sharkova, "O biblioteke Sheremetevykh," *Kniga v Rossii XVI—seredina XIX v. Knigorasprostranenie, biblioteki, chitatel'*, L. 1987, pp. 96–101.
Prokopovic, Feofan, *De Arte Rhetorica Libri X. Kijoviae 1706*, Renate Lachman, ed., Köln/Wien, 1982. =Rhetorica Slavica Band II.
——, *Istoriia imperatora Petra Velikago Ot Rozhdeniia Ego do Poltavskoi batalii . . .*, St. Petersburg, 1773.
——, *Slova i Rechi*, 3 vv. St. Petersburg, 1760–1765.
——, *Sochineniia*, M-L. 1961.
Prüsener, Marlies, "Lesegesellschaften im achtzehnten Jahrhundert. Ein Beitrag zur Lesergeschichte," *AGB*, XIII (1973), 369–594.
Ptashitskii, S. L., "Ivan Fedorov, Moskovskii pervopechatnik. Prebyvanie ego vo L'vove. 1573–1583 gg. Ocherk po arkhivnym materialam," *Rs*, 1884, No. 3, 461–478.
Pumpianskii, L. V., "Lomonosov i nemetskaia shkola razuma," *Russkaia literatura XVII—nachala XIX veka i obshchestvenno-kul'turnom kontekste*, L. 1983, pp. 3–45. =XVIII vek. Sbornik 14.
Pushkarev, L. N., "Kul'turnye sviazi Ukrainy i Rossii posle ikh vossoedineniia (vtoraia polovine XVII v.)," *Istoriia SSSR*, 1979, No. 3 (May–June), 85–95.
Pushkarev, L., "Simeon Polotskii," in Dm. Zhukov & L. Pushkarev, eds., *Russkie pisateli XVII veka*, M. 1972, pp. 197–335.
Raabe, Paul, "Aufklärung durch Bücher," in Paul Raabe & Wilhelm Schmidt-Biggermann, eds., *Aufklärung in Deutschland*, Bonn, 1979, pp. 87–104.
——, "Der Verleger Friedrich Nicolai, ein preussischen Buchhändler der Aufklärung," in his *Bücherlust und Lesefreuden*, Stuttgart, 1984, pp. 141–164.
——, "Die Zeitschrift als Medium der Aufklärung," *WSA*, I (1974), pp. 99–136.
——, "Gelehrtenbibliotheken im Zeitalter der Aufklärung, in Werner Arnold & Peter Vodosek, eds., *Bibliotheken und Aufklärung*, Wiesbaden, 1988, pp. 103–122.

=Wolfenbütteler Schriften zur Geschichte des Buchwesens. 14.

——, "Zum Bild des Verlagswesens in der Spätaufklärung. Dargestelt an Hand von Friedrich Nicolais Lagerkatalog von 1787," in his *Bücherlust und Lesefreuden*, Stuttart, 1984, pp. 66–88.

Rabb, Theodore K., *The Struggle for Stability in Early Modern Europe*, New York, 1975.

Rabil, Albert Jr., ed., *Renaissance Humanism. Foundations, Forms, and Legacy*, 3 vv. Philadelphia, 1988.

Radishchev, Alexander, *A Journey From St. Petersburg to Moscow*, Leo Wiener, trans., Cambridge, Mass., 1958.

——, *Izbrannye filosofskie i obshchestvenno-politicheskie proizvedeniia*, M. 1952.

Raeff, Marc, "On the Heterogeneity of the Eighteenth Century in Russia," in R. P. Bartlett et al., eds., *Russia and the World of the Eighteenth Century*, Columbus, Ohio, 1986, pp. 666–679.

——, *Origins of the Russian Intelligentsia. The Eighteenth-Century Nobility*, New York, 1966.

——, "Perspectives on the 18th Century in Russia," in Eberhard Müller, ed., ". . . aus der anmuthigen Gelehrsamkeit." *Tübinger Studien zum 18. Jahrhundert. Dietrich Geyer zum 60. Geburtstag*, Tübingen, 1988, pp. 169–178.

——, ed., *Russian Intellectual History, an Anthology*, New York, 1966.

——, "Seventeenth-Century Europe in Eighteenth-Century Russia?," *SR*, Vol. 41, No. 4 (Winter, 1982), 611–619.

——, "The Enlightenment in Russia and Russian Thought in the Enlightenment," in John G. Garrard, ed., *The Eighteenth Century in Russia*, Oxford, 1973, pp. 25–47.

——, *The Well-Ordered Police State. Social and Institutional Change through Law in the Germanies and Russia, 1600–1800*, New Haven/London, 1983.

——, "Ukraine and Imperial Russia: Intellectual and Political Encounters from the Seventeenth to the Nineteenth Century," in Peter J. Potichnyj et al. eds., *Ukraine and Russia in Their Historical Encounter*, Edmonton, 1992, pp. 69–85.

——, *Understanding Imperial Russia*, Arthur Goldhammer, trans., New York, 1984.

Rainov, T., *Nauka v Rossii XI–XVII vekov. Ocherki po istorii do nauchnykh i estestvenno-nauchnykh vozzrenii na prirody*, 3 vv. M-L. 1940.

Rammelmeyer, Alfred, *Studien zur Geschichte der russischen Fabel des 18. Jahrhunderts*, Leipzig [1938]. =Veröffentlichungen des Slavischen Instituts an der Friedrich-Wilhelms-Universität Berlin, 21.

Ransel, David L., "Ivan Betskoi and the Institutionalization of the Enlightenment in Russia," *CASS*, Vol. 14, No. 3 (Fall, 1980), 327–338.

Rayfman, Irina, *Vasilii Trediakovsky. The Fool of the 'New' Russian Literature*, Stanford, 1991.

Redston, David, "Kantemir's Translation of Horace," *SGECR*, No. 4 (1976), 7–10.

Reedy, Jeremiah, "Cultural Literacy and the Classics," *CJ*, Vol. 84, No. 1 (Oct.–Nov., 1988), 41–46.

Reinhold, Meyer, *Classica Americana. The Greek and Roman Heritage in the United States*, Detroit, 1984.

——, "Eighteenth-Century American Political Thought," in R. R. Bolger, ed., *Classical Influences on Western Thought A.D. 1650–1870*, Cambridge, 1979, pp. 223–243.

Rexine, John E., "The 350th Anniversary of the Boston Latin School," *CJ*, Vol. 82, No. 2 (Feb–Mar, 1987), 236–241.

Reynolds, Beatrice Kay, ed., *Spokesmen of the French Revolution: Historical Issues, 1790–1794*, New York, 1974.

Rezanov, V. I., *Iz istorii russkoi dramy. Shkol'nye deistva XVII–XVIII vv. i teatr iezuitov*, M. 1910.

Rice, James, L., "The Memoirs of A. T. Bolotov and Russian Literary History," in A. G. Cross, ed., *Russian Literature in the Age of Catherine the Great*, Oxford, 1976, pp. 17–44.

Rice, Tamara Talbot, *Elizabeth Empress of Russia*, New York/Washington, 1970.

Richard, Carl J., *The Founders and the Classics. Greece, Rome, and the American Enlightenment*, Cambridge, 1994.

Richard, John, *A Tour from London to Petersburgh, from thence to Moscow*, London, 1780.
Riedel, Manfred, "Aristoteles-Tradition am Ausgang des 18. Jahrhunderts. Zur ersten deutschen Übersetzung der "Politik" durch Johann Georg Schlosser," *Alteuropa und die Moderne Gesellschaft. Festschrift für Otto Brunner*, Göttingen, 1963, pp. 278–315.
Robel, Gert, "Die Siberienexpeditionen und das deutsche Rußlandbild im 18. Jahrhundert," in Erik Amburger et al., eds., *Wissenschaftpolitik im Mittel- und Osteuropa*, Berlin, 1976, pp. 271–294.
Roberts, C. B., ed., *The Slavonic Calvinist Reading-Primer in Trinity College Dublin Library*, 2 vv. München, 1986–87. =Specimina Philologiae Slavicae Vols. 61 & 71.
Robinson, A. N., "Avtobiografiia Epifaniia," *Issledovaniia i materialy po drevnerusskoi literature*, [1], M. 1961, pp. 101–132.
——, *Bor'ba idei v russkoi literature XVII veka*, M. 1974.
——, "Pervyi russkii teatr kak iavlenie evropeiskoi kul'tury," *Novye cherty v russkoi literature i iskusstve*, M. 1976, pp. 1–18. =Issledovaniia i materialy po drevnerusskoi literature [4].
——, "Zarozhdenie kontseptsii avtorskogo stilia v ukrainskoi i russkoi literaturakh kontsa XVI–XVII veka," *Russkaia literatura na rubezhe dvukh epokh (XVII—nachalo XVIII v.)*, M. 1971, pp. 33–83. =Issledovaniia i materialy po drevnerusskoi literature [3].
Roche, Daniel, "Noblesses et culture dans la France du XVIIIe: les lectures de la Noblesse," *Buch und Sammler. Private und öffentliche Bibliotheken im 18. Jahrhundert*, Heidelberg, 1979, pp. 9–28. =Beiträge zur Geschichte der Literatur und Kunst des 18. Jahrhunderts. Band 3.
[Rogov, A. N.], "Shkola i prosveshchenie," "Knigopechatanie," *Ocherki russkoi kul'tury XVII veka*. Vol. II, M. 1979, pp. 142–154, 155–169.
Rosenberg, Karen, "The Quarrel between Ancients and Moderns in Russia," in A. G. Cross, ed., *Russia and the West in the Eighteenth Century*, Newtonville, Mass., 1983, pp. 196–205.
Rosenfeld, Günter, "Justus Samuel Scharschmid und seine Bedeutung für die deutsche Rußlandkunde am Anfang des 18. Jahrhunderts," *Zeitschrift für Geschichtswissenschaft*, Vol. II, No. 6 (1954), 866–902.
Rosenthal, Bernice Glatzer & Martha Bohachevsky-Chomiak, eds., *A Revolution of the Spirit. Crisis of Value in Russia 1890–1924*, New York, 1990.
Rothe, Hans, *Religion und Kultur in den Regionen des russischen Reiches in 18. Jahrhundert. Erster Versuch einer Grundlegung*, Opladen, 1984. =Rheinisch-Westfälische Akademie der Wissenschaften. Geisteswissenschaften Vorträge. G. 267.
——, "Zur Frage von Einflüssen in der russischen Literatur des 18. Jhs.," *ZSP*, Vol. XXXIII, No. 1 (1967), 21–68.
Rozhdestvenskii, S. V., *Ocherki po istorii sistem narodnago prosveshcheniia v Rossii v XVIII–XIX vekakh*, I, St. Petersburg, 1912. =Zapiski istoriko-filologicheskago fakul'teta imp. S.-Peterburgskago universiteta, No. 104.
Rozov, N. N., "Chitateli russkoi knigi pervykh vekov ee sushchestvovaniia i ikh izuchenie," *Trudy: Leningradskii gos.-yi institut kul'tury im. N. K. Krupskoi. XXV. Istoriia russkogo chitatelia*, Vyp. 1, L. 1973, pp. 20–36.
——, "Iz istorii kirillo-belozerskoi biblioteki," *Trudy gosudarstvennoi publichnoi biblioteki imeni M. E. Saltykova-Shchedrina*, Vol. IX (12) (1961), 177–188.
——, *Kniga drevnei rusi XI–XIV vv.*, M. 1977.
——, *Kniga v Rossii v XV veke*, L. 1981.
——, "K opredeleniiu poniatiia "kniga" v istoricheskom aspekte (po russkim materialam XI–XIV vv.)," *Rukopisnaia i pechatnaia kniga*, M. 1975, pp. 11–19.
——, "Nekotorye problemy izucheniia istorii knigi i bibliotechnogo dela v drevnei Rusi," *Trudy gosudarstvennoi publichnoi biblioteki im. M. E. Saltykova-Shchedrina*, Vol. X (13) (1962), 153–160.
——, "O kul'turno-istoricheskom znachenii rukopisnoi knigi posle vvedeniia

knigopechataniia v Rossii," *Russkie knigi i biblioteki v XVI—pervoi polovine XIX veka*, L. 1983, pp. 13–22.

——, "Russkie biblioteki XV v. i ikh chitateli," *Russkie biblioteki i ikh chitatel'*, L. 1983, pp. 51–59.

——, "Solovetskaia biblioteka i ee osnovatel' igumen Dosifei," *Todl*, Vol. XVIII (1962), 294–304.

Ruppert, Hans, *Goethes Bibliothek. Katalog*, Weimar, 1958.

Russkaia literatura i fol'klor (XI–XVIII vv.), L. 1970.

Russko-angliiskii literaturnye sviazi (XVIII vek—pervaia polovina XIX veka), M. 1982. =Literaturnoe nasledstvo, Vol. 91.

Russko-belorusskie sviazi vo vtoroi polovine XVII v. (1667–1686 gg.). Sbornik dokumentov, Minsk, 1972.

Rutledge, Harry C., "Greece and Rome in the Twentieth Century: Observations on the Classical Tradition and Modernization," *CJ*, Vol. 78, No. 2 (Dec–Jan, 1983), 143–149.

Rykov, Aleksandr, *Rukovodstvo, vedushchee k udobnomu izucheniiu Rossiiskago chistopisaniia*, St. Petersburg, 1782.

Sacharov, A. M., "Über den Kampf gegen das "Lateinertum" in Rußland am Ende des 15. und zu Beginn des 16. Jahrhunderts," in W. Steinitz et al., eds., *Ost und West in der Geschichte des Denkens und der kulturellen Beziehungen*, Berlin, 1966, pp. 92–105.

Sakulin, P. N., *Istoriia novoi russkoi literatury. Epokha klassitsizma*, M. 1918.

Sapunov, B. V., "Antichnaia literatura v russkikh bibliotekakh XVII v. i moskovskoe barokko," *Russkie biblioteki i ikh chitatel'*, L. 1983, pp. 70–80.

——, "Ivan Fedorov i Renessans na zemliakh iugo-zapadnoi Rusi," *Kniga i knigotorgovlia v Rossii v XVI–XVIII vv.*, L. 1984, pp. 27–35.

——, "Izmenenie sootnoshenii rukopisnykh i pechatnykh knig v russkikh bibliotekakh XVI–XVIII vv.," *Rukopisnaia i pechatnaia kniga*, M. 1975, pp. 37–50.

——, "Kniga i chitatel' na Rusi v XVII v.," in A. A. Sidorov & S. P. Luppov, eds., *Kniga v Rossii do serediny XIX veka*, L. 1978, pp. 61–74.

——, "Sotsial'naia baza moskovskogo barokko," *Kniga i ee rasprostranenie v Rossii v XVI–XVIII vv.*, L. 1985, pp. 59–78.

——, "Ukrainskaia kniga v Rossii v XVII v. (Iz istorii russko-ukrainskikh kul'turnykh sviazei)," *Istoriia knigi i izdatel'skogo dela. Sbornik nauchnykh trudov*, L. 1977, pp. 5–21.

Sauder, Gerhard, "Die Bücher des Armen Mannes und der Moralischen Gesellschaft im Toggenburg," *Buch und Sammler. Private und öffentliche Bibliotheken im 18. Jahrhundert*, Heidelberg, 1979, pp. 167–186.

Saunders, David, *The Ukrainian Impact on Russian Culture 1750–1850*, Edmonton, 1985.

(Savel'eva, E. A.), *Biblioteka Ia. V. Briusa. Katalog*, L. 1989.

Savel'eva, E. A., "Biblioteka Ia. V. Briusa v sobranii BAN SSSR," *Russkie biblioteki i ikh chitatel'*, L. 1983, pp. 123–134.

——, "Izdatel'stvo Plantena v XVI–XVII vv.," *Sbornik statei i materialov Biblioteki AN SSSR po knigovedeniiu*, III, L. 1973, pp. 408–422.

——, "Perevodnye istoricheskie trudy v Rossii v pervoi polovine XVIII v.," *Rukopisnaia i pechatnaia kniga v Rossii. Problemy sozdaniia i rasprostraneniia*, L. 1988, pp. 118–130.

Savel'eva, L. I., *Antichnost' v russkoi poezii kontsa XVIII—nachala XIX veka*, Kazan', 1980.

Saverkina, I. V., "K istorii biblioteki A. D. Menshikova," *Kniga v Rossii XVII—seredina XIX v. Knigorasprostranenie, biblioteki, chitatel'*, L. 1987, pp. 37–45.

—— & V. A. Somov, "Reestr knig A. D. Menshikova," *Kniga v Rossii v epokhu prosveshcheniia*, L. 1988, pp. 145–160.

Sazonova, L. I., "Ot basni barokko k basne klassitsizma," *Razvitie Barokko i zarozhdenie Klassitsizma v Rossii XVII—nachala XVIII v.*, M. 1989, pp. 118–148.

——, *Poeziia russkogo barokko (vtoraia polovina XVII—nachalo XVIII v.)*, M. 1991.

Schama, Simon, *Citizens. A Chronicle of the French Revolution*, New York, 1989.

Schamschula, Walter, "Zu dem Quellen von Lomonosovs 'kosmologischer' Lyrik," *ZSP*, Vol. XXXIV, No. 2 (1969), 225–253.

Scharf, Claus, "La Princesse de Zerbst Catherinisée": Deutschlandbild und Deutschlandpolitik Katharinas II," in Dagmar Herrmann, ed., *Deutsche und Deutschland aus russischer Sicht. 18. Jahrhundert: Aufklärung*, München, 1992, pp. 271–340.

Shcherbatov, M. M., *On the Corruption of Morals in Russia*, A. Lentin, trans., Cambridge, 1969.

Schenda, Rudolf, *Volk ohne Buch. Studien zur Sozialgeschichte der populären Lesestoffe 1770–1910*, Frankfurt am Main, 1970. =Studien zur Philosophie und Literatur des neunzehnten Jahrhunderts, 30/11.

Schibli, Roland, *Die altesten russischen Zeitungsübersetzungen (Vesti-Kuranty), 1600–1650. Quellenkunde, Lehnwortschatz und Toponomastik*, Bern, 1988.

Schlafly, Daniel L., "The Popular Image of the West in Russia at the Time of Peter the Great," in R. P. Bartlett, et al., eds., *Russia and the World of the Eighteenth Century*, Columbus, Ohio, 1986, pp. 2–21.

[Schlözer, A. L.], ed., *Neuerändertes Rußland oder Leben Catharina der Zweyten Kayserinn von Rußland aus authentischen Nachrichten Geschrieben*, Riga/Leipzig, 1767.

——, ed., *M. Johann Joseph Haigolds Beylagen zum Neuerändeten Rußland*, Riga/Leipzig, 1770.

Schmidt, Horst, "Die russische Literatur der Aufklärung (1650–1825)," *ZS*, Vol. 30, No. 4 (1985), 602–608.

——, ed., *Die russische Literatur der Aufklärung (1650–1825)*, Halle (Saale) 1985. = Wissenschaftliche Beiträge 1985/53. =Beiträge zur Geschichte der UdSSR No. 13.

Scholder, Klaus, "Grundzüge der theologischen Aufklärung in Deutschland. Unterschiedlicher Charakter der Aufklärung in Deutschland und Westeuropa," *Geist und Geschichte der Reformation. Festschrift für Hanns Rükkert*, Berlin, 1966, pp. 460–486. =Arbeiten Zur Kirchengeschichte, Band. 38.

Schütz, Werner, "Die Kanzel als Katheder der Aufklärung," *WSA*, I (1974), 137–171.

Scott, H. M., "Reform in the Hapsburg Monarchy, 1740–1790," in H. M. Scott, ed., *Enlightened Absolutism. Reform and Reformers in Later Eighteenth-Century Europe*, London, 1990, pp. 145–188.

Segel, Harold B., "Baroque and Rococo in Eighteenth Century Russian Literature," *CSP*, Vol. XV, No. 4 (1973), 556–566.

——, "Classicism and Classical Antiquity in Eighteenth- and Early Nineteenth-Century Russian Literature," in J. G. Garrard, ed., *The Eighteeth Century in Russia*, Oxford, 1973, pp. 48–71.

Selle, Götz, ed., *Die Matrikel der Georg-August-Universität zu Göttingen 1734–1837*, Hildesheim/Leipzig, 1937.

Semennikov, V. P., *Knigoizdatel'skaia deiatel'nost' N. I. Novikova i tipograficheskoi kompanii*, St. Petersburg, 1921.

——, *Sobranie stariushcheesia o perevode inostrannykh knig, uchrezhdennoe Ekaterinoi II. 1768–1783 g.g. Istoriko-literaturnoe izsledovanie*, St. Petersburg, 1913.

Serman, Il'ia Z., "Lomonosovs Oden und die Poetik des Schuldramas," *Slavische Barockliteratur II. Gedankschrift für Dmitrij Tschizewskij 1894–1977*, München, 1983, pp. 129–141. =Forum Slavicum 54.

——, *Mikhail Lomonosov. Life and Poetry*, Jerusalem, 1988.

——, *Russkii klassitsizm. (Poeziia, Drama. Satira)*, L. 1973.

Setin, F. I., "'Bukvari' Simeon Polotskogo v riadu drevnerusskikh uchebnikov XVI–XVII vv.," in A. N. Robinson, ed., *Simeon Polotskii i ego kniznoizdatel'skaia deiatel'nost'*, M. 1982, pp 93–104.

——, ed., *Russkaia detskaia literatura*, M. 1972.

Sevcenko, Ihor, "The Many Worlds of Peter Mohyla," *HUS*, Vol. VIII, No. 1/2 (June, 1984), 9–44.

Scharf, Claus, "'La Princesse de Zerst Catherinisée.' Deutschlandbild und Deutschlandpolitik Katharinas II," in Dagmann Herrmann, ed., *Deutsche und Deutschland aus russischer Sicht. 18. Jahrhundert: Aufklärung*, München, 1992, pp. 271–340.

Shatz, Marshall S., trans., "'Evgenii Onegin and His Ancestors' by V. O. Kliuchevskii," *CASS*, Vol. 16, No. 2 (Summer, 1982), 227–246.

——, trans., "'Western Influences in Russia after Peter the Great' by V. O. Kliuchevskii," *CASS*, Vol. 20, No. 3/4 (Fall-Winter, 1986), 467–84, Vol. 24, No. 4 (Winter, 1990), 431–55.

Shchepkina, E., "Populiarnaia literatura v seredine XVIII v. (Po zapiskam Bolotova)," *ZMnp*, Vol. 244 (Apr. 1886), Otd. 2, 238–276.

Shcherbatov, Prince M. M., *On the Corruption of Morals in Russia*, A. Lentin, trans., Cambridge, 1969.

Shliapkin, I. A., *Sv. Dmitrii Rostovskii i ego vremia (1651–1709 gg.)*, St. Petersburg, 1891. =Zapiski Istoriko-filologicheskago fakul'teta imp. S.-Peterburgskago universiteta, Vol. XXIV.

Sholom, F. A., "Prosvetitel'skie idei v ukrainskom literature serediny XVIII veka," *Problemy russkogo prosveshcheniia v literature XVIII veka*, M-L. 1961, pp. 45–62.

Shtrange, M. M., *Demokraticheskaia intelligentsiia v Rossii v XVIII veke*, M. 1965.

——, "'Entsiklopediia' Didro i ee russkie perevodchiki," *Frantsuzskii ezhegodnik 1959*, M. 1961, pp. 76–88.

Silbajoris, R., *Russian Versification. The Theories of Trediakovsky, Lomonosov, and Kantemir*, New York/London, 1958.

Simeon Polotskii i ego knigoizdatel'skaia deiatel'nost', M. 1982. =Russkaia staropechatnaia literatura (XVI—pervaia chetvert' XVIII v.) 3.

Simonov, P. A., "Predystoriia rukopisnoi i pechatnoi russkoi matematicheskoi knigi (drevnerusskii uchebno-matematicheskii 'fol'klor' i 'posobiia' tablichnogo tipa," *Rukopisnaia i pechatnaia kniga*, M. 1975, pp. 205–212.

Siromakha, V. G., "Nikonovskaia knizhnaia spravka v iazykovom vospriiatii staroobriadtsev vtoroi poloviny XVII v.," *Izvestiia Akademii nauk SSSR. Seriia literatury i iazyke*, Vol. 45, No. 5 (1986), 445–451.

Sitnikov, L. A., "Zapadnoevropeiskaia kniga v Sibirii vo vtoroi polovine XVIII veka," *Kniga v Sibiri XVII—nachala XX vv.*, Novosibirsk, 1980, pp. 78–98 & 9 pp. prilozhenie.

Sivkov, K. V., "Chastnye pansiony i shkoly Moskvy v 80-kh godakh XVIII v.," *Ia*, Vol. VI (1951), 315–323.

Slovar' knizhnikov i knizhnosti drevnei Rusi, 2 vols. L. 1988, 1989.

Slukhovskii, M. I., *Bibliotechnoe delo v Rossii do XVIII veka. Istorii knizhnogo prosveshcheniia*, M. 1968.

——, *Iz istorii knizhnoi kul'tury Rossii. Starorusskaia knigi v mezhdunarodnykh kul'turnykh sviaziakh*, M. 1964.

——, *Russkaia biblioteka XVI–XVII vv.*, M. 1973.

Smagina, G. I., "Iz istorii narodnogo obrazovaniia i rasprostraneniia uchebnoi literatury v Latvii vo vtoroi polovine XVIII veka," *Kniga v Rossii XVII—nachala XIX v. Problemy sozdaniia i rasprostraneniia*, L. 1989, pp. 93–98.

——, "Iz istorii sozdaniia i rasprostraneniia uchebnykh knig v Rossii vo vtoroi polovine XVIII v.," *Kniga v Rossii XVI—seredina XIX v. Knigorasprostranenie, biblioteki, chitatel'*, L. 1987, pp. 71–78.

Smirnov, N., "K voprosu o pedagogike v Moskovskoi Rusi XVII st.," *Russkii Filologicheskii Vestnik* (Warsaw), Vol. XXXIX, No. 1–2 (1898), 8–36.

Smirnov, V. I. & E. S. Kuliabko, *Mikhail Sofronov. Russkii matematik serediny XVIII veka*, M-L. 1954.

Smith, G. S., "The Most Proximate West: Russian Poets and the German Academicians 1728–41," in R. P. Bartlett et al., eds., *Russia and the World of the Eighteenth Century*, Columbus, Ohio, 1986, pp. 360–370.

——, "The Reform of Russian Versification: What More is There to Say?," *SGECR*, No. 5 (1977), 39–44.

Smith, Preserved, *Origins of Modern Culture 1543–1687*, New York, 1962 (orig. 1934).

Smotrit'skii, Meletii, *Gramatika*, 2 vv. V. V. Nimchuka, ed., Kiev, 1979.

Sobolevskii, A. I., *Perevodnaia literatura Moskovskoi Rusi XIV –XVII vekov*, St. Petersburg, 1903.

Sobornoe Ulozhenie 1649 goda, L. 1987. Also, *The Muscovite Law Code (Ulozhenie) of 1649. Part 1. Text and Translation*, Richard Hellie, trans., Irvine, Cal., 1988; *Das Sobornoe Ulozhenie von 1649*, Halle-Wittenberg, 2 vv. 1985–87. =Beiträge Zur Geschichte der UdSSR, No. 9, 10.

Somov, V. A., "Frantsuzskaia 'Rossika' epokhi Prosveshcheniia i tsarskoe pravitel'stvo (1760-e–1820-e gg.)." *Russkie knigi i biblioteki v XVI—pervoi polovine XIX veka*, L. 1983, pp. 105–120.

—— & M. I. Fundamenskii, "Biblioteka Akademii nauk—dostoprimechatel'nost' Peterburga XVIII v.," *Kniga v Rossii XVIII—serediny XIX v. Iz istorii Biblioteki Akademii nauk*, L. 1989, pp. 13–41.

Sparn, Walter, "Vernünftiges Christentum. Über die geschichtliche Aufgabe der theologischen Aufklärung im 18. Jahrhundert in Deutschland," in Rudolf Vierhaus, ed., *Wissenschaften im Zeitalter der Aufklärung*, Göttingen, 1985, pp. 18–57.

Spernaskii, M. N., "Odin iz istochnikov Triiazichnogo leksikona" Fedorova Polikarpova—rukopisnyi belorussko-latinsko-pol'skii slovar' XVII v.," in his *Iz istorii russko-slavianskikh literaturnykh sviazei*, M. 1960, pp. 198–210.

——, *Rukopisnye sborniki XVIII veka. Materialy dlia istorii russkoi literatury XVIII veka*, M. 1983.

Stahlin, Karl, *Geschichte Russlands von den Anfängen bis zur Gegenwart*, II, Graz, 1961. (Orig, Berlin, 1930).

Startsev, A., *Universitetskie gody Radishcheva*, M. 1956.

Stennik, Iu. V., *Russkaia satira XVIII veka*, L. 1985.

Stieff, Christian, "Relation von dem gegenwärtigen Zustande des Moscowitschen Reichs," in Mechthild Keller, ed., *Russen und Rußland aus deutscher Sicht. 18. Jahrhundert: Aufklärung*, München, 1987, pp. 85–108. =West-Östliche Spiegelungen, Reihe A. Band 2.

Stoeffler, F. Ernest, *German Pietism During the Eighteenth Century*, Leiden, 1973.

——, *The Rise of Evangelical Pietism*, Leiden, 1965.

Stökl, Günther, "Das Echo von Renaissance und Reformation im Moskauer Rußland," *JfGO*, Vol. 7 (1959), 413–430.

——, *Russische Geschichte von den Anfangen bis zur Gegenwart*, Stuttgart, 1962.

Stupperich, Robert, "Die kirchlichen Beziehungen zwischen West und Ost im Zeitalter Peters I," *Miscellanien Historiae Ecclesiasticae*, IV (1972), 113–130.

Subtelny, Orest, *Ukraine. A History*, Toronto, 1988.

[Sul'tser] [Sulzer, Johann George], *O poleznom s iunoshestvom chtenii drevnikh klassicheskikh pisatelei*, St. Petersburg, 1774.

Svetlov, L. B., *Izdatel'skaia deiatel'nost' N. I. Novikova*, L. 1946.

——, "'Obshchestvo liubitelei rossiiskoi uchenosti' pri Moskovskom universitete," *Ia*, Vol. V (1950), 302–322.

——, "Russkie perevody proizvedenii frantsuzskikh prosvetitelei," *Frantsuzskii ezhegodnik 1962*, M. 1963, pp. 421–441.

Sydorenko, Alexander, *The Kievan Academy in the Seventeenth Century*, Ottawa, 1977.

Syromiatnikov, B. I., *"Reguliarnoe" gosudarstvo Petra Pervogo i ego ideologiia*, Chast' I, M-L. 1943.

Sysyn, Frank E., "Concepts of Nationhood in Ukrainian History Writing, 1620–1690," *HUS*, Vol. X, No. 3–4 (Dec., 1986), 393–423.

——, "Peter Mohyla and the Kiev Academy in Recent Western Works: Divergent Views on Seventeenth-Century Ukrainian Culture," *HUS*, Vol. VIII, No. 1/2 (June, 1984), 155–187.

Tatarintsev, A. G., "Biblioteka R. M. Tsebrikova," *Russkie biblioteki i chastnye knizhnye sobraniia XVI–XIX vekov*, L. 1979, pp. 5–12.

Tatarskii, Ierofei, *Simeon Polotskii (ego zhizn' i deiatel'nost')*, M. 1886.
Tatishchev, V. N., *Izbrannye proizvedeniia*, L. 1979.
Ternovskii, A. V., *Detskaia literatura*, M. 1977.
Tetzner, J., "Bücher deutscher Autoren in Prokopovics Bibliothek," in E. Winter, et al., eds., *Die deutsch-russische Begegnung und Leonhard Euler*, Berlin, 1958, pp. 124–142.
Thaden, Edward C., "V. N. Tatishchev, German Historians, and the St. Petersburg Academy of Sciences," *RH*, Vol. 13, No. 4 (Winter, 1986), 367–398.
Tiemann, Barbara, "Die Butenbach-Bibliothek in der Reformierten Kirche zu Lübeck. Der Sammler und seine Sammlung," *Zeitschrift des Vereins für Lübeckische Geschichte und Altertumskunde*, Vol. 65 (1985), 143–221.
Tikhomirov, M. N., "Moskva i kul'turnoe razvitie russkogo naroda v XIV–XVII vv.," in his *Russkaia kul'tura X–XVIII vekov*, M. 1968. pp. 255–276 (orig. 1947).
——, "Nachalo knigopechataniia v Rossii," in his *Russkaia kul'tura X–XVIII vekov*, M. 1968, pp. 292–320 (orig. 1940).
——, "O biblioteke moskovskikh tsarei (Legendy i deistvitel'nost')," in his *Russkaia kul'tura X–XVIII vekov*, M. 1968, pp. 281–291 (orig. 1960).
Titov, F., *Materialy dlja istorii knyznoi spravky na Ukraini v XVI–XVIII vv.*, Kiev, 1924. (reprint, Köln/Wien, 1982). =Bausteine zur Geschichte der Literatur bei den Slaven, 16.
Tiulichev, D. V., "Klassifikatsionno-statisticheskii analiz akademicheskikh izdanii 1747–1753 gg. kak metod izucheniia russkoi kul'tury serediny XVIII v. (Po novym materialam)," *Sbornik statei i materialov Biblioteki AN SSSR po knigovedeniiu*, III, L. 1973, pp. 299–318.
——, *Knigoizdatel'skaia deiatel'nost' Peterburgskoi Akademii nauk i M. V. Lomonosov*, L. 1988.
——, "Knizhnaia torgovlia Peterburgskoi Akademii nauk v seredine XVIII veka (tematiko-otraslevye i obshchie kolichestvennye kharakteristiki," *Kniga v Rossii XVIII—nachala XIX v. Problemy sozdaniia i rosprostraneniia*, L. 1989, pp. 21–36.
——, "Prodazha v Moskve izdanii Peterburgskoi Akademii nauk v nachale 60-kh gg. XVIII veka," *Russkie knigi i biblioteki v XVI—pervoi polovine XIX veka*, L. 1983, pp. 85–104.
——, "Tsenzura izdanii Akademii nauk v XVIII v.," *Sbornik statei i materialov Biblioteki AN SSSR po knigovedeniiu*, II, L. 1970, pp. 71–114.
Tolstoi, D. A., *Akademicheskaia gimnasiia v XVIII stoletii, po rukopismym dokumentam arkhiva Akademii Nauk*, St. Petersburg, 1885.
——, "Gorodskie uchilishcha v tsarstvovaniie Ekateriny II," *ZIAn*, Vol. 41 (1886), Prilozhenie, 1–213.
Tolstoi, P. "Putevoi Dnevnik P. A. Tolstago," *Russkii arkhiv*, 1888, xxvi, T. 1, pp. 161–204, 321–68, 505–52; T. II, pp. 5–62, 113–56, 225–64. *The Travel Diary of Peter Tolstoi, A Muscovite in Early-Modern Europe*, Max J. Okenfuss, trans., DeKalb, IL, 1987. L. A. Ol'shevskaia and S. N. Travnikov, eds., *Puteshestvie stol'nika P. A. Tolstogo po Evrope 1697–1699*, M. 1992.
Tolstoy, Nikolai, *The Tolstoys. Twenty-Four Generations of Russian History 1353–1983*, New York, 1983.
Tooke, W., *History of Russia*, 3 vv. London, 1800.
Torke, Hans-Joachim, *Die staatsbedingte Gesellschaft im Moskauer Reich. Zar und Zemlja in der altrussischen Herrschaftsverfassung 1613–1689*, Leiden, 1974. =Studien zur Geschichte Osteuropas XVII.
——, "The History of Pre-Revolutionary Russia in the Current Debate of Soviet Historians," in Takayaki Ito, ed., *Facing Up to the Past. Soviet Historiography under Perestroika*, Sapporo, Japan, 1989, pp. 97–109.
——, "The Unloved Alliance: Political Relations between Muscovy and Ukraine in the Seventeenth Century," in Peter J. Potichnyj et al. eds., *Ukraine and Russia in Their Historical Encounter*, Edmonton, 1992, pp.
Treadgold, Donald W., *The West in Russia and China. Vol. I, Russia 1472–1917*, Cambridge, 1973.

Trofimova, N. S. & P. I. Khoteev, "Katalog biblioteki P. P. Shafirova," *Kniga v Rossii v epokhu prosveshcheniia*, L. 1988. pp. 161–168.

Tschizewskij, Dmitrij, "Das Barock in der russischen Literatur," *Slavische Barockliteratur*, I, München, 1970, pp. 9–39. =Forum Slavicum, 23. [see also Cizevskij].

——, *Skovoroda. Dichter, Denker, Mystiker*, München, 1974. =Harvard Series in Ukrainian Studies Vol. 18.

Tuck, Richard, "Humanism and Political Thought," in Anthony Goodman and Angus Mackay, eds., *The Impact of Humanism on Western Europe*, London/New York, 1988, pp. 43–65.

Tukalevskii, Vl., "Glavnyia cherty mirosozertsaniia Lomonosova (Leibniz i Lomonosov)," in V. V. Sipovskii, ed., *1711–1911. M. V. Lomonosov. Sbornik statei*, St. Petersburg, 1911, pp. 13–32.

Tvorogov, O. V., *Drevne-russkie khronografy*, L. 1975.

Unbegaun, B. O., "Lomonosov und Luther," *ZSP*, Vol. XXXVII, No. 1 (1973), 159–174.

Undol'skii, V. M., "Biblioteka Pavla, mitropolita Sarskogo i Podonskogo, i knigi i imushchestvo Epifaniia Slavinetskogo," *Vremenik Moskovskogo obshchestvo istorii i drevnosti rossiiskikh*, 1850, Kn. 5, Otd. 3, 65–83.

Uspenskij, Boris A. & Victor M. Zivov, "Zur Spezifik des Barock in Rußland. Der Verfahren der Äquivokation in der russischen Poesie des 18. Jahrhunderts," *Slavische Barockliteratur*. *II. Gedenkschrift für Dmitrij Tschizewskij (1894–1977)*, München, 1983, pp. 25–56. =Forum Slavicum. 54.

Valitskaia, A. P., *Russkaia estetika XVIII veka. Istoriko-problemnyi ocherk prosvetitel'skoi mysli*, M. 1983.

Valkina, I. V., "K voprosu ob istochnikakh Tatishcheva," *Rol' i znachenie literatury XVIII veka v istorii russkoi kul'tury*, L. 1966, pp. 74–85. =XVIII vek. Sbornik 7.

Vasetsky, G., *Lomonosov's Philosophy*, M. 1968.

"Vedomost', chto po opisi iavilos' v dome . . . Iakova Vilemovicha Briusa v biblioteke knig nemetskikh raznykh dialektov i rossiiskikh . . . ," *Materialy dlia istorii Imperatorskoi Akademii nauk. Vol. 5 (1742–1743)*, St. Petersburg, 1889, pp. 152–245.

Venturi, Franco, *Utopia and Reform in the Enlightenment*, Cambridge, 1971.

Verkhovskoi, P. V., "Biblioteka Feofana Prokopovicha," *Uchrezhdenie dukhovnoi kollegii i dukhovnyi reglament*, Rostov na Donu, 1916, Vol. II, Otdel 5-yi, pp. 3–71.

Vernadskii, George, *The Tsardom of Moscow 1547–1682*, 2 parts, New Haven/London, 1969.

Vierhaus, Rudolf, "Aufklärung als Lernprozeß," in his *Deutschland im 18. Jahrhundert*, Göttingen, 1987, pp. 84–95.

——, "Kulturelles Leben im Zeitalter des Absolutismus in Deutschland," in Ulrich Herrmann, ed., *"Die Bildung des Bürgers." Die Formierung der bürgerlichen Gesellschaft und die Gebildeten im 18. Jahrhundert*, Weinheim/Basel, 1982, pp. 11–37.

Vladimirskii-Budanov, M., "Iz istorii nashego prosveshcheniia. Pervaia gimnasiia v Rossii," *Pedagogicheskii Musei*, 1878, No. 1, 17–27, No. 2, 91–112, No. 3, 183–194.

Vomperskii, V. P., *Ritoriki v Rossii XVII–XVIII vv.*, M. 1988.

Voronov, A., *Fedor Ivanovich Iankovich de-Mirievo ili narodnyia uchilishcha v Rossii pri imperatritse Ekaterine II-i*, St. Petersburg, 1858.

Vucinich, Alexander, *Science in Russian Culture. A History to 1860*, London, 1963.

Wade, Ira O., *The Intellectual Development of Voltaire*, Princeton, 1969.

Watson, Foster, *The Beginnings of the Teaching of Modern Subjects in England*, London, 1909.

Waugh, Daniel Clarke, "The Library of Aleksei Mikhailovich," *FzoG*, Vol. 38 (1986), 299–324.

——, "The Unsolved Problem of Tsar Ivan IV's Library," *RH*, Vol. 14, No. 1–4 (1987), pp. 395–408.

Weber, Friedrich Christian, *The Present State of Russia*, London, 1723. (reprint 1969).

Weiss, Anton, ed., "Die allgemeine Schulordnung der Kaiserin Maria Theresia und J. J. Felbigers Forderungen an Schulmeister und Lehrer," *Neudrucke Pädagogischer Schriften*, Vol. XV (1896), 1–79.

Weltin, E. G., *Athens and Jerusalem. An Interpretative Essay on Christianity and Classical Culture*, Atlanta, 1988. =American Academy of Religion Studies in Religion, No. 49.

Wes, Marinus A., *Classics in Russia 1700–1855. Between Two Bronze Horsemen*, Leiden/New York/Köln, 1992. =Brill's Studies in Intellectual History, Vol. 33.

Whittaker, Cynthia H., *The Origins of Modern Russian Education. An Intellectual Biography of Count Sergei Uvarov, 1786–1855*, DeKalb, 1984.

Wiegand, Günther, "Rußland im Urteil des Aufklärers Christoph Schmidt genannt Phiseldek," in Erna Lesky, et al., eds., *Die Aufklärung in Ost- und Südosteuropa*, Köln/Wien, 1972, pp. 50–86.

Winter, Eduard, ed., *August Ludwig v. Schlözer und Russland*, Berlin, 1961.

——, *Byzanz und Rom im Kampf um die Ukraine 955–1939*, Leipzig, 1942.

——, "Die Aufklärung bei den slawischen Völkern und die deutsche Aufklärung," *ZS*, Vol. II, No. 2 (1957), 153–162.

——, "Die Aufklärung in der Literaturgeschichte der slawischen Völker," *Sbornik Slavianskaia filologiia*, III, M-L. 1958, 283–294.

——, "Die Jesuiten in Russland (1772 bis 1820). Ein Beitrag zur Auseinandersetzung zwischen Aufklärung und Restauration," *Forschen und Wirken. Festschrift zur 150-Jahr-Feier der Humboldt-Universität zu Berlin 1810–1960*, III, Berlin, 1960, 167–191.

——, "Euler und die Begegnung der deutschen mit der russischen Aufklärung," in E. Winter et al., eds., *Die deutsch-russische Begegnung und Leonhard Euler*, Berlin, 1958, pp. 1–18.

——, "Feofan Prokopovich i nachalo russkogo prosveshcheniia," *Rol' i znachenie literatury XVIII veka v istorii russkoi kul'tury*, M-L. 1966, pp. 43–46. =XVIII vek. Sbornik 7.

——, *Frühaufklärung. Der Kampf gegen den Konfessionalismus in Mittel- und Osteuropa und die deutsch-slawische Begegnung*, Berlin, 1966. =Beiträge zur Geschichte des religiosen und wissenschaftlichen Denkens, Band. 6.

——, *Halle als Ausgangspunkt der deutschen Russlandkunde im 18. Jahrhundert*, Berlin, 1953.

—— et al, eds., *Lomonosov Schlözer Pallas*, Berlin, 1962.

——, *Rußland und das Papstum*, 2 vv. Berlin, 1959–61. =Quellen und Studien zur Geschichte Osteuropas, Vol. VI.

——, "Zum geistigen Profil Feofan Prokopovics," in Helmut Grasshoff & Ulf Lehmann, eds., *Studien zur Geschichte der russischen Literatur des 18. Jahrhunderts*, I, Berlin, 1968, pp. 24–28.

Wittmann, Reinhard, "Der lesende Landmann. Zur Rezeption aufklärischer Bemühungen durch die bäuerliche Bevölkerung im 18. Jahrhundert," in Dan Berindei, et al., eds., *Der Bauer Mittel- und Osteuropas in sozio-ökonomischen Wandel des 18. und 19. Jahrhunderts*, Köln/Wien, 1973, pp. 142–196.

——, "Die frühen Buchhändlerzeitschriften als Spiegel des literarischen Lebens," *AGB*, XIII (1973), 613–931.

——, "Soziale und ökonomische Voraussetzungen des Buch- und Verlagswesens in der zweiten Häfte des 18. Jahrhunderts, in Herbert G. Göpfert et al. eds., *Buch- und Verlagswesen im 18. und 19. Jahrhundert*, Berlin, 1977, pp. 5–27.

Wolff, Christian, *Vernünftige Gedancken von dem gesellschaftlichen Leben der Menschen*, Leibzig, 1721.

Wynar, Lubomyr, *History of Early Ukrainian Printing 1491–1600*, Denver, 1962. =Studies in Librarianship, University of Denver Graduate School of Librarianship, Vol. 1, No. 2.

Zabelin, Ivan, *Domashnyi byt russkikh tsarei v XVI–XVII st.*, 2 vv. 3rd ed., M. 1895.

Zaitseva, A. A., "Assortment knizhnoi lavki Akademii nauk v kontse XVIII v.," *Kniga i knigotorgovlia v Rossii v XVI–XVIII vv.*, L. 1984, pp. 140–167.

——, "Inostrannye knigotorgovtsy v S.-Peterburge v kontse XVIII—nachale XIX v.," *Knigotorgovoe i bibliotechnoe delo v Rossii v XVII—pervoi polovine XIX v.*, L. 1981, pp. 29–51.

——, "K 15-letiiu nauchno-issledovatel'skogo otdela istorii knigi Biblioteki Akademii nauk SSSR," *Kniga v Rossii XVIII—serediny XIX v. Iz istorii Biblioteki Akademii nauk*, L. 1989, pp. 5–12.

——, "Novye materialy o russkikh knizhnykh lavkakh v S.-Peterburge v kontse XVIII—nachale XIX v.," *Knizhnoe delo v Rossii v XVI–XIX vekakh*, L. 1980, pp. 116–43.

Zarubin, N. N., comp., *Biblioteka Ivana Groznogo. Rekonstruktsiia i bibliograficheskoe opisanie*, L. 1982.

Zenkovskii, Sergei, *Russkoe staroobriadchestvo*/Zenkovsky, Serge A., *Russia's Old-Believers*, München, 1970. =Forum Slavicum 21.

——, "The Ideological World of the Denisov Brothers," *HSS*, Vol. III (1957), 49–66.

——, "The Russian Church Schism: Its Background and Repercussions," *RR*, Vol. XVI, No. 4 (1957), 37–58.

Zhivov, V. M., *Kul'turnye konflikty v istorii russkogo literaturnogo iazyka XVIII—nachala XIX veka*, M. 1990.

Zhukov, Dm., "Avvakum Petrov," in Dm. Zhukov & L. Pushkarev, eds., *Russkie pisateli XVII veka*, M. 1972, pp. 9–196.

Ziolkowski, Margaret, *Hagiography and Modern Russian Literature*, Princeton, 1988.

Zizani, Lavrentij, *Hrammatika Slovenska*, Gerd Friedhof, ed., München, 1972. =Specimina Philologiae Slavicae, 1. Also, M. Voznjak, ed., *Hramatyka Lavrentija Zyzanija z 1596 g.*, München, 1990. =Specimina Philologiae Slavicae, 88.

INDEX

Abélard et Eloise, 126
Academy of Sciences, gymnasium, 92,
    161–171, 174, 182, 183
Academy of Sciences, university,
    161–165
Adrian, Pariarch, 36, 78, 162
Aepinus, F. U. T., 214
Aeschylus, 54, 57
Aesop, 25, 56, 93, 94–95, 122, 124,
    130, 155, 158, 168, 192, 206
Afanasii, Archbishop, 32, 69
Afanasii, monk (Kondoidi), 107 fn. 106
Albertus Magnus, 182
Alcibiades, 36
Alekseev, M. P., historian cited, 51
Aleksei Alekseevich, 58, 66
Aleksei Petrovich, Tsarevich, 63, 117,
    127–128, 129–130
Aleksei Mikhailovich, Tsar, 3–6, 32,
    33, 55, 63–69, 72, 214, 231, 233
Alexander the Great, tales of, 34, 40,
    72, 118, 130
Alexander I, Emperor, 93, 226, 235,
    237
Allen, English divine, 83, 139
Alvarez, E., 156
Amburger, Erik, historian cited, 8
Ambrose, Saint, 23, 50, 111, 175
Amyot, Jacques, 90
Anacreon, 17, 56, 109, 122, 174
Andrusovo, Treaty of, 46, 47
Anna, Empress, 126, 135, 165, 181
Annenkov, Ivan Petrovich, 183
Ansbach, Markgräfin von, 86
Apollos, Archimandrite, 217
Apothecary Prikaz, 65, 108
Appolodorus Atheniensis, 130
Appolonius of Tyre, 64
Apuleius, 25
Aquinas, Thomas, 105, 140, 182
Archimedes, 75
Arescine, Robert, 108
Ariosto, L., 24
Aristeas, 56
Aristides, 1
Aristippus, 62
Aristophanes, 17, 56
Aristotle, 24, 25, 28, 42, 50, 53, 54,

55, 56–57, 58, 62, 65, 66, 67, 69,
    90–91, 97, 105, 109, 122, 123, 125,
    162, 175, 185, 191
Arndt, Johann, 85, 86, 111, 159
Arnold, Gottfried, pietist, 128, 133
Arsenii the Greek, 53–4
Ashmole, Elias, 81
Athenagoras Atheniensis, 216
Athenasius, Saint, 55, 67, 106, 110
Augustine, Saint, 47, 55, 60, 65, 105,
    111, 115 fn. 142, 129, 140, 175,
    216
Ausonius, 22, 105
Avedikovich, Nikolai, 55
Avicenna, 181
Avraamy, *starets*, 43, 44
Avvakum, 41–44, 63, 74, 103, 115,
    224

Bacon, Francis, 86, 106, 112, 181
Baillet, 141
Baranovych, Lazar, 68, 78
Barclay, R., 182, 192
Barkov, Ivan, 163
Barlaam and Josaphat, tale of, 35, 39,
    68, 123
Baronius, C., 63, 105, 130
Barsov, Anton, 163
Basil the Great, 69, 93, 111, 115, 175,
    216
Baumeister, F. C., 167
Baxter, Andrew, 83, 139
Bayle, Pierre, 121, 123, 129, 130, 133,
    141, 143, 181
Beaumont, Madame, 146
Beccaria, C., 195
Becker, R. Z., 146
Belinskii, V., 178, 226, 235
Bellarmine, Cardinal, 24
Bellegarde, Abbe, 86, 124, 126, 146
Belorussia, see Humanism, Polish-
    Lithuanian State
Bennet, Elisabeth, 193
Bentham, J., 195
Berkeley, George, 139
Berkov, P. N., historian cited, 8, 10,
    225, 226–227
Bertrand, Elie, 140

DATE DUE